DRAGONOMICS

CAROL WISE

Dragonomics

HOW LATIN AMERICA
IS MAXIMIZING (OR MISSING OUT ON)
CHINA'S INTERNATIONAL DEVELOPMENT STRATEGY

Yale

UNIVERSITY PRESS

NEW HAVEN & LONDON

Published with assistance from the foundation established in memory of
Henry Weldon Barnes of the Class of 1882, Yale College.

Yale University Press books may be purchased in quantity for
educational, business, or promotional use. For information, please e-mail
sales.press@yale.edu (U.S. office) or sales@yaleup.co.uk (U.K. office).

Set in Scala type by Integrated Publishing Solutions,
Grand Rapids, Michigan.
Printed in the United States of America.

Library of Congress Control Number: 2019946343
ISBN 978-0-300-22409-2 (hardcover : alk. paper)

A catalogue record for this book is available from the British Library.

This paper meets the requirements of ANSI/NISO Z39.48-1992
(Permanence of Paper).

10 9 8 7 6 5 4 3 2 1

For Roger

CONTENTS

PREFACE

THIS IS NOT A BOOK ABOUT CHINA. It is, rather, a book about Latin America's reaction to and political economic interaction with China over the past two decades. This is admittedly a huge topic and a relatively new one. Since the explosion of trade, loans, and investment between the People's Republic of China (PRC) and Latin America and the Caribbean (LAC) in the early 2000s, Chinese politicians and policy makers have sought to cast this burgeoning relationship as largely economic in nature. However, the very magnitude of these economic ties is eroding the PRC's apolitical spin on them. The numbers are indeed significant: in 2018 total China–LAC trade (exports and imports) hit US$306 billion, up from just a few billion dollars in 2000. China's total outflow of foreign direct investment (FDI) to LAC in 2018 was around US$129.8 billion, accounting for about 15 percent of LAC's total FDI inflows. Total development lending from China's two big policy banks to the LAC region since 2005 reached around US$150 billion in 2017. What are we to make of these numbers? Why now and why Latin America? How is tighter economic integration with China since the early 2000s shaping the political economies of its strongest LAC partners?

My first impulse was to research the ways in which Chinese exports had quickly burrowed through the North American market following China's 2001 entry into the World Trade Organization (WTO). Seemingly overnight, in 2003 China bumped Mexico down a notch in its ranking as a US trade partner, and Chinese exports of intermediate manufactured inputs to both Mexico and the US were displacing products and producers within both of these markets. Was this just a one-shot phenomenon related to China's having gained most favored nation status at the WTO? In violation of WTO rules Mexico responded with four-digit tariffs on over a thousand Chinese imports but to little effect. Was China becoming a de facto member of the North American Free Trade Agreement (NAFTA), regardless of Mexico's efforts to shut it out with high tariff walls? These questions may have been compelling at the time, but editors at the big presses all deemed them too narrow. Think bigger, they all said.

Fast-forward seven years. In the aftermath of the 2008–9 global financial crisis (GFC) this picture had enlarged considerably. First, with a brief interruption during the GFC, it became clear that the biggest commodity boom ever had been under way since 2003, driven by China's escalating need for precisely those commodities that some Latin American countries hold in abundance, such as copper, iron ore, crude oil, soybeans, and fish meal. Given China's scarcity of natural resources, these commodities were essential for propelling the country's ambitious manufacturing export-led model to ever-greater heights. Second, although the Latin American region went into the new millennium with anemic growth, Chinese demand for regional commodities helped to push average annual growth for the region as a whole to 4.8 percent between 2003 and the boom's end in 2013—almost double the historical rate of growth. Third, while most of South America revived quickly from the GFC, countries in Central and North America were just surviving. Chinese imports had inundated Mexico and Central American markets, but these countries had little that China wanted to buy in return. North American trade deficits became the mirror image of the commercial surpluses that were accruing in South America.

This greater complementarity between China and the South American commodity-producing countries helps explain their rapid exit from the GFC. The financial crisis actually struck these countries on the trade side, and once China restored its growth with a huge fiscal stimulus they were back in business by 2010. Mexico, with its overwhelming dependence on the US market, took a major hit on both the current and capital accounts, registering the lowest returns on aggregate and per capita income growth

among the top six Latin American countries between 2003 and 2013. Although the decade-long commodity price cycle had cooled by 2014, in 2017
prices on copper, fish meal, and iron ore remained two to three times above
their 2000 levels. Nevertheless, this did not stop Argentina and Brazil from
entering a downward economic spiral with no clear exit in sight, and Mexico continued to tread water. And yet the two smaller South American countries, Chile and Peru, held steady with positive rates of aggregate and per
capita GDP growth.

I now had a book-length take on China–LAC ties, but how to make sense
of these from the Latin American angle? I began with the premise that
China, despite projecting the image of a behemoth Asian developmental
state, faces serious natural resource constraints. The country's leaders face
the urgent need to feed the world's largest domestic population and to fuel
the world's soon-to-be largest economy. Of necessity China has had to internationalize its development strategy. In his tour de force *Chinese Economic
Statecraft*, William Norris analyzes China's deft orchestration of foreign
economic policy to these ends from the Chinese perspective. The task I have
set here is to capture the ways in which China's strategic foreign economic
policies have crystallized within Latin America, which since the turn of the
new millennium has served as one of several regional arenas in which this
internationalized development strategy is playing out. This strategy is viable due to China's accumulation of the world's highest level of foreign exchange reserves—the first emerging economy to accomplish this feat.

What about the Latin American side of this equation? Once the dust had
settled on the commodity price bonanza, the winners in terms of Chinese
inflows of FDI were Brazil, Peru, and, a distant third, Argentina. Mexico
had the strongest trade ties with China, although the bulk of this was on the
import side, while Brazil, Chile, and Peru followed, in that order; furthermore, all three have maintained a more even trade balance with China since
2001. China has now displaced the US as the top trade partner for Brazil,
Chile, Peru, and Uruguay. The other major capital inflow from China is lending from its two policy banks. As of 2017 the top loans went to Venezuela
(US$67.2 billion), Brazil (US$28.9 billion), Ecuador (US$18.4 billion), and
Argentina (US$16.9 billion). All of these figures flagged some initial puz-
zles. Why, for example, would Ecuador and Venezuela score so large on

policy bank loans from China but rank quite low on FDI inflows from the PRC? How could a small, open economy like Peru attract nearly double the amount of Chinese FDI that Argentina had received up until 2017? Finally, why has Mexico, where high-value-added manufactured goods count for nearly 80 percent of exports, been virtually paralyzed in standing up to Chinese competition and instead resorted to self-defeating protectionism?

I tackled these puzzles with a three-pronged approach. First, I looked for lessons and themes that could build on and update long-standing theories and models of development. Second, I constructed a comparative macro-economic database that measured everything from per capita growth to capital formation to long-term institutional performance. Third, I compiled three analytical development narratives along the lines of the methodological approach taken in Dani Rodrik's edited collection *In Search of Prosperity*. It is too soon to attribute causality in the context of the China–LAC relationship. However, the development economics literature offers rich insights that help frame the emergent country scenarios.

I begin with three small, open economies—Chile, Costa Rica, and Peru—which out-performed Argentina, Brazil, and Mexico by a wide margin during the China boom and thereafter. All three of these smaller states had advanced considerably on macroeconomic and institutional reforms prior to the boom and were thus well positioned to accept China's offer to each to negotiate a bilateral Free Trade Agreement (FTA). The proliferation of FTAs between developed and developing countries in the 1990s triggered a wave of mainly neoliberal analyses that touted their benefits based on computable-general-equilibrium models and comparative advantage. As my analysis shows, entering into a South–South FTA with China opened up new options for these countries while also defying narrow neoliberal parameters. China's FTAs with Chile and Peru allowed for numerous exceptions in each country's manufacturing sector, and all three FTAs offered immediate access for up to 90 percent of the Chinese market. Services and investment are covered in all three of these bilateral accords, which was a great leap forward for China.

I then turn to Argentina and Brazil, countries that ostensibly have it all in terms of rich factor endowments and strong trade complementarities with China. These countries are the most closely integrated into China's internationalized development strategy and ostensibly industrialized enough to have avoided a full-blown episode of the resource curse. However, the boom caught each in the immediate aftermath of economic crisis and reform fatigue. I turned to recent work on the resource curse that broadens its definition to include the institutional landscape. From this angle, during the China price boom both countries suffered an institutional resource curse, if you will, signaled by the erosion of state and economic institutions, the adoption of seriously misguided public policies, and the stalling of essential reforms. Broad questions for analyzing an institutional resource curse include how did a critical juncture like the China boom work to strengthen (or weaken) domestic institutions, lower (or elevate) the threshold for achieving significant reform, and open (or obstruct) the way for new leadership, organizational change, and policy innovation? Both Brazil and Argentina come out on the negative side of this ledger. In Brazil, for instance, the boom set the backdrop for one of the world's biggest corruption scandals—the skimming of billions of dollars from the state majority-held oil company (Petrobras)—while in Argentina it enabled executive interference and resource grabbing from a handful of private and public entities, including the reserves of the Central Bank of Argentina.

Mexico is my third country narrative. With the country's accession to NAFTA in 1994, policy makers kicked away Ha-Joon Chang's iconic development ladder (*Kicking Away the Ladder: Development Strategy in Historical Perspective*), jettisoning industrial policy and state intervention. Ironically, the triumph of securing this groundbreaking deal distracted subsequent Mexican administrations from carrying out the considerable backlog of reforms that would be required for the country to thrive in the global economy, NAFTA or no NAFTA. The trade deal alone and the neoliberal macro- and micro-economic policy approaches that framed it simply failed to trigger the kind of transformation that policy makers in the ruling party had promised. Instead, they delivered rampant corruption, burdensome regulation, a credit drought, and a mammoth infrastructure deficit. As Mexico has learned the hard way, an FTA is one possible venue for development but not an ultimate destination. The results depend largely on the hard work of public and private actors on the domestic front. With Washington's renegotiation of NAFTA—now renamed the US–Mexico–Canada–Agreement, or USMCA—into a mercantilist manifesto that favors the US market, and China continuing to crowd out Mexican exports abroad, Mexican policy makers literally need to get a new life. This means climbing back up the ladder with better state guidance, articulating a formidable trade and competition strategy along Chinese (versus US) lines, and, finally, closing some mutually favorable investment deals with the PRC outside of the oil sector.

At least one external reviewer of this manuscript challenged my decision to exclude the cases of Venezuela and Ecuador as a fourth narrative. My rationale for doing so is as follows: because neither of these oil-abundant countries has made a convincing effort to diversify its economic base and both have rejected the kinds of institutional and macroeconomic reforms that could have helped to harness the China boom more productively, there is little more than an old-fashioned resource curse on which to base a narrative. Neither case contributes to theory building or to the larger body of rich literature on this topic by pioneering scholars like Terry Karl and Michael Ross. As this manuscript goes to press, postboom Venezuela remains mired in hyperinflation, authoritarian backsliding, and a tragic humanitarian crisis. The postboom milieu in Ecuador is not as dire, although by some estimates the government has mortgaged the bulk of the country's oil reserves to China.

For China, both countries were low-hanging fruit, an easy way to get its foot in the door of the LAC region with infrastructure contracts that were high in Chinese content (labor, equipment, etc.) and low on environmental precautions. Venezuela has little to show for the billions lent to it by China's policy banks. In his pathbreaking work on "patient capital," Stephen Kaplan finds that in both Venezuela and Ecuador these were state-to-state loans made by China with no transparency or conditionality. Some were "loans-for-oil" deals, on which both countries are now in steep arrears; former presidents in both countries funneled other Chinese loans through special projects that are now largely untraceable. Ecuador, at least, has some highways and bridges to show for its Chinese loans. But it also has the US$19 billion. China-backed Coca Codo dam, already infamous for its corruption scandals and for shorting out the country's electrical grid. The overall scenario is one of capital squandering and corruption. Sadly, this is nothing new in Latin America. Although Trump's Washington has accused

China of setting a debt trap for developing countries, the Venezuelan situation is playing out in the reverse: in the absence of conditionality and woefully behind in servicing its debt payments to China, Venezuela has ensnared Beijing in a creditor trap. Ecuador is not far behind it.

The China boom threw LAC's reform gaps and institutional weaknesses into stark relief while also highlighting multiple paths forward for the very diverse mix of countries considered here. While the opportunities for closer economic integration with China are seemingly infinite, so too are the risks. This book shows that "success" has varied according to issue areas, sectors, and projects across these countries. For reasons analyzed throughout the book, the three small, open economies fared best by advancing institutional and macroeconomic reforms during and after the boom, whereas Argentina, Brazil, and Mexico were not able to seize the opportunities at hand for reform and restructuring. The work of the Nobel Prize–winning economist Douglass North (*Institutions, Institutional Change, and Economic Performance*) reminds us that the tedious Venezuelan pattern of the past repeatedly recurring in the present is far from inevitable. I note the tremendous room for maneuver afforded by the China boom and the opportunity for human agency in undertaking the kinds of reforms and promotional policies that could strengthen a given country's ability to benefit most from its increased economic ties with China.

Although China has become a steady feature of the political-economic landscape in Latin America, this book makes clear that the China–LAC relationship is still a work in progress. Inevitably, the best outcomes have stemmed from China-related endeavors where rule of law, regulatory oversight, and a clear strategy exist on the Latin American side. As the China–LAC relationship moves into its third decade, this analysis suggests that political leaders, policy makers, and economic elites across the LAC region need to step up in brokering deals around the rich trade, lending, and investment opportunities China is offering, while also finding creative ways to minimize the risks.

ACKNOWLEDGMENTS

THIS BOOK WAS A LONG TIME IN THE making. I conducted fieldwork in all six of my case study countries, and I met with country representatives at the Beijing embassies of Argentina, Brazil, Chile, Mexico, and Peru. During the book's completion I made presentations on this research at numerous universities and institutions, including Renmin University in Beijing, Carleton University (Ottawa), the University of Chicago, Boston University, Carleton College, the University of Virginia, the University of Alberta (Canada), the University of Illinois at Urbana-Champaign, Pacific University (Lima, Peru), FLACSO-Buenos Aires (Argentina), EAFIT University (Medellín, Colombia), FLACSO-Quito (Ecuador), Sergio Arboleda University (Bogotá, Colombia) and the University of the Andes (Bogotá, Colombia). Colleagues in the Latin American Institute at the Chinese Academy of Social Sciences in Beijing have been so very helpful. I received other valuable feedback during presentations I made at the Central Reserve Bank of Peru, the Guadalajara International Book Fair, at Canada's Ministry of International Trade, the National Business Federation of Bogotá, and the Inter-American Dialogue in Washington, DC. Although it is simply not possible to mention everyone by name, I want to express my gratitude to all for their hospitality and collegiality.

My home department, Political Science and International Relations at USC, could not have been more supportive of this project. From funding to research assistance to a manuscript review seminar, my colleagues really came through. In my department (and in no special order), I thank Erin Baggott Carter, Gerry Munck, Pat James, David Kang, Ben Graham, Joshua Aizenman, Brett Carter, and Wayne Sandholtz for their feedback, support, and encouragement of my work. Ben Graham and his research assistant, Claire He, worked their magic in formatting the book's figures for me. David Kang hosted the manuscript review seminar at our Center for International Studies and brought in Richard Feinberg and Barbara Stallings as external discussants. I want to acknowledge the very helpful insights from Richard and Barbara as well as the feedback from our doctoral students who participated in the seminar: Jennifer Roglá, Victoria Chonn Ching, Mariana Rangel, and Stephanie Kang. Many of my former and present doctoral students have also helped to sharpen my thoughts, including Christina Faegri, Cíntia Quiliconi, Fabian Borges-Herrero, Hai-vu Phan, Shiming Yang, Juvenal Cortes, and Nicolás Albertoni.

As for research assistance, I am proud to say that I relied almost entirely on our brilliant undergraduate students at USC. The provost's office generously awarded me two Provost Undergraduate Research Fellows each year over the course of this project. The dean's office also kicked in, providing research funding under the auspices of our Student Opportunities for Academic Research program. I thank David Glasgow in the USC Provost's office and Steve Lamy in the Dean's office of Dornsife College for their commitment to these programs and their support in pairing me with so many vibrant undergraduate research assistants. Because these are mentoring programs, many of these research assistants started during their sophomore year and worked with me all the way through to their graduation. I had fantastic number crunchers in Vijeta Tandon, Chengxi Shi, Scotty Huhn, and Hannah Kwon; bilingual whizzes in Dawn Powell, Erin Piñeda, Daniel Paly, Lucy Santora, and Qiong Wu; and other genuine talents in Becky Turner, Brittney Kidwell, Savannah Wiseman, Nick Engler, Chris Roman, Susan Ye, Felix Tam, Victor Paredes, Michael Lampe, Lauren Deife, Maureen Clougherty, Jason Tse, and Chenyan Zhou. Scotty Huhn, who left me long ago for Silicon Valley, compiled the final database for this project and graciously agreed to stick with me on a consulting basis through the publication of the book. Thank you so much, Scotty.

Five close friends—Debby Brautigam, Helen Shapiro, Cynthia Sanborn, Monica DeHart, and Erin Baggott Carter—read the entire manuscript word for word. They were hard critics, and I so appreciate the truthful feedback. Other supportive colleagues include Kevin Gallagher, Rebecca Ray, Tom O'Keefe, Shaun Breslin, Jonathan Fox, Leonardo Stanley, Margaret Myers, Guo Jie, Manuel Pastor, Michael Shifter, Stan Rosen, Rolando Avendano, Jeff Dayton-Johnson, Diana Tussie, Clay Dube, Shoujun Cui, Carol Graham, Stephen Kaplan, Alison Brysk, Martin Monsalve, and Benjamin Creutzfeldt. Enrique Dussel Peters has been an indefatigable force in gathering data on and promoting the study of China–Latin America relations. I rely heavily on Enrique's data analyses. Because I knew little about China prior to undertaking this project, I want to acknowledge some of the authors and scholars whose work was instrumental in my increased understanding of this wondrous, complex country. I have cited them all in the book: Yasheng Huang, Minxin Pei, Yuen Yuen Ang, Justin Yifu Lin, Xiaolan Fu, Hu Angang, Susan Shirk, Barry Naughton, William Norris, Elizabeth Economy, William Overholt, Arthur Kroeber, and, finally, Ezra Vogel, for his masterful biography of Deng Xiaoping.

It was my luck to meet Jaya Chatterjee, my editor at Yale University Press, at the very point when she was launching a new series on Latin America. Thank you, Jaya, for your enthusiasm and unwavering support and for guiding me through this project. Eva Skewes and Dorothea Halliday at Yale University Press could not have been more helpful in finalizing the manuscript for publication. Lawrence Kenney did the copyediting, Bill Nelson finalized the figures, and Jeff Schier brought the galley proofs to life. They are all perfectionists, and for this I thank them. The editor of *Pacific Affairs*, Hyung-Gu Lynn, has the patience of a saint. He mentored me through my first publication in an Asia Pacific journal, and for this I am grateful.

In January 2018 I attended an exhibit called *Winds from Fusang: Mexico and China in the Twentieth Century* at the USC Pacific Asia Museum. The centerpiece of the exhibit was a large mural entitled *Winds from Fusang* painted in the tradition of the Mexican mural artist Diego Rivera by the Chinese artists Jingbo Sun and Shengtian Zheng. The mural blended powerful images from the Mexican and Chinese revolutions, and it featured iconic figures like Rivera, Frida Kahlo, Zhou Enlai, and Leon Trotsky. In

1956, at a very young age, Shengtian Zheng had seen the large Rivera mural *The Victory of War* at a rare exhibit of Mexican art in Beijing. This confluence of Mexican and Chinese culture confirms that the history between China and Latin America goes back much further and the ties have been closer than the "mainstream narrative" suggests. I thank these artists for granting me the privilege of using their work for the cover of my book.

INTRODUCTION

Debating the New Terrain

The United States is no longer our privileged partner. Now the privileged partner is China.

Ricardo Patriño, former foreign minister of Ecuador[1]

BEGINNING IN THE EARLY 2000S, when most of the region was still reeling from the effects of the dot.com bust in the US and the deepening of this recession by the 9/11/01 terrorist attacks on New York City and Washington, DC, China became a much bigger player in Latin America and the Caribbean (LAC). Whereas LAC's growth was in the dumps in 2001, this trend turned around almost overnight (fig. I.1). As Mother Nature would have it, the LAC region is home to those very commodities that China needed to propel its high-growth, export-led development model to a more mature stage. Under the impulse of voracious Chinese demand, prices for oil, copper, iron ore, soybeans, and fish meal soared (table I.1). For South America in particular the decade from 2003 to 2013 would turn out to be the biggest commodity lottery ever. Average annual growth for the region as a whole was 4.8 percent between 2003 and 2013—almost double the historical rate of growth for the region.[2] While there is certainly more to this story than the simple rise of China in Latin America, China's trade demand and capital supply have helped to grease the wheels of LAC's growth since the turn of the new millennium.

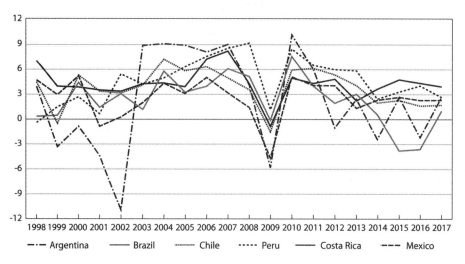

Figure I.1. Percentage growth of gross domestic product (GDP), 1998–2017.
Source: The Conference Board Total Economy Database™ (Adjusted version), March 2018.

Latin America's growth spurt came on the heels of a major reform effort that had been under way in the region since the late 1980s and early 1990s. Dubbed the Washington Consensus (WC) by the economist John Williamson, this market-based approach rested on three pillars: privatization, liberalization, and deregulation.[3] Nearly three decades later the record shows that LAC countries have indeed made strong inroads with the privatization of state-held assets; trade regimes have been liberalized, and there has been a diversification of trade partners; financial markets have been opened, deepened, and deregulated; external debts have been reduced; and a number of countries have built up large arsenals of foreign exchange reserves.[4] This is another world altogether from earlier times in Latin America, when short-lived price spurts reaped large returns for the region but in the absence of sound macroeconomic policies or resilient economic institutions. This latter scenario, for example, was the backdrop to the 1982 debt shocks, which hurled LAC into the "lost decade" of high inflation, capital flight, and zero growth during the 1980s.

When we skip ahead twenty-five years to LAC's responses to the 2008–9 global financial crisis (GFC), the difference is like that between night and day: not a single country was forced to turn to the International Monetary

Table I.1. Annual commodity price trends in real (2010) dollars, 2000–18

Year	Copper, $/metric ton	Crude oil, @ spot price, $/barrel	Soybeans, $/metric ton	Fish meal, $/metric ton	Iron ore, $/dry metric ton unit
2000	2,279	35	266	519	36
2001	2,061	32	256	636	39
2002	2,061	33	281	801	39
2003	2,235	36	332	767	40
2004	3,371	44	360	763	45
2005	4,195	61	313	833	74
2006	7,475	71	299	1,297	77
2007	7,459	75	402	1,234	129
2008	6,764	94	508	1,102	152
2009	5,339	64	453	1,275	83
2010	7,535	79	450	1,688	146
2011	7,955	94	487	1,385	151
2012	7,226	95	537	1,414	117
2013	6,682	95	491	1,592	123
2014	6,354	89	455	1,582	90
2015	5,645	52	400	1,596	57
2016	5,192	46	433	1,601	62
2017	6,834	61	387	1,477	72
2018	6,075	54	381	1,480	69

Source: World Bank Global Economic Monitor (GEM). Available at http://databank.worldbank .org/data/views/variableselection/selectvariables.aspx?source=global-economic-monitor-%28 gem%29-commodities.

Fund (IMF) for assistance. Neither has the LAC region ever fully rebounded, as it did in 2010, from a crisis of this magnitude without relying on a kick-start from the motor of the US economy. Although the GFC was a financial crisis at heart, it hit Latin America, China, and most other emerging economies (EEs) on the trade side. This is because EE banks, for the most part, had avoided the reckless high-risk financial instruments that brought the US banking system to the brink in 2008. The impacts of the GFC clearly varied across the EEs and developed countries, but the responses were quite similar. Both China and the US moved quickly, with policy makers in both countries infusing a huge fiscal stimulus into their respective domestic economies. In 2009 alone the US spent 5.9 percent of GDP in its efforts to fend off a full-blown economic depression, while China's fiscal stimulus amounted to 4.8 percent of GDP that same year.[5]

Argentina, Brazil, Chile, and Peru were able to ride out the recovery on China's shirttails, enabling each to similarly engage in counter-cyclical policies when the GFC struck.[6] Recent research conducted by the Inter-American Development Bank (IDB) economist Ambrogio Cesa-Bianchi and his colleagues has found that "the long-run impact of a [positive] Chinese GDP shock on the typical Latin American economy has increased three times since 1990."[7] Thus for all but Mexico the quick pickup in Chinese growth and demand for LAC's commodities put these countries back in business long before the US recovery. Mexico, being more tightly integrated with the US market, was beholden to US economic recovery and thus much slower to rebound. The overall picture, however, looked rosy. Brazil made the November 9, 2009, cover of the prestigious *Economist* magazine under the title "Brazil Takes Off."[8] Even Argentina, the bête noire of international financial markets following its messy US$100 billion bond default in 2001, was lauded by the IMF for making a much stronger than expected rebound from the GFC.[9]

Yet in the world of commodity price booms what goes up inevitably comes back down. Prices on all but crude oil began to drop in 2014–15 (see table I.1); by early 2016 oil prices had gone into their own freefall, dipping to just below US$30 per barrel.[10] By 2019 they had stabilized at around US$62 per barrel. Reminiscent of the 1986 crash in oil prices, the combination of excess production and the slowing of Chinese growth from its thirty-year average of 9–10 percent annually down to about 6.5 percent showed how swiftly a negative GDP shock from China could dampen world growth. For the LAC region, just as China's positive GDP shock was a godsend in 2003–13, its reversal was a negative jolt. The pain has been acute for those that were the most celebrated countries just three years earlier—Brazil and Argentina. In both cases the economy has shrunk, deficits are exploding, and social tensions are palpable.[11] Argentina, after paying off its IMF debt in 2006 and declaring a public relations war on the institution, was forced to return to the fund in mid-2018 with egg on its face. The IMF demonstrated that it held no grudges, cobbling together a new loan package for Argentina in the range of US$57 billion.[12]

According to Beijing, China's slowing of growth has been partly intentional, as policy makers there seek to shift away from a heavy reliance on manufactured exports and big investment projects at home toward more services, technology, and domestic consumption. But China's slower growth also reflects domestic reform bottlenecks across the board, especially in the financial (bloated state enterprise debt and other nonperforming loans) and real estate sectors. The pass-through for the LAC region as a whole has been a slowing of growth to 1–2 percent on average since 2014.[13] Moreover, as the aura of plenty fades, long-standing reform gaps on both sides of the Pacific have become more glaring. China and LAC both face stern challenges in the realm of government effectiveness, regulatory quality, rule of law, and the control of corruption. But LAC, much more so than China, still lags sorely on indicators of efficiency, competitiveness, and productive investment.[14]

This current juncture is the impetus for this book. Commodity lotteries are seemingly random and unpredictable, and rarely do they leave a positive footprint once they taper down. In much earlier times Peruvian guano (fertilizer) producers and Brazilian rubber barons found this out the hard way. For price swings on more cyclically volatile commodities like oil, the present postboom economic plight of petroleum-producing Venezuela is like the rerun of a B-grade movie.[15] Unlike past booms, though, China's presence in the LAC region continues to hold strong. In fact, according to statements made by President Xi Jinping of China at a forum hosted by Beijing in January 2015 with thirty-three member countries of the Community of Latin American and Caribbean States (CELAC), the Chinese government is committed to doubling China–LAC trade to US$500 billion by 2025 and to investing US$250 billion in Latin America over the next decade.[16] It is this commitment to stick around that has triggered debates concerning China's "true" intentions in the region. At the same time, scholars and policy analysts have worried openly about the trade and investment asymmetries that are coming to characterize China–LAC economic relations.

Debating the New Terrain

Despite the emergence of a rich literature on the political economy of China–LAC relations, we are still scratching the surface in terms of our grasp of this phenomenon.[17] Was the recent China boom just another flash in the pan for Latin America, or will there be some staying power to the apparently thick trade and investment ties that have been forged? Is it true, as the realist gurus John Mearsheimer and Stephen Walt have recently argued, that Washington needs to focus more on "preserving US dominance in the Western Hemisphere"?[18] Since the advent of the administration of Donald Trump this call has been partially answered, as hardliners at the State Department and the National Security Council have sought to cast the China–LAC relationship as a threat to US hegemony in the Western Hemisphere. Within the ivory tower a slew of recent articles point to the emerging patterns of trade and investment asymmetry between China and the LAC region, casting this as a form of "neo-dependency."[19]

In a similar vein, a new wave of scholarship cautions that stronger trade ties with China can lead to a convergence on foreign policy stances between LAC and China that represent a setback on the LAC side. For example, although based on thin data, Gustavo Flores Macías and Sarah Kreps report a dissemination of China's less favorable voting preferences on country-specific human rights issues to its strongest LAC trade partners within the UN General Assembly.[20] At the same time, another quantitative study by Georg Stuver found that "matching patterns of policy convergence between China and South American countries . . . at the bi- and multilateral level of relations did not reveal any consistent picture."[21] Opinions on this matter of the dissemination of China's darker political impulses to its LAC partners appear to be a wash and for now seem best left at that.

My answer to the other three questions posed above is the following. Despite some highly credible doubters, the China–LAC relationship is now an enduring part of LAC's political economic landscape;[22] this complements rather than threatens US hegemony in the Western Hemisphere; and dependency theory, with its focus on the structure of international capitalism, tends to overlook the divergent domestic outcomes that are emerging across these countries as a result of their closer engagement with

China.[23] As such, dependency theory remains lucid as a description of the features of underdevelopment, and it keeps us honest by pointing to the large asymmetries between China and its LAC partners as problematic; yet this systemic approach cannot account for the differential performance of EEs within the international political economy (IPE).

This book is precisely about the variation in political economic outcomes that has emerged as a result of China's closer integration with six of its ten designated "strategic partners" (SPs) in Latin America: Argentina, Brazil, Chile, Costa Rica, Mexico, and Peru. Like many gestures of Chinese diplomacy, the designation of an SP is open to interpretation. Although the practice of naming SPs began in 1993, there is no formal list of China's SPs, as foreign ministry officials fear that "it could lead to confusion and unnecessary discontent on behalf of important countries which are not labelled as China's strategic partners."[24] My usage here follows the work of Yanran Xu, who culls a definition from the speeches of former premier Wen Jiabao: "strategic" means that cooperation is long-term and stable and that it transcends ideology and individual events; "partner" suggests that the bond between China and a given country is mutually beneficial, win–win, and established on equal footing.[25] In chapter 1 I clearly define the nature of China's integration with these SPs, and I analyze the effects of this engagement through the lens of various theories and models of economic development. But before going to the heart of this matter, let me put my own spin on these aforementioned debates.

Is China Just a Fair-Weather Friend?

At this point it has become customary to rattle off the data that confirm that the China–LAC relationship is much more than a passing fancy. Indeed, I took this blitzkrieg approach in the preface. Now, let me briefly restate the argument that runs throughout the book. China, despite projecting the image of a behemoth Asian developmental state, faces serious natural resource constraints. Most pressing are its urgent needs to feed the world's largest domestic population and to acquire the resources needed to fuel the world's soon-to-be largest economy. Of necessity it has internationalized its development strategy. What started as Deng Xiaoping's promotion of the

Chinese Communist Party's (CCP) "reform and opening" strategy in the late 1970s has gradually evolved into a development model that relies on the incorporation of select resource-rich EEs in Africa, Southeast Asia, and increasingly Latin America. This internationalized development strategy has been made possible by China's accumulation of the world's highest level of foreign exchange reserves, which sat at US$3.09 trillion in March 2019. China's unique status as a capital-abundant EE reflects its tenacious pursuit of an export-led development model—much like the earlier Japanese and South Korean strategies—based on a huge pool of cheap labor, low domestic consumption, an undervalued currency, and, in the case of China, enormous economies of scale. However, as in Japan and South Korea, this approach has run its course in China. With the mixed returns and saturation of domestic investment in big infrastructure and industrial projects, Chinese policy makers and entrepreneurs are now hard-pressed to put these funds to more productive and efficient use. At a time when the Western multilateral banks are focused on poverty reduction and the UN's Sustainable Development Goals, China has stepped in to fund projects that fill crucial infrastructure gaps in other EEs as part of its own internationalized development strategy.[26]

Bushra Bataineh and his colleagues estimate that China's lending for infrastructure projects has grown "from around a quarter of the development lending industry in 2002 (measured in total assets) to more than three-quarters of it by 2016."[27] These same authors note that China's approach to infrastructure investments abroad is an offshoot of the country's domestic buildup over the past thirty years, and, contrary to the Western lenders, China's projects "are evaluated more on their impact than on the specific viability of the project in question." As such, these infrastructure projects are closely linked to the production of goods and the extraction of resources that are then shipped back to spur Chinese development. China's emphasis on trade, lending, and FDI related to all aspects of overseas resource extraction reflects its continued status as an EE.

Inadvertently or not, China is promoting the development of its aforementioned SPs in LAC, most of which have factor endowments that are complementary to those of China. Now, to reiterate the considerable numbers that underpin the burgeoning China–LAC relationship: at US$306 billion in 2018, total China–LAC trade had increased exponentially from just a few billion dollars in 2000; as for the six countries considered in this study—Argentina, Brazil, Chile, Costa Rica, Mexico, and Peru—in 2017 China accounted for 9 percent of exports and 16 percent of their imports.[28] On Chinese investment in LAC, from 2000 to 2018 China's total outflows of foreign direct investment (OFDI) to the LAC-5 (I omit Costa Rica here, as Chinese FDI inflows are negligible there) is estimated to be US$129.8 billion, accounting for around 15 percent of LAC's total FDI inflows.

According to official Chinese data, the bulk of Chinese FDI inflows to Latin America are channeled through the Cayman and British Virgin Islands, mainly for tax purposes, which makes it difficult to gauge the precise amount that has actually been invested within each country. Therefore I rely on data compiled by Enrique Dussel Peters at the Universidad Nacional Autónoma de México in Mexico City.[29] As for country destination, the biggest recipients have been Brazil, Peru, and Argentina, in that order (table I.2). Raw materials, on average, accounted for about 60 percent of Chinese OFDI to LAC in 2000–2017; Chinese OFDI in manufacturing was minor until 2017, when it increased nearly fourteen times from its level in 2010 (table I.3). Chinese OFDI in services heated up in 2016, averaging about 33 percent of the total from 2000 to 2017. Chinese aid to LAC was approximately US$560 million in 2013, and these funds were allocated in some combination of traditional grants and concessional or interest-free loans.[30]

In 2010–19 various LAC countries have also received loans from China's two big policy banks, the China Development Bank (CDB) and the China Export-Import Bank (CHEXIM), whose joint commitments to LAC since 2005 come to about US$150 billion.[31] In 2015 alone lending to Latin America from these Chinese policy banks was nearly double the total combined funds lent to the region by Western multilateral banks.[32] Most of the projects China has funded in LAC tend to be capital intensive, with huge economies of scale and high barriers to exit. Examples include the building of railroads and dams in Argentina; a dam, highways, bridges, and hospitals in Ecuador; and the modernization of major ports in Brazil, Mexico, and Peru.[33] Fixed assets, large overhead costs, and joint ventures are other features of China's rapidly growing ties with LAC. Given the political and economic chaos to which Venezuela has succumbed, a Chinese-sponsored high-speed

Table I.2. Chinese outflows of foreign direct investment to Latin America
by destination country (2000–2017)

	2000–2005	2010	2014	2015	2016	2017	2000–2017
Argentina							
Number of transactions	0	3	3	0	3	3	19
Amount ($M)	0	5,597	523	0	215	1,283	11,870
Employment	0	2,601	480	0	670	3,874	11,210
Brazil							
Number of transactions	6	10	13	19	16	13	107
Amount ($M)	3,565	12,867	1,747	5,319	13,903	2,902	48,021
Employment	6,303	15,208	7,128	13,950	37,163	32,955	138,613
Chile							
Number of transactions	0	1	2	1	3	4	22
Amount ($M)	0	18	36	286	215	2,764	6,091
Employment	0	0	43	175	4,284	5,691	10,721
Mexico							
Number of transactions	4	4	10	9	4	19	68
Amount ($M)	563	84	1,140	1,001	81	2,498	6,010
Employment	6,354	478	2,470	4,915	1,455	17,524	40,615
Peru							
Number of transactions	0	4	5	1	0	3	33
Amount ($M)	0	296	518	2,500	0	1,635	19,347
Employment	0	3,552	5,381	3,000	0	8,300	34,090

Source: Enrique Dussel Peters, *Monitor of Chinese OFDI in Latin America and the Caribbean 2018*, available at http://www.redalc-china.org/monitor/images/pdfs/menuprincipal/DusselPeters_MonitorOFDI_2018_Eng.pdf.

railway project collapsed halfway through its construction. Stephen Kaplan and Michael Penfold report that "railroad factories along the construction corridor were ransacked for their power generators, computers, metal siding and copper wiring."[34] Nevertheless, Chinese "red elephants" like this

Table I.3. Chinese outflows of foreign direct investment to Latin America by activity (2000–2017)

	2000–2005	2010	2014	2015	2016	2017	2000–2017
Raw materials							
Number of transactions	40.00	36.67	19.05	11.43	25.71	13.33	29.88
Amount ($M)	85.35	61.47	54.89	68.29	28.72	23.61	57.93
Employment	50.69	76.64	60.70	15.22	27.35	18.13	41.04
Manufacturing							
Number of transactions	26.67	23.33	40.48	48.57	34.29	51.11	36.28
Amount ($M)	2.67	2.61	3.66	19.76	1.90	35.82	8.58
Employment	6.86	5.00	14.29	74.44	13.80	26.16	25.27
Services and domestic market							
Number of transactions	33.33	40.00	40.48	31.43	40.00	33.33	32.62
Amount ($M)	11.98	35.91	41.45	11.25	69.38	38.36	33.19
Employment	42.45	18.36	25.01	7.80	58.85	53.39	32.89
Purchase of technology							
Number of transactions	0.00	0.00	0.00	8.57	0.00	2.22	1.22
Amount ($M)	0.00	0.00	0.00	0.70	0.00	2.21	0.29
Employment	0.00	0.00	0.00	2.54	0.00	2.32	0.80

Source: Enrique Dussel Peters, *Monitor of Chinese OFDI in Latin America and the Caribbean 2018*, available at http://www.redalc-china.org/monitor/images/pdfs/menuprincipal/DusselPeters_MonitorOFDI_2018 _Eng.pdf.

one do not take away from the fact that China's commitment to the LAC region is long-term and now an integral part of its own internationalized development strategy.[35]

Chinese OFDI into massive resource-related projects within other EEs has been going on since about 2010.[36] Again, and as is the case in these other EEs, LAC is beginning to see a shift in the sectoral makeup of Chinese OFDI away from resource exploitation and toward related manufacturing and services. As indicated in China's 13th Five-Year Plan, President Xi is looking to launch a "New 30 Years" initiative that seeks to modernize

China into a more mature developmental state. Further infrastructure projects will seek to build regional economies of scale and closer integration via transport networks. In Asia this is personified by the One Belt One Road (BRI) initiative launched in 2013 under Xi, which includes the land-based Silk Road Economic Belt and the 21st Century Maritime Silk Road. The financial centerpiece of this project is the Asian Infrastructure Investment Bank (AIIB), launched by China in 2015. Embedded within the 13th Five-Year Plan is a development manifesto issued by the Central Committee of the CCP which indicates that competition and efficiency will underpin the overhaul of Chinese fiscal, financial, foreign trade and OFDI policies.

With regard to Latin America, China's reforms could have significant multiplier and spillover effects. The allocation of BRI funds, it seems, has become synonymous with China's earlier "go out" mandate. LAC is getting in on some of this action, although it does appear that the BRI imprimatur has been attached to projects that would go forward with or without it. Such is the case with a US$2.1 billion contract won in 2018 by China's State Construction Engineering Corporation for highway construction in Argentina.[37] As with many Chinese projects in Argentina, that government has signed on to a large percentage of Chinese input with this project, including engineering, construction, upgrades, and operational maintenance.[38] Other China–LAC deals seem to fit this same bill, like the construction of a fourth bridge over the Panama Canal by the China Communications Construction Company for US$1.42 billion. Although nineteen Latin American countries have now signed BRI memoranda of understanding (MOU) with China, most of these are vaguely worded. Such is the case with the MOU between China and the government of Guyana for a BRI loan to build public infrastructure.[39]

Significantly, Brazil and Mexico have sat out the BRI for the time being, and at the G-20 meeting in Buenos Aires in 2019 Argentina declined President Xi's offer to sign on to any further BRI projects. Worries over debt sustainability for BRI country participants outside of LAC (e.g., Malaysia, Pakistan, Sri Lanka, and Montenegro) and controversies over the opaque, exploitative nature of some of these contracts means it is probably a good thing that the BRI has yet to catch on significantly in the LAC region. To quote a *Financial Times* editorial, "89 per cent of contractors on China-funded [BRI] transport projects were Chinese. Chinese projects court further publicity by failing to publicise impact studies."[40]

Already the lack of serious environmental impact assessments and the deleterious effects of some BRI projects have cast a pall over this initiative. But there is more here than meets the eye. A study by the Rhodium Group found that in China's thirty-eight debt renegotiations with twenty-four developing countries over the past decade, "debt write-offs were found in 14 cases, deferments in 11 cases, and refinancing and debt term changes accounting for most other cases."[41] With no conditionality, China has little choice but to work with its debtors, some of which have drawn China into a creditor trap. In fact, China's only asset seizure during this time was Sri Lanka's Hambantota port in 2017, a decision that Beijing has yet to live down.

As the process of deepening China–LAC relations has now entered its third decade, outflows of Chinese FDI to the region have leveled off. Some of this leveling is due to China's own slowing growth but also to its weak record of due diligence. Environmental transgressions, conflicts with local communities, and numerous allegations of old-fashioned corruption have also caught up with Chinese investors.[42] At the same time, China–LAC trade hit US\$306 billion in 2018, its highest level yet, and Chinese soft power is enriching cross-Pacific ties, including some forty-one Confucius Institutes that offer Mandarin training in the region and fellowship exchange programs back and forth for Chinese and LAC students. Premier Li Keqiang of China has raised the possibility of relocating Chinese industrial production to Latin America, including proposals for joint ventures between Chinese companies (state held and private) and local Latin American firms in high-tech and manufacturing projects (e.g., telecommunications, logistics, rail, and shipbuilding). Even if these proposed projects, BRI or otherwise, turn out to be mere pipe dreams, there are no two ways about it: China's roots in Latin America are still deepening and are seemingly permanent.

US Hegemony over LAC—Looking for Threats in All the Wrong Places?

Especially since its 2001 accession to the WTO China has actively engaged in every region of the global economy and in developed and developing countries alike. It has become the top emerging market destination for FDI and has risen to the upper ranks of world trade more quickly than any other developing country during the post–World War II period. In just a matter of a decade, for example, China has displaced Germany as the top exporter of goods to the rest of the world, and in this process "has gone from being one of the most insignificant high-technology exporters to the number-one high technology manufacturer in the world."[43] This is not to be confused with technological independence. As we saw from the near collapse in 2018 of ZTE, one of China's biggest telecom equipment makers, when the US imposed sanctions on China for its violation of an agreement to halt dual-purpose exports with both commercial and military uses to North Korea and Iran, China is still dependent on external suppliers (and US companies in particular) for 95 percent of the high-end chips and manufacturing components.[44] Despite the wishful thinking expressed by Ecuador's finance minister in the epigraph to this introduction, the US is still the top economy in the world, the main political and economic broker in Latin America, and China remains beholden to US companies for crucial technology inputs.

The data I have presented thus far delineate the ways in which China's global reach has crystallized in Latin America, all of which falls under the umbrella of standard economic diplomacy. As further evidence of its growing commitment to the region, China obtained permanent observer status at the Organization of American States (OAS) in 2004, and in 2008 it paid the US$300 million entry fee to become a full-fledged member of the IDB. Under an arrangement between the CHEXIM and the IDB, China also established a US$1.8 billion Latin American Fund to spur equity investments in the region's infrastructure, medium-sized enterprises, and natural resources.[45] As noted, the January 2015 China–CELAC summit in Beijing produced commitments from the People's Republic of China (PRC) for ever-higher levels of trade and investment in the region. Already China has set up three separate regional finance platforms that together total US$35 billion in credit for industrial cooperation, infrastructure, and other productive projects.[46]

Nevertheless, from the standpoint of the US, China's meteoric rise in the Western Hemisphere has periodically invoked cries of concern. China's ascendance and projected displacement of the US by 2027 (if not sooner) as the country with the largest GDP in the world has triggered worry about the decline of US hegemony and with it the waning of US prestige and leadership on the international front.[47] This sense of the US being under increasing political and economic siege was accentuated by the severity of the Wall Street–induced GFC of 2008–9 and exacerbated by the hard-fought but expensive and interminable wars the US has waged in Afghanistan and Iraq since the 9/11 terrorist attacks. The advent of the Trump administration and its America First program has magnified fears about the decline of the US—both politically and economically. Trump's aggressive unilateral style reflects a loss of US relative power and an attack on the liberal economic order that his predecessors worked hard to construct and nurture over the post–World War II era. However, a confrontation between China and the US over hegemony in the Western Hemisphere is still a very remote possibility.[48]

Yet this improbability has not stopped some Trump appointees from trying to hasten an East–West clash over the region. For example, on the eve of his first tour of Latin America in early 2018 Trump's short-lived secretary of state Rex Tillerson declared the Monroe Doctrine to be "as relevant today as it was the day it was written."[49] This echoed comments made in 2005 by the former Republican congressman Dan Burton of Indiana, who stated at a hearing of the Western Hemisphere Subcommittee of the House International Relations Committee, "Until we know the definitive answer to this question of whether China will play by the rules of fair trade and engage responsibly on transnational issues, I believe we should . . . perhaps go so far as to consider China's actions in Latin America as the movement of a hegemonic power into the hemisphere."[50] During his LAC tour Tillerson taunted his hosts about the rise of Chinese imperialism in the Western Hemisphere, as did his successor, Secretary of State Mike Pompeo.

Some officials in Peru and Chile publicly refuted Tillerson's China bashing, noting that their respective countries had been able to establish a better working relationship with Beijing than with Washington. For the record, John Kerry, the former Obama administration secretary of state, had laid the Monroe Doctrine to rest in a speech he made before the OAS in 2013: "The era of the Monroe Doctrine is over. . . . The relationship that we seek and that we have worked hard to foster is not about a United States declaration about how and when it will intervene in the affairs of other American states. It's about all of our countries viewing one another as equals, sharing responsibilities, cooperating on security issues, and adhering . . . to the decisions that we make as partners to advance the values and the interests that we share."[51] For the time being Washington itself has dropped this soft-power, liberal internationalist stance and replaced it with reassertions of US dominance in the region. Neither are there any of the proclamations characteristic of the Clinton and Obama administrations about the need to prioritize and revitalize US–Latin American ties. It is no wonder that polling by the Pew Research Center found "the U.S. image in Latin America . . . has taken a major hit since Trump took office." Unthinkable even a decade ago, in all of Latin America except for Brazil, Colombia, and parts of Central America China is outpacing the US as a preferred partner in the LAC region.[52]

To conclude this section, I want to compare the role of China and the US in the Western Hemisphere according to some of the traditional measures of hegemonic might: arms sales, trade, and FDI. Since China sells arms only to developing nations, I will compare the two countries on that measure. On a global scale, in 2015 the US accounted for 41 percent of arms transfer agreements with developing nations and China just 9 percent.[53] In the Western Hemisphere China's arms transfers to Latin America have more than tripled since 2008 and averaged US$2.7 billion annually from 2012 to 2015; average US arms transfers to LAC held steady at US$2.6 billion annually during the same period. To put these numbers in perspective, from 2012 to 2015 China's arms sales to LAC averaged 16.3 percent of its total whereas around 46 percent went to Africa and 10 percent to Asia over the same time period. Nevertheless, given that China and the US are now running neck and neck in arms sales to LAC, should Washington be more wary?

Ted Piccone of the Brookings Institution quotes a report from the hawkish US–China Economic and Security Commission (USCESC) which states that China poses no obvious security threat to the region at this time.[54] USCESC identifies two phases of Chinese arms sales to LAC: "First, low-level military sales and exchanges of items like transport aircraft and anti-tank missiles (1990–2000), and second, sales worth approximately US$100 million a year of more sophisticated equipment such as aircraft, radar, and air-to-air missiles, mainly to Venezuela but also to Ecuador, Peru, Bolivia, and Argentina (2000–2015)."[55] More recently, China has ventured into higher-tech military agreements with LAC countries, for example, the February 2015 deal for Argentina and China to coproduce amphibious armored vehicles and the integration of Chinese fighter airplanes into the Argentine fleet. The former Peronist party president Cristina Fernández de Kirchner negotiated a number of clandestine agreements with China, including the construction of a satellite and space control station in Patagonia that could plausibly be converted to a Chinese military base. It was up to the subsequent center-right administration of Mauricio Macri to secure an agreement from Beijing stating that this base could be used only for "peaceful purposes."[56]

Others are more equivocal about these trends. Allan Nixon points to China's lower prices and lack of conditionality in selling arms to these LAC countries: "This could pave the way for China to reap the benefits of enhanced diplomatic relations and economic ties, such as helping secure the lucrative energy deals it so doggedly seeks."[57] As Nixon cautions, "China's influence-building endeavors through these sales would likely negatively impact US influence over the long term in the process." This is an important consideration, especially given that in 2017 China built its first overseas military base in Djibouti, Africa, and this was surely just the beginning of its foreign military expansion. If it attempted to do the same in Buenos Aires or Rio de Janeiro, though, this would indeed be a geopolitical catastrophe from the standpoint of the entire Western alliance. Michael Beckley argues why this scenario is so improbable: "Inefficiencies and barriers drag down China's military might. On average, Chinese weapons systems are roughly half as capable as those of the United States in terms of range, firepower, and accuracy. Chinese troops, pilots, and sailors lack combat experience and receive less than half the training of their American counterparts. Moreover, border defense and internal security consume at least 35 percent of China's military budget and bog down half of its active-duty force."[58]

On trade, in 2018 total exports and imports between China and Latin America amounted to nearly US$306 billion whereas total US–LAC trade was about US$896 billion this same year. On FDI, the US accounted for 35 percent of LAC's FDI in "greenfield," or new investments, in 2016 (US$24.2 billion) compared with China's 5 percent share (US$3.7 billion). It is true that China has become the most important partner in terms of total trade for Brazil, Chile, Peru, and Uruguay.[59] Yet in the bigger scheme of things Latin America still represents a small slice of China's go out strategy and internationalized development model. Ever mindful of this being the US sphere of influence and of its own dependence on investing in and exporting to the US market, China has trod cautiously in the Western Hemisphere.[60]

Regardless of the erratic attention the US has paid to the region in the 2000s, Latin America's importance to the US is still evident in terms of economic weight, long-standing political influence, and security ties. Occupying a huge chunk of the Western Hemisphere, LAC is also a crucial factor in the ability of the US to project power globally. Further examination of the participation of both the US and China in Latin America suggests an emerging division of labor. The US will no doubt continue to promote democracy, property rights, the rule of law, and investment in services and manufacturing in the region, while China will do the heavy lifting with trade expansion, resource extraction, infrastructure investment, and a range of other development endeavors. In essence, China's participation in Latin America has largely been developmental in nature, which reflects its own status as an EE. A pathbreaking article by Francisco Urdinez and his colleagues titled "Chinese Economic Statecraft and US Hegemony in Latin America," argues that, if anything, "Beijing has filled a void left by a diminished US presence in the latter's own backyard."[61] For the US, a more sensible approach to the China–LAC phenomenon would be to deepen economic and diplomatic ties with both sides on matters concerning the Western Hemisphere.

The breakdown of democracy in Venezuela in August 2017—with President Nicolás Maduro staging a rigged election for an assembly that would enable him to write a new constitution and rule by dictatorial fiat—is the most recent example of this division of labor between China and the US in the Western Hemisphere. The US, the UK, the EU, and a number of Latin American states refused to recognize the fraudulent Venezuelan vote, and the US, Mexico, and Colombia promptly announced sanctions against Maduro and a number of his appointed officials. The Venezuelan crisis offered a concrete opportunity for China to step into the fray and thus intrude on US hegemony. At least one Chinese scholar has in fact argued that Beijing is waiting in the wings "to create a 'sphere of influence' in the traditional 'backyard' of the United States ... in retaliation for the US containment and encirclement of China" in the Asian region.[62] In fact, China shirked any semblance of a showdown.[63]

At this stage China's strategic partnerships (SPs) in the region are trade, investment, and resource-based, and it is best not to read too much more into them. China has cloaked these SPs in its own version of soft power and laced them with euphemisms about mutual trust, reciprocity, special understanding, and so on. The bottom line is that China has brokered loans-for-oil deals with Ecuador and Venezuela but does not intend to spend political capital in support of their anti-US follies.[64] Brazil, moreover, may be the top recipient of Chinese OFDI to the region, but the two countries have been at loggerheads over China's refusal to support Brazil's bid for a permanent seat on the UN Security Council. China also has a running battle with its top LAC trade partners—Argentina, Brazil, and Mexico—over anti-dumping complaints filed by all three countries against the PRC at the WTO. Although realist thinkers have not been able to wrap their heads around the notion or implications of China's internationalization of its development strategy into the Western Hemisphere, there is little sign that China's activities in the region pose a threat to US hegemony.[65]

The Dependency School Revival: Thick Description, Thin Explanation

With regard to the political economic dynamics that have been unfolding since the explosion of China–LAC trade and investment ties in the 2000s, the two most common dependency school diagnoses have been "unequal exchange" and "Dutch disease,"[66] or the "resource curse." Unequal exchange refers to the dependence of a developing region like LAC on primary exports, which are plagued by cyclical price downturns, and the reliance of these countries on the import of manufactured goods, for which prices tend to rise in an upward secular pattern. This concept became a mainstay of the dependency school's emphasis on the international system and this core–periphery relationship, in particular, as the perpetuator of underdevelopment.[67] However, the transformation of Japan, Taiwan, and South Korea from poor (10 percent or less of US per capita GDP) to rich (50 percent or more of US per capita GDP) countries since the 1970s suggests that the structure of international capitalism is less important than the domestic institutions and actual policies which a given state relies on to engage in global markets.[68]

The rise of China in the global economy is further evidence of the shortcomings of this paradigm when it comes to explaining the widely varying political economic performance of the EEs. Although China still has some way to go in order to cross over the threshold into developed country status, Beijing's policy makers clearly have their eye on this prize. According to World Bank estimates, at the outset of the reform era in 1979 China's per capita GDP was US$182; at last count, in 2017, that same figure was US$7,329. When calculated by purchasing power parity, Chinese per capita GDP was US$15,308 in 2017.[69] China's total GDP was about US$76.9 billion in 1979 and now stands at around US$11.2 trillion. The dependency school has always been adept at describing policy failures and downward mobility in the developing world but struggles to explain these successful Asian breakout cases.

On this question of unequal exchange, with the exception of Costa Rica and Mexico it is true that the pattern of trade between China and its SPs has mirrored the old-fashioned comparative advantage model that existed in the region at the beginning of the twentieth century: South American countries mainly export commodities and raw materials to China and import value-added manufactured goods back from China. Another reality is the asymmetrical nature of the China–LAC relationship in terms of FDI. Total LAC OFDI to China from 2003 to 2018 is estimated to be around US$5.3 billion[70] versus the roughly US$109.1 billion in Chinese outflows of FDI to LAC from 2000 to 2017.[71] Yet whereas the earlier experience with this pattern of trade and FDI inspired policies of import-substitution industrialization (ISI) and a widespread critique of the unfavorable terms of trade for the region, the structural conditions that now prevail within most of these economies are radically different.[72]

Table I.4. Average manufacturing rates in LAC 2000–2017

Country	Manufactures exports (% of merchandise exports)	Manufacturing, value added (% of GDP)
Argentina	30.9	16.5
Brazil	44.4	12.5
Chile	14.9	13.0
Costa Rica	60.6*	14.9
Mexico	78.6	16.5
Peru	16.4*	15.3

*Data available only through 2016.
Source: World Development Indicators; data computed as average value of 2000–2017 statistics, available at http://databank.worldbank.org/data/home.aspx.

With the exception of Chile and Peru, considerable inroads have been made with industrialization in the LAC EEs, and manufactured goods accounted for at least 44.4 percent of total exports on average from Brazil, 60.6 percent from Costa Rica, and 78.6 percent from Mexico between 2000 and 2017 (table I.4). Moreover, for all but Costa Rica and Mexico, the terms of trade during the China boom were highly favorable. The downside of this story is that, although forward linkages in terms of manufactured exports have clearly improved in LAC, backward linkages to the domestic market are still too weak. This is the case with Mexico, for example, where manufacturing production relies on incoming FDI to the extent that local producers of intermediate goods are still not competitive as suppliers in these production zones.[73] To a lesser extent, Argentina and Brazil face this same dilemma: hence the ease with which China has captured export niches for intermediate inputs in Argentina, Brazil, and Mexico. Put simply, those intermediate goods that producers in all three of these LAC EEs are importing from China are higher in value-added and technological content, and they are priced more competitively.

LAC EEs have not kept pace with the gains in competitiveness that China has registered in its manufacturing sector over the past twenty years, advances that are the result of highly focused expenditures and policies that have promoted science, technological adaptation, advanced education in hard science fields, and research and development since the early 1980s.[74] Based on his econometric analysis, Jaime Ortiz argues that LAC "has reached a point in its production possibilities frontier at which it is not feasible to further increase its level of output unless technology and innovation come into play. Latin America must broaden its productivity base, move into more sophisticated endeavors, and diversify its export basket to gain market share."[75] Despite their advocacy of import-substitution and protectionism, even the earlier theorists of unequal exchange advocated technology adaptation, the strengthening of backward linkages, and export diversification.[76] With the rise of China in regional markets, LAC countries are more pressed than ever before to climb quickly up the value-added production ladder and to articulate a longer-term vision for a growth model based on efficiency, innovation, and competitiveness.[77]

Diagnoses of the resource curse hold more weight. This term relates to a country's dependence on commodity exports at the expense of the industrial sector, job creation, and sound macroeconomic policy making.[78] Although this label originated with reference to the natural gas boom and accompanying currency appreciation in the Netherlands, it caught on quickly as an analytical lens through which to explain this similar resource curse occurrence in the developing countries. In days of old the cluster of macroeconomic policies that underpinned the resource curse in Latin America— trade protectionism, financial repression, fiscal profligacy, and overvalued exchange rates—readily set the stage for a full-blown balance-of-payments crisis once commodity prices began to tumble. As I suggested earlier, the GFC unveiled the merit of the macroeconomic, financial sector and trade reforms that were undertaken by many LAC countries over the past two decades. These reform advances helped to fend off the old-fashioned balance-of-payments implosions that used to erupt in the wake of a commodity price boom. Venezuela, which has obstinately refused to move forward on economic policy reforms and the modernization of domestic financial institutions, provides the counterfactual here, as the economy sank to new depths when petroleum prices plummeted in 2014–15 (see table I.1).[79]

For the other LAC EEs, the exchange rate has been the most difficult variable to control. In response to the GFC the US Federal Reserve Bank ran a near-zero interest rate policy from December 2008 until late 2015, and since then inflation and interest rates have remained low. As a result, there has been a sizeable spread in EE interest rates vis-à-vis those of countries that are in the Organization of Economic Cooperation and Development (OECD) bloc. This situation encouraged massive capital inflows to some LAC EEs in the 2000s and, when combined with the aforementioned commodity price boom, the accumulation of unprecedented levels of foreign exchange reserves. One consequence was the considerable overvaluation of the LAC currencies up through the devaluation of the Chinese yuan in August 2015. Back in 2011 the former Colombian finance minister Mauricio Cárdenas called attention to this "financial Dutch disease," cautioning that some LAC countries were losing exchange rate and export competitiveness at the hands of enthusiastic global speculators and thus becoming "too expensive for their own good."[80]

To be clear, financial Dutch disease is just one possible outcome in this scenario. For example, Chile and Peru were even harder hit by falling commodity prices and the drop in Chinese demand post-2013, although policy makers in both countries weathered this storm much better than their South American neighbors did. Guillermo Perry and Alejandro Forero attribute the success of both Chile and Peru to "a combination of higher previous TFP [total factor productivity] growth in industry in Peru and Chile and to two macro policy factors that mitigated the extent of real exchange rate appreciation in both countries: first, they were the only two countries in the region that kept a fiscal surplus during the boom . . . and second, they accumulated larger fractions of reserves to GDP than the rest."[81] The authors add that Chile and Peru also undertook the most significant countercyclical fiscal interventions in the throes of the GFC but tapered these policies down to precrisis levels once the recovery was under way. Although Brazil and Argentina successfully executed counter-cyclical policies in 2008–9, both countries simply continued to spend in the postcrisis period.

While I have questioned the usefulness of falling back into this dependency school paradigm in search of explanations, I would not rule them out entirely. But both must be viewed from the vantage point of the twenty-first century. Whereas earlier reference to unequal exchange pertained to commodity exporters with low levels of industrial development, the cases of Argentina and Brazil confirm that this dynamic can also take hold when a country has achieved a sizeable level of industrial capacity and exports. As for the resource curse, the initial emphasis on manufacturing sector decline during a commodity price boom misses the mark, as LAC's average level of manufactured exports was roughly 47 percent in 2013.[82] Financial Dutch disease, and the steep currency appreciation that tends to accompany it, is another matter. Under the thrust of massive capital inflows, soaring commodity prices, and the accumulation of unprecedented levels of foreign exchange reserves, currency appreciation was most dramatic in Brazil post-2006 and in Argentina post-2009.[83] In Argentina currency overvaluation was exacerbated by the resort to 1960s-style financial repression as once-competent counter-cyclical policies overstayed their welcome and remained in place long after the country's successful rebound from the GFC.

A twenty-first-century rendition of the resource curse is perhaps best captured by a rich and evolving body of literature which highlights the quality of domestic institutions as the variable that most decisively explains differences in development outcomes between countries that are abundant in natural resources.[84] This literature raises two interrelated questions that will inform my own analysis in chapter 5: (1) In what ways might institutional weaknesses condition the effects of natural resource abundance on economic performance? (2) How might otherwise effective institutions deteriorate under the force of a major commodity boom?[85] In line with the distinction that Daron Acemoglu and James Robinson make between efficient and extractive institutions when explaining economic trajectories,[86] Halvor Mehlum and his coauthors frame this phenomenon in terms of "grabber-friendly" versus "producer-friendly" institutions: "With grabber-friendly institutions there are gains from specialization in unproductive influence activities, for instance due to a weak rule of law, malfunctioning bureaucracy, and corruption. Grabber-friendly institutions can be particularly bad for growth when resource abundance attracts scarce entrepreneurial resources out of production and into unproductive activities. With producer-friendly institutions, however, rich resources attract entrepreneurs into production, implying higher growth."[87]

Just how low Argentine institutions, broadly defined, sank during the 2003–13 China boom can be easily detected in their rankings (table I.5). Brazil, on this count, came out of the boom marginally better. China, which

Table I.5. Latin America's and China's institutional rankings, 2018
(percentile rank among all countries)

Country	Doing business—total countries: 189 (closer to 0 = favorable)	Competitiveness report—total countries: 144 (closer to 0 = favorable)	Corruption perceptions— total countries: 175 (closer to 100 = favorable)	Economic freedom—total countries: 178 (closer to 100 = favorable)
Argentina	119	81	49	52
Brazil	109	72	35	52
Chile	56	33	67	75
China	46	28	39	58
Costa Rica	67	55	56	65
Mexico	54	46	28	65
Peru	68	63	35	68

Sources: World Bank, http://doingbusiness.org/rankings; World Economic Forum, http://reports.we forum.org/global-competitiveness-report-2018/competitiveness-rankings/;Transparency International, https://www.transparency.org/cpi2018; and Heritage Foundation, http://www.heritage.org/index /ranking.

deplores these indicators and has repeatedly asked to be deleted from these databases, actually ties with the low rankings of Argentina and Brazil on crucial measures like regulatory quality, rule of law, and corruption perceptions.[88] At the same time, in overall competitiveness rankings China sits at 27, whereas Argentina and Brazil sit at 92 and 80, respectively. This suggests a scenario in China in which, despite massive rent seeking and corruption, producer-friendly institutions function to the extent that economic growth has not been significantly deterred. Yuen Yuen Ang describes the wider setting that has facilitated China's higher competitiveness ranking: "It was . . . Beijing's willingness to allow and direct local improvisation that enabled the nation's economic dynamism. . . . [T]he country leveraged local knowledge and resources, promoted diversity, and motivated people to contribute their ideas and effort."[89]

Thus far political leaders and policy makers in both Argentina and Brazil have not been able to muster the institutional cohesion and esprit de corps that stand out in Ang's quote. In both countries the China boom unleashed numerous instances of institution grabbing. In Argentina, for example, political elites led by Fernández de Kirchner (2007–15) extracted mounds of cash by directly taxing soybean exports and channeling these revenues into populist subsidies on energy and other consumer necessities. During this same period Brazilian elites pocketed billions from Petrobras and ran down both the company and the country's credit rating from investment grade to junk bonds in just a matter of months. But other resource-abundant countries, like Chile and Peru, were able to maintain growth and significantly raise per capita GDP both during and after the China boom. While table I.5 sheds light on the institutional foundations of this relative success, the dependency school offers few insights into these markedly different development stories.

The broader question, it seems, should be how a critical juncture like the China boom worked to strengthen (or deter) political and economic institutions, lower (or raise) the barriers to reform, and open (or close) the way for new leadership, organizational change, and policy innovation.[90] Two insights come to mind. First, as Douglass North reminds us and the Chilean and Peruvian cases suggest, development need not be "a story of inevitability in which the past neatly predicts the future."[91] There is, in other words, nothing deterministic about these trends; rather, they reflect how domestic institutions and interests have interacted over time within a fiercely changing global environment. Second, hindsight shows the considerable leeway for human agency and policy innovation that LAC policy makers have been afforded by the rise of China in Latin America. If anything, this phenomenon has confirmed the extent to which institutions, leadership, and sound policy making truly matter.

Plan of the Book

The book is written in two parts. First, in chapters 1–3 I build my argument about the nature of China's internationalized development strategy, Latin America's role in it, and the interactive effects of this rapidly growing bond on six of China's designated SPs in the LAC region: Argentina, Brazil, Chile, Costa Rica, Mexico, and Peru. In chapter 1 I argue that the rise of

China in both LAC and the world economy has forced us to rethink established paradigms and emergent debates in the fields of IPE and development economics. I also review the empirical evidence—trade, FDI, lending, and aid flows—on how LAC has been incorporated into China's internationalized development strategy, and I explain how I have grouped the three case studies. In chapter 2 I situate the China–LAC relationship in its proper historical context, going back to the founding of the PRC in 1949, as opposed to the tendency of the recent literature on this topic to take the onset of the commodity boom as the beginning of a new relationship.[92] From there, in chapter 3, follows a comparative political economy analysis of the markedly different economic reforms undertaken since the 1980s by China, on one side of the Pacific, and the LAC countries, on the other.

The second half of the book, chapters 4–6, probes the ways in which the impact of China's political economic engagement in the region has varied according to a given country's endowment factors, institutional rigor and depth, and the nature of the development model in place at the turn of the twenty-first century. I identify three political economic clusters that have sprung to life over the past two decades: (1) the three small open economies (Chile, Costa Rica, and Peru) that have made openness work in their respective relationships with China. By entering into separate bilateral Free Trade Agreements (FTAs) with China all three have expanded the conceptual contours of bilateral integration and raised expectations about the potential for south–south FTAs to bear more fruit; (2) the complementary advantage Argentina and Brazil enjoy in their respective relationships with China. These countries are the most closely integrated into China's internationalized development strategy and ostensibly industrialized enough to have avoided a full-blown episode of the resource curse; however, a broadened definition of this term points to institutional erosion as a main drag on growth in the wake of the China boom; and (3) Mexico's position of competitive disadvantage vis-à-vis China, despite its standing as the most industrialized of the six SPs considered here.

The trends are not all positive, and news on the rise of China in Latin America is not all good. Nevertheless, I believe that this phenomenon offers plenty of reasons for optimism. First, although Chinese demand for LAC's raw commodities has clearly waned, patterns of commercial exchange

across the Pacific are still vibrant. Second, LAC has quickly become a bene-
ficiary of China's status as a capital-abundant EE. But unlike the 1970s,
when the mass of loans flowing into the region was propelled by a capital
glut related to the 1974–75 oil price shocks, Chinese loans and OFDI are
tied to specific productive projects where the barriers to exit are quite high.
Finally, China's entry into LAC has both highlighted the need for yet another round of reforms to improve efficiency and competitiveness and provided policy makers with considerable financial room to forge ahead with
these reforms. It is now up to political leaders, policy makers, and economic
elites in these countries to focus on seizing the rich trade and investment
opportunities China is offering while also looking for creative ways to minimize the risks.

Dragonomics: An Internationalized Development Strategy

Development is a hard truth.

Deng Xiaoping[1]

SINCE THE FOUNDING OF THE People's Republic of China (PRC) in 1949 and that country's search for allies of like minds, the relationship between China and Latin America and the Caribbean region (LAC) has gone on to surpass anyone's wildest expectations. What began as a political outreach effort on the part of the PRC some seventy years ago is well on its way to becoming one of the most compelling new south–south economic bonds across the Pacific region. Researchers at Boston University's Global Economic Governance Initiative have been the most prolific and accurate in charting this trend. I quote from their 2015 headlines: "China surpassed the United States as South America's most important destination for exports"; "China's policy banks have become the largest annual public creditors to LAC governments"; "Chinese investment in LAC spiked in 2013, with China comprising over half of new (greenfield) projects in LAC that year."[2] Underpinning these dazzling numbers is China's historically unprecedented average annual growth rate of 9–10 percent over three decades, its amassment of the world's highest level of foreign exchange reserves, and its approximation of Japan to become one of the largest holders of US Treasury securities.

For the PRC, the story of the rise of China in Latin America is yet another angle on the phenomenal economic progress of this country since policy makers there declared their "reform and opening" project in 1978, followed by their go out strategy in 1999. To this day Chinese officials have set their sights almost single-mindedly on spurring growth and development.[3] For LAC, the spectacular figures just cited basically apply to fewer than half of the countries in the region, including Argentina, Brazil, Chile, Peru, and, secondarily, Colombia, Ecuador, and Venezuela. For this group, which fortuitously holds an abundance of precisely those natural resources China needs to sustain its high-growth development model, the period 2003–13 was an unprecedented boon. Prices on copper, oil, and iron ore tripled on global commodity markets, and those for soybeans and fish meal doubled.

The price boom caught these LAC countries at very different points on their respective political economic trajectories. Argentina, for example, was just coming off a massive US$100 billion debt default and rolling back market reforms that had been implemented in the 1990s; Brazil had just elected its first Workers' Party candidate, who turned out to be more market friendly (and corrupt) than expected; Chile had just completed its decade-long quest to launch a bilateral free trade agreement (FTA) with the US; Mexico, for better or worse, had finally made its prolonged transition to an electoral democracy; and Peru's president had just faxed in his resignation from Japan, where he had fled to evade charges of murder, graft, and conspiracy.

For all of these countries, massive inflows of foreign exchange in the 2000s opened up new opportunities for poverty reduction, domestic credit expansion, fiscal reform, and productive investment. At the same time, the boom fostered conditions that were ripe for corruption, populist spending sprees, and general reform backsliding. While prices on China's most prized commodity imports have been on the wane since 2013 (see table I.1), these still remain well above their 2000 baseline. Nevertheless, the slowing of Chinese demand has meant a drop in LAC exports and foreign exchange earnings and thus the inevitable period of adjustment as commodity markets settle back down to normal.

This postboom period raises a rich array of questions concerning the effect of China's rise on these countries. As I stated in the introduction, my argument is that China has of necessity internationalized its development strategy in ways that have had dramatic consequences for the LAC region. As a middle-income, developing region with a sophisticated consumer base, LAC countries have provided buoyant demand for China's finished consumer goods and for its intermediate inputs for manufacturing and industry. In addition, for the handful of LAC countries with rich natural resource endowments Chinese demand has been a game-changer, not only in terms of the massive revenues this has generated but also due to Chinese financing of the infrastructure and transportation networks necessary for extracting these resources and shipping them across the Pacific. The domestic political economy and developmental logic of these key LAC countries have been unavoidably influenced by their incorporation into China's internationalized development model.

To be clear, my approach is not to be confused with that of Francis Fukuyama, who argued in a 2016 essay that "China is seeking to export its development model to other countries."[4] The comment refers to China's ambitious launching of the One Belt One Road (BRI) infrastructure initiative in 2013, which intends to connect the ancient Silk Road and seaborne transit routes from China through Central Asia, South Asia, the Middle East, and Europe. Fukuyama aptly depicts BRI as unilateral on China's part; in contrast, the China–LAC relationship is both bilateral and mini-lateral, the latter taking shape in two summits between China and the Community of Latin American and Caribbean States (CELAC) that were held in 2015 in Beijing and 2018 in Santiago, Chile. As of yet Latin America has attracted modest BRI support—for a highway in Argentina and a bridge in Panama. Chile, too, signed on to BRI in 2018, although thin details were offered on this memorandum of understanding. Five years into BRI participating countries in Asia are already accruing unforeseen debt on BRI projects, and it has become clear that host governments must hold China's feet to the fire if they hope to honor their own project-related environmental impact assessments.[5]

My point is that China does not have the natural resources to go it alone in its quest to maintain steady growth and has had to incorporate resource-rich emerging economies (EEs) into its development model in order to sustain it. Fukuyama cautions, "The US and other Western countries need to ask themselves why infrastructure has become so difficult to build, not just in developing countries but at home as well. Unless we do, we risk ceding the future of Eurasia and other important parts of the world to China and its development model." My response to this zero-sum view is that the West and certainly the US have been out of the business of infrastructure investment in mega-projects in the developing countries since the "lost decade" of the 1980s. Bushra Bataineh and his colleagues attribute this withdrawal of the US and development institutions like the World Bank to two factors. First is the increasingly risk averse lending milieu in the West, whereby transaction costs on infrastructure loans have ballooned due to strict fiduciary guidelines and social / environmental standards.

Second, the prospect for increased Western infrastructure investment in the developing countries has been mitigated by domestic politics. In the case of the US, right–left considerations around corruption and corporate welfare on the part of conservatives and labor / environmental concerns on the part of liberals account for the steep contraction in spending allocated for infrastructure over the past decade. But there is another angle on this matter: Chinese involvement in building infrastructure in Latin America is actually complementary to that of the US, where services, manufacturing, and finance dominate its LAC trade and investment. Apparently meant to counter China's BRI initiative, the Trump administration reactively rescued rather than terminated the US Overseas Private Investment Corporation in 2018 and even doubled its budget to US$60 billion.[6] However, these funds would be better spent in coordination with some of China's ongoing development projects in the region, not in competition with them.

A Brief Historical Backdrop to China–LAC Relations

China's entry into the World Trade Organization (WTO) in 2001 had a profound effect on its ability to greatly increase trade with the rest of the world. From 1993 to 1998 policy makers there had launched a wave of reforms meant to correct for previous errors and to deepen the country's commitment to an export-led industrialization strategy. Susan Shirk observes that on the political front Deng, "although falling short of democratization, proposed a system governed by rules, clear lines of authority, and collective decision-making institutions to replace the overconcentration of power and patriarchal rule that had characterized China under Mao." In terms of China's economic progress prior to WTO entry, Barry Naughton writes that fiscal, corporate, foreign, and financial sector measures amounted to "a burst of remarkably decisive and effective reform policymaking [that] transformed every aspect of the Chinese economy."[7] This political economic reform momentum, combined with WTO entry, set the stage for China's voracious demand for those commodities needed to fuel its modernization drive and take it to the next level. Yes, LAC producers of these commodities were poised to step up and meet Chinese demand, but these relationships had been established decades earlier. In fact, these LAC countries had been selling the very same products to China throughout the post–World War II period.

Long before the normalization of diplomatic ties between China and these LAC countries, and even midst the US embargo against trade with China, "people-to-people" commercial relations had been established between China and various countries in the region.[8] For example, Argentina and Mexico both sold wheat to the PRC in the early 1960s as the severe mismanagement of grain stocks under Chairman Mao Zedong's Great Leap Forward industrial strategy led to widespread death and famine.[9] Large Chinese-sponsored trade exhibitions were staged in both Chile and Mexico in 1964, resulting in numerous informal bilateral deals to promote trade between private actors in China and in these host countries.[10] By the 1970s Brazil was trading iron ore in exchange for Chinese oil; China had become the third largest buyer of Chilean copper, and Chile was importing back from China light industrial goods, chemical products, tools, and machinery;[11] Mexican producers, moreover, had met with considerable success in selling value-added manufactured goods to their Chinese counterparts.

Despite these growing economic ties, from roughly 1949 to 1979 cross-Pacific relations were weighted more heavily toward politics. First were the efforts of the PRC to gain diplomatic recognition from afar and to isolate the so-called renegade province of Taiwan (Republic of China, or ROC); second, the Chinese Communist Party (CCP) also saw Latin America as a possible ally and recruiting ground for fellow radicals of a socialist-communist bent. In the spirit of third world solidarity and advancing the "people's revolution," China hosted delegations of students, teachers, lawyers, journalists, and individual investors from across the region. Cuba's revolutionary victory of 1959 and the eventual siding of Fidel Castro with the Soviets against the PRC saw the majority of LAC leftist political parties and would-be revolutionaries follow suit. Yet China continued to pursue its people-to-people strategy with Latin America, still looking to spruce up its foreign image and to drum up business deals. Countries like Argentina, Brazil, Chile, and Mexico returned these invitations in-kind. Numerous deals were cut between private actors, and these initiated a pattern of exchange that has prevailed to this day.

It was Mexican president Luis Echeverría's impassioned speech before the UN in 1971, which argued for the expulsion of Taiwan and the admission of China in its place, that helped rally the LAC vote which contributed to China's entry into the UN later that year—including a permanent seat on the UN Security Council. By 1974 Argentina, Brazil, Chile, Mexico, and Peru had all formally recognized the PRC and normalized diplomatic relations with Beijing—five years earlier than the opening of the US embassy there. From here followed a slew of cross-Pacific delegations at higher, more official levels. China's 1966–76 Cultural Revolution put a damper on China–LAC ties, although political and economic exchanges were resurrected by the mid-1970s. Up until Deng and his visionary cohort launched deep reforms in the late 1970s China continued to voice political support for LAC on issues of sovereignty, economic justice, and the right to self-determination even as LAC countries grappled steadily with challenges on all of these fronts. The PRC also tended to vote steadily with LAC on issues before the UN during this period.

Following the 1989 military massacre of Chinese student protesters in Tiananmen Square, China was widely condemned by the West. Perhaps the one exception was the LAC countries, which actively reached out in hosting delegations of distinguished Chinese officials in the immediate aftermath of this tragedy. Post-Tiananmen, the CCP dropped its rhetorical political support of fellow revolutionaries and developing countries and stuck mainly to economic exchanges and business relations.[12] Throughout this book it will become evident that Beijing's attempt to cordon off politics in the China–LAC relationship has been itself profoundly political. At any

rate, by 1990 five LAC countries dominated trade with China in the following order: Brazil, Chile, Argentina, Peru, and Mexico. In the case of the first
four of these South American countries, the same products (iron ore, copper, and soybeans) have topped the list of exports to China ever since the
forging of these trade ties. By 2000 Mexico registered the highest total
trade with China, but of note here is that its trade with China had burgeoned on the import side. Since 1989 Mexico has consistently traded at a
deficit with China; as of 2013 this deficit accounted for some 85 percent of
the entire LAC trade deficit with China.

Up through the 1980s the LAC countries carried a trade surplus with
China in most years; during the people-to-people trade period from 1949 to
1979 producers in the LAC region actually complained that their Chinese
counterparts were not turning out the quality or kinds of goods they sought
to buy. The tables have now turned, although Mexico has since been the
only country to consistently carry a trade deficit with China. Apart from
Mexico and Costa Rica, from which China purchases a small amount of
value-added manufactured goods, the remainder of the countries considered here (Argentina, Brazil, Chile, and Peru) have exponentially increased
their sales of commodities to China but with little diversification of their
exports to China.

Costa Rica is the newcomer here, as it made a diplomatic about-face in
2007 and recognized China over Taiwan. This resulted in the implementation of the PRC–Costa Rica FTA in 2011, China's designation of Costa
Rica as a strategic partner (SP) in 2015, and Costa Rica's opportunity to
extend its information technology (IT) cluster into Chinese and other Asian
production-export chains.[13] Mexico remains the outlier in this scenario.
From 2001 to 2017 Mexico's value-added manufactured exports to China
averaged about 28 percent of its total exports to China, although China accounts for just roughly 2 percent of Mexico's overall exports. Competition
from China in domestic and third markets (mainly the US) continues to
overwhelm Mexican producers.

At the aforementioned Beijing–CELAC forum in January 2015 the Chinese government committed to doubling China–LAC trade and China's
outward foreign direct investment (OFDI) to LAC by 2025.[14] As ambitious
as this may sound, total LAC–China trade increased to US$306 billion in

2018, up from just a few billion dollars in 2000. China's stated outward FDI goals could be a reach, as a number of mega-infrastructure projects led by Chinese consortia have slowed in the face of local political complications, allegations of corruption, environmental damage, and red tape on both sides.[15] Nevertheless, two decades ago these sums were simply unthinkable. The rise of China in both LAC and the world economy has shown just how quickly the unimaginable can become a reality.

Reconceptualizing International Political Economy (IPE) and Development Models in the Wake of China's Rise

China, the West, and the International Political Economy: Parallel Worlds

The spectacular ascendance of China has breathed new life into the field of development economics, and it has forced us to ask new questions and rethink long-standing expectations and paradigms in the fields of international relations (IR) and IPE. The world has simply never seen anything like this: the rapid rise of a behemoth authoritarian developmental state with a diehard commitment to high growth and fast economic advancement—which also happens to be home to the largest population on earth. China may be poised to surpass the US and the rest of the OECD bloc in terms of GDP size, but at least for now the nature of its political regime works directly against membership in this developed country club. The surge of China and its potential to fulfill expectations for global leadership are obviously tainted by the dogged commitment that the country's political leaders have shown toward maintaining an authoritarian regime and with this a domestic economic policy approach that lacks transparency.[16]

Based on earlier generations of IR / IPE scholarship, China's sheer amassment of wealth, not to mention its greatly increased military capabilities, would be considered synonymous with an increase in power. Under these earlier theoretical assumptions China's projected ascendance to the largest GDP in the world economy and thus the top country in the IPE by 2027 (if not sooner) would equate with its playing a stronger leadership role and providing the kinds of international public goods (e.g., aid, security, lender-of-last-resort) that Great Britain and the US offered during the respective hegemonic heyday of each. This worldview was long ago challenged by the advent of a multipolar power-sharing arrangement and hence new patterns of "complex interdependence."[17] China's rise, however, defies both the old liberal hegemonic and the new multipolar IPE paradigms. This new phenomenon, in short, does not fit neatly into long-standing molds.

This reality does not mean that IR / IPE scholars have stopped working off of old theories, rather than seizing the opportunity of China's rise to engage in theory expansion. For example, Realist scholars, including those that identify as classical and structural, agree on one main point: "The rise of China must be seen as a potentially dangerous destabilization of the international system."[18] Writing in the structural / offensive vein, the premier realist John Mearsheimer counsels, "The optimal strategy for dealing with a rising China is containment . . . [this] is an alternative to war against a rising China. Nevertheless, war is always a possibility."[19] Liberal internationalist scholars are more sanguine but also naïve. Their expectation that China will eventually be absorbed into a US-led liberal hegemonic order— through persuasion, incentives, and, if necessary, disincentives—has already proven elusive.[20] Yes, China's ascendance in the Western Hemisphere does reflect its overall strategy of participating vigorously in the global economy as well as signing on to those multilateral norms that embody the liberal international ethos of Bretton Woods; however, China has not always reciprocated, and hence the aggressive unilateral measures of the Trump administration meant to penalize China for its supposed unfair trade and investment practices.

Disappointment toward China's illiberal stance vis-à-vis the West took hold during the Obama administration. Two frontline policy officials who worked on East Asian affairs under Obama, Kurt Campbell and Ely Ratner, have written on the numerous ways in which "Washington got China wrong."[21] Briefly, they complain, "rather than opening the country up to greater competition, the Chinese Communist Party, intent on maintaining control of the economy, is instead consolidating state-owned enterprises and pursuing industrial policies . . . that aim to promote national technology champions in critical sectors, including aerospace, biomedicine, and robotics."[22] Perhaps most egregious from the standpoint of the developed countries and the US in particular are China's requirements that foreign investors form joint ventures with Chinese partners which hold a majority position and that those foreign companies (some 20 percent of US firms) share technology with the Chinese partner company. At a less sophisticated level, Latin American entrepreneurs also complain about how difficult it is to access the Chinese market in terms of both exports and direct investment.

But the Western resentment of China raises at least two questions. First, could it be that this projection of liberal internationalist expectations onto China is precisely that? Chinese leaders have been quite articulate and succinct in expressing their long-term goals, which resonate with recapturing the glory of the past. Consider the joint publication of *China 2030: Building a Modern, Harmonious, and Creative Society* by the World Bank and the PRC's Development Research Center of the State Council (2013): this is hardly a treatise on how China intends to incorporate into a US-led liberal hegemonic order. Similarly, President Xi's goal of achieving developed country status by 2049—the one-hundredth anniversary of the Chinese revolution—is couched in "we'll do it our way" language. Peace, prosperity, and security are the catchwords here, and considerations of how these endeavors will jibe with the Western world are implicit at best. There is also a realistic chance that the CCP has gotten too far ahead of itself and that the catch-up phase will take much longer. In other words, liberal internationalists and realists alike may be misgauging China's true power capabilities.

My second question: To a certain extent don't some of these Western disappointments run in both directions? The emerging economies (EEs) have been clamoring for a larger spot at the G-7 decision-making table for years. The launching of the WTO's Doha Development Round in 2001 marked the first time they had enough economic muscle to thwart G-7 business as usual. At heart, the failure of that round hinged on the inability of the G-7 to table authentic proposals for the reduction of barriers in agriculture and to offer greater market access for nonagricultural finished goods from the EEs. Doha also fell victim to unprecedented US disengagement, although US negotiators held steady in demanding the deep liberalization of investment and services in the developing countries.

Now that the developing countries constitute a majority at the WTO, there would have to be much more give-and-take for the completion of any future multilateral trade agreement at the WTO. Another point of North–

South tension has been the unwillingness of the G-7 to increase significantly the weighted vote of the top EE members in the International Monetary Fund and the World Bank. The most noticeable reform, in 2016, saw
a near doubling of China's voting share in the IMF, from 3.81 to 6.16 percent.[23] This meant minor decreases for the G-7 countries, although there
was no change in the 16.73 percent that the US alone controls. Given pro-
jections that the Chinese and US economies will reach parity in less than a
decade, why should China's weighted vote in these Bretton Woods institutions trail the US by ten percentage points?[24]

Recall that the Obama economic team did all it could to thwart China's
launching of the Asian Infrastructure Investment Bank (AIIB) in 2015,
while four of its G-7 partners broke loose and joined on. Interestingly, the
World Bank and the Asian Development Bank are now partnering with
AIIB on a number of projects which surpass the resources of any one of
these institutions. The AIIB is just one example of what Oliver Stuenkel
refers to as China's efforts at parallel institution building, endeavors not
necessarily meant to undermine the Western order but rather to open alternative venues for trade, investment, and financial transactions in areas
that are still hardwired by the G-7 countries and thus less accessible to
outsiders.[25] With regard to finance, for example, Stuenkel points to the creation of China Union Pay as a non-Western alternative to Visa and Master-
Card and to the BRICs-led New Development Bank as parallel to the World
Bank. On trade and investment, Stuenkel refers to the China-led Regional
Comprehensive Economic Partnership (RCEP) as a correlate to the newly
resurrected Comprehensive and Progressive Agreement for Trans-Pacific
Partnership (CPTPP) and to China's Silk Road Fund, which has no Western
equivalent.

In a benign sense, we could interpret the mutual attraction of China and
LAC over the past two decades as a similar instance of parallelism. Although
the US–LAC relationship is distinctly different from the China–LAC one, I
have argued here that they are complementary and possibly positive-sum.
For the likes of Evan Ellis, the most prolific of the China–LAC hawks, my
position is far too soft. His take on the rise of China in the region is that the
PRC's "success is deceptively dangerous because economic and political
subjugation of the rest of the world is not their explicit goal, but simply an

unavoidable consequence . . . of their ascension to the top."[26] It is true that China will continue to pursue foreign economic policies toward LAC that uphold its own development goals and narrowly defined interests; but I insist that China's endeavors in Latin America tend to complement, rather than conflict with, US interests and concerns. Realist scholars in search of zero-sum interactions will have to set their sights elsewhere, as there has been no consistent attempt at alliance building or leverage tactics in the region on China's part.[27] Otherwise, the overview in this chapter suggests that those LAC countries which can help to promote China's ambitious development agenda can expect loans, trade deals, and outward FDI from China; those countries that do not fit this bill will see much less.

Development Economics and the Rise of China: The Asian Developmental State Redux

Like Japan and South Korea before it, China has made its way to the top of global markets by relying on a state-led strategy that has explicitly bolstered and incorporated the private sector into the economy. Long before China's widely hailed takeoff, a flourishing academic and policy literature had analyzed and debated the contours of the East Asian developmental state.[28] Based largely on the impressive economic boom that occurred in Japan, South Korea, and Taiwan from the 1960s on, this literature was a forerunner to the more recent deluge of books and articles on the rise of China. Certainly China shares with these forebears some of the long-recognized features of the East Asian developmental state: policy making placed in the hands of technocrats and bureaucrats within the government, close state–business collaboration, agricultural and land tenure reform, the accumulation of capital and its channeling toward productive endeavors, tying investment to export-led growth, offering incentives to promote competitiveness, and a long-term vision of a given country's growth and development path.

With regard to both domestic and foreign economic policy China nevertheless differs from these earlier cases in some significant ways. Whereas Japan, South Korea, and Taiwan were privy to large amounts of US aid, assistance, and easy access to the US market as part of the post–World War II reconstruction effort, the PRC was beholden to the USSR for economic aid, military assistance, and strategic advice until the Sino–Soviet split in 1960. Thereafter, the PRC found itself increasingly isolated in the Cold War climate of the 1960s and 1970s. The development strategy of China's communist regime was such that nearly all assets were controlled by the state up until the beginning of the reform era in 1978. At this juncture it was actually Japan that came forward to assist with Chinese reforms. Realizing that Japan could be of help to China in its pursuit of the four modernizations (agriculture, industry, national defense, and science and technology),[29] Deng signed the Sino–Japanese Treaty of Peace and Friendship in 1978 as a way of engaging Japanese support and policy advice for Chinese reform.[30] Although, the current acrimony in this bilateral relationship makes it difficult to imagine, from 1978 to 1992 Japan was more engaged with China than any other country and offered assistance with industrial restructuring and technology adaptation in particular.[31]

Nevertheless, in contrast with these other East Asian developmental states, China's reform effort took off some twenty-five years later, started from ground zero in terms of the complete economic dominance of state-owned enterprises (SOEs), lacked the initial institutional cohesion that has been so widely touted in the other East Asian cases,[32] and had few of the technological advantages that had been afforded to Japan, South Korea, and Taiwan by virtue of their postwar alliance with the US.[33] At the same time, although China was much more welcoming toward FDI at the outset than were these other so-called Asian miracles, it did not openly embrace its own private entrepreneurs or admit them to the CCP until the early 2000s.

As a late-late-late developer, China at the outset of reforms embraced the typically East Asian strategy of export-led growth based on exchange rate devaluation, financial repression, and constricted domestic consumption. Like their East Asian peers before them, Chinese policy makers moved boldly in 1980 with the creation of special economic zones, which dynamically joined FDI, trade, and cross-border production. The country's massive pool of cheap labor and huge economies of scale reaped a magnitude of returns that caught even Chinese policy makers by surprise.[34] In turn, the rapid accumulation of capital allowed for ambitious investments in infrastructure, industry, technology, research, and education. This quickly catapulted China from a position of severe capital scarcity to one of utmost capital abundance and to the world's top exporter of manufactured goods and the leading EE destination for FDI.

On the foreign economic policy front, Chinese OFDI and other capital outflows are a more recent phenomenon but have taken a path similar to that of Japan and South Korea. For example, Japanese and South Korean outgoing FDI to LAC gradually diversified away from commodities and labor-intensive operations. As of 2012, 35 percent of Japanese outgoing FDI to LAC was concentrated in services and 34 percent in manufacturing;[35] for this same year, data on outgoing Korean FDI to LAC show a breakdown of 24 percent in manufacturing and 44 percent in services and commerce.[36] After a heavy initial concentration of Chinese outgoing FDI in LAC's extractive industries, these investments are just beginning to diversify along lines similar to those of Japan and Korea (see table I.2 in the introduction). One contrast is that outgoing Chinese FDI to LAC has been largely undertaken by SOEs versus the greater private sector role in FDI outflows from Japan and South Korea.[37] Other foreign economic policies that distinguish China from the standard East Asian developmental state depicted in the literature include its initiation of currency swaps (e.g., with Argentina, Brazil, and Chile) and the granting of significant loans and foreign aid (e.g., to Bolivia, Costa Rica, Cuba, and the Caribbean Basin countries) while China itself is still an aid recipient.[38] Like Japan, China has also negotiated loan-for-oil agreements (e.g., with Brazil, Ecuador, and Venezuela), as the PRC is now the world's largest consumer of oil.[39]

China's Internationalized Development Strategy

Again, of particular interest here is the unique way that China has relied on foreign economic policy to quicken its reform pace and overcome its more difficult development challenges. In his tour de force *Chinese Economic Statecraft* William Norris identifies this as an understudied phenomenon and analyzes China's masterful orchestration of foreign economic policy from the Chinese perspective.[40] My task here is to capture the ways in which the China phenomenon has crystallized within Latin America—a similarly under-researched topic—which, since the turn of the new millen-

nium, has served as one of several regional arenas where this internationalized development strategy is playing out. First, China has engaged Latin
America as part of its larger goal to promote the internationalization of its
currency, the renminbi (RMB), also known as the yuan. In October 2016
the IMF board approved the inclusion of the Chinese yuan as a "freely us-
able" currency in the IMF's basket of reserve currencies, the first new currency to be added in fifty years.[41] Moreover, in 2018 230 A-share stocks from
mainland China were incorporated into the prestigious MSCI emerging
market index. Doubters remain, as some private sector analysts still reject
yuan-denominated financial instruments as far too risky.[42] The yuan, moreover, accounted for just 1.1 percent of foreign reserve holdings by the world's
governments in 2017 versus 64 percent for the US dollar.[43] Chinese policy
makers have thus vigorously promoted currency swaps with numerous
countries as a way of further promoting the yuan's circulation.[44] In the case
of LAC such swaps have been made between the People's Bank of China
and the central banks of Argentina (US$17.6 billion), Brazil (US$30 billion), and Chile (US$3.6 billion).

Second, given China's scarcity of natural resources and its dependence
on external suppliers to sustain its export-led manufacturing model, the
LAC region has become integral to the country's development strategy. The
quest to fuel industry (crude oil, copper, iron ore) and to feed (soybeans,
fish meal) the world's largest and increasingly prosperous population has
forced Chinese policy makers to find creative ways to secure these resources. One way China has sought to address this dilemma is by establishing strategic partnerships (SPs) with ten LAC countries: Brazil (1993), Venezuela (2001), Mexico (2003), Argentina (2004), Peru (2008), Chile (2012),
Costa Rica (2015), Ecuador (2015), Uruguay (2016), and Bolivia (2018).[45]
Although "strategic" tends to imply matters related to military cooperation
and security concerns in the Western setting, for China it is more of an
economic endeavor—albeit one cloaked in platitudes of friendship, trust,
and a long-term bilateral commitment between China and a given signa-
tory.[46] Yet it is no coincidence that nine of these LAC countries are highly
abundant in oil, soya beans, iron ore, copper, and other natural resources
that are vital inputs for Chinese growth. Finally, China's lending, grants,

and foreign aid to Latin America have also played a sizeable, if ill-defined, role in the incorporation of Latin America into China's internationalized development strategy.

Some of China's capital outflows to LAC have been harnessed in pursuit of its One-China policy. However, despite the public proclamations of Costa Rican and Panamanian leaders about "having seen the light" when deciding to diplomatically recognize China over Taiwan, the plain truth is that the decision to establish new diplomatic ties with a given country is made in Beijing. As Gastón Fornés and Álvaro Méndez have written, "Panama tried for years to convince Beijing to open the door to them, but China refused it and several other nations in order to avoid precipitating a diplomatic crisis by stripping Taipei of international personhood."[47] This was the case while Ma Ying-jeou and the Kuomintang were in power in Taiwan from 2008 to 2016, during which the PRC–ROC relationship improved. With the election of Tsai Ing-wen and the Democratic Progressive Party in May 2016 and the framing of a decidedly less favorable policy toward the mainland, Beijing returned to its One-China policy with vigor.[48] It is no coincidence, then, that Dominica, Grenada, and Costa Rica joined on to the One-China policy in 2005–7 while Panama, the Dominican Republic, and El Salvador followed suit in 2017–18.

Still, some of the last countries to recognize China—Belize, Guatemala, Haiti, Honduras, Nicaragua, Paraguay, Saint Kitts and Nevis, Saint Lucia, Saint Vincent, and the Grenadines—are located in the LAC region.[49] China has laid the groundwork for establishing diplomatic ties with these countries by joining the Caribbean Development Bank, launching the China–Caribbean Economic and Trade Cooperation Forum and offering US$1 billion in preferential loans to these very small players in 2011.[50] Once Beijing decides to incorporate a given country into the One-China fold, the rewards can be considerable. Costa Rica, for example, received US$180 million in grants for projects of that government's choosing, rendering China the largest source of foreign aid for Costa Rica. Barbara Stallings writes that "China also agreed to purchase US$300 million of Costa Rican government bonds on very favorable terms: 12 years for repayment and an interest rate of 2 percent."[51] As mentioned earlier, in 2011 Costa Rica also completed a bilateral FTA with China that afforded it considerable access to the Chinese market.

Chinese loans and aid to LAC have been bundled together with large outlays from the country's policy banks, in particular, the China Development Bank (CDB) and the China Export-Import Bank (CHEXIM). These bundled financial packages to select LAC countries go to the heart of China's internationalized development strategy, as they are channeled into the construction of transport networks, power plants, telecommunications, and the upgrading of oil and mining infrastructure—all related to building up a given country's productive and export capacity. Through numerous joint ventures China is contributing to the development of select LAC countries so that they can become stronger partners in the provision of primary exports and offer the kinds of market opportunities China needs to propel its own growth and development.

One caveat here is the poor quality of data on aid and outward FDI flows from China to LAC. China simply does not make its foreign aid data available;[52] and the figures on outward FDI from China to LAC are clouded by the fact that the bulk of these flows have been channeled through offshore tax havens in the Cayman Islands and the Bahamas. The lack of accurate data has led to wild, questionable guestimates of the kind found in a recent Rand Corporation study.[53] Rather than try to redesign this wheel, I rely here on the very best of this research, including the data on China–LAC trade and Chinese FDI to LAC compiled by Boston University's Global Development Policy Center; the "Monitor of China's OFDI in Latin America and the Caribbean 2018" compiled by Enrique Dussel Peters;[54] Stallings's work on Chinese foreign aid flows to LAC;[55] and the extensive work of Kevin Gallagher and Margaret Myers in building the "China–Latin America Finance Database" at the Inter-American Dialogue in Washington, DC.[56]

This latter source tracks lending to LAC from China's policy banks. Together, CDB and CHEXIM have lent approximately US$150 billion to LAC countries between 2005 and 2017; in 2015 alone lending from these two banks was nearly double the total combined funds lent to the region by Western multilateral banks, including the World Bank, the Inter-American Development Bank (IDB), and the Latin American Development Bank.[57] Chinese outward FDI to LAC between 2010 and 2017 was roughly US$109.1 billion; about US$27 billion went toward greenfield investments, and US$63.4 billion was for mergers and acquisitions. While the early emphasis of outward Chinese FDI was on raw materials, Chinese data from 2000 to 20017 show that a diversification into services began in 2010 (totaling US$33.1 billion over the 2000 to 2017 time period); Chinese outward FDI in raw materials totaled US$57.9 billion over this same time frame, and manufacturing showed its first big bump in 2017 (see table I.2).[58]

Chinese foreign aid is nestled into some of these figures but also exhibits a small life of its own. Whereas the aforementioned Rand report states that China's "first aid deliveries to the region occurred in 2005, with peaks of $11 billion in 2006 and of $6.6 billion in 2010," Stallings offers estimates based on more than just data mining.[59] She notes that the Chinese rarely use the term "aid" and that, going back to Premier Zhou Enlai's original articulation of it, the PRC prefers to use the term "south–south cooperation." Reading between the lines on Chinese foreign policy proclamations, Stallings discerns that this means mutual benefit, equality between donor and recipient, "all-weather friends," and no strings attached.[60]

Based on fieldwork research interviews, a close reading of the government's two White Papers titled *Chinese Foreign Aid* published in 2011 and 2014, and a careful analysis of the data at hand, Stallings estimates that Chinese aid to LAC was approximately US$560 million in 2013 and that these funds were allocated in some combination of traditional grants, concessional loans, and interest-free loans.[61] Of the LAC SPs analyzed in this book, and keeping in mind the importance of the One-China policy to Beijing, only Costa Rica is on the list of nineteen countries that receive Chinese foreign aid. The remaining eighteen, all of which recognize China over Taiwan, have received Chinese foreign aid for such endeavors as the modernization of port facilities (Cuba), the construction of a new ministry of housing (Bolivia), the rehabilitation of a hospital (Saint Lucia), and other highly visible infrastructure and public works projects.[62] Dominica, on establishing diplomatic relations with China and dropping the ROC in 2004, was rewarded by Beijing with a six-year aid package worth US$117 million.[63]

Back to my argument: whether by trade, loans, aid, or outward FDI, China has assertively incorporated the Latin American region into its own ambitious development strategy. In fact, China's internationalized development strategy and these windfall trade and investment inflows to LAC from China are two sides of the same coin: China's capacity building in the region guarantees it a steady flow of raw material imports to fortify its own economy. The more recent surge of outward Chinese FDI into manufacturing and services is the next phase of this strategy and one that is especially promising for the LAC region.

The extension of China's state-led development model across the Pacific has also thrown the political economic strengths and weaknesses of its SPs into stark relief, and it has forced a rethinking of the assumptions that have underpinned the varying development themes and models embraced by these countries. The prolonged postboom slump in Latin America suggests that the old status quo is no longer a policy option. But neither is there a clear path forward for exiting these economic doldrums, especially in Argentina and Brazil.

Case Studies and Emerging Political Economy Clusters

Long-standing theories of economic development tell us that countries that have traditionally relied on a primary export-led model would be the first to benefit during a commodity price boom but also the first to crash once the boom fades. Although it is thirty-five years since Max Corden and Peter Neary published their seminal work on the "Dutch disease," this is exactly what Venezuela and Ecuador are now suffering.[64] Neither of these oil-dependent countries has made a serious effort to diversify its economic base, and both have rejected the kinds of institutional and macroeconomic reforms that could have helped mitigate a postboom economic crisis.[65] Venezuela and Ecuador top the list of China's country borrowers in LAC: as of 2017 Venezuela had received seventeen loans from CDB and CHEXIM totaling US$67.2 billion over the course of the boom, and Ecuador received thirteen loans from the banks totaling US$18.4 billion.[66] That said, part of these funds are loans-for-oil deals that could just as easily be treated as export credits from China.[67] The remainder, as Stephen Kaplan writes, were state-to-state loans granted with no transparency or conditionality, meaning that in both countries the funds were channeled through special presidential projects, some of which are now largely untraceable.[68]

Opinions are mixed as to China's motives for getting in so deep with Venezuela and Ecuador—apart from gaining access to massive oil reserves.

Those who attribute these ties to political affinities overlook the extent to which China has tried to avoid projecting this very image in the Western Hemisphere, that is, openly befriending self-avowed US enemies. Explanations based on China's resource diplomacy also take us just so far,[69] as neither country has been especially diplomatic about falling into serious arrears on debt payments to Beijing. Although we could be looking at the next big Latin American debt crisis (with Chinese characteristics), we are not there yet. With Venezuela's annual inflation approaching 1 million percent in 2018 and Ecuadorians still reeling from the corruption and crime that marked the China boom in that country, these cases offer little in the way of theory building or the reconceptualization of standing development strategies. Thus I omit them from my list of empirical cases studies. As for China's 2016 strategic partnerships with Uruguay and Bolivia, these bilateral relationships are too incipient and the political economic ties too weak to treat as case studies.

The other six SPs, each in its own way, offer more compelling insights into how closer trade and financial integration with China are transforming their domestic political economies as well as our thinking about the development strategies on which they are based. As I mentioned in the introduction, China's designation of an SP has become a prime tool in its foreign policy outreach. Although the actual list of SPs is not reported by Beijing for fear of offending a nonpartner, Feng Zhongping and Huang Jing estimate that China has established SPs with some forty-seven countries, most of them since the early 2000s.[70] The first SPs, however—Brazil, Russia, and the US—were struck in the 1990s, the first to help mend China's diplomatic bridges in the aftermath of the Tiananmen Square massacre and the latter two in recognition of the new post–Cold War era. China has also designated about half of the G-20 countries as SPs, and it has recently upgraded its ties with Russia and the US as a "New Type of Major-Power Relationship."[71]

China's SPs with emerging economies, including those with the LAC countries considered here (Argentina, Brazil, Chile, Costa Rica, Mexico, and Peru), invariably touch on trade, investment, and economic cooperation as well as the One-China policy: "In nearly every strategic partnership document, concepts such as non-interference in domestic affairs, different understandings of democracy and human rights, or different development paths have been asserted."[72] China's SP documents are also laced with terms like "win-win," "mutual respect," and "all-weather friend." As I mentioned earlier, all of the LAC SPs, with the exception of Costa Rica, are richly abundant in natural resources; the Costa Rican SP is the product of the One-China policy. Are these SPs worth the paper on which they are printed? In the introduction, I pointed out that PRC leaders have taken their noninterference pledge quite literally in the case of the China–Venezuela SP, even though Venezuela has fallen behind in its oil repayments to the PRC to the tune of an estimated US$20–30 billion. But the all-weather friendship is wearing thin, as reflected in the 2017 decision of one of China's mammoth state-held oil companies (SINOPEC) to sue the Venezuelan state oil company for back payments in a US district court in Houston.[73]

Nevertheless, China's policy banks issued another US$5 billion in loans to Venezuela in 2018. Stephan Kaplan and Michael Penfold report that these funds have "been linked to directly financing joint ventures in the oil industry to help boost production, and hence, recover China's outstanding oil collateral under its loans-for-oil deals."[74] As one Chinese expert on China–Latin America relations told me in an off-the-record interview, "The Chinese government should take control in getting Venezuela back on track with a viable repayment plan, but as long as the oil and mining resources are there China will stick around." China, despite its own immediate losses, will adhere to its noninterference stance even if this means standing by as President Maduro runs the Venezuelan political economy into the ground. This is one variant on China's SP diplomacy toward Latin America.

China–Mexico relations are another variation on the SP relationship (see chapter 6). China and Mexico have trudged along in the 2000s against a backdrop of two SP upgrades, the final one being a Comprehensive Strategic Partnership in 2013. This merits the cachet of "reliable all-weather friends," which Mexico and China have been anything but.[75] Throughout the 2000s little love has been lost between the two countries, although each has sought to maintain some outward semblance of civility. As I mentioned earlier, Chinese SPs with LAC say less about the quality of the diplomatic relationship between the countries and more about their importance as resource-rich EEs. Because China appears to value the SP framework as its

main means of deepening ties with the LAC countries, I rely on it as an
entry point and organizing theme for my analysis. But moving beyond the
SP concept, I group these six countries (Argentina, Brazil, Chile, Costa Rica,
Mexico, and Peru) according to size, factor endowments, institutional rankings, and the nature of their political economic relationship with China.
Again, what might these cases offer in the way of theory building and / or
the reconceptualization of standing development strategies?

I begin with the three small open economies—Chile, Costa Rica, and
Peru—each of which has pursued an FTA with China. The proliferation of
FTAs between developed and developing countries in the 1990s triggered
a wave of mainly neoliberal analyses that touted their benefits based on
computable-general-equilibrium models and comparative advantage.[76] As
my analysis will show, entering into an FTA with China opened up new
options for these countries while also defying these narrow neoliberal parameters. I then turn to Argentina and Brazil, countries with rich factor
endowments and strong trade complementarities with China. Argentina
and Brazil fell into deep recession when the boom cooled in 2013, and neither has yet to fully recover (see fig. I.1). I situate both within the literature
on the institutional resource curse and show how both countries suffered
institutional erosion and reform backsliding during the China boom. Mexico is my third case study. With the country's accession to NAFTA in 1994,
policy makers kicked away the ladder, jettisoning industrial policy and state
intervention. This FDI-driven neoliberal industrial strategy has pushed
Mexico into a low-growth trap and has left the country vulnerable and
overexposed to China's competitive state-led strategy.

Country Sketches

Chile, Costa Rica, and Peru—Making Openness Work

Several decades ago Chile, Costa Rica, and Peru would have easily sunk
along with Venezuela in the wake of the China boom. Yet Chile and Peru
have outpaced their larger, more industrialized LAC neighbors in terms of
growth rates and capital formation since the turn of the millennium (fig.
I.1).[77] As Peter Katzenstein argued in his classic work *Small States in World*

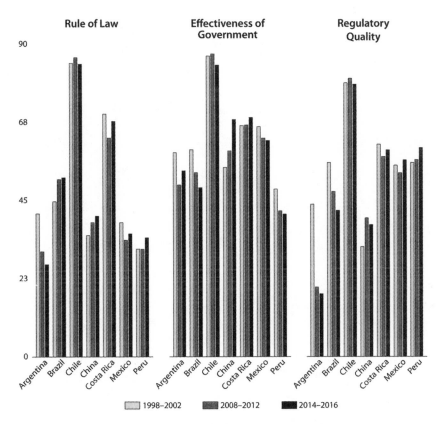

Figure 1.1. Institutional measures for Argentina, Brazil, Chile, Costa Rica, Mexico, and Peru (closer to 100 = better performance).
Source: World Bank's Worldwide Governance Indicators (WGI) Project (2017, Total Countries, 215): WGI is produced by the Revenue Watch, Brookings Institution, World Bank Development Research Group, and the World Bank Institute, available at http://info.worldbank.org/governance/wgi/index.aspx#home.

Markets, because small states are by definition more dependent on external markets, protectionism is a less viable option for them. Instead, elites in small states are prone to "letting international markets force economic adjustments," while employing a range of economic and social policies to help smooth the process.[78] But contrary to neoliberal nostrums on the fruits of joining an FTA, policy makers in these three countries have worked overtime to construct the institutional depth and macroeconomic stability that are necessary conditions for an FTA to deliver on growth and per capita gains (table 1.1). Whereas average growth rates in Chile, Costa Rica, and

Table 1.1. Comparative macroeconomic performance for LAC-6

	GDP growth (annual %)			GDP per capita growth (annual %)			Gross fixed capital formation		
	2003–2013	2014–2017	2001–2018	2003–2013	2014–2017	2001–2018	2003–2013	2014–2017	2003–2017
Argentina	5.4	0.3	2.4	4.3	-0.7	1.3	17.0	15.2	16.5
Brazil	3.8	-1.3	2.3	2.7	-2.1	1.3	18.9	17.1	18.4
Chile	4.7	1.7	3.8	3.6	0.9	2.7	22.4	23.0	22.6
Costa Rica	4.4	3.7	4.1	3.0	2.6	2.6	20.7	18.4	20.0
Mexico	2.2	2.8	2.0	0.7	1.4	0.8	21.6	22.2	21.8
Peru	6.2	3.0	5.0	4.9	1.7	3.9	21.0	22.4	21.4

Source: World Development Indicators, http://databank.worldbank.org/data/home.aspx.

Peru were in the 3.8 to 5 percent range from 2001 to 2018, the comparable figures for Argentina, Brazil, and Mexico were 2 to 2.4 percent.

As Mexico has learned the hard way, an FTA is one possible venue for development but not an ultimate destination. It is, rather, a given country's commitment to pursue growth jointly with one or more countries through the reciprocal liberalization of trade and investment flows. The results depend largely on the hard work of public and private actors on the domestic front. In the case of these three small, open economies, institutional reform has long surpassed the minimalist criterion of upholding property rights, on which neoliberal analysis rests.[79] First, Chile, Costa Rica, and Peru have undertaken crucial macroeconomic reforms since the early 1990s, including the modernization of financial institutions, fiscal, currency, and monetary reform, and a complete overhaul of their respective trade regimes.

Second, Chile and Costa Rica and, secondarily, Peru have forged ahead on indicators of institutional performance that bring them closer to the standards upheld in the OECD countries. For instance, the most recent data show that Chile and Peru are the only two countries in the LAC region that have persistently reduced their per capita income gap vis-à-vis the US between 1990 and 2013.[80] In 2010 Chile became a member of the OECD, and Costa Rica is now in the process of joining. On measures that are crucial for attracting productive investment, such as effectiveness of government and regulatory quality, Chile and Costa Rica top the charts in the World Bank's Worldwide Governance Indicators (see fig. 1.1). Third, all three countries had advanced considerably on these reforms prior to entering into FTAs with both the US and China between 2002 and 2011.

An overriding goal of all three countries was to secure preferential access to the two largest markets in the world, the US and China.[81] The FTAs each signed with the US covered agriculture, intellectual property rights (IPRs), national treatment for FDI, dispute resolution, and protection for labor rights and the environment. In this respect, the three countries' FTAs with the US are considered WTO-plus, as they went much further than what had been accomplished in the Uruguay Round (1986–94) and succeeded in issue areas where the Doha Round patently failed. The WTO-plus nature of these FTAs meant that China, which has yet to obtain market economy status at the WTO, would have to concede on some WTO-plus coverage with all three countries for these FTAs to be credible. Credibility was especially of concern for Chile and Peru, as both countries have relied on a dense network of bilateral FTAs as one aspect of their respective development strategies.

But what did China want? China's Ministry of Commerce vaguely states that "the Chinese government deems FTAs as a new platform to further opening up to the outside and speeding up domestic reforms."[82] China's first policy statement on Latin America, issued in 2008, offers more clarification on the development challenges that are shaping its pursuit of FTAs with these particular countries.[83] First, as I have argued throughout, is China's concern over resource security and its need for Latin America's abundant raw materials to fuel economic growth.[84] Second, the statement prioritizes the pursuit of the One-China principle as fundamental to the establishment of closer relations with the Latin American region. China was the initiator of all three FTAs, as Chile and Peru obviously fit the first criterion, and Costa Rica the second. Yet despite quite divergent motives for negotiating the FTAs, the outcomes for all three are quite similar in the sense that all had achieved rapid access to the Chinese market as well as WTO-plus status by 2012, including some coverage of services, investment, IPRs, and competition policy.[85] Moreover, China's FTAs with Chile and Peru allowed for numerous exceptions in each country's manufacturing sector, clearly not a worry for China.

As south-south accords, these three FTAs defy standing explanations in the political economy literature which rest on cross-border industrial lobbies, market- and efficiency-seeking investor coalitions, and the lock-in of market reforms as the impetus for pursuing these deals.[86] Rather, as part of China's internationalized development strategy these were demand-side FTAs initiated by the PRC. Since the implementation of these agreements Chile–China trade has quadrupled, and China's trade with Costa Rica and Peru has doubled. Peru is the second largest recipient of Chinese FDI; Chile is second only to France in the export of wine to the Chinese market and has surpassed Thailand to become the top exporter of tropical fruits to the PRC. With the PRC–Costa Rica FTA, Costa Rica and China gained market access for 60 percent of each other's exports, with an increase of 30 percent to be implemented over a fifteen-year time period. In 2016 alone Chinese tourism contributed to a 34 percent increase in this Costa Rican sector. To its credit, Costa Rica has stood up to Chinese investors in upholding environmental standards. This plus other regulatory and legislative complications have led to the stalling or cancellation of Chinese-financed projects in energy and transport infrastructure.[87]

In 2008 Ken Shadlen wrote about the pitfalls of LAC's bilateral FTAs with the US, which lean toward exaggerated liberalization, and he cautioned that LAC countries "may be relinquishing the very tools they would need to move into higher value-added positions in industrial value chains."[88] With its offering of rapid market access, granting of industrial sector exceptions, and readiness to lend for productive projects, China is loosening the bilateral straightjacket that Shadlen highlighted with regard to earlier LAC FTAs with the US.

Argentina and Brazil—An Institutional Resource Curse

In 2017 the previous presidents of Argentina and Brazil—Cristina Fernández de Kirchner (2007–15) and Luiz Inácio Lula da Silva (2003–10), respectively—threw their hats back into the electoral ring, as election to even a congressional seat would provide both with immunity from the numerous corruption allegations and indictments each faced from their time in office. The interim Brazilian president, Michel Temer (2016–18), considered it a major victory when the Brazilian congress exempted him from a criminal trial in which he was sure to be found guilty of accepting bribes from Brazil's JBS, the world's largest meatpacking company.[89] The JBS saga, however, pales next to Operation Car Wash, the ongoing scandal since 2014, which has seen Brazil's political and economic elites help themselves to millions in bribes and graft related to the majority state-held oil company, Petrobras. Lula failed to gain immunity via elected office and is serving a twelve-year prison term. Fernández de Kirchner succeeded in securing a senate seat on the Peronist party ticket, although the domestic fight to reverse her immunity continues.

In the introduction I identified a twenty-first-century rendition of the resource curse, which is partly exemplified by the scenario just described. In the wake of the China boom, for example, Brazil's political structures collapsed under the weight of unprecedented corruption and graft. In 2018 Brazilian voters took matters into their own hands and elected the far right candidate Jair Bolsonaro—a self-proclaimed "Trump of the tropics"—on a law-and-order platform with the additional promise to implement orthodox liberal economic reforms.[90] Argentine political institutions have also been put through the wringer but are still standing. The beating taken by political institutions in both countries and the unbridled corruption in both are reflected in the reform backsliding that simultaneously occurred. Argentina gave up on crucial measures like rule of law and regulatory oversight during the China boom (see fig. 1.1). Brazil outpaced Argentina's ranking on these same measures but not enough to prevent reckless policy decisions that prolonged an economic depression in that country in the aftermath of the boom.

This deterioration of political institutions and a devil-may-care pattern of reform reversal is precisely what scholars of the institutional resource curse are referring to when they ask, in what ways might institutional weaknesses condition the effects of natural resource abundance on economic performance?[91] The data (see fig. 1.1 and table I.5) speak directly to the Argentine case, where comparative analysis shows that those institutional reforms most likely to foster growth and productive investment never reached a point of effectiveness despite a decade of so-called neoliberal restructuring from 1991 to 2001.[92] Although Brazil outpaced Argentina and saw less backsliding on institutional reforms, hindsight shows that institutional frailties most likely did condition the negative effects of the China boom on postboom economic performance in both countries.

A second question asked by scholars of the institutional resource curse concerns how otherwise effective institutions might deteriorate under the force of a major commodity boom.[93] In Brazil the Brazilian National Development Bank (BNDES) was the main entity for channeling the mass of incoming revenues for project lending to the public and the private sectors. In their analysis of BNDES, Kathryn Hochstetler and Alfred Montero argue that the bank held its own over the time period under study, making "significant numbers of smaller loans to firms in all sectors, as well as renewed support for internationalisation and innovation."[94] In Argentina, President Fernández de Kirchner assaulted the once-respected Central Bank of Argentina, firing the president and gutting its reserves to cover mounting deficits. Otherwise effective institutions did indeed deteriorate in Argentina; in Brazil, BNDES survived, Petrobras—where an investment-grade rating was downgraded to junk bond status in a matter of days—did not.

Mexico: Ratcheting Down the Ladder

In his treatise on development economics *Kicking Away the Ladder: Development Strategy in Historical Perspective* Ha-Joon Chang disputes the widely touted notion that the earlier development path for advanced countries in the OECD bloc was one based on laissez-faire economic policies.[95] He argues instead that throughout history state guidance in the form of infant industry promotion, public credit, tax breaks, trade tariffs, and so on was key to the development of most nations. Once countries like the UK and the US had achieved industrial and technological supremacy based on protectionism and state largesse, they kicked away these statist ladders and preached the merits of economic liberalism to those nations still trying to climb up the ranks of the world economy.[96]

Under the influence of the structuralist / dependency arguments I discussed in the introduction, most Latin American countries bucked postwar liberal economic prescriptions and launched ambitious state-sponsored programs of import-substitution industrialization (ISI). The pitfalls of this strategy as it was adopted in LAC were the failure to add value to the manufacturing sector and to promote industrial exports anywhere near on par with the East Asian developmental states that were quickly climbing their own ladders at this time. Mexico seemed the one exception, as an electoral-authoritarian, single-party (the Revolutionary Institutional Party, or PRI) regime succeeded in designing a "stabilizing development" ISI strategy that yielded average annual growth rates of 6 percent (3 percent per capita) from World War II up through the early 1970s. But the PRI did a desperate about-face in the debt-laden 1980s and embraced the Washington Consensus. Although the prospect of negotiating an FTA with the US had once been anathema to the country, by 1994 Mexico had negotiated its way into NAFTA.

Under NAFTA the government set its sights on the manufacturing sector—now exposed to much higher levels of import competition and

streamlined state support—as the anchor for growth and the overall modernization of the economy.[97] Mexico's expectation was that it could count
on FDI and the heightened competition from US imports to force a restructuring of the domestic industrial sector.[98] Policy makers, in other words,
bought into prevailing neoliberal arguments in favor of joining an FTA.
Industrial policy was scrapped, and the tough tasks of technology acquisition and adaptation were turned over to foreign, mainly US, companies
operating in export processing zones located in central and northern Mexico. Industrial exports soared, FDI poured into the manufacturing sector,
and Mexico seemed to be poised for the trade- and investment-driven takeoff that had inspired it to join NAFTA. There was a glitch, however, and this
was the failure of average annual growth to surpass 2.4 percent from 1994
to the eve of the China boom. To this day Mexico has continued to grow at
less than half the rate maintained during the stabilizing development era.[99]

During the early 1990s a nagging sideshow was that commitments made
for deeper trade liberalization under NAFTA also left Mexico vulnerable to
China's aggressive export-led policies, which were bolstered by a cheap exchange rate and quickly flooding goods into the Mexican market. As early
as 1993 Mexico began filing antidumping complaints against Chinese producers under the General Agreement on Tariffs and Trade (GATT). Moreover, with an eye toward preserving its privileged access to the US market
under NAFTA, Mexico was the very last holdout vote on China's 2001 entry
into the WTO.[100] By 2014 measures of "revealed comparative advantage" in
Mexico's manufacturing sector came closest to those of China when compared with other LAC countries, and its manufacturing value-added as a
percent of GDP is the highest in the region (table 1.2), but growth remained
elusive. The country's apparent technological strength stems from intermediate inputs developed in the advanced economies and increasingly in
China, processed in Mexico, and shipped back out.

As the record has thus far shown, China's strategy has been growth promoting whereas Mexico's has not. By 2003, for example, China had displaced Mexico in the ranking of US trade partners. Over the period 2000–
2005 Mexico had increased its share of US imports by 25 percent, while
China's share in US imports grew by 143 percent; from 2008 to 2013 some
27 percent of Mexico's manufacturing exports were under "direct threat"

Table 1.2. Manufacturing, value added (% of GDP): 2000–2017

Country	2000	2001	2002	2003	2004	2005	2006	2007	2008
Argentina	16.5	16.1	20.3	22.5	18.9	18.3	17.9	17.0	16.5
Brazil	13.1	13.1	12.4	14.5	15.1	14.7	14.1	14.2	14.0
Chile	16.9	17.5	17.6	17.0	16.0	14.3	12.9	12.0	11.1
Costa Rica	18.4	17.5	17.5	17.2	17.0	16.9	16.6	16.2	15.2
Mexico	19.0	18.1	17.3	16.6	16.7	15.7	16.7	15.9	15.8
Peru	15.2	15.6	15.5	15.4	16.4	16.6	16.5	16.5	16.3

Country	2009	2010	2011	2012	2013	2014	2015	2016	2017
Argentina	15.6	15.8	15.9	15.2	15.0	14.8	14.2	13.6	13.0
Brazil	13.1	12.7	11.8	10.7	10.5	10.3	10.5	10.3	10.2
Chile	11.2	10.8	11.0	10.8	11.1	11.1	11.6	10.8	10.2
Costa Rica	14.2	14.5	14.0	13.5	12.6	12.2	11.4	11.4	11.8
Mexico	15.1	15.6	15.4	16.3	15.8	15.9	17.1	16.9	17.2
Peru	15.3	15.6	15.1	15.2	14.8	13.9	13.8	13.2	

Source: World Development Indicators, http://databank.worldbank.org/data/home.aspx.

from Chinese competition, and another 48 percent were classified as being under "partial threat."[101] China accounted for around 9.8 percent of Mexico's total trade in 2016, but just 2 percent of its exports go to the Chinese market. This percentage of Mexico's exports going to the Chinese market has changed little over the past decade. Despite Mexico's obvious geographic advantage over China, the latter has gradually eclipsed Mexico in the US manufacturing market by actively deploying public policy in the expansion, upgrading, and infusion of technology into its manufacturing sector.[102] While China continues to thrive near the top of Ha-Joon Chang's ladder, Mexico has somehow relegated itself to the lower rungs.

The effect of China's rise on both global and regional markets has generated more questions than answers at this point in time. Rather than strive for a big theoretical splash here, I have taken an incremental approach toward portraying how China is pushing long-standing conceptual contours in the fields of IPE and development economics. As a field, development economics has lent itself more readily to theory expansion. I grouped the effect of the China–LAC relationship on its six SPs into three development themes: the FTA option chosen by the three small, open economies—Chile, Costa Rica, and Peru; the institutional resource curse scenario which crystallized in Argentina and Brazil; and the simultaneous export-led industrialization strategy and ratcheting down of Ha-Joon Chang's ladder that Mexico has committed to since its 1994 entry into NAFTA.

In the first two cases I argued that the tighter economic ties with China opened up more space for policy making and innovation. The three FTAs with the PRC, for example, are at once WTO-plus *and* more lenient when it came to China's willingness to agree to numerous exceptions in the domestic industrial sector. In the case of the institutional resource curse, the experiences of Argentina and Brazil show that the downside of a commodity price boom could still creep in, even when countries have achieved much higher levels of industrialization than those that existed for countries on which resource curse theories were originally based. With the exception of Mexico, there has been a huge silver lining for LAC in the form of China's generous policy bank loans (Argentina, Brazil, Costa Rica, and Peru), Chinese outward FDI (all but Chile), Chinese currency swaps (Argentina, Brazil, and Chile), and Chinese aid (Costa Rica). The astronomical increase in trade with these five SPs is the glue that holds these burgeoning relationships together. Again, China's internationalized development strategy has been less a choice than a necessity, and its flourishing economic ties with these five countries has everything to do with meeting these needs.

Mexico, with its neoliberal, FDI-driven industrial export strategy, is the odd one out here. Hindsight tells us that those policy makers' resort to NAFTA as a way to lock in market reforms had the unfortunate effect of stalling the vital follow-up reforms (see fig. 1.1) needed to render NAFTA a success. The counterfactual here would be the considerable progress on institutional reforms made by the three small open economies *prior* to negotiating an FTA with the PRC. That more favorable record speaks for itself (see table 1.1). The decision of Mexican policy makers to scrap industrial policy upon the country's entry into NAFTA coincided with China's burst of reforms geared precisely toward escalating its prowess as a manufacturing exporter. Bad luck and unfortunate timing are one thing, but for Mexico to continue with its industrialization-sans-industrial policy approach defies logic. The competitive losses over the past decade alone in both domestic and third markets as well as the stagnant record on aggregate and per capita growth rates suggest the severity of this decision. The running of a tight "macro-prudent" monetary and fiscal policy alongside this laissez-faire strategy has further exacerbated this weak performance.

A Slow Thaw across the Pacific: From Socialist Revolution to Pragmatic Reform

The Latin American peoples are standing in the forefront of . . . [the] struggle against US imperialism.

Zhou Enlai[1]

THE LITERATURE ON CHINA–LATIN AMERICA relations during the post–World War II period is rich with political intrigue and the steady efforts of the Chinese Communist Party (CCP) to bond with a number of countries in the region around a third world revolutionary agenda. Chinese leaders had interpreted Fidel Castro's 1959 victory in Cuba as the same kind of anti-imperialist struggle for liberation that characterized their own triumph a decade earlier. As the epigraph above suggests, Beijing assumed that the Latin American region as a whole was ripe for the organization of similar revolutionary movements that could succeed along "nationalist-socialist" lines, as had those in both China and Cuba.[2] No matter that the prevailing levels of development both within the Latin American and Caribbean (LAC) region (e.g., Argentina versus Paraguay) and between China and LAC were highly diverse, the CCP's application of class analysis to the LAC countries deemed them ready to fight a "people's war."[3]

This period in China–LAC relations is riddled with contradictions. The first is China's acrimonious split with the Soviet Union in 1960 and then with Cuba by 1965. At heart was Castro's initial insistence on remaining neutral toward both China and the Soviets, but then his firm decision to side with the latter. Prior to this there had been a series of cross-Pacific spats between the Chinese leader Mao Zedong and Castro over political strategy, Marxist–Leninist doctrine, and agricultural trade between China and Cuba.[4] A second irony was China's understandable appeal and support for the socialist administration of President Salvador Allende (1970–73) of Chile, but its equal willingness to recognize Allende's successor, the rabidly anti-communist general Augusto Pinochet, who displaced Allende in a bloody coup and went on to rule Chile with an iron fist until 1990.[5] From this point on China's affinity for democrats and authoritarians alike would continue, for example, in its relations with Argentina and Brazil.[6] Finally, when a homegrown Maoist guerrilla insurgency openly launched its own people's war in Peru in 1980 Beijing wanted nothing to do with it![7]

From an economic standpoint it takes a bit of digging to piece together the economic ties that were being formed between China and various LAC countries prior to the 1980s. Reliable data on this period are hard to find. Whereas the narrative on China–LAC political interactions in the postwar era is quite lively and engaging, any parallel analyses of economic exchange between the two have been relegated to dry, dusty tomes.[8] However, the record that does exist offers some interesting insights. For instance, it lays to rest the claim made by some that the LAC nations were reticent to interact with China during the Cold War years due to Washington's economic blockade and Beijing's equally hostile anti-US stance.[9] Rather, as early as the 1950s and long before President Richard Nixon's trip to China in 1972, there was a vibrant, albeit informal, pattern of China–LAC interactions, both political and economic.[10] Moreover, on the economic side the actual products being traded and the main LAC countries involved with China closely presage the nature and content of China–LAC economic ties that would later explode at the turn of the millennium. Twelve LAC countries had established diplomatic relations with the PRC prior to the 1979 opening of the US embassy in Beijing (table 2.1).

Taken together, all of these loose political and economic ends reveal perhaps the biggest contradiction in China–LAC relations during this era: radical revolutionary political gestures *and* pragmatic economic overtures

Table 2.1. Establishment of diplomatic relations between Latin American countries and the People's Republic of China

Cuba	28 September 1960
Chile	15 December 1970
Peru	2 November 1971
Mexico	14 February 1972
Argentina	19 February 1972
Guyana	27 June 1972
Jamaica	21 November 1972
Trinidad and Tobago	20 June 1974
Venezuela	28 June 1974
Brazil	15 August 1974
Suriname	28 May 1976
Barbados	30 May 1977
Ecuador	2 January 1980
Colombia	7 February 1980
Antigua and Barbuda	1 January 1983
Bolivia	9 July 1985
Uruguay	3 February 1988
Bahamas	22 May 1997
Dominica	23 March 2004
Grenada	27 January 2005
Costa Rica	1 June 2007
Panama	13 June 2017
Dominican Republic	1 May 2018
El Salvador	25 August 2018

Sources: Republic of China, Government Information Office, *The Republic of China Yearbook* (Taipei: ROC Government Information Office, 1996), 792–96; Dennis Van Vranken Hickey, *Taiwan's Security in the Changing International System.* (Boulder: Lynne Rienner, 1997), 116, 118; Francisco Haro Navejas, "China's Relations with Central America and the Caribbean States: Reshaping the Region," in *China Engages Latin America: Tracing the Trajectory,* ed. Adrian H. Hearn and José Luis León-Manríquez (Boulder: Lynne Rienner, 2011), 203–20; Neil Connor, "Panama Cuts Ties with Taiwan in Major Diplomatic Coup," *The Telegraph,* June 13, 2017, http://www.telegraph.co.uk/news/2017/06/13/panama-cuts-ties-taiwan-major-diplomatic-coup-china/; Austin Ramzy "Taiwan's Diplomatic Isolation Increases as Dominican Republic Recognizes China," *New York Times,* May 1, 2018, https://www.nytimes.com/2018/05/01/world/asia/taiwan-dominican-republic-recognize.html); Tracy Wilkinson, "U.S. Decries Salvadoran China Policy," *Los Angeles Times,* August 25, 2018, A.4.

were simultaneously exchanged back and forth between China and LAC up through the 1970s. By the time of Mao's death in 1976, China had stopped funding communist parties and training communist insurgents from various LAC countries. As the Chinese leadership quietly shed its aim of promoting a worldwide proletarian revolution and moved from its "third-worldist" stance toward the advocacy of multilateralism and nonintervention, China–LAC relations began to take on the more apolitical, businesslike tone which best characterizes them today.[11]

I want to set a baseline of sorts here, one that traces the evolution of postwar China–LAC relations from that of third world peers with markedly distinct political and economic interactions, all the way up to the takeoff in China–LAC ties at the turn of the millennium. As I argued in the previous chapter, by the advent of the twenty-first century the China–LAC relationship was largely an economic one. If anything, both sides have been overly cautious by sweeping possible political conflicts under the carpet, be it China's dismal human rights record, the unsuccessful bids by Bolivia, Ecuador, and Venezuela to draw China into their strident anti-US rhetoric, or the open social contestation around environmental concerns that both Chinese investors and LAC host governments have faced in the launching of numerous mining deals.[12]

My focus here is on five of the six strategic partners (SPs) that I identified at the outset as now having the strongest bonds with China: Argentina, Brazil, Chile, Mexico, and Peru (I exclude my sixth country case, Costa Rica, as it did not recognize China diplomatically until 2007 and was not designated as an SP by China until 2015.) Although local experts in some of these countries express surprise at the rapidity of China's ability to become such a significant force within their respective economies, I suggest that the sudden burst in commodity prices around 2003 merits this reaction, as the timing, pace, and longevity of such lotteries hinge on any number of complicated factors.[13] However, the actual nature of the ties formed is largely an extension and exaggeration of much earlier trends. Thus the sheer magnitude of the expansion in China–LAC economic relations in the 2000s may have caught policy makers and producers off guard, but the relationship itself was already under way and fairly well defined.

1949–1959: Economic Realities amid Ideological Proselytizing

At the outset of this period the political differences between China and Latin America were stark.[14] To China, "politics" meant the actualization of a communist / socialist regime on the mainland and the isolation of Taiwan as both the People's Republic of China (PRC) and Taiwan (ROC) fought for international legitimacy and recognition. For the Latin American countries, "politics" generally meant the oscillation between democratically elected civilian governments and authoritarian military regimes. Three of the countries considered here—Argentina, Brazil, and Chile—saw the installation of especially brutal military governments in the 1960s and 1970s, and these lasted well into the 1980s. Peru also was ruled by a military junta, from 1968 to 1980; however, Peru's so-called Revolutionary Government of the Armed Forces talked a socialist-reformist line, was less harsh, and more ideologically flexible than the adamantly anticommunist Southern Cone juntas.[15] During this entire period an electoral-authoritarian single party, the Revolutionary Institutional Party (PRI), ruled Mexico.

1949–59

The evolution of the China–LAC relationship from 1949 to 1979 can be roughly broken down by decade.[16] The period 1949–59 was marked by recognition on both sides of the vast geographical distance between China and Latin America and the low level of knowledge and understanding each had of the other. China, moreover, had launched a massive program of economic reconstruction and a centrally planned economic model based on the Soviet system of five-year plans. Much of this effort relied on heavy Soviet economic assistance.[17] Even though Latin America was admittedly remote in terms of the PRC's ability to interact closely with this region, after the overthrow of pro-US leaders like Gustavo Rojas Pinilla in Colombia in 1957 and Marcos Pérez Jiménez in Venezuela in 1958 CCP leaders did take note of the possibilities for joining in the struggle against US imperialism in Latin America.[18] But it was Castro's triumph in ending the authoritarian regime of Fulgencio Batista in 1959 that clinched the PRC's interest in the region.

Prior to this the PRC had engaged in a policy of "propaganda and invitations," which entailed the hosting in China of some fifteen hundred Latin Americans from twenty-one countries between 1949 and 1960.[19] These people included mainly educated Latin Americans, from doctors and lawyers to university professors, students, and journalists. Apart from wooing fellow or prospective communists, the goals here were to enhance China's reputation within the Latin American region, to tarnish the image of the US, and to champion the benefits of the Chinese model in overcoming political and economic challenges.[20] But this low-key diplomacy was more than a one-sided exchange. William Ratliff writes that, beginning in 1953 "small groups of Chinese visited Latin America in cultural, trade, journalist, and youth delegations; larger numbers went in performing troupes on tour. Leading members of the Chinese delegations met outstanding political figures and attended legislative sessions in the countries they visited. They talked with university presidents and newspaper editors, visited overseas Chinese communities, and went to meetings of local friendship associations."[21]

On the propaganda side the Central Committee of the CCP and the Radio Broadcasting Agency of the Council of State succeeded in securing airtime for pro-China Spanish language programs in Central and South America. China's airtime allotment in these subregions had expanded to twenty-eight hours a week by 1966.[22] With the establishment of Latin American branch offices by China's only newspaper at the time, the New China News Agency (NCNA, or *Xinhua News Agency*), the written word was also utilized. By 1960 NCNA was operating in seven countries, including Argentina, Brazil, and Peru. Given the Cold War context and China's diplomatic recognition by just one Latin American country (Cuba), the NCNA branch offices became important vehicles for political outreach, intelligence gathering, and communist recruitment.[23] As such, they were also the locus of frequent crackdowns by staunch anticommunist authorities in most countries, Cuba being the exception.

Underpinning these open diplomatic overtures was a more targeted effort by the Chinese to cultivate and nurture pro-PRC communist parties in LAC. Following the 20th Congress of the Communist Party of the Soviet Union in 1956, the Latin American guest delegates were invited to China to meet personally with Mao and to participate in a six-month course in indoc-trination.[24] But it was the CCP's increasingly strict adherence to Maoist doctrine, whereby "the only correct road of revolution for the Latin Ameri-can people is to . . . wage guerrilla warfare, unfold an agrarian revolution, build rural base areas, [and] use the countryside to encircle the cities and finally capture them," that prompted the exodus of the majority of LAC communist parties over to the Soviet camp.[25] Given the comparatively high levels of industrialization and urbanization in Latin America at that time, Mao's doctrine lost its punch for most communist party organizers in the region. Of the fifty-nine Latin American communist parties that existed across the region in 1970, only eight still looked to Beijing for guidance.[26]

Economically, as the PRC's first decade ended in 1959 CCP leaders were faced with the dire results of Mao's Great Leap Forward, a Soviet-style pro-gram of heavy industrialization that was to be financed with grain proceeds from the hastily collectivized agricultural sector. The outright devastation, including upward of forty million deaths due to grain shortages and famine, compelled China to search abroad for agricultural resources.[27] Argentina, Brazil, and Chile had all signed informal trade agreements with China—based on private, people-to-people contacts—even before each country's diplomatic recognition of the PRC. Argentina, with its rich abundance of grains, sold 28,000 tons of wheat and 50,000 tons of millet to China in 1962, as reports of drought and starvation in the Chinese countryside con-tinued through that year.[28] By 1965 Argentina had sold over 1 million tons of wheat to China, who paid in cash. Similarly, Mexico sold 450 tons of wheat to China in 1964 for the reported cost of US$30 million in hard currency.[29]

1960–69: Deepening Contradictions

Both China and LAC entered the 1960s against a tumultuous backdrop. While China was still reeling from the political and economic effects of what had become known as the Great Famine, the South American coun-tries considered here were living from one balance-of-payments crisis to the next. Under policies of ISI, average growth in the top twenty LAC countries was an impressive 5.2 percent from 1945 to 1972.[30] Yet the failure to tackle mounting structural bottlenecks and the incursion of military officials into the halls of government during this period fostered growth patterns that were uneven, highly inequitable, and ultimately unsustainable. The Brazilian military coup of 1964 signaled a wave of authoritarian takeovers that would dominate regional politics and economic management for more than two decades. Such regimes were adamantly opposed to China *and* the Soviet Union.

With the onset of the Sino–Soviet split in 1960 over which country would lead the communist world, along with the Sino–Cuban rift in 1965 as Cuba sided with the Soviets, China continued to voice its support for those revolutionary groups in Latin America that were earnest about overthrowing the purportedly reactionary governments.[31] This decade was increasingly overshadowed by volatile domestic politics in China. The CCP elite turned its wrath on those within the party whose response to the dislocations of the Great Leap Forward had been to challenge Mao's reckless experiment with their more rational economic proposals and to diminish the importance of class struggle. This prompted the Cultural Revolution in 1966, a movement to restore Mao's vision of communism as a "proletarian-led, anti-imperialist, and anti-feudal culture of the broad masses."[32] China–LAC political exchanges waned during this period. Having peaked in the 1960–65 period, China–LAC political ties were further strained by the rise of Soviet aid to some LAC countries, aid which was six times that of China, and by the Soviet's growing ideological influence over the radical left in a number of Latin American countries.[33] By 1967, moreover, China had managed to pick a fight with some thirty-two countries, most of them in the developing world.[34]

Still, despite China's deepening international isolation and diplomatic testiness during the Cultural Revolution, China–LAC economic ties were on the rise. China–LAC trade, for example, increased more than fourfold during this decade (table 2.2). Sino–Cuban trade accounted for the lion's share (approximately 75 percent) of China–LAC trade in the 1960s and continued apace even after the acrimonious rupture between Castro and Mao in 1965–66.[35] Yet it is important not to exaggerate the China–LAC commercial relationship, as the levels of trade were still low as a percentage of overall trade on both sides. Cuba's dominant position reflected the CCP's initial political enthusiasm and ideological support for the Castro regime.

Table 2.2. China's trade with Latin America, 1950–1980 (millions of USD)

Year	1950	1960	1970	1980
Total	1.96	31.3	145.8	1,331
Exports	0.05	10.3	75.2	488
Imports	1.91	21.0	70.6	843
Balance	–1.86	–10.7	4.6	–355

Sources: Almanac of China's Foreign Economic Relations and Trade, 1984, 1985, and 1986 (Hong Kong: China Resources Trade and Consultancy Co., 1984, 1985, 1986); General Administration of Customs of the PPC, *China's Customs Statistics, 1990,* no. 1 (Hong Kong: Economic Information Agency, 1990).

China exported rice, soybeans, cotton cloth, tools, and medicine to Cuba and in return imported brown sugar and mineral ores back from Cuba. Much of this bilateral trade was conducted through barter. As well, Beijing donated considerable amounts of wheat, corn, cement, and steel to the Cubans and issued some US$100 million in interest-free loans to Havana from 1960 to 1964.[36] In the end, China's inability to compete with Soviet levels of aid, trade and lending to Cuba became another factor in the deterioration of Sino–Cuban relations.

By the mid-1960s China's three main imports from LAC were wheat (90 percent), cotton (5.4 percent), and maize (3.9 percent).[37] After Cuba, Argentina and Brazil were next in the LAC trading queue with China during this decade, followed by Mexico and Chile. Prior to the Sino–Cuban split and the onset of the Cultural Revolution in 1966, Beijing had continued its efforts at commercial outreach and exchange with the region. But owing to their open alliance with Cuba up until 1965–66, Chinese delegates to both Argentina and Brazil were now given the cold shoulder. Conservative elements in both countries blocked Chinese proposals to stage a trade exhibition locally, and military officials in both countries reduced the actual levels of goods traded, including Argentina's earlier promises for wheat sales. Beijing met with considerable more success in Chile and Mexico during the 1960–66 window of time. Large Chinese-sponsored trade exhibitions were staged in the two countries in 1964, resulting in numerous informal accords for the promotion of bilateral trade between private actors in China and these host countries.[38] In 1961 China had been allowed to open an office of commercial information in Santiago and in 1965 established its own commercial mission there.

Of course the irony of this period is that China's advances into the region were eclipsed by the country's descent into domestic violence as the Cultural Revolution took on a grim life of its own. The remainder of the 1960s was a hiatus in China–LAC relations, although Latin American countries like Argentina and Brazil brought their own political baggage to the table as well. For example, after the 1964 military coup in Brazil nine Chinese citizens who worked for the NCNA and the China Council for the Promotion of International Trade in Brazil were jailed and charged with espionage.[39] Similarly, the NCNA's offices were shut down and Chinese nationals expelled from Mexico and Ecuador, as US-inspired anticommunist paranoia shaped the political decisions of authoritarian leaders in the Western Hemisphere.[40] As for China, historians equate the end of the Cultural Revolution with Mao's death in 1976. Although hard to imagine at the time, the remainder of the 1970s would turn out to be a turning point in all respects for China, with eventual implications for the flourishing of China–LAC economic relations.

1970–79: From Isolation to International Outreach

By the early 1970s Chinese leaders were split between hardliners in favor of perpetuating the political and economic chaos of the Cultural Revolution and reformers like Deng Xiaoping and Chen Yun, who had begun to articulate the need for a "socialist modernization" strategy that could usher a more developed China into the twenty-first century.[41] Even before Mao's death in 1976 this more forward-thinking internationalist coalition had scored several foreign policy victories in rapid succession. The first was China's admission to the UN in 1971, which included a permanent seat on the UN Security Council. This meant the ejection of Taiwan as the Chinese representative at the UN, which was obviously a monumental boost for the PRC's One-China policy.

Having spent most of the post–World War II period on the diplomatic margin, China's entry into the UN opened the floodgate for the normalization of diplomatic relations with a number of countries, including all five of the Latin American countries considered in this chapter (see table 2.1). Prior to 1971 China was able to rally just two votes (Chile and Cuba) from the LAC countries in support of its admission to the UN. But as China had begun to emerge from its diplomatic shell and to preach the importance of third world solidarity and the need to design a New International Economic Order, China–LAC relations began to rebound. China's resumption of hosting delegations and a wide range of guests from the region also helped to pave the way for a favorable UN vote in October 1971. On that vote, twelve of the twenty-four LAC UN members took a favorable or neutral stand.[42] Peru, Mexico, and Argentina moved almost immediately thereafter to formalize diplomatic ties with China (see table 2.1). Brazil officially recognized China in 1974, mainly in an act of economic pragmatism, as an anticommunist military regime reluctantly switched its allegiance from Taiwan to China.

The second foreign policy triumph was China's rapprochement with the US in 1972, a notion that had been completely unthinkable just a decade earlier. In his historical memoir *On China*, Henry Kissinger writes that Mao had returned "to a classical Chinese stratagem: pitting the barbarians against each other, and enlisting faraway enemies against those nearby."[43] Alas, with tensions and open aggression erupting along the Sino–Soviet border, the CCP came around to the idea of normalizing China's relations with the US as a way of further undermining and isolating the Soviets. Moreover, as some Chinese policy makers had begun to think seriously about the dire need for economic reform and deepening the country's trade and investment ties with the rest of the world, the pursuit of closer links with the US economy seemed the most promising option.

The establishment of formal diplomatic relations between China and the US did not occur until 1979, when the US converted its American Liaison Office in Beijing to the US embassy proper. In the interim between Nixon's 1972 visit and the launching of the new US embassy, China was gaining a foothold in Latin America under the new guise of its anti-Cuban, anti-Soviet stance, one that was now "leaning toward the U.S. side."[44] This is an ironic historical twist, as most military regimes that prevailed in the region at this time had cast themselves in the same political mold.[45] This also sheds some light on Mao's willingness to accept the avidly anti-Soviet Pinochet regime in Chile following the 1973 military overthrow of the democratically elected socialist president, Salvador Allende. The PRC had provided the Allende administration with a US$65 million loan that included a generous fifty-year repayment period.[46] However, Allende, a victim of his own hasty macroeconomic and nationalization policies, angered the Chinese by turning to the Soviet Union for additional economic assistance when the Chilean economy had virtually collapsed. Beijing exercised restraint but quietly judged the rash economic policy decisions of the Allende administration. However, Premier Zhou Enlai did write to Allende just months before the coup, warning that only by "acting in accordance with actual conditions and possibilities, and in a planned and gradual manner, can one achieve, step by step, the objective of changing the face of economic backwardness and improve the conditions of the people's lives."[47]

While formal diplomatic recognition between China and the first twelve LAC countries (see table 2.1) predated the formalization of China–US ties, certainly the China–US rapprochement of the early 1970s eased the way for LAC's increased economic interaction with China. Moreover, China had all but done away with its earlier revolutionary rhetoric and rabble-rousing. With China now taking a "flexible, pragmatic, and non-ideological" approach in its dealings with countries in the region, its more developmentalist line clearly resonated with LAC political leaders and policy makers at this time.[48] As a result, a number of noteworthy agreements were brokered between China and the LAC countries in the 1970s. These covered such key issues as maritime transport, science and technical cooperation, tourism, and barter trade (e.g., Brazilian iron ore for Chinese oil). China–LAC trade increased nine-fold between 1970 and 1980, with LAC consistently running a highly favorable trade surplus with China from 1950 to 1970 (see table 2.2). This is remarkable, as all parties concerned, with the exception of Chile, were still highly protected economies.

The bulk of trade in the 1970s was on the side of LAC exports to China (table 2.3). Tellingly, only about 11 percent of these goods (machinery and transport) could be classified as value-added. Brazil and Mexico, in particular, had borrowed billions in easy petrodollar loans from the international banks through the 1970s, ostensibly to ramp up their industrial sectors and launch a major manufactured export drive. Although China was desperately

Table 2.3. Main Chinese imports from Latin America (1984)

Product	Percentage of total imports	SITC
Agricultural products	21	1–2
Processed food items	20	0
Steel and iron	29	67
Chemical products	10	5
Machinery and transport	11	7

Source: United Nations, *Commodity Trade Statistics,* Series D. 34, no. 17 (New York: United Nations, 1986), 1–8.

in need of manufactured imports at this time, having broken off with its former Soviet supplier, it was mainly Mexico that had begun to export some value-added industrial goods to the PRC. As I mentioned earlier, China's large trade deficit with the LAC region stemmed from its lack of sufficient commodities and value-added goods to sell to these countries. Natural resources and primary goods thus continued to constitute about 90 percent of LAC exports to China at this time.

In terms of individual LAC countries, Cuba's trade with China waned substantially in the 1970s and Chile had moved up, as China became the world's third largest buyer of Chilean copper.[49] Among other things, Chile purchased from China light industrial goods, chemical products, tools, and machinery.[50] Peru also moved up in the trading queue with China, and the PRC responded in kind with major purchases of copper, lead, and zinc from Peru, for which it paid US$45 million in hard currency. Like Chile, Peru also received a loan from China (US$42 million) that came with highly favorable repayment conditions. As for Argentina and Brazil, although prickly anticommunist military leaders had not made it easy for the PRC to conduct business in the two countries, trade still managed to trump politics. Argentina continued to be an important source of wheat and maize for the PRC in the 1970s, and Brazil a crucial supplier of iron ore.[51]

Mexico had the lowest level of total trade with China at this time in terms of both imports from and exports to (cotton, coffee beans, sulphur, and lead oxide) the PRC. But not for lack of trying. The early 1970s saw Mexico taking a more independent political stand from the US, for example, with President Luis Echeverría's 1971 speech to the UN that championed the expulsion of Taiwan and the admission of China in its place. One result of this show of solidarity was the PRC's voting in unison with Mexico at the UN up through the 1990s. Echeverría, furthermore, made history as the first Latin American president to visit China, as a special guest of Zhou.[52] Such high-level diplomatic exchanges would become commonplace from the 1980s on, but Mexico was the trailblazer in this respect. As time would tell, this diplomatic triumph failed to translate into a more buoyant commercial relationship between China and Mexico.

This brief overview of China–LAC relations from 1949 to 1979 suggests that, despite the huge geographical distances and cultural chasm, there was nothing random or casual about this relationship. Up until the eve of the 1966 Cultural Revolution in China the CCP was motivated to reach out politically to a number of Latin American countries where the possibilities for instigating a Maoist-style people's war looked especially promising. CCP operatives working in the region, mainly in a journalistic or cultural capacity, took this task quite seriously. Economically, the PRC was in desperate need of raw materials to fuel its Soviet-style strategy of heavy industrialization and Latin America was blessed with an abundance of these resources. With the exception of Cuba, where economic ties were more ideologically motivated, the PRC forged pragmatic trade ties with mainly those countries that could fill its orders for copper (Chile), iron ore (Brazil), wheat and maize (Argentina), and cotton (Mexico).

On the Latin American side the enchantment of radical left parties and socialist leaders with China's brand of revolution was brief. By the late 1960s the Soviet model and more generous amounts of economic assistance and lending from the Soviet Union all but quashed the political affinities the Latin American left may have once had for China. But the economic appeal of partnering with China was another matter entirely. Although LAC political movements had quickly soured on doctrinaire Maoist principles, commercial relations held steady during this period. As China and Latin America headed into the 1980s it was this pragmatic economic relationship and the turn toward an outward orientation that would continue to unite China and the handful of countries that are the focus of this book. By the turn of the century politics, as such, would become platitudes to embellish the more narrow business-oriented evolution of China–LAC relations going forward.

1980–2000: From Surrealism to Realism

For both China and Latin America, the run-up to the final two decades of the twentieth century was surely surreal but for markedly different reasons. On China's side the political gyrations and severe economic hardship wrought by the Great Leap Forward and the Cultural Revolution were seemingly over. The radical discourse of earlier years had faded, and in its place was Deng's "open-door policy" based on external trade, foreign investment, and increased cooperation in science and technology. In the aftermath of these self-destructive domestic experiments the PRC went into the 1980s with the single-minded goal of promoting development through policy flexibility, gradual reform, industrialization, exports, and international economic cooperation. China's stance toward the Latin American region was increasingly nonideological and pragmatic. Its new focus, for example, included such issues as the right to self-determination, the establishment of a two-hundred-nautical-mile economic boundary, a nuclear-weapon-free zone, and support for Panama's demand for sovereignty over the Canal Zone.[53]

If China went into the 1980s focused, politically determined, and economically driven, the LAC region was the opposite: politically fragmented, economically besieged by external debt and macroeconomic disequilibria, and no clear development strategy. The 1973–74 oil price shocks had hit the LAC countries like a ton of bricks, causing balance-of-payments deficits to balloon across the region. At the same time, the recirculation of petrodollars through the international banking system created a global financial glut. Suddenly the international commercial banks were willing to lend to developing countries in Latin America regardless of macroeconomic instability and balance-of-payments difficulties, a region that heretofore had been considered too risky. The result was the implosion of LAC's long-term debt between 1975 (US$45.2 billion) and 1982 (US$333 billion).[54] When the bubble burst in 1982 the region entered a prolonged period of recession and adjustment that reduced average growth for the 1980s to near zero levels. Amid these economic doldrums China–LAC relations began to pick up where they had left off in 1965 as both were hit with the political and economic realities of the 1980s.

This renewal can be seen in the continued negotiation of a number of bilateral protocols, treaties, and agreements and in the increasing flow of both political and commercial delegations back and forth across the Pacific. However, the PRC's post–Cultural Revolution rapport with LAC was laced with much less of the earlier acrimony toward Cuba and the Soviet Union. Although both continued to assail the PRC leadership, including Castro's scathing attack on China and the US at the 1979 Havana Summit Conference of the Non-Aligned Movement, Beijing took the high road.[55] The CCP continued to mingle with anti-Soviet regimes in Latin America, including invitations to two decidedly disreputable authoritarian heads of state— General Jorge Rafael Videla of Argentina and General João Figueiredo of Brazil—to visit China in 1980 and 1984, respectively. But the demise of the Soviet Union in 1989 was China's vindication for most of what had gone on before. As Cuba lost its lifeline of Soviet aid, trade, and lending, commercial exchange between China and Cuba basically continued.

As for the rest of the LAC region, bilateral deals with China proliferated during this period, covering everything from commodities to the peaceful utilization of nuclear energy to maritime transport to scientific and technical cooperation.[56] By the late 1980s two things could be said about these various deals: they began to focus more explicitly on development projects and exchanges; and, despite the capital scarcity that characterized both China and LAC at this time, considerable sums were exchanged in the form of trade credits and loans. Development projects included such ventures as Argentina's 1988 contract to build a model farm in China, the joint Brazil–China accord to construct and launch two satellites in 1988, and China's provision of small hydropower stations to Peru beginning in 1981. Financial exchange took the shape of reciprocal credit lines between Argentina and China from 1980 to 1985, reciprocal credits for bilateral trade between China and Mexico beginning in 1987, and China's loan of US$6.3

million and a grant for US$630,000 to Peru in 1990—in the midst of that country's struggle against hyperinflation and a violent guerrilla insurgency which continued to advocate a Maoist-inspired insurgency that the CCP had long since rejected.[57]

Official visits back and forth across the Pacific involving prominent figures also became the order of the day. Foreign Minister Huang Hua, who toured Colombia, Mexico, and Venezuela, led the first high-level delegation from China in 1981. From there followed a slew of exchanges, including Premier Zhao Ziyang's 1985 tour of Argentina, Brazil, Colombia, and Venezuela. The CCP had already made a 180-degree turn toward economic pragmatism, with Zhao reiterating China's Latin American policy as one based on trade, investment, technology transfers, and the extension of credit.[58] Politics, however, had still not been eliminated from Chinese discourse on the region.

As Wolfgang Deckers points out, through the 1980s visiting Chinese leaders emphasized their support for Argentina's claim over the Falkland / Malvinas Islands; for the efforts of the Contadora Group to mediate the violent Central American conflict under way at that time; and for the Cartagena Group's efforts to broker a more reasonable sharing of the debt burden with commercial lenders.[59] All three issues raised questions of sovereignty, external interference, and the inequities intrinsic to the structure of the international economy—matters that politically united China with many LAC countries.

It appears to be the 1989 Tiananmen tragedy, marked by the CCP's deadly military crackdown of the student democracy movement, that stunted the reference to real-world politics within China–LAC relations. As Frank Mora writes, "Images in the Western press of the People's Liberation Army tanks rolling through Tiananmen Square and soldiers beating and shooting students threatened to reverse everything Deng and his cohort had accomplished in the diplomatic and economic realm since the late 1970s."[60] Although China was castigated by most Western democratic governments, newly democratizing regimes in Latin America hardly missed a beat in welcoming the country back into their fold. Indeed, Mexico had similarly committed (and subsequently sought to sweep under the carpet) its own version of Tiananmen twenty years earlier, with the army's massacre of protesting students just prior to the start of the 1968 Olympics in Mexico City.[61]

Just a year after Tiananmen President Yang Shangkun made China's first executive-level visit to Argentina, Brazil, Chile, Mexico, and Uruguay, reiterating the country's priorities for engaging with LAC (trade, joint ventures in foreign direct investment (FDI), collaboration in the extraction of natural resources, and exchanges in science and technology) and touting the distinctly apolitical "Five Principles of Peaceful Coexistence."[62] From there followed a chain of executive-level delegations to China from the LAC region, including those led by the presidents Patricio Aylwyn (1992) of Chile, Carlos Salinas de Gortari (1993) of Mexico, Itamar Franco (1993) of Brazil, Alberto Fujimori (1995) of Peru, Carlos Saúl Menem (1995) of Argentina, Eduardo Frei (1995) of Chile, and Fernando Henrique Cardoso (1995) of Brazil.[63] The PRC went so far as to designate Brazil its first SP in 1993, an added enticement to sweep Tiananmen under the carpet while vaguely bestowing on Brazil the status of a great power![64]

To be fair, while all but Mexico and Peru (both ruled by electoral-authoritarian regimes at this time) represented newly democratized governments, these executive delegations were more than unapologetic gestures toward China in the aftermath of Tiananmen. Rather, the post-1990 period saw the unleashing of centrally planned economies across Eastern Europe and the new reality that the LAC region, still in the economic doldrums, would now have to compete with the likes of Russia, Poland, Hungary, and other extra-regional market reformers for scarce capital flows and FDI.[65] These economic concerns would continue to eclipse politics in China–LAC relations from here on out.

It would be China, which had eschewed the big bang market shock strategies in vogue at the IMF and World Bank at the time, that would offer up the fiercest competition of all for emerging economies, including those in Latin America. Moreover, with the exception of Chile, the LAC countries studied here were just starting to get serious about market reform, whereas China was now into its second decade of economic restructuring. In fact, the parade of Latin American executives traveling to China in search of trade and investment opportunities coincided with a formidable shift in China's reform trajectory that began in 1993. Barry Naughton captures this moment:

> Under the new decisive policy regime, a succession of milestone reforms were rolled out over the years. The most striking of these were the fiscal, corporate, foreign, and financial reforms that were adopted between 1993 and 1998, in a burst of remarkably decisive and effective reform policymaking [that] transformed every aspect of the Chinese economy. After 1998, the pace of new policy introduction slowed somewhat, but important initiatives have continued. The World Trade Organization (WTO) accession negotiations culminated in late 1999 with dramatic promises of progressive marketization, commitments that required a substantial leadership effort to alter the status quo.[66]

Trade tensions were already surfacing in China–LAC relations, as China's industrial sector was increasingly opened to private ownership and began to overtake agriculture and services as the largest contributor to GDP growth.[67] Having complained during earlier times about the absence of Chinese goods worth buying, LAC countries now felt the force of China's concerted manufactured export drive. Thus, with the exception of Mexico, the asymmetry that had prevailed through the 1980s in terms of LAC's running trade surplus with China was now starting to even out. (The dollar amounts and products traded between China and the six countries in this book between 1980 and 2000 are given in tables 2.4–2.9.) Brazil emerged as China's leading trade partner over these two decades, with total trade reaching nearly US$25 billion. Argentina, Chile, and Peru followed, with total trade hitting US$13.8 billion, US$9.5 billion, and US$4.7 billion, respectively. Peru is the only country to retain a trade surplus with China over the two decades.

While these four countries held their own against China in the 1990s, Mexico did not. Policy makers there had moved quickly with unilateral trade liberalization as the country prepared to join the General Agreement on Tariffs and Trade (GATT) in 1986. With trade reforms in place, financial markets were also quickly liberalized, leading to a flood of capital inflows and imports.[68] As the Mexican peso steeply appreciated up to the December 1994 "tequila crisis" and the Chinese yuan was clearly undervalued in the

Table 2.4. Argentina's trade with China

Argentina trade patterns with China, 1993–2017 ($B)			
Year	Exports	Imports	Total
1993–2000	4.1	6.1	10.2
2001	1.1	1.1	2.2
2003	2.5	0.7	3.2
2005	3.2	1.5	4.7
2007	5.2	5.1	10.3
2009	3.7	4.8	8.5
2011	6.0	10.6	16.6
2013	5.5	11.3	16.8
2015	5.2	11.7	16.9
2017	4.3	12.3	16.6
Total	40.8	65.2	106.0

Top products, 1993–2000		
Imports from China	$MM USD	% of total
Electrical, electronic equipment	1,212	20
Nuclear reactors, fuel elements, isotope separators	852	14
Exports to China	$MM USD	% of total
Animal, vegetable fats and oils, cleavage products	883	21
Oil seed, oologic goods (eggs), grain, seed, fruit	874	21

Top products, 2001–2017		
Imports from China	$MM USD	% of total
Electrical machinery and equipment	33,628	31
Nuclear reactors, boilers, machinery	23,829	22
Exports to China	$MM USD	% of total
Oil seeds and oleaginous fruits	40,483	58
Animal or vegetable fats and oils	11,595	17

Source: IMF, *Directions of Trade Statistics Yearbook.* "Top Products Data" sourced from ComTrade Database. Export/Import totals and categories sorted from top 100 commodity categories worldwide. All available historical data included.

Table 2.5. Brazil's trade with China

Brazil trade patterns with China, 1993–2017 ($B)			
Year	Exports	Imports	Total
1993–2000	8.7	7.0	15.7
2001	1.9	1.3	3.2
2003	4.5	2.1	6.7
2005	6.8	5.4	12.2
2007	10.7	12.6	23.4
2009	20.2	15.9	36.1
2011	44.3	32.8	77.1
2013	46.0	37.3	83.3
2015	35.6	30.7	66.3
2017	47.5	27.3	74.8
Total	226.4	172.5	398.9

Top products, 1993–2000		
Imports from China	$MM USD	% of total
Electrical, electronic equipment	1,474	21
Nuclear reactors, fuel elements, isotope separators	757	11
Exports to China	$MM USD	% of total
Animal, vegetable fats and oils, cleavage products	2,064	24
Ores, slag and ash	1,701	19

Top products, 2001–2017		
Imports from China	$MM USD	% of total
Electrical machinery and equipment	97,640	31
Nuclear reactors, boilers, machinery	61,572	19
Exports to China	$MM USD	% of total
Oil seeds and oleaginous fruits	137,316	34
Ores, slag, and ash	128,407	32

Source: IMF, *Directions of Trade Statistics Yearbook.* "Top Products Data" sourced from ComTrade Database. Export/Import totals and categories sorted from top 100 commodity categories worldwide. All available historical data included.

Table 2.6. Chile's trade with China

Chile trade patterns with China, 1993–2017 ($B)			
Year	Exports	Imports	Total
1993–2000	3.5	4.7	8.2
2001	1.1	1.0	2.1
2003	1.9	1.6	3.6
2005	4.9	3.2	8.1
2007	10.5	6.1	16.6
2009	13.0	6.2	19.2
2011	18.6	12.7	31.3
2013	19.1	15.6	34.7
2015	16.7	14.8	31.5
2017	19.1	15.5	34.6
Total	108.3	81.5	189.8

Top products, 1990–2000		
Imports from China	$MM USD	% of total
Articles of apparel, accessories, not knit or crochet	809	17
Electrical, electronic equipment	604	13
Exports to China	$MM USD	% of total
Copper and articles thereof	1,283	37
Ores, slag, and ash	1,006	29

Top products, 2001–2017		
Imports from China	$MM USD	% of total
Electrical machinery and equipment	30,970	21
Nuclear reactors, boilers, machinery	18,961	13
Exports to China	$MM USD	% of total
Copper and articles thereof	100,052	52
Ores, slag, and ash	63,409	33

Source: IMF, *Directions of Trade Statistics Yearbook.* "Top Products Data" sourced from ComTrade Database. Export/Import totals and categories sorted from top 100 commodity categories worldwide. All available historical data included.

Table 2.7. Costa Rica's trade with China

Costa Rica trade patterns with China, 1993–2017 ($B)			
Year	Exports	Imports	Total
1993–2000	0.1	0.3	0.4
2001	0.0	0.1	0.1
2003	0.1	0.2	0.2
2005	0.2	0.4	0.6
2007	0.8	0.8	1.6
2009	0.8	0.7	1.5
2011	0.2	1.5	1.7
2013	0.4	1.7	2.1
2015	0.1	1.9	2.0
2017	4.7	15.6	20.3
Total	7.4	23.2	30.6

Top products, 1994–2000		
Imports from China	$MM USD	% of total
Electrical, electronic equipment	37	12
Footwear, gaiters and the like, parts thereof	28	9
Exports to China	$MM USD	% of total
Sugar and sugar confectionery	31	34
Fish, crustaceans, mollusks, aquatic invertebrates	28	31

Top products, 2001–2016		
Imports from China	$MM USD	% of total
Electrical machinery and equipment	3,524	23
Nuclear reactors, boilers, machinery	1,756	12
Exports to China	$MM USD	% of total
Electrical machinery and equipment	3,638	77
Nuclear reactors, boilers, machinery	623	13

Source: IMF, *Directions of Trade Statistics Yearbook.* "Top Products Data" sourced from ComTrade Database. Export/Import totals and categories sorted from top 100 commodity categories worldwide. All available historical data included.

Table 2.8. Mexico's Trade with China

Mexico trade patterns with China, 1993–2017 ($B)			
Year	Exports	Imports	Total
1993–2000	1.1	7.6	8.7
2001	0.4	4.0	4.4
2003	1.0	9.4	10.4
2005	1.1	17.7	18.8
2007	1.9	29.7	31.6
2009	2.2	32.5	34.7
2011	6.0	52.2	58.2
2013	6.5	61.3	67.8
2015	4.9	70.0	74.9
2017	6.7	74.1	80.9
Total	31.7	358.7	390.4

Top products, 1990–2000		
Imports from China	$MM USD	% of total
Electrical, electronic equipment	2,975	28
Nuclear reactors, fuel elements, isotope separators	1,528	14
Exports to China	$MM USD	% of total
Nuclear reactors, fuel elements, isotope separators	443	34
Manmade staple fibers	300	23

Top products, 2001–2017		
Imports from China	$MM USD	% of total
Electrical machinery and equipment	286,500	43
Nuclear reactors, boilers, machinery	154,259	23
Exports to China	$MM USD	% of total
Ores, slag, and ash	13,712	24
Vehicles; other than railway or tramway rolling stock	11,060	19

Source: IMF, *Directions of Trade Statistics Yearbook.* "Top Products Data" sourced from ComTrade Database. Export/Import totals and categories sorted from top 100 commodity categories worldwide. All available historical data included.

Table 2.9. Peru's trade with China

Year	Exports	Imports	Total
1993–2000	3.1	1.9	5.0
2001	0.6	0.5	1.1
2003	1.2	0.8	2.0
2005	2.3	1.6	3.9
2007	3.7	4.1	7.8
2009	5.4	5.1	10.6
2011	7.8	7.8	15.7
2013	7.0	8.9	15.9
2015	7.3	8.7	16.0
2017	11.6	8.9	20.5
Total	50.2	48.2	98.4

Peru trade patterns with China, 1993–2017 ($B)

Top products, 1992–2000

Imports from China	$MM USD	% of total
Electrical, electronic equipment	223	15
Nuclear reactors, fuel elements, isotope separators	202	13

Exports to China	$MM USD	% of total
Residues, wastes of food industry, animal fodder	1,958	73
Ores, slag, and ash	524	20

Top products, 2001–2017

Imports from China	$MM USD	% of total
Electrical machinery and equipment	18,278	24
Nuclear reactors, boilers, machinery	13,131	17

Exports to China	$MM USD	% of total
Ores, slag, and ash	55,203	69
Food industries, residues and wastes thereof	11,304	14

Source: IMF, *Directions of Trade Statistics Yearbook.* "Top Products Data" sourced from ComTrade Database. Export/Import totals and categories sorted from top 100 commodity categories worldwide. All available historical data included.

1990s, the stage was set for a massive run-up in Mexico's trade deficit with China. This deficit had reached US$6.5 billion by 2000 (see table 2.8). Moreover, a 30 percent devaluation of the Mexican peso post-1994 had little effect in boosting Mexico's exports to China.

Herein lies the tension between Mexico and China, as Mexican policy makers imposed tariffs and quotas on supposedly cheap Chinese imports in 1993 and initiated antidumping measures on 70 percent of China's imports in 1995.[69] In 1994, for example, Mexico imposed an antidumping duty of 379 percent on Chinese clothing and textile imports.[70] Even countries like Brazil, whose trade endowments are more complementary to those of China, moved to impose import quotas on Chinese textiles in 1996.[71] In time, China's entry into the WTO would help alleviate some of the protectionist measures that it, too, had used to combat its trade deficits.

However, trade frictions with the more industrialized LAC emerging economies—Argentina, Brazil, and Mexico—would remain a constant theme in China's relationship with these countries. Mexico's manufactured exports to China averaged around 35 percent of its total exports to China through the 1990s, whereas Argentina and Brazil were still exporting mainly primary products to China (see tables 2.4, 2.5, 2.8). In essence, a not-so-subtle role reversal had occurred, and it was now China that found little in the way of higher value-added goods to purchase from these Southern Cone countries. Mexico, having diversified away from selling cotton and wheat to China, was simply overwhelmed by the rapidity with which Chinese policy makers and producers were climbing the industrial and technological learning curve.[72] Hence, Mexico continues to carry a seemingly irreversible trade deficit with China.

For Chile and Peru, small, open economies with negligible manufacturing sectors, the challenge was to hedge from becoming too dependent on commodity sales to China. Both managed to diversify their trade partners, if not their actual export products, through this period.[73] By the turn of the new century China accounted for about 9 percent of Chile's exports and the US around 18 percent. In Peru's case China represented 8 percent of its exports while the US captured another 20 percent.[74] For both countries the remainder of trade was split between other Asian countries, the European Union, and intraregional trade within LAC. An added bonus for Peru was the purchase of the Hierro iron ore mine in 1992 by the Chinese company Shou-hang for US$120 million. Not only was this China's largest outgoing FDI to date, but also the asset had been run into the ground by poor state management.[75] Asset quality and the potential for political risk also seemed moot for China in a second round of purchases made in Peru between 1993 and 1995, the window within which China became a net importer of oil. The ink had barely dried on Peru's long overdue Hydrocarbons Law in 1993,[76] when China National Petroleum Corporation (CNPC) successfully bid on service contracts to drill for oil in two blocks of Peru's dilapidated Talara oilfields.[77]

Still, China was now getting its foot in the door in terms of investing directly in those LAC countries with which it had normalized relations. The numerous pacts, memoranda, and agreements brokered between China and the LAC countries were now converting to hard deals. As China's ability to sustain its industrializing export-led model ran up against its natural resource deficit in both energy and agriculture, the search for raw goods rapidly escalated in the 1990s. China had already undertaken joint ventures, for example, in lumber mills and iron ore in Brazil, fisheries in Argentina, copper in Chile, and even a Chinese restaurant in Mexico.[78] On the LAC side, expectations were fast rising that FDI and joint ventures would be undertaken by LAC in China's home market, although these hopes have remained ephemeral.

Economic crisis and a new outward orientation united China and most of LAC in the last two decades of the twentieth century. Yet the roots of these economic crises varied considerably, and the very nature of economic restructuring in China and in LAC, including the content, timing, and sequencing of key policy reforms, were worlds apart. The key points I make here are that Beijing had already begun to articulate and vigorously execute an industrialization strategy based on the import of raw materials and intermediate inputs not available in the home market; and that by selling manufactured goods and fuels abroad China earned the hard currency needed to deepen and expand its new pattern of capital accumulation. Trade was pivotal to this strategy, and the LAC countries became one of many global players that were incorporated into it in order to diversify and solidify Deng's go out strategy.

Whereas politics and the search for common political ground had mattered to both sides at the outset of the 1980s, any effort at forging political bonds around mutual concerns had all but faded by the late 1990s. By the turn of the new century even trade disputes (such as the filing of antidumping complaints at the GATT / WTO), which can be quite political, have been treated mainly as technocratic matters by both sides. LAC is hardly alone in its propensity both to step gingerly with China for fear of rocking the economic boat and to look the other way on China's continued political infractions, environmental damages, and human rights abuses. During President Bill Clinton's second term Chinese President Jiang Zemin hailed his 1997 visit to the US as the "second normalization" of China–US relations. Jiang had secured US renewal of China's most-favored-nation trade status, all the while refusing to express remorse for the student deaths at Tiananmen. A former Clinton aide described these encounters with China as a rigid form of "ask-no-quarter, give-no-quarter bargaining" when it came to discussing China's domestic politics as part of the diplomatic relationship.[79]

Post-2000: The Boom of a Century

Just as China's prowess in conquering international markets with its increasingly competitive manufactured exports caught LAC and the world by surprise in the 1990s, the explosion in commodity prices at the turn of the century came as a second shock of sorts. Driven largely by heightened Chinese demand, the 2003–13 commodity price boom was akin to that which had occurred in the period up to the onset of World War I in 1914.[80] For Argentina, Brazil, Chile, and Peru, the gains have been spectacular, as documented earlier. Be it average growth rates, highly favorable terms of trade, or China's rising FDI inflows to the region, all four of these countries experienced massive windfalls in varying degrees during this decade. Mexico, although benefiting from high commodity prices driven by Chinese demand, continued to struggle with an ever-burgeoning deficit in its trade with China.

Yet as much as things appeared to change in China–LAC relations in the new millennium, in some remarkable ways each country's relationship with China either remained similar to the preboom period or actually worsened (in the case of Mexico). With politics on the back burner, the sweeping over-haul of China's economic reform strategy in 1993, and economics the focus in China's interactions abroad, trade rapidly escalated and became the clos-est bond in China–LAC relations. (The dollar amounts and products traded in the period that covers 2001–17 are given in tables 2.4 to 2.9.) Brazil, Chile, and Peru have held steady with their respective trade balances with regard to China. Argentina has seriously slipped since the 2008–9 global financial crisis and is now exporting around half as much to China as it imports back. In addition, Mexico is now running a record-breaking deficit with China, exporting just 10 percent of the amount that it imports back from China.

On the export side there is little discernible difference in the actual prod-ucts that Argentina, Brazil, Chile, and Peru shipped to China during the preboom (1980–2000) and boom (2003–13) periods (see tables 2.4–2.6 and 2.9). In all four countries primary products have dominated the export profile from 1980 to 2016. On the import side China's gains in climbing the value-added learning curve stand out most vividly for Argentina and Brazil, where the average percentage of manufactured imports from China jumped from 34 percent to 57.7 percent for the former and from 29.6 per-cent to 57.4 percent for the latter. For Chile and Peru, with their much smaller manufacturing sectors, the increase in higher value-added imports from China was less accentuated. Chile's manufactured imports from China went from an average of 38.6 percent to 44.8 percent, and for Peru the in-crease was an average of 33 percent to 49 percent.[81]

Mexico was the only country in this group that exported high value-added goods to China in the 1980–2000 period; however, in the 2001–17 period that figure had dropped from an average of 35 percent of Mexico's total ex-ports to China in the earlier period to 27 percent during the boom years (see table 2.8). At the same time, the average level of Mexico's raw material exports to China saw a slight bump up in the 2001–17 period. On the im-port side, an average of 46.6 percent of Mexico's imports from China could be classified as high value-added from 1980 to 2000, whereas this same figure averaged 71.2 percent from 2001 to 2017. What is new for Chile and Peru is that both have increased the variety of commodities each is now exporting to China, and each has covered the liberalization of agriculture,

services, and investment within the respective bilateral FTAs they have negotiated with the PRC.

Obviously, these facts and figures are difficult to decipher without situat-
ing them within their proper political economic context. I will seek to bring
these data to life with a review of the reforms within which they were en-
shrouded (chapter 3) and the institutions, interests, and actors that framed
policy making during the boom period, in particular (chapters 4, 5, and 6).

Three main insights can be gleaned from this historical overview. The
first concerns cross-Pacific political relations. Common wisdom has long
held that the LAC region was held hostage by the Cold War and, in particular, by the exceedingly acrimonious US–China relationship up through the
early 1970s and thus deterred from interacting with China during this
time.[82] Yet in the interim between 1949 and the onset of China's reform era
in 1978 any number of rich tales can be told with regard to China–LAC
political dialogue and exchange. As reflected in the epigraph to this chapter,
there were some clear political affinities (whether socialist or communist)
between China and certain segments of Latin American civil society in the
early post–World War II period, especially within the South American region. Leftist political parties and movements within the region were ultimately put off by Mao's dogmatism and misreading of the structural realities they faced and ultimately sided with the Soviet Union. However, the
LAC region could still count on China to voice support and third world
solidarity, for example, at the United Nations, on matters related to sovereignty and anti-imperialism.

The second insight concerns commercial ties between China and LAC.
China and Chile had engaged in people-to-people trade relations as early as
1952, and Argentina and Brazil became similarly engaged during the early
1960s as the Great Leap Forward had quickly deteriorated into the Great
Famine. Until China's entry into the United Nations in 1971 its informal
commercial exchange with LAC took any number of forms, including minerals, agricultural commodities, and science and technological sharing. As
the five SPs analyzed in this chapter (Argentina, Brazil, Chile, Mexico, and
Peru) all diplomatically recognized the PRC between 1970 and 1974, these
trade relationships were formalized. By the late 1980s economic concerns

had superseded politics in the China–LAC relationship, although economic structures have held steady since the early 1950s. By this I mean that, with the exception of Mexico, the nature of each SP's trade relationship with China has continued with the sale of raw materials and, since the reform era, the import of manufactured and durable goods from China. What is different is the magnitude of these cross-Pacific trade flows and the voicing of defensive concerns about unequal exchange by some LAC policy makers and political leaders.

This observation segues into my final insight: while slow to evolve, China has formulated a concrete economic development strategy toward the LAC region, but the same cannot be said for all of the LAC countries considered in this book. The UN Economic Commission for Latin America and the Caribbean, the World Bank, the IDB, and even the OECD have published data and insightful reports concerning the various aspects of the China–LAC relationship. These efforts, however, do not add up to a cohesive political economic strategy on the part of the countries at hand. The route taken by Chile, Costa Rica, and Peru, the three countries that negotiated a bilateral FTA with China, comes the closest, but the ability of each to achieve designated goals via these FTAs with China is not guaranteed.[83] Although Argentina and Brazil may lack a clearly defined China strategy, their strong economic ties with China in terms of trade, loans, and FDI have thus far meant that neither side is going to walk away from the negotiating table. Mexico is the most vulnerable, given its adverse factor endowments, serious reform bottlenecks, and the expression of little goodwill toward China.[84]

The lack of an explicit foreign economic strategy toward China on the part of the LAC region, let alone the individual countries involved, was most obvious at the aforementioned China–CELAC meeting in January 2015, when China's proposals to increase its LAC trade and FDI by billions of dollars was met with passivity. This lackadaisical response to China's ambitious trade and investment proposals seems to have spilled over to the broader commitment to economic reform since 2000, most notably in the three larger emerging economies, Argentina, Mexico, and Brazil.

3

From State to Market:
A Fork in the Reform Road

The notion, which dies hard, that development takes place spontaneously, without a rational and deliberate effort to achieve it, has proved to be an illusion, both in Latin America and in other peripheral regions of the world.

Raúl Prebisch, 1963, Director, UN Economic
Commission for Latin America, 1950–63[1]

BY THE EARLY 1980S BOTH CHINA AND the Latin American region had bottomed out economically, but for radically different reasons. China's leaders were faced with the cumulative fallout from two decades of political turmoil and reckless economic management, beginning with the Great Leap Forward in 1958 and culminating with the end of the Cultural Revolution in 1976. Although China's average annual growth rate was 5.1 percent from 1950 to 1978, with its huge population some 80 percent were still living on less than US$1.25 per day by 1981.[2] An internal Chinese Communist Party (CCP) document estimated that grain consumption per capita in 1978 was slightly less than it had been in 1957 and that average annual per capita income in the rural sector was running at around US$39 per year.[3] Even then, reformers within the CCP like Deng Xiaoping and Chen Yun were fiercely attacked for their bourgeois "comprador mentality" by foes within the party who still championed the Cultural Revolution and rejected reform proposals that would tackle these abysmal indicators. Despite having once achieved a standard of living on par with some in Great Britain at the height of the Celestial Empire in the seventeenth and eighteenth centuries, the Chinese political economy had sputtered out by the late 1970s.[4]

While China's woes were mainly a domestic phenomenon, Latin America's doldrums stemmed from a combination of foreign and domestic factors. The top five LAC countries, Argentina, Brazil, Chile, Mexico, and Peru, had almost inadvertently integrated into global markets by borrowing around US$333 billion between 1975 and 1982.[5] It was the last hurrah for the pursuit of import-substitution industrialization (ISI) strategies, which were already in serious trouble when the oil price shocks of 1973–74 struck. For the first time ever international banks, now flush with petrodollars, were willing to lend to sovereign borrowers in Latin America. LAC countries dependent on oil imports ostensibly borrowed to cover their balance-of-payment shortfalls; oil-rich countries purportedly borrowed to ramp up their industrial sectors and complete the region's elusive industrial revolution once and for all. In short, everyone borrowed, until the day of reckoning struck in 1982, when one country after another found itself unable to service its foreign debt. But contrary to the LAC bond defaults in the 1930s, innovations in the commercial lending market—including flexible interest rates and loans packaged by large banking consortia—meant that the barriers to exit were infinitely higher than any barriers to entry had been for these countries.

On both sides of the Pacific policy makers could no longer ignore the exigencies of economic reform. Both China and Latin America were faced with the task of relying on less state intervention and opening up to greater market exposure, including international markets. My subtitle for this chapter, a fork in the reform road, refers to the dramatically different approaches each side took in this quest. As noted, China has moved gradually and cautiously and has experimented boldly with what works and what doesn't in its pursuit of a high-growth development model. Latin America, both within the region and when this group as a whole is compared with China, obviously took differing paths in its efforts to spur growth and development; unlike China, all five of the top countries were starting from a base of state capitalism and middle-income status. Moreover, whether it was Chile's "neo-conservative" market policies of the mid-1970s or Mexico's "stabilizing development" model of the 1960s and 1970s, by 1982 all of these countries faced similar problems in the way of recession, inflation, capital flight, and in some cases the outright collapse of public finances.[6] All five of the LAC countries considered here (Argentina, Brazil, Chile, Mexico, and Peru) ended up in the lap of the IMF by the mid-1980s.

The Prelude to Reform

Latin America

The combination of two world wars and the Great Depression between 1914 and 1945 had dealt severe economic blows the world over, and Latin America was no exception. During World War II economic cooperation between the US and the LAC region had reached one of its few high points, in terms of both trade and aid. To guarantee a steady supply of raw materials the US had signed commodity agreements with various LAC countries, and it had negotiated bilateral defense agreements, most notably with Brazil and Mexico.[7] Funds were also granted by the US for the modernization of regional infrastructure, including the construction of the Pan-American Highway.[8] Political leaders in early post–World War II Latin America were therefore taken aback when Washington made clear that this would all come to a halt. The postwar focus of US foreign economic policy would be the reconstruction of Europe and northeast Asia. Not only would there be no equivalent of the Marshall Plan for Latin America, but also, from the early 1950s on, US attention toward the LAC region would turn narrowly on the imperative to block the spread of communism to the Western Hemisphere.

From this period all the way up to the fall of the Berlin Wall in 1989 Latin America was a pawn of sorts in the game of Cold War politics. We have seen that during the 1950s and 1960s the newly installed communist regime in China did indeed set its sights on the recruitment of Latin American radical parties to its own communist cause, efforts which mostly came to naught. But it was the more developed and established communist regime in the Soviet Union that instilled the fear in US policy circles of Soviet encroachment into the LAC region. As in times past, Washington stood ready to intervene in the event of a perceived threat, this time from the Soviet bloc. US political protagonists, however, proved inept in their efforts to distinguish between honestly elected democratic reformers in the region and those with an explicit Marxist/socialist agenda.[9] Ironically, it was this combination of benign economic neglect on the part of the US and the rapidly transforming political and economic conditions wrought by two wars and the Great Depression that prompted some LAC countries to experiment with their own brand of socially minded reforms.

With the exception of Colombia, all the LAC countries had resisted the US call for Latin American troops to join the US in fighting the so-called communist threat in Korea in 1951.[10] Also in 1951 Guatemala saw the inauguration of a committed reformer, President Jacobo Arbenz, with a platform based on expanded labor rights, land redistribution, and the nationalization of foreign companies, including the expropriation of the notoriously exploitative United Fruit Company. This being the first Cold War test case in the region, Washington overreacted to what in the end was an ambitious reform agenda led by a democratically elected president. From there, other radical political highlights—at least from Washington's vantage point—included the Cuban revolution of 1959 and the advent of Fidel Castro; the attempted return of the liberal democratic reformer Juan Bosch (also misread by Washington as far too radical) in the Dominican Republic in 1965, as the military regime that had interrupted his administration crumbled; the election of the avowed socialist candidate Salvador Allende as Chilean president in 1970; and the revolutionary Sandinista victory in Nicaragua in 1979. In each of these cases Washington thwarted, meddled, and connived until it succeeded in unseating all but Castro.

Some carrots were thrown in with this big stick approach, the most prominent being President John F. Kennedy's launching of the Alliance for Progress in the wake of the Cuban revolution.[11] From 1961 to 1969 an estimated US$10.2 billion in US aid was administered across the region under the auspices of the Alliance for Progress. The goals set out by the Kennedy administration were a precursor to the more grandiose Millennium Development targets established by the UN some forty years later.[12] Following Kennedy's death, his successors quietly began to reduce the alliance budget, which dwindled to around US$335 million by 1969.[13] Hindsight shows that this would be the last big burst of US development aid allotted to the LAC region, as subsequent administrations began advocating private enterprise and self-help. In their classic account *The Alliance that Lost Its Way* Jerome Levinson and Juan de Onís conclude that "without the Alliance the Latin American experience in the 1960's might have been even more turbulent. . . . It was a dramatic and noble crusade, deriving from excessive idealism and over optimism, a momentum that was slowly but indisputably dissipated in encounter with harsh realities—economic, political, and social."[14]

Import-Substitution Industrialization (ISI) and the ECLA Critique

It was against this backdrop that the UN Economic Commission on Latin America (ECLA) was created in 1948.[15] Under the directorship of the Argentine economist Raúl Prebisch from 1950 to 1963, analysts there had begun to question the region's mode of insertion into the postwar international political economy (IPE). ECLA launched a policy research agenda that encouraged the LAC region to rely less on primary exports and to deepen the industrialization inroads that had been made in some countries during World War II.[16] Import substitution had become a necessity during the war, the result being that a small but sophisticated capital goods industry had evolved in Argentina, Brazil, Chile, and Mexico. In his sweeping economic history of Latin America, Victor Bulmer-Thomas points to the creation of two entities by the Roosevelt administration in 1940—the Inter-American Financial and Economic Advisory Committee and the Inter-American Development Commission—which provided US personnel and technical assistance in the cultivation of these industrial sectors.[17] Add to this a wartime boom in intra–Latin American trade and the branching of these nascent industries into the production of intermediate goods, and the stage was ostensibly set for the effective continuation of ISI into the postwar era.

In the introduction I briefly reviewed the ECLA position as advocated by Prebisch, and I argued that the current resurrection by some scholars of such ECLA / Prebisch concepts as "unequal exchange" and "declining terms of trade" to capture the contemporary China–LAC relationship overlooks the dramatic gains in industrialization and export-led growth that have been made in much of the LAC region. However, in the Latin America of the early 1950s the work of Prebisch and his colleague Hans Singer resonated widely.[18] They argued that (1) volatility in commodity prices, versus the secular rise in prices for manufactured goods, undermined LAC's development prospects and exacerbated the gap between rich and poor nations; and (2) in order to overcome this disadvantage the LAC countries needed to deepen and expand their industrial sectors through the use of moderate and selective policy instruments based on trade protection and strong state promotion.[19] Thus was born the structuralist school, whereby protectionism and state intervention in the economy were afforded a considerable degree of respectability.

The rise and demise of ISI in postwar Latin America is a well-told story. As I noted in chapter 2, under ISI policies average annual growth for the top twenty LAC countries was an amazing 5.2 percent from 1945 to 1972.[20] Nevertheless, by the 1960s there had emerged a sizeable laundry list of ISI's shortfalls. The usual rent seeking and corruption had blemished the fast-growing state-owned enterprise (SOE) sector across the region, many of which lacked proper legal frameworks and regulatory oversight. High import tariffs and blanket subsidies for industry had deterred producers from pursuing competitive gains, rendering their goods mainly suitable for sale in domestic or regional markets. Over time this inward orientation fostered a mood of export pessimism, which in turn placed a heavy burden on the balance of payments. Rising income inequality, fiscal profligacy, financial repression, and a blighted agricultural sector became the more common scenario for those LAC countries that engaged most heavily in the ISI strategy. By the 1960s inflation, which ate away at savings, investment, and productivity, had become a serious problem. The basic lack of macroeconomic acumen and technical expertise in the face of these challenges is summed up well by the former Panamanian president Nicolás Ardito Barletta:

> Exchange rates were fixed relative to several of the main hard currencies. Import controls were part of the import substitution policies. Reserves were normally kept low and were not built up with favorable movements in the terms of trade. Fiscal policy consisted in deciding how much of the government deficit would be financed domestically because this would determine

the increase in the quantity of money and inflation. Monetary policy was used mainly to keep interest rates low, producing excess demand for credit to priority sectors, which they [policy makers] defined.[21]

The 1973–74 oil price shocks and severe balance-of-payment shortfalls may well have put an end to ISI. Yet the LAC region, cut off from international capital markets due to the bond defaults of the 1930s, quite suddenly found itself eligible for commercial bank loans comprised largely of recycled petrodollars and issued by institutions operating in the less regulated Euromarkets.[22] Interest rates on these loans were flexible but much lower than average growth rates at the time of issue, and lenders asked little of country borrowers in the way of conditionality. The extra leeway created by foreign borrowing through the 1970s permitted most governments to postpone the necessary macroeconomic adjustments. Moreover, at least temporarily political leaders were able to avoid confrontation with domestic producers and organized labor by delaying significant reforms. The first warning sign of things to come was 1978, as the US Federal Reserve Bank turned to a combination of high interest rates and a strong dollar as its main inflation-fighting strategy. As interest rates quickly outpaced growth and exports and commodity prices began to slide, most of these sovereign borrowers found themselves in a state of de facto default on their dollar-denominated debts after 1982.

ISI, as the region had known it, was officially over, as was the external borrowing that had helped sustain it. The record would show that in the period from 1960 to 1982 consumption had tripled and investment had quadrupled in the LAC region. Brazil and Mexico were fairly successful at channeling borrowed funds into productive investments, while Chile, Argentina, and Peru were not;[23] industry, moreover, grew rapidly in Brazil and Mexico but stagnated in Argentina, Chile, and Peru.[24] Although the region's exports expanded two and a half times during these two decades, the increased levels of investment did little to diversify the composition of trade.[25] Aside from a phenomenal 40 percent level of manufactured exports achieved by Brazil and Mexico under their respective ISI programs, by 1982 traditional primary exports still accounted for 80 percent of all exports from the region. At the same time, debt-backed development based on ISI fell far short of promoting more productive and equitable patterns of growth. On the eve of the 1982 crisis LAC had long surpassed the rest of the developing world in terms of income inequality.

1982–1990: False Starts and Hyperinflation

It would take the remainder of the 1980s for LAC policy makers to fully grasp the implications of the price, capital, and commodity shocks that had hit the region early in the decade. In the wake of the debt crisis the lax macroeconomic scenario described above was no longer an option. Public and private lending to the region had turned to a net negative outflow, and official aid flows were negligible. Suddenly, the main sources of foreign exchange were export earnings, FDI, and portfolio investment (primarily stocks and bonds), all of which required a more stable and convincing legal framework and accompanying set of favorable market signals. Policy makers gradually discerned that they had little choice but to launch the kinds of market-oriented stabilization and adjustment measures that would appeal to private investors.[26] In the initial phases of adjustment, crisis managers generally turned to the IMF and the World Bank, both of which prescribed the usual orthodox fiscal and monetary tightening.[27] Yet by 1985 it was quite clear that a strong dose of austerity, or "cutting your way to growth," was not working.[28]

Of the main borrowers, only Chile found its way out of these tangled economic woods in the 1980s, registering an annual average growth rate of 3.9 percent from 1981 to 1990 (table 3.1). Since 1973 a harsh military regime had provided policy makers there with ample political leeway to experiment with market reforms until the desired results were obtained. While Chile had not been spared the crisis, progress on fiscal and trade reforms prior to the 1982 meltdown had laid the groundwork for a sustainable recovery.[29] As time would tell, the crisis also triggered an important process of institutional reform in Chile, a springboard that has served it well all the way up to the country's accession to the OECD in 2010.[30] The other big borrowers, Argentina, Brazil, Mexico, and Peru, had a much rougher go of it (table 3.1). In these four countries growth was elusive, inflation continued unabated (table 3.2), and the debt burden mushroomed under steep

Table 3.1. Average growth rates, 1981–2018

GDP growth (annual %)	1981–1990	1991–2000	2001–2018
Argentina	−1.4	4.7	2.4
Brazil	1.8	2.6	2.3
Chile	3.1	6.3	3.8
Costa Rica	2.6	4.9	4.1
Peru	−0.7	4.0	5.0
China	9.3	10.5	9.7
Mexico	1.9	3.6	2.0

Source: The Conference Board Total Economy Database™ (Adjusted version), November 2018.

dollar appreciation. In all but Chile the costs of this messy pattern of adjustment fell disproportionately on per capita income (table 3.3).

Argentina, Brazil, and Mexico sought to service their debt by running massive trade surpluses achieved through competitive exchange rate devaluations and high import tariffs. However, as inflation hit triple digits in Argentina, Brazil, and Peru by 1985, policy makers lost faith in IMF remedies. All three countries launched heterodox anti-inflation shock programs that relied on fixed exchange rates and wage and price controls. The out-

Table 3.2. Average inflation, 1981–2016

Inflation, GDP deflator (annual %)	1981–1990	1991–2000	2001–2016
Argentina	765.3	14.6	20.8
Brazil	570.7	582.3	8.3
Chile	21.3	8.7	4.9
Costa Rica	30.8	15.6	8.2
Peru	1008.7	56.6	3.0
China	5.5	7.2	3.6
Mexico	67.4	20.2	4.9

Source: World Development Indicators; Inflation (GDP deflator), http://databank.worldbank.org/data/home.aspx.

Table 3.3. Average growth rates (per capita), 1981–2018

GDP per capita growth (annual %)	1981–1990	1991–2000	2001–2018
Argentina	−2.9	3.4	1.3
Brazil	−0.3	1.0	1.3
Chile	1.4	4.8	2.7
Costa Rica	0.0	2.4	2.6
Peru	−3.0	2.2	3.9
China	7.8	9.3	9.1
Mexico	−0.2	1.8	0.8

Source: The Conference Board Total Economy Database™ (Adjusted version), November 2018.

come in each case was disastrous, with outbursts of higher hyperinflation and huge GDP losses in all three countries.[31] In Argentina and Peru the state had literally collapsed by 1989, while in democratizing Brazil the state had reasserted itself with a vengeance. In Mexico, as much as policy makers there may have tried to tow the orthodox line, they were still struggling by the end of the 1980s to accomplish basic macroeconomic stabilization goals that had been established back in 1982. Together, these abysmal results provided yet another reality check on the steep costs of reckless policy interventions in this new age of deeper international financial integration and higher capital mobility.

China

In his book *On China* Kissinger assigns Deng Xiaoping most of the credit for China's astounding takeoff that began in the 1980s: "Only those who experienced Mao Zedong's China can fully appreciate the transformations wrought by Deng Xiaoping. . . . [A]ll of these were inconceivable in Mao's drab China of agricultural communes, a stagnant economy, and a population wearing standard jackets while professing ideological fervor from the 'Little Red Book' of Mao quotations."[32] Indeed, Deng had been at Mao's side through the revolution and founding of the PRC and was a chief protagonist in the launching of China's heavy industry strategy in the

1950s. This had earned Deng the nickname "steel factory," due to both his fortitude in implementing the CCP's big push industrial plan and the stubbornness with which he stood by his convictions.[33] Purged twice by Mao, Deng returned to political life in Beijing in the summer of 1977 and eventually became China's paramount leader. He was not a one-man show, as there were any number of other important frontline CCP economic reformers at the helm, for example, Chen Yun, Li Xiannian, and Zhao Ziyang.[34]

After Mao's death in September 1976 party leaders were able to make a realistic assessment of the economic setbacks the country had incurred under the decade-long Cultural Revolution (1966–76). The toll was considerable. Agriculture was in shambles, living standards were still dismal, and both urban unemployment and inflation were hovering at levels that, by this time, would have set off another military coup in places like Argentina or Chile. Chinese universities had been closed or gutted through most of the Cultural Revolution, with a huge contingent of the country's most skilled and educated workers sent down to the countryside in an effort to cleanse the populace of any residual capitalist inclinations. Planning mechanisms were depleted, and administrative structures that had been honed since the 1950s were now skeletal. The reformist elements within the CCP moved quickly but carefully, as the formidable old guard of status quo Mao loyalists continued to throw up barriers at every turn.

The initial reform impulse, however, was to renew and deepen the Soviet-style command economy based on heavy industry, with special attention paid to energy, transport, and the development of materials (e.g., plastics, artificial leather, synthetic rubber). The four modernizations (agriculture, industry, national defense, and science and technology)—articulated in the early sixties by Zhou and tirelessly promoted by him and Deng—were still at play but rearticulated in an ambitious Ten Year Plan for Economic Development (1976–1985). At once the plan sought to tackle bottlenecks, revive and restore the institutional moorings of the command economy, and trigger a higher level of growth. Policy makers had assumed, erroneously, that China's petroleum reserves were vast and that further exploitation would yield the revenues needed to finance the plan.[35] China was selling crude oil even to Brazil in the 1980s, as noted above. Although the plan projected that

China's petroleum output would reach five million barrels / day by 1985, ranking it fourth in world production after Saudi Arabia, in fact by 1993 China would become a net importer of oil.

By 1978 the Ten Year Plan was collapsing amid a scarcity of resource-rich land and a huge abundance of labor and underutilized human capital. Those who had been purged during the Cultural Revolution needed to be reintegrated into society and the economy. The portfolio of massive projects that ministry heads had bid for was drastically downsized, and the blight of the agricultural sector now required immediate attention. With billions of dollars in canceled investment projects in 1978, the Soviet-style command economy was now collapsing under its own weight. The CCP revived a slogan that had been used to unite the population in the 1960s in the wake of the wrenching Great Leap Forward: Readjustment, reform, rectification, and improved standards. With the country still reeling from Mao's reckless experiments, Deng reached out to Japan for assistance in pursuing the four modernizations. Ezra Vogel writes,

> From 1978 until 1992, China had received more help from Japan than from any other country. At that time . . . China had very little money and badly needed outside help to promote economic growth. The Japanese government, through JETRO (Japan External Trade Organization), responded with technology and industrial advice, and JETRO in turn called on Japanese officials and even Japanese firms, which dispatched officials to China to provide assistance. By 1992, China was no longer in such desperate need, and other countries began to remove the sanctions imposed in response to the 1989 Tiananmen incident.[36]

Herein lies the beginning of what would become the most successful developing country reform effort ever.

Market Reforms across the Pacific: Ex Ante versus Ex Post Policy Frameworks

Considerable ink has been spilled on attempts to conceptualize and capture the diverse paths to reform that China and the LAC region have taken.[37] We know from the analysis thus far that the LAC countries considered here did not get down to serious business until the late eighties and early nineties, whereas China had buckled down to its reform efforts a full decade earlier. The two reform trajectories are frequently contrasted as the big bang (LAC), meaning that market reforms were adopted quickly and simultaneously, versus China's gradual, experimental opening that has come in waves of policy packages since the early 1980s.[38] The former was coined the Washington Consensus (WC) in a 1990 collection of essays titled *Latin American Adjustment* edited by John Williamson, a senior fellow at the Peterson Institute for International Economics in Washington, DC;[39] the latter was anointed the Beijing Consensus (BC) by Joshua Cooper Ramo in a 2004 paper published by the Foreign Policy Centre in London.[40]

The WC was an ex ante attempt by a group of Washington economists and former LAC finance ministers (many of whom had done their training in the US) to design a set of market-oriented policy prescriptions that would put an end to the low-growth, high-inflation decade of the 1980s. Of the ten recommendations on the WC agenda (table 3.4), the first five would be found in any IMF stabilization program undertaken over the postwar period: fiscal reform toward the goal of halting inflation and capital flight; the reorientation of public expenditure toward its traditional role of financing health, education, and infrastructure; the expansion of the tax base and the setting of moderate tax rates; maintaining positive interest rates to deepen financial markets and combat capital flight; and establishing a competitive exchange rate. The remaining five policy prescriptions included trade and investment liberalization, privatization, deregulation, and the enforcement of property rights. Twenty-five years down the road, the first five policy reforms on the WC agenda are more or less in place in most of the LAC emerging economies (EEs). The remainder have been implemented in varying degrees across the region (see following section).

But back in 1990 the WC triggered mainly negative reactions across the region—from labor unions to domestic producers and the more ECLA-cultivated institutions like ministries of planning, labor, industry, and agriculture as well as in SOEs and the various sectoral development banks. Left-leaning political parties would base their entire campaigns on anti-WC platforms. The challenge for the WC opposition was twofold. First, the Berlin Wall had just come down, signaling the collapse of state-command plan-

Table 3.4. Ten policy recommendations of the Washington Consensus

Policy recommendation	Description
1. Curtailing fiscal deficits	Fiscal deficits lead to inflation, and capital flight; moderate deficits should occur only when being used to finance productive infrastructure investments
2. Reducing subsidies	Subsidies are a major drain on the government's budget and cause market distortion; subsidies should be reduced or, preferably, eliminated
3. Tax reform	As an alternative to reducing subsidies, taxes can be raised to address fiscal deficits; tax regimes should be broad-based with moderate marginal rates
4. Interest rate management	Interest rates should be market-based, with real interest rates being positive in order to discourage capital flight and encourage saving
5. Competitive exchange rates	Exchange rates need to be competitive to support exports
6. Liberalizing trade	Protection leads to "costly distortions that penalize" exports; instead, limited tariffs should be used to protect infant industries for limited time horizons or promote diversification
7. Encouraging foreign direct investment	Economies should encourage foreign direct investment, as it provides the "necessary capital, skills, and know-how, either producing goods needed for the domestic market or contributing new exports"
8. Privatizing state-owned enterprises	Proceeds from privatization can combat fiscal deficits both immediately and in the longer term; privatized entities are generally more competitive than their state-owned equivalents
9. Deregulation	Regulations that impede the establishment of new businesses and investments, price controls, and restrictions on capital flows hinder growth, spur corruption, and should be curtailed
10. Enforcing property rights	Fundamental to a capitalist system, property rights must be rigidly enforced

Source: Compiled by the author, based on John Williamson, "What Washington Means by Policy Reform," in *Latin American Adjustment: How Much Has Happened?* ed. John Williamson (Washington, DC: Institute for International Economics, 1990), 8–17, http://piie.com.

ning models and any credibility they may have once enjoyed. Second, there was no concrete alternative on the horizon for these inflation-prone, recession-riddled LAC economies. The Asian miracle had been well under way, and a rich literature was already emerging on the nature of those developmental states that had underpinned high growth and rapid modernization since the 1970s, for example, in Japan, South Korea, and Taiwan.[41] The Latin American state, however, was in no shape to take any further lead in the development process at this point in time. By default the West's triumph of liberal democratic capitalism based on open borders and free markets was superimposed on these capital-starved countries.

To be clear, within the LAC region there was a consensus that something new had to be done, but there was little unanimity that that something should take the shape of a big bang market shock—especially after a decade of failed attempts by LAC policy makers at cutting their way to growth via tight austerity measures. This unfounded claim to a consensus is something the WC shares with the BC. Like the WC, the idea of a BC caught fire due to the timing of its release in 2004. China's pace of integration into global markets for trade and FDI was catapulting upward. Heretofore a development strategy that some mainstream economists and policy analysts from afar had discounted as too unstable and risky, the rise of China in the IPE began to command renewed attention, if not respect.[42] Publications on China's success, both academic and popular, proliferated, as did writings on China as a new economic threat. Ramo seized the moment and published an ex post tract that attributed China's rise to innovation-based development; economic success measured not by per capita income but by its sustainability and level of equality; and self-determination for China and for other countries vis-à-vis the US.[43]

There are a number of subpoints to Ramo's scheme, such as leading by example, opposition to the WC, China's globalizing on its own terms, and the use of China's asymmetric capabilities to balance against the US. Like the WC, the BC invoked considerable opposition, but not along sectoral, ideological, or North–South lines; rather, the uproar against the BC had to do with its being "a misguided and inaccurate summary of China's actual reform experience. It not only gets the empirical facts wrong about China, it also disregards the similarities and differences China's experience shares with other countries, and it distorts China's place in international politics."[44] Even so, the BC has been the subject of numerous conferences and the topic of books, academic journals, and policy magazines, and it continues to surface at times in prominent media outlets like the *Financial Times* and *The Economist*. Within the halls of academe it can be difficult to deter aspiring undergraduates from delving into the BC as the subject for a senior honors thesis.

It is truly remarkable that these two simple ideas, sprung from think tank researchers, have assumed such a lasting and tenacious hold on development policy debates since their respective emergence—the WC in 1990 and the BC in 2004. William Easterly, in his best-selling book *The Elusive Quest for Growth,* laments how multilateral institutions like the World Bank have run through a series of theoretical models in the developing world over the past sixty years without ever hitting the right one.[45] The LAC region had been a guinea pig of sorts for many of these ill-fitting models in the 1950s and 1960s. However, freakishly high levels of capital liquidity in the 1970s prompted LAC policy makers to throw macroeconomic caution and textbook models to the winds. The magnitude of the 1982 debt shocks opened the door for the IMF and the World Bank, and both returned to the region with the same reform recipes they had been advocating since their creation in the late 1940s. From this seemingly random string of events the WC was born.

Again, the first five tasks on the WC agenda now constitute basic measures that are essential for reigniting growth that any country, North or South, would embark on. The second five tasks dig into deeper tissue, both politically and economically, the result being that these remain only partially completed in some of the countries considered here. At its worst, antiglobalization activists and nongovernmental organizations (NGOs) have declared the entire WC agenda a neoliberal disaster. This stance still resonates strongly with some domestic constituencies in Latin America, as witnessed in the 2018 election of President Andrés Manuel López Obrador (AMLO) in Mexico and the resurgence of the former Argentine president Cristina Fernández de Kirchner in 2019. Williamson himself has expressed shock that the WC became a prime departure point for global policy debates, and he has continually revised, clarified, and expanded on it since the 1990s.[46]

My point: the WC was anchored in at least a half century of debate about state versus market approaches and was a response to real-world trends and material conditions in the LAC region. Williamson and his cronies got it wrong in proclaiming the victory of markets over states in the post–Cold War era, and they completely missed the mark in declaring a consensus about the need for a fast-moving implementation of market reforms. Domestic elites in the region made their fortunes off rapid privatizations, and international banks thrived on the quick opening of financial markets and the capital account. Nevertheless, the WC was much more than an ex post narrative about what appeared to be happening in Latin America.

This last point highlights the prime shortcoming of the BC: it bears little relationship to the facts and unfolding outcomes of China's far-reaching reform program. Top scholars, both Chinese and foreign, have reacted vehemently to the three key BC pillars mentioned above.[47] For example, here are the objections raised by Scott Kennedy, one prominent critic:

- Innovation-based development: "Technological innovation has not been the centerpiece of China's growth. . . . [F]or the most part Chinese enterprises make products and provide services that have been designed or invented outside of China."[48]
- Economic success measured by its sustainability and level of equality: "The evidence that China is pursuing sustainable and equitable development is highly limited. . . . [W]hen there appears to be a tradeoff between the environment and growth, the latter wins. . . . Similarly, inequality, not equality, has been the chief hallmark of China's growth experience."[49]
- Self-determination for China vis-à-vis the US: "If there is a consensus in China, it is that the BC is wrong and overly antagonistic to the United States and the global community."[50]

With regard to Ramos's contention that the BC stands in direct opposition to the WC, this prominent group of BC doubters further begs to differ. For example, Arthur Kroeber, a senior fellow at the Brookings–Tsinghua Center in Beijing, has analyzed the extent to which China's reforms match up to the WC.[51] Returning to the WC agenda (see table 3.4), Kroeber answers a "resounding yes" on the degree to which China's fiscal discipline, trade and investment liberalization, and competitive exchange rate management have all closely followed the dictates of the WC. He assigns a "qualified yes" on China's performance with regard to the setting of public expenditure priorities (there has been a clear shift away from nonmerit subsidies to infrastructure and other public goods); tax reform (the effective tax rate is moderate, and the revenue base has been broadened and diversified); deregulation (easing barriers to entry and exit); and property rights (ambiguous but gradually moving forward). Kroeber assigns a definitive "no" to interest rates and privatization. The privatization of China's large SOEs has been one of the main reform delays. The government has introduced competition into the economic system by allowing private firms to steadily increase their share in the economy. At the same time, Elizabeth Economy notes the expansion of SOEs under Xi Jinping.[52]

Because my focus here is on the cross-regional comparison, I have not engaged with the more nuanced debates about the processes and outcomes of Chinese reform since 1978. Three iconic books stand out: *China's Trapped Transition: The Limits of Developmental Autocracy* by Minxin Pei; *Capitalism with Chinese Characteristics* by Yasheng Huang; and *How China Escaped the Poverty Trap* by Yuen Yuen Ang.[53] Pei argues that the authoritarian nature of the Chinese political regime is a structural impediment that limits the realization of China becoming a fully developed country. The self-elevation of Xi Jinping to "paramount leader" in 2017 does seem to raise the probability of policy mistakes given that this signals an even lower level of transparency and accountability. In his book Huang also laments the lack of political reform and argues that the "true Chinese miracle" occurred in the 1980s under the thrust of rural sector reforms that unleashed growth and entrepreneurship. He contends it was the shift away from this market-fueled phenomenon in the 1990s and toward state-led urban sector policies that slowed the buoyant patterns of poverty reduction and expanding household incomes.

Ang's book is the most recent, and she argues provocatively that China's impressive growth and development since 1978 is based on "directed improvisation . . . the introduction of some democratic qualities through bureau-

cratic reforms and Beijing's willingness to allow and direct local improvisation that enabled the nation's economic dynamism."[54] From the standpoint
of Latin America, the debates about how China has arrived to become the
second biggest economy in the world are ancillary in that they do not necessarily chart a viable reform path forward for the LAC region. Taken at face
value, the 2003–13 commodity boom and buoyant growth rates on both
sides of the Pacific drove home the fact that China, in its own unique way,
had combined sound macroeconomic policy reforms with the institutional
might of the Asian developmental state.[55] Add to this some of the established features of the developmental state—policy making placed in the
hands of technocrats and bureaucrats within the government, high savings
and investment rates, investment tied to productive sectors, the use of tax
and credit incentives to promote export-led growth—and it becomes clear
that the phenomenon of China's rise cannot be neatly categorized into the
likes of the BC. Nor can it be replicated in the LAC region, despite the rhetoric of some Latin America leaders who claim to embrace the BC as the
opposite of the WC.

Blueprints and Stepping-Stones

Widely differing reform paths within and across the Pacific Basin make
it tricky to compare reform progress and outcomes. I want to briefly review
the various measures of reform progress, none of which is entirely satisfac-
tory. First is the challenge of diversity in reform approaches between LAC
and China. Second, the measures and indices that have been generated by
the international financial institutions (e.g., the World Bank and the Inter-
American Development Bank [IDB]) and other global institutions such as
the World Economic Forum and Transparency International have differing
timelines and emphases, meaning they are rough guidelines at best. Third,
China's own data are widely considered to be unreliable, meaning that it is
possible to speak only in terms of general trends.[56] Moreover, the Chinese
government has vigorously objected to the country's inclusion in some
World Bank databases, for example, the bank's "Doing Business" survey.[57]
Admittedly, some of the data presented must be taken with a grain of salt.

Latin America

At the outset of this book I argued that reform paths and progress would depend on a given country's endowment factors, institutional rigor and depth, and the nature of the development model in place at the time a major reform effort is launched. Due to these variables, LAC's ostensible big bang was less of a market shock than has been broadly alleged by WC critics.[58] Two of the hyperinflationary cases, Argentina and Peru, did act quickly, as the economy of each had literally spun out of control. Having started its reforms much earlier, Chile moved at a steady pace through the 1990s. Brazil, despite its exceedingly high inflation (see table 3.2), moved more gradually on market reforms, but so did Costa Rica, although the latter has advanced on par with Chile in terms of institutional modernization. Mexico's initial reform pace was more in line with that of Argentina and Peru, except for the fact that its reform zeal quickly waned after policy makers secured the 1994 NAFTA deal. It was not until the *sexenio* (the six-year term) of the PRI president Enrique Peña Nieto (2012–18) that significant reforms were launched, for example, in the realm of education, elections, labor, banking, taxes, telecom, and economic competition;[59] ending the state monopoly over petroleum exploration and extraction was the ultimate victory.

For all the consternation and criticism surrounding the WC, there is, interestingly, a paucity of studies on the actual outcomes of market reforms. A 2002 report produced by two IDB economists, Eduardo Lora and Ugo Panizza, remains one of the most careful analyses undertaken to date.[60] Lora and Panizza set 1985 as the reform baseline and measure the accomplishments that had been made by 1989, 1994, and 1999 (fig. 3.1).[61] LAC countries went the farthest with trade liberalization, and nearly half of them made considerable inroads on financial sector reform. Progress on privatization and tax reform was slower, while the reform of labor markets through the 1990s was minimal. Growth did rebound in the 1990–99 period (see fig. I.1), but it did so from the very low level registered in the 1980s. When growth slowed during the recessionary window between 1999 and 2002 reform fatigue took over.

Again, a first phase of macroeconomic reforms, based largely on points

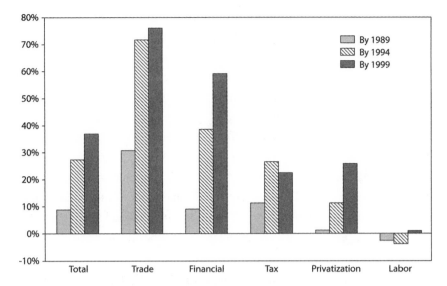

Figure 3.1. Progress of market reforms in Latin America
(margin of reform put to use, 1989–99).
Source: Eduardo Lora and Ugo Panizza, "Structural Reform in Latin America under Scrutiny,"
Inter-American Development Bank Research department, March 2002, 9.

one to five on the WC agenda (see table 3.4), had met with some success. With the restoration of both aggregate and per capita growth, inflation moved downward in all but Brazil for the first time since the 1982 shocks had hit. The simultaneous transition to democracy in all but Mexico saw the entry of a new generation of talented and more technically skilled policy makers into the halls of government. Newly elected executives were able to cash in on a democracy dividend, as mass constituencies in the region looked forward to future gains rather than backward at past losses. Moreover, the pain and gains from macroeconomic stabilization were perceived to be widely shared and quite tangible. Growth was up, inflation was easing down, and the consumer surplus was finally reemerging. Although presidential terms in most of the LAC-5 countries prohibited incumbents from running for a second consecutive term, voters in Argentina, Brazil, and Peru granted their presidents a second term for the sake of continuity in the implementation of key economic policies and reforms.

Alas, the implementation of a second phase of reforms in the mid-1990s proved to be a much trickier endeavor. Necessary follow-up policies were needed for the successful sustainability of a market-based development model. However, as policy makers sought to create new mechanisms for regulatory oversight and to promote efficiency, competitiveness, and greater transparency within the public and private sectors distributional conflict quickly set in. The winners and the losers in the reform process became more discernible, as the costs (downsizing, bankruptcy, antitrust oversight) became more concentrated and the benefits (productivity gains, greater public accountability, increased efficiency in the delivery of key services) far less tangible.[62] Moisés Naím has written on the institutional backdrop to this reform impasse in the LAC region and on the kinds of reform strategies that could help to overcome it.[63] Suffice it to say that second-term executives in Argentina, Brazil, and Peru accomplished little in the way of second-phase reform.

The slowing of regional growth in 1999 came on the heels of two exchange rate crises—Mexico in 1994 and Brazil in 1998–99—and seemingly endless efforts by the LAC EEs to periodically fend off international contagion, for example, from the 1997–98 Asian crises, the 1998 Russian debt default, and Turkey's financial crash of 2000–2001. While I have argued that the implementation of WC policies in the LAC-5 countries was less the big bang than some have written about, the simultaneous implementation of trade and capital account liberalization, coupled with aggressive privatization efforts, contributed greatly to these exchange rate meltdowns.[64] In this respect, the sequencing and timing of market reforms were poorly coordinated, and, although it is a counterfactual, one could reasonably argue that a more gradual approach could have eliminated or greatly eased the magnitude of these shocks.[65] A reform hiatus set in amid the 2000–2003 global recession, and there appeared to be no end in sight. Then, quite suddenly, the commodity lottery struck, and the LAC region would ride high on China's tailwinds for the next decade (2003–13).

China

China's reform strategy remains a work in progress (table 3.5). Because the literature is saturated with definitions and analyses of the China Model, my purpose here is not to add value to this concept but rather to use it as a comparative reference point in analyzing the Latin American experience.[66]

Both the aggregate data on GDP growth (see table 3.1) in China since 1981 and the corresponding data on per capita GDP growth (see table 3.3) highlight the extent to which the country's economic rise is simply unprecedented in the developing world. Hu Angang, the prominent Chinese economist, has commented, "China's quick ascent into the ranks of great powers not only outstripped the expectations of the international community but has also surpassed the Chinese government's own expectations."[67] While the potential for success was not entirely obvious at the outset of the reform period, Hu cites several preexisting factors that enabled China's economic takeoff:

- A strong industrial foundation due to the "big push" strategy under Mao
- High investment and savings rates
- Solid social infrastructure in the realms of public transportation, telecommunications, postal services, and urban utilities
- An abundance of cheap labor and a relatively well-educated population
- The sheer size of the domestic market[68]

As early as 1993 William Overholt observed this synergy in *The Rise of China: How Economic Reform Is Creating a New Superpower:*

> China's leaders have shown remarkable insight into the institutional requirements of market systems, and have thoughtfully constructed a sequence of steps that build the necessary institutions while avoiding fatal damage to price stability, social welfare, or political support for future economic reform. They have made many mistakes, but so far their analysis has demonstrated the intellectual bankruptcy of the spasmodic strategies favored in the West. Above all, the Chinese experience has shown that a socialist economic system can indeed move to a market system without an intervening social catastrophe—a conclusion that would be very much in doubt if the world had only experienced the Russian and East European approaches.[69]

Published on the heels of the Tiananmen massacre and just fifteen years into the reform era, this assessment surprised external scholars of China.

Table 3.5. Highlights of Chinese reform, 1978–present

1978	Open-Door Policy initiated, allowing foreign trade and investment to begin
1978	"Household-responsibility system" in the countryside gave some farmers ownership of their products
1979	Collective farms assigned plots to individual families
1979	Township and village enterprises encouraged
1979	Most urban families limited to one child to slow population growth
1980	Special economic zones created for export; PRC became member of the International Monetary Fund
1981	Household responsibility reform allowed farmers to retain surpluses as opposed to surrendering them
1982	The new constitution promised to protect "the lawful rights and interests of foreign investors"
1984	Self-proprietorship (*getihu*) encouraged, fewer than eight persons
1986	The Contract Responsibility System implemented: enterprises required to pay a set amount of profits to the government but may retain profits above the contract requirement
1986	Student-led protests against corruption and political control spread in Beijing and other cities
1987	The very first email in China was sent in September
1988	Economic turbulence stirred public discontent. Rising inflation peaked at over 30 percent in urban areas
1989	The massacre at Tiananmen Square was followed by strong measures to cool the economy, to alleviate negative social externalities, along with renewed political campaigns to suppress dissent
1990	Stock markets opened in Shanghai and Shenzhen; lending to nonpriority sectors increased
1992	The price control "rectification program" was abandoned; foreigners were allowed to purchase and sell B shares, which were issued by some enterprises; shares that were limited to purchase and sale by domestic residents were called A shares
1993	Decision made to establish a "socialist market economic system"

1993	The 1993 Company Law allowed SOEs to become corporatized, with a corporate board, and to establish joint stock companies
1994	Company Law introduced; multiple exchange rate system ended and tax reforms introduced; China–ASEAN Joint Committee on Economics and Trade Cooperation established
1995	Contractual terms for staff of state–owned enterprises established
1996	Full convertibility offered for current account transactions
1997	Plan to restructure many state-owned enterprises began; China implemented reforms to maintain stability after Asian Financial Crisis; extended $4 billion in aid to other Asian states
1997	Beijing enacted its first Internet laws
1998	Program for recapitalization created commercial banks
1999	Announcement of the "go out" policy encouraged Chinese firms to invest abroad
1999	Clean Vehicle Action Program called for 10% of all taxis and 20% of all buses in twelve cities to run on alternative fuels, such as natural gas or liquefied petroleum gas
2000	State Council issued Order No. 292, which introduced new content restrictions that required Internet service providers to make sure that the information sent out on their services adhered to the law and that domain names and IP addresses be recorded for providers engaged in media or online bulletin boards
2001	China joined the World Trade Organization
2002	Communist Party endorsed the role of the private sector, inviting entrepreneurs to join
2003	Decision made to perfect the socialist market economic system; A-share markets opened to foreign investors
2004	Constitution amended to guarantee private property rights
2005	Exchange rate reformed
2006	Three Gorges Dam project and a railway to Tibet completed
2006	China's foreign currency reserves reached US$1 trillion
2006	The State Environmental Protection Administration established five regional supervision centers to oversee local governments' implementation of environmental oversight efforts

(table continues)

(continued)

2007	Government acknowledged economic growth is unbalanced and unsustainable and agreed to increase market access to foreigners
2008	In response to the global financial crisis China implements US$586 billion stimulus package which is invested largely in infrastructure and social welfare projects
2008	Beijing hosted the Summer Olympic Games
2009	Beijing blocked Facebook after protestors in Xinjiang used it to communicate
2010	State Council Information Office's white paper "The Internet in China" called on governments at every level to address all the problems reported by the Chinese people via the Internet
2010	The IMF promised a restructuring of shares that would increase China's voting weight
2011	Government announced the 12th Five-Year Plan aimed at rebalancing the economy
2011	Communist Party General Secretary Hu Jintao offered a stark assessment on corruption in the Communist Party
2012	Government increased flexibility of exchange rate, lowered cap on deposit rates, opened foreign access to capital markets; the state committed to environmental protection; policies aimed at increasing social safety nets were implemented to boost consumption
2012	President Xi Jinping called for the party to play an increased role in supervising higher education
2013	Xi's economic plan directed at reforming markets and the financial sector
2014	The high capital exports encouraged by the balanced growth policy caused China's reserve holdings to fall by US$150 billion, which led to a capital account deficit
2015	The IMF declared reserve currency status for the RMB, meaning it joined the dollar, yen, euro, and British pound as one of the world's main central bank reserve currencies (took effect in October 2016)
2015	Xi's anticorruption campaign disciplined more than three hundred thousand officials, two hundred thousand of whom received "light punishment" and an additional eighty thousand who received harsher punishment

2015	China's Ministry of Environmental Protection reported that 280 million Chinese did not have access to safe drinking water
2015	Government put forth a new set of regulations under the guise of national security designed to force technology companies involved in providing computing and networking equipment to China to provide their source code
2015	National Credit Information Sharing Platform established
2016	At the Fifth Plenum of the 18th Party Congress, the most notable announcement was that Xi would be recognized as the paramount leader of the Communist Party
2016	Xi put to rest the notion that the party would reduce its role in the management of SOEs
2016	Chinese military established its first overseas military logistics base in Djibouti
2017	Jack Ma (CEO of Alibaba) pledged that Alibaba would create one million jobs for American small businesses through the Alibaba platform by 2022
2017	China and the Association of Southeast Asian Nations adopted a draft framework on a code of conduct for the South China Sea
Next 5–10 years	China intends to fully liberalize its deposit rate (as it already has with the lending rates), further globalize the RMB, increase exchange rate flexibility, and foster more high value-added industries
2020	Commitment to double incomes and recapture China's historic centrality and greatness in the international system
2030	RAND and the Institute for Mobility Research estimate that the number of automobiles produced in China could reach fifty million annually.

Sources: Robert Devlin, "China's Economic Rise," in *China's Expansion into the Western Hemisphere: Implications for Latin America and the United States,* ed. Riordan Roett and Guadalupe Paz (Washington, DC: Brookings Institution Press, 2008), 127; Xiaodong Zhu, "Understanding China's Growth: Past, Present, and Future," *Journal of Economic Perspectives* 26, no. 4 (2012): 103–24; various issues of *Xinhua News,* http//news.xinhuanet.com/English; Eswar Prasad, "The Path to Sustainable Growth in China," testimony before the US–China Economic and Security Review Commission, April 22, 2015, http://www.brookings.edu/~/media/research/files/testimony /2015/04/22-path-sustainable-growth-china-prasad/uscesrctestimony22apr15.pdf; https://www .reuters.com/article/us-china-reforms-chronology-sb/timeline-china-milestones-since-1978 -idUKTRE4B711V20081208; Elizabeth C. Economy, *The Third Revolution: Xi Jinping and the New Chinese State* (New York: Oxford University Press, 2018).

Overholt was attacked as a pro-Beijing, Hong Kong–based investment banker who produced nothing more than "a better written version of an official account by the Chinese government."[70] However, a pathbreaking book on the political correlates to Chinese economic reforms, *The Political Logic of Economic Reform in China* by Susan Shirk, also published in 1993, gave weight to Overholt's analysis. Early on Shirk identified five key dimensions of China's political institutions within which the reforms were generated, hashed over, modified, and implemented: authority relations among institutions; leadership incentives; the bargaining arena; the enfranchisement of groups in the policy-making process; and decision rules by consensus.[71]

From these prescient 1993 analyses on, the story of China's rise would become almost mythical. What stands out is the ability of a developmental state to make way for and crowd in the private sector, while treading lightly when reforms came too close to upsetting entrenched interests within the CCP. This "dual track" strategy was part of the gradual nature of China's reform path.[72] Within this framework the government channeled savings and investment into SOEs, which became engines of industrial growth. Growth, in turn, helped to quell reform opponents and placate veto players. The government also delegated authority to policy banks, the China Development Bank (CDB) in particular, to fund massive infrastructure and industrial projects. The four big state banks—Bank of China, China Construction Bank, Industrial and Commercial Bank of China, and the Agricultural Bank of China—took the lead on sectoral lending at low rates in order to expand the productive capacity of the economy. With the liberalization of investment within special economic zones, the opening of trade with the country's accession to the WTO in 2001, and the ongoing incorporation of the private sector into the domestic political economy, China's private sector is increasingly the driver of output, productivity, and employment creation.[73]

The quality and availability of economic data on China do not lend themselves to the kind of index building that Lora and Panizza have constructed for Latin America. As mentioned earlier, though, there is agreement within the rich literature on the Chinese political economy that policy makers there have made considerable inroads on the WC reforms (see table 3.4). When we look at how China fares on Western measures of institutional reform and rankings, there is good reason to believe that this combination of WC reforms undertaken by a developmental state has compensated for some of China's purported institutional weaknesses. For example, China outranked all of the LAC cases in this book on the World Economic Forum's measure of overall competitiveness.[74] But it performed abysmally on the World Bank's "Doing Business" index, which is no doubt why the Chinese government has so adamantly opposed China's inclusion in this database.[75] Its rankings on the Worldwide Governance Indicators (WGI) are just as poor.[76]

Granted, China's inclusion in these Western databases may be like trying to fit a square peg into a round hole, but when those same WGI indicators are analyzed over time and compared with the LAC cases here (see fig. 1.1) a different reality emerges. On key measures like rule of law, government effectiveness, and regulatory quality, China outpaces the performance of three to four LAC cases in each category. Moreover, in all three categories China's institutional modernization moved forward during the China boom, whereas the same cannot be said of the LAC countries. Argentina and Brazil, for example, experienced considerable reform backsliding during this period. China's progress on this count may be incremental, but it is steady forward movement. Yuen Yuen Ang attributes China's successful rise to policy makers' strategy of "building markets with weak institutions and, more fundamentally, by crafting environments that facilitate improvisation among the relevant players."[77] This, along with the country's huge economies of scale, is one of many ways that we can account for China's leap from one-half the size of all LAC economies combined in 1990 to nearly twice the total regional GDP in 2013.[78]

The Global Financial Crisis (GFC): Macro Convergence, Micro Divergence

Macroeconomic Convergence

Looking back on the 1990s, the EEs seemed to be ricocheting from one financial crisis to another.[79] Mexico's 1994 "tequila" crisis was emblematic of a new phase in which securitized capital inflows came to count for the bulk of funds pouring into the LAC economies. This, combined with the rise of computerized trading, meant that stocks, bonds, and equities could exit in a flash when a given EE's fundamentals began to look shaky. In most of the abovementioned cases (Brazil, Russia, Asia—Thailand, Korea, Malaysia, Indonesia—Turkey, and Argentina) the massive exit of securitized capital flows provoked an exchange rate crisis, which in turn brought the domestic banking system to the brink. These blowups, as painful as they were, prompted a concerted effort at banking and financial sector reform that would serve these countries well when the GFC began to erupt with the bankruptcy of Lehman Brothers in September 2008. China, too, had progressed on financial sector and banking reforms, although not to the extent of the LAC EEs. Yet China was able to move swiftly with a huge stimulus package when the GFC struck, which the IMF declared to be a "quick, determined, and effective" response to the crisis.[80]

Hindsight shows that policy learning and reforms adopted in response to these previous crises positioned EE policy makers to respond effectively to the GFC, despite the obvious differences between China and the LAC-5 and within the LAC region itself. In terms of the most common indicators of macroeconomic performance—external debt, public or government-held debt, and inflation—sound progress had been made on all three fronts prior to the GFC. Although LAC's public debt as a percentage of regional GDP had previously been about 20 percent higher than that of the Asian EEs, the 2000s saw a close convergence in public debt levels across the Pacific. Moreover, on the eve of the GFC, LAC's external debt had been reduced to its 1980 levels and was now running neck to neck with the less indebted Asian EEs. In the period from 2005 to 2009 inflation, also more common to LAC, was running in single digits on average in China and the LAC countries, with the exception of Argentina. However, even Argentina, having jettisoned WC-style reforms in the wake of its 2001–2 meltdown, was able to navigate the crisis due to the financial sector reforms carried out in the 1990s.[81]

It helped that the LAC-5 had built up huge arsenals of foreign exchange thanks to the commodity price boom, and this enabled them to respond counter-cyclically to the GFC. The transmission of the crisis was mainly on the trade side for China and the LAC-5, given China's dependence on exporting to the US market and LAC's growing reliance on exports to China. Both China and Brazil loosened fiscal and monetary policy, and both infused relief funds into the national economy through their formidable development banks. To a lesser extent Chile and Mexico (with a delayed response) followed suit. In varying degrees the LAC-5 reduced reserve requirements, lowered interest rates, and pumped liquidity into the domestic economy through different currency swap arrangements. To halt the erratic flow of capital in and out of the country all of the LAC-5 relied on some semblance of capital controls, such as early withdrawal penalties and taxes on cross-border financial transactions. Such measures, once considered anathema to the IMF, have now been recast as part of the larger package of macroprudential policies.[82] Moreover, more than seventy years after its creation the fund finally conceded that full capital account liberalization may "only be optimal after a nation has reached a certain threshold of financial and economic development, one that many emerging market and developing countries have not yet reached."[83]

In the period from 1985 to the eve of the GFC notions of convergence centered largely on the OECD bloc, where policy makers touted the "Great Moderation," meaning that sound macroeconomic management and mature institutions had basically insured the developed countries from the volatility witnessed in the EE countries during this period.[84] How wrong this assumption turned out to be! Over a decade out from the GFC, it is the convergence of macroeconomic policy approaches across EEs in the Pacific Rim that has been more noteworthy. First, policy makers in the EEs stepped outside of their usual comfort zones to embrace a combination of market-based and state-led policies that rendered old labels like "neoliberal" and "developmentalist" much less relevant.

Second, on the LAC side it was the increased confidence gained from policy learning during previous crises that prompted officials to experiment with temporary capital controls and counter-cyclical fiscal policies. While EE responses deny neat categorization, the overall trend in response to the GFC was the adoption of pragmatic, flexible policies. As I alluded to in chapter 1, it was the continuation of these pragmatic crisis-response policies long after the GFC that rendered them profligate in countries like Argentina and

Brazil. Perhaps the main Achilles heel of all of the LAC-5 has been the failure to consistently link macroeconomic reform with a sound microeconomic strategy at the level of the individual and the firm.

Microeconomic Divergence

On August 21, 2016, a front-page story in the *Los Angeles Times* reported "A Manufacturing Boom Lifts More than Mexico."[85] The article stated, "Around 40 cents of every dollar that the United States imports from Mexico comes from the US, compared with 4 cents of every dollar in Chinese imports. . . . [S]imply put, Mexico needs to consume a chunk of US goods in order to make its own." This is obviously good for producers and US workers but damning for Mexico, and it illustrates Mexico's lack of backward linkages to the domestic economy. Remarkably, the article failed to mention the anemic growth that has underpinned Mexico's FDI-driven, export-led manufacturing model over the past two decades, and it skimmed over the fact that stagnant Mexican wages are the flip side of this supposed boom. Again, this is the country that abruptly tapered its industrial policies in 1992 and has heretofore had no concrete strategy in place for promoting higher value-added in manufacturing or raising per capita income growth on par with the country's productivity gains. The hollowed-out nature of Mexican manufacturing is reflected in the country's low ranking on measures of innovation (table 3.6).

Since the onset of slower growth in China and LAC, a number of reports have bemoaned the eroding effect of Chinese manufactured exports on the region's industrial base. The World Bank commissioned a 2012 study that condones a new industrial policy for Latin America, and the IDB has rolled out its own report on the need to rethink productive development in the LAC region.[86] The Atlantic Council, a Washington, DC, think tank, has even advocated that LAC employ "trade defensive strategies" and antidumping remedies and cast a regional veto of China's quest to obtain market economy status at the WTO.[87] Achievement of the latter by China would render these various defensive trade remedies by LAC much less credible. What is new here is the enthusiasm with which these multilateral banks and a conventional beltway think tank are now advocating state intervention in the

Table 3.6. Global innovation index LAC-6 and China

Country	Score (0–100)*	Rank
China	52.5	22
Chile	38.7	46
Costa Rica	37.1	53
Mexico	35.8	58
Brazil	33.1	69
Peru	32.9	70
Argentina	32.0	76

*Closer to 1 on the ranking = more innovative
Source: Soumitra Dutta et al., "GII 2017 Report," Global Innovation Index, Cornell INSEAD WIPO, January 2017, www.globalinnovation index.org/gii-2017-report.

promotion of Latin American industry in ways that were unthinkable during the heyday of the WC.

What's not at all new, unfortunately, is the sluggishness with which the three most industrialized LAC countries in this study—Argentina, Brazil, and Mexico—have gotten down to business with the kinds of institutional and microeconomic reforms that could rectify the decline of productivity, efficiency, and market share in their respective domestic markets. These, after all, equate with the so-called second-phase reforms that were placed on the back burner once the commodity price boom took off at the turn of the millennium. It is true that Chinese industrial exporters have a leg up over LAC in that they benefit from opaque subsidies, cheap credit, and other supports from the government; but it is also true that political and economic elites in all three of these LAC countries have simply not embraced competitiveness policies with the seriousness and tenacity of their Asian counterparts. Ironically, the biggest overall gains have been achieved by the three small open economies considered here, two commodity exporters (Chile and Peru) and one aspiring export-led industrializer (Costa Rica).

Whereas China is posed as the LAC region's main reference point in these aforementioned studies, China's main reference point is the US. As

Xiaolan Fu demonstrates in her study of *China's Path to Innovation,* China has climbed the techno-industrial ladder through promotional policies implemented over time at the national, regional, and firm levels that have combined technological adaptation and upgrading with sizeable investments in education and skill acquisition.[88] For example, in its transition from assembler to innovator China has outpaced the US in the global ranking of supercomputers, with its Sunway Taihu Light supercomputer (which uses entirely Chinese-made chips) now the world's top-ranked machine. According to its most recent five-year plan, this is part of China's intention to deepen its commitment to innovation and technology as the main drivers in the country's next stage of growth. Then again, Xiaolan Fu's narrative has not gone unchallenged.

First, it is true that China's initial phase of technological acquisition was based on so-called borrowing, that is, demanding that foreign companies form joint ventures with Chinese firms, which included the transfer of their technology and intellectual property to the latter. About 20 percent of US companies operating in the country's mammoth domestic consumer market took the leap and transferred their technological know-how to Chinese firms through these joint ventures. It is a bone of contention as to whether China is actually maturing past the imitation stage of innovation and becoming capable of inventing its own electric vehicles, industrial robots, high-speed trains, and so on.[89] One good sign is that China has gone increasingly legal by purchasing technology-intensive companies and intellectual property from abroad.[90] Second, Barry Eichengreen and his colleagues caution that China's ability to become an innovation economy that can generate exports with high local technological content requires a pool of highly skilled workers. Despite the country's considerable investment in human capital, this is still not guaranteed.[91] Company surveys in China suggest that the domestic educational system still falls short of producing graduates with the truly high-tech skills employers require.

Even if China's path to becoming a major innovator in the global economy is more arduous than Beijing policy makers care to divulge, it is certainly light years ahead of LAC's EEs on this count. In 2010 Kevin Gallagher and Roberto Porzecanski published *The Dragon in the Room: China and the Future of Latin American Industrialization,* a study that cautioned that LAC was at risk of falling seriously behind in the absence of cohesive policies to promote manufacturing productivity and competitiveness.[92] At this time China was readily out-competing Brazil and Mexico as a high-technology exporter and had already emerged as the world's top manufacturer of high-tech goods. The task now for the LAC EEs, it seems, is to catch up on their own terms and to begin by greatly strengthening the position of firms and individuals within the domestic market. For Brazil and Mexico this means less red tape, better access to affordable credit, and, in the case of the more vulnerable small and medium-sized enterprises, a much more proactive approach to integrating the latter into production and export chains. Both countries also need heightened investment in science, technology, engineering, and math (STEM) programs and the matching of skill training with the actual job demands being generated by companies operating in the domestic market.

Finally, a better linking of macro- and microeconomic policy for LAC would mean to lighten up on the tight macro-prudent policies and budget surplus targets that have been a deterrent to higher growth—a relic of the WC that is now even spurring doubt within some corners of the IMF. As three prominent members of the IMF's own research department recently wrote, "In the case of fiscal consolidation, the short-run costs in terms of lower output and welfare and higher unemployment have been underplayed, and the desirability of countries with ample fiscal space of simply living with high debt and allowing debt ratios to decline organically through growth is underappreciated."[93]

I have traced here the developmental paths of China and the LAC-5 since the onset of market reforms on both sides of the Pacific. Despite the obvious differences in timing, pace, economies of scale, and geopolitical backdrop, there are some similarities between China and the LAC-5 in the pre-reform era. Most obvious is that all of the countries in question began the reform process by embracing an inward-looking development model; at the same time, the respective relationship with the US of all of these countries was contentious, ranging from hostile (China) to conflictual (the LAC-5). This stands in direct contrast to the Asian "tigers" (Japan, Korea, and Taiwan), which benefited from generous US aid and policy support for an outward-looking development model in the early post–World War II period. For both China and the LAC-5, when the inward-looking model had run its course there was a crash landing. In retrospect, perhaps one of the biggest lost opportunities for LAC during the twentieth century occurred when it turned its back on foreign markets at the very moment when the early postwar trade and investment boom was taking off.

From the 1980s on, China and the LAC-5 have taken decidedly different forks in the road to market restructuring. China's path has been endogenously driven, in the sense that policy makers were largely on their own in drawing up the content and sequence of reforms (see table 3.5). Although diplomatically isolated and communist in every sense of the term, Chinese officials could hardly ignore that their next-door neighbor and longtime foe Japan had surged to become the world's second largest economy by 1979—thanks largely to its export-oriented model driven by a formidable developmental state. Nevertheless, China's embrace of the market was gradual, experimental, and done mainly on its own terms. For the LAC-5, the embrace of market reforms was an exogenous process. Although the IMF's economically conservative remedies for countries in the throes of a balance of payments crisis had been around since the fund's founding in the 1940s, this policy advice prevailed throughout the lost decade of the 1980s. Remarkably, with the end of the Cold War and the political and economic liberalization of the former Soviet bloc countries, the West held steady in prescribing these same policies, which had been repackaged into the WC.

I have argued in this chapter that by now both China and the LAC region have implemented more than half of the WC policies. Moreover, the first five of these policies (listed in table 3.4) have become standard practices for any economic team operating in today's global economy, whether within a developed or an emerging economy context. The more rapid pace and timing in the implementation of market reforms within the LAC region and the less than spectacular returns in terms of GDP growth and per capita gains had fostered a clear pattern of reform fatigue by the turn of the millennium. Any concerns about remaining reform gaps, however, were quickly swept under the carpet by the China boom and commodity price bonanza that came seemingly out of nowhere in 2002–3.

The postboom period that had set in by 2014 would reveal new reform challenges on both sides of the Pacific. For China, the 13th Five-Year Plan acknowledged the saturation of a model based on heavy investment and an aggressive manufactured export-led strategy and elucidated on the numerous paths that the country will now pursue in the way of services, consumption, information technology, innovation, and R&D. Without stirring up an academic hornet's nest, some historians have argued persuasively that the demise of the earlier Chinese Empire by the nineteenth century was due to the indifference of consecutive rulers to the kinds of transformative technologies that had originated in seventeenth- and eighteenth-century England and then disseminated to the Continent.[94] My point: the current Chinese leadership seems intent on leaving no technological stone unturned this time around. Higher consumer demand, investments in human capital, more sophisticated technical training, and a bigger burst of outward foreign direct investment are some of the other highlights of China's stated goals in the twenty-first century.[95]

For LAC, the marked differences among the countries analyzed below make it difficult to summarize any one vision of where to go from here. The small open economies have set their sights on maximizing the exploitation of their endowment factors, diversifying exports by adding value to the commodities and goods they hold in abundance, and deepening the crucial process of institutional reform. The three EEs (Argentina, Brazil, and Mexico), despite their earlier achievements in the industrial sector and in exporting higher value-added goods, appear to be stuck in either a traditional "industrial policy" vacuum (Argentina and Brazil) or "let the market do it" mindset (Mexico). Their collective challenges are to seriously update their mindsets on an industrial development strategy and get busy climbing up Ha-Joon Chang's ladder; to come to grips with the fact that China's competitive prowess is only going to get stronger; and to buckle down on the kinds of institutional and microeconomic policy reforms that have been pending since the late 1990s.

4

Making Openness Work:
Chile, Costa Rica, and Peru

We were sort of prejudiced that it would be a complex negotiation, in which China would act very conservatively where opening its market was concerned. But, it proved not to be so. In the end, the negotiation . . . took just ten months, which is also almost unheard of in a trade negotiation.

Marco Vinicio Ruiz, 2016, principal trade negotiator for the
PRC–Costa Rica free trade agreement[1]

ON NOVEMBER 8, 2016, THE seventy-year-old rule-based global trading system took its last breath—or at least that is what President-elect Donald Trump and his rust-belt "base" wanted us to believe. It is true that the turn of the millennium marked a waning of the multilateral commitment to global trade that had been crafted as part of the post–World War II Bretton Woods order. Although the 1990s saw the completion of the Uruguay Round in 1994 and the creation of the World Trade Organization (WTO) in 1995, the launching of the Doha Development Round in the immediate wake of the 9/11/01 terrorist attacks on the US was ill-timed and, in the end, a losing proposition. With Doha falling into limbo nearly a decade after it was launched, the new century's most notable trade accomplishment has thus far been China's accession to the WTO in 2001. Like three of the LAC emerging economies (EEs) considered in this book (Chile, Mexico, and Peru), China read the tea leaves on the Doha impasse and began to negotiate minilateral (e.g., the China–ASEAN free trade agreement [FTA])[2] and bilateral (e.g., Australia, New Zealand, Singapore, Chile, Peru, Costa Rica) trade deals on the heels of its WTO entry.[3]

Underpinning the failure of the Doha Round was the lack of US leadership on par with that invested by Washington in the successful completion of the Uruguay Round and the creation of the WTO. New issues on the trade agenda held dear by the OECD bloc, such as the liberalization of services and investment and the protection of intellectual property rights (IPRs), quickly clashed with the interests of powerful EEs like Brazil, China, and India, which were most adamant about the liberalization of "old" issues and sectors like agriculture and manufacturing in developed country markets.

Domestic politics in the US were a further drag on Doha. US voters soured on trade agreements soon after the 1994 implementation of the North American Free Trade Agreement (NAFTA) between Canada, Mexico, and the US, as Mexico's massive peso devaluation of December 1994 quickly shifted a sizeable US trade surplus with Mexico into the red column. The US manufacturing sector was hard hit. But it is the cumulative effects of China's 2001 WTO entry, the "jobless recovery" from the 2000–2003 global recession, and rising automation in the industrial workplace that most account for an estimated 30 percent loss of US manufacturing jobs since 2000.[4] The loss of some eight to ten million jobs from the 2008–9 global financial crisis (GFC) struck an additional blow.

Hence Trump's electoral victory and the wrath he unleashed against US trade agreements, even if these are not the main culprit. Trump made good on his vow to renegotiate NAFTA and rashly ripped up the Trans-Pacific Partnership (TPP) treaty—the key economic pillar of President Barack Obama's "pivot toward Asia"—without even vetting it through the US Congress. The demise of the US-led TPP was music to Beijing's ears. Of the twelve countries participating in the TPP negotiations (Australia, Brunei, Canada, Chile, Japan, Malaysia, Mexico, New Zealand, Peru, Singapore, US, and Vietnam), all but Japan and the NAFTA countries had already signed an FTA with China. The TPP, however, did not include China. Rather, it was largely a US power play to control the membership and write the rules for future economic integration across the Pacific Basin. The TPP was nearly a decade in the making and ostensibly on track to become the largest regional trade deal in terms of economic size.[5] By canceling it the Trump administration cleared the way for China to advance quickly with its own counterproposal, the Regional Comprehensive Economic Partnership (RCEP), which includes ASEAN, Australia, China, India, Japan, South Korea, and New Zealand.

Whereas TPP was all about advancing quickly on the new trade agenda, including the removal of opaque barriers to government-procurement contracts and foreign direct investment (FDI), RCEP is expected to move more gradually on the old trade agenda, including tariff reductions and greater market access.[6] For the Asian TPP participants, deeper access to the US market was a strong incentive for concession making around the new trade agenda and a lever of sorts for member countries to further advance with structural reforms on the domestic front. TPP was also appealing as a way for the smaller Asian countries to use their economic relationship with the US to balance China's rising power in that region.[7] As for RCEP, with China, a country in need of further market reforms, as its industrial anchor, some have questioned whether the incentives for making significant breakthroughs will be especially compelling. Nevertheless, due to the heightening of protectionist rhetoric in Washington and Trump's rash trade war against China, Japan, and the EU, the China-led RCEP was at the time perceived as the only Asia–Pacific integration path available in the short-to-medium term.[8]

Still, the eleven remaining TPP members (Australia, Brunei, Canada, Chile, Japan, Malaysia, Mexico, New Zealand, Peru, Singapore, and Vietnam) regrouped and agreed on a new Comprehensive and Progressive Agreement for Trans-Pacific Partnership (CPTPP) which covers about 15 percent of the global economy. Approved by all eleven member nations in March 2018, CPTPP will cut tariffs on goods and services flowing between member markets, and it covers labor and environmental standards. China, which is not a member, has an open door to join.

What does this highly unpredictable turn of events around US foreign economic policy mean for the six strategic partner countries considered in this book? First, Mexico is once again the outsider, with the US launching the renegotiation of NAFTA in August 2017 and Trump's insistence on building a US$18 billion wall to reinforce the fence that already exists along the US–Mexico border. Things worsened in 2018 as Washington bullied both Canada and Mexico in negotiating a supposedly new US–Mexico–Canada FTA (USMCA) and the White House sent troops to protect the US–Mexico border. The USMCA draft agreement broke new ground as the first US economic treaty to raise, rather than lower, barriers to trade and investment. The uncertainties of this situation have deterred FDI in Mexico and periodically sent the Mexican peso into a tailspin.

Second, Argentina and Brazil, having fortified their trade and investment relationship with China since 2003 and relying less on the US market, can perhaps seek economic solace in their respective ties with China. It would behoove both to throw their hat in the ring for RCEP membership in order to deepen and formalize their access to the Chinese market. However, as members of the Southern Cone Common Market (Mercosur) they are committed to negotiating any outside deals as a bloc (Argentina, Brazil, Paraguay, and Uruguay; Venezuela is a suspended member due to its authoritarian regime). After nearly two decades of negotiations the EU–Mercosur FTA has finally been completed. A China-Mercosur FTA could take just as long to negotiate. Paraguay, moreover, does not recognize China diplomatically, which is a nonstarter from the standpoint of the Chinese. Third, although still not formal members of RCEP, Chile, Costa Rica, and Peru, by virtue of having negotiated separate bilateral FTAs with the US and with China, will be the *only* countries in Latin America to enjoy privileged access to the two largest markets in the world. In the spirit of competitive regionalism, Chile and Peru are in the queue to join RCEP, as more than half of the CPTPP members will have combined membership in these two megaregional deals.[9]

In tandem with the rise of China in Latin America has been the proliferation of a dense network of bilateral FTAs across the Pacific Basin. Beginning with the pathbreaking Chile–Korea FTA in 2004 up to the Costa Rica–Singapore FTA in 2013, at least twenty-two cross-Pacific accords have been negotiated, a fact which reflects the richness and diversity of trade and investment ties that are quickly strengthening across the Pacific (table 4.1 lists sixteen of these). I analyze here China's bilateral FTAs with Chile (2006), Peru (2010), and Costa Rica (2011).[10] My argument is twofold: first, these FTAs are part and parcel of China's internationalized development strategy, as the combined export of copper and other ores to China accounts for 85

Table 4.1. Asia–Latin American FTAs, 2004–2013

FTA	Level of development	Tariff liberalization	Services coverage	Investment chapter	Competition policy	Intellectual property rights	Government procurement
1. Korea–Chile FTA (2004)	Advanced–Developing	Relatively fast	Comprehensive	Standard	Standard	Above standard	Above standard
2. Taipei, China–Panama FTA (2004)	Advanced–Developing	Relatively fast	Comprehensive	Above standard	Standard	Above standard	No provision
3. Japan–Mexico EPA (2005)	Advanced–Developing	Relatively fast	Comprehensive	Above standard	Standard	Above standard	Standard
4. PRC–Chile FTA (2006)	Developing–Developing	Relatively fast	Some	No provision	No provision	Above standard	No provision
5. Trans-Pacific Strategic EPA P4-Agreement, Chile, New Zealand, Singapore, (2006)	Advanced–Developing	Relatively fast	Comprehensive	No provision	Above standard	Above standard	Above standard
6. Singapore–Panama FTA (2006)	Advanced–Developing	Relatively fast	Some	Above standard	Standard	No provision	Above standard
7. Taipei, China–Guatemala FTA (2006)	Advanced–Developing	Relatively fast	Comprehensive	Above standard	No provision	Above standard	No provision

FTA							
8. Japan–Chile FTA (2007)	Advanced–Developing	Relatively fast	Comprehensive	Standard	Standard	Above standard	Standard
9. Taipei,China–Nicaragua FTA (2008)	Advanced–Developing	Relatively fast	Comprehensive	Above standard	Standard	Above standard	No provision
10. Australia–Chile FTA (2009)	Advanced–Developing	Relatively fast	Comprehensive	Above standard	Standard	Above standard	Above standard
11. Singapore–Peru FTA (2009)	Advanced–Developing	Relatively fast	Comprehensive	Above standard	Above standard	No provision	Standard
12. PRC–Peru FTA (2010)	Developing–Developing	Relatively fast	Some	Standard	Standard	Above standard	No provision
13. Korea–Peru FTA (2011)	Advanced–Developing	Relatively fast	Comprehensive	Above standard	Standard	Above standard	Above standard
14. PRC–Costa Rica FTA (2011)	Developing–Developing	Relatively fast	Some	Standard	Standard	Above standard	No provision
15. Japan–Peru EPA (2012)	Advanced–Developing	Relatively fast	Comprehensive	Non-provision	Standard	Above standard	Above standard
16. Singapore–Costa Rica FTA (2013)	Advanced–Developing	Relatively fast	Comprehensive	Above standard	Standard	Above standard	Above standard

Source: Ganeshan Wignaraja, Dorothea Ramizo, and Luca Burmeister, "Assessing Liberalization and Deep Integration in FTAs: A Study of Asian–Latin American FTAs," *Journal of East Asian Economic Integration* 17, no. 4 (2013), table compiled by the author based on Annexes 1 and 2, 408–11.

percent of Chile's and 78 percent of Peru's exports to that country. More-over, both of these bilateral FTAs with China, which lock in essential raw material exports to the PRC, represent the most institutionalized version of this internationalized development strategy in the Western Hemisphere.

Second, these FTAs departed from neoliberal notions concerning the ben-efits of free trade based on computable-general-equilibrium models and comparative advantage.[11] Rather, entering into an FTA with China allowed rapid access to that market, the granting of industrial sector exceptions, and China's readiness to lend for infrastructure and other productive proj-ects. Although the PRC–Costa Rica FTA had its roots in the One-China policy, as Costa Rica cut its diplomatic ties with Taiwan in 2007, it would be a mistake to dismiss it as a simple diplomatic perk. This third FTA may defy all of the theoretical premises concerning why countries choose to enter into these arrangements, but it is every bit as serious as the accords Chile and Peru brokered with China.

What's New about Latin America's FTAs with China?

The three cross-Pacific FTAs break new ground in several ways. First, these are the only agreements of those listed in table 4.1 that depart from the bilateral advanced–developing country pattern, as China's FTAs with Chile, Peru, and Costa Rica are all categorized as developing–developing country accords. The Latin American experience with developing–develop-ing country regional schemes that involve two or more member states has not been particularly successful, Mercosur and the Andean Community being prime cases in point.[12] However, whereas these intraregional accords have shied away from the World Trade Organization's (WTO) "new trade agenda" (which covers such issues as services, investment, IPRs, competi-tion policy, and government procurement),[13] and even eschewed it at times, all three of the China–Latin America FTAs discussed here reflect some attempt by the signatories to approximate twenty-first-century standards vis-à-vis the WTO and its new trade agenda. This suggests, at least in the cross-Pacific context, that not all developing–developing country FTAs are doomed to the vicissitudes of populism and protectionism.

Second, a comparison of these three China–Latin American FTAs re-flects a learning curve over time on both sides. With regard to the Latin American side, each of the three countries has made relatively strong, if uneven, progress in the realm of institutional reform over the past two de-cades, as measured by the World Bank's Worldwide Governance Indicators (see fig. 1.1). Chile, Costa Rica, and Peru also score much higher on mea-sures of trade and investment openness than the larger Latin American (LAC) economies like Argentina, Brazil, and Venezuela;[14] and the macro-economic performance of each of these smaller countries in the 2000s (see table 1.1) has surpassed that of the larger LAC EEs. In other words, as small, vulnerable economies all three have responded to the challenges of global-ization by modernizing domestic institutions, sticking tenaciously to their respective reform agendas, and integrating more tightly into world mar-kets. In contrast to so many developing country FTAs, which have sought to lock in economic reforms at an early stage, these three accords were ne-gotiated once reforms were better consolidated.

On the Chinese side, the 2006 Chile–China FTA followed in the footsteps of China's negotiation of an FTA with the ASEAN bloc, its first FTA ever. This being China's first FTA foray into the Latin American region and its second FTA ever, the learning curve for China is evident in its increased willingness to cover items on the new trade agenda. For example, the Chile–China FTA is the least comprehensive of the three China–Latin American FTAs dis-cussed here. This is so even though Chile had just completed an FTA with the US in which coverage was so deep and binding that some have referred to it as "new age." China's later FTAs with Peru and Costa Rica, respectively, reflect a greater inclination on its part to include chapters on investment and competition policy, which are lacking in the Chile–China FTA. Peru and Costa Rica had similarly concluded "new age" FTAs with the US prior to negotiating with China. Following in Chile's footsteps, both were able to push a bit harder in negotiating the coverage of investment and services in their respective FTAs with China.[15] This matters, as China's outward FDI flows to the LAC region began to shift significantly toward services in 2013, including "everything from electricity generation and transmission to infor-mation technology [IT] and communication, finance, and transportation."[16]

Conceptualizing FTAs in the Twenty-First Century

A Cumulative Argument

Despite econometric evidence that suggests that multilateralism remains the most efficacious way to achieve Pareto-optimal gains, i.e., all member countries would be better off under a new multilateral agreement, departures from multilateralism have now become the new normal.[17] Debates over multilateralism versus regionalism will continue, including the standoff over whether FTAs of the kind analyzed here constitute "building blocs or stumbling blocs" for realizing dynamic trade and investment gains in the international political economy (IPE); however, the increasing diversity in development levels and economic goals among the WTO membership suggests that subregional FTAs are here to stay.[18] Of the more than three hundred bilateral or subregional FTAs negotiated over the past two decades, the bulk of these deals were struck between developed (US, EU, Japan, etc.) and developing countries. The upshot is that most of the recent theorizing about FTAs is based on those North–South agreements that comprise the mainstay of the sample.

Mexico's pioneering entry into NAFTA opened the floodgate for the numerous other North–South FTAs that quickly followed. Apart from the obvious goals of gaining greater market access through the reduction of tariff and nontariff barriers, three overlapping arguments have evolved for explaining the proliferation of North–South FTAs. First, in terms of the domestic political economy, there is a broad consensus that leaders in various developing countries have sought FTAs with the US and the EU in order to lock in liberalizing economic reforms and further deepen them.[19] The negotiation of a North–South FTA with a major power becomes a strategy to at once internationalize the challenges of economic liberalization and signal a legally binding reform commitment to foreign investors and other potential trading partners.

A second argument is the designation of cross-border lobbies comprised of intra-industry producers, state technocrats, and workers / consumers as a main independent variable in the finalization of North–South FTAs. In this North–South context, the argument goes, manufacturing interests and intra-industry producers are motivated by the prospect of achieving scale

economies related to greater specialization, increased technological capabilities, and a more rapid and efficient deployment of endowment factors
across the border.[20] In order to maximize efficiency gains North–South FTAs
have generally encompassed a combination of issues on the aforementioned
old and new trade agendas at the WTO.

A third argument highlights the role played by private investors, foreign
and domestic, who have utilized FTAs as a way of capturing investment
opportunities, both market and efficiency-seeking.[21] Especially in the 2000s
the negotiation of North–South FTAs that include investment and services
liberalization has resulted in developing country commitments that surpass the inroads that have been made thus far in the WTO's 1995 General Agreement on Trade in Services (GATS). As the relationship between
services and investment has become increasingly interwoven,[22] this has
spawned a North–South FTA pattern whereby "concentrated interests in
FDI-exporting countries have a strong incentive to lobby for preferential
agreements because they confer specific advantages over competitors."[23]

What explanatory light do these standing arguments shed on the Chile–
China, Peru–China, and Costa Rica–China FTAs? Actually, very little. The
third argument, which emphasizes the role of efficiency and market-seeking
investors and their lobbies in various service sectors (e.g., banking / finance,
telecom, and pharmaceuticals), captures most fully the logic of the FTA
that each country negotiated with the US in the 2000s, while none of the
above arguments explains these FTAs with China.[24] First, in contrast with
Mexico, these three countries had already advanced significantly on their
respective reform agendas prior to negotiating FTAs with both the US and
with China; second, for Chile and Peru, the small size of the industrial sector and low levels of intra-industry trade render the second explanation above
a moot point; Costa Rica, in contrast, has developed an intra-industry high-
tech manufacturing sector over the past two decades, but more than 30
percent of this cross-border trade and production is conducted with the US.
Third, while Chinese FDI inflows are still negligible in Costa Rica, some 85
percent of Chinese outward investment in Chile and Peru has been of a
"resource-seeking" nature and concentrated almost solely in mining.[25]

So how might we account for these cross-Pacific FTAs between China
and Latin America? Another body of promising literature treats the FTA

itself as the explanatory variable. While this begs causality, econometric analyses undertaken in this literature do bolster the rationale for these China–Latin America FTAs. For example, based on a sample of ninety-six countries including China and the three LAC countries considered here, Baier and Bergstrand find that "an FTA will on average increase two member countries' trade 100% after ten years."[26] While only Chile fits this ten-year horizon, it has more than met Baier's and Bergstrand's 100 percent benchmark. Moreover, both Costa Rica and Peru are well on their way to doing so (see tables 2.7 and 2.9). In related work, Saggi and Yildiz focus their econometric analysis on the asymmetries intrinsic to a given FTA. They find that bilateral FTAs that involve large differences in size and GDP between the two partners, as these China–LAC FTAs do, can indeed constitute building blocks toward global trade liberalization.[27] Although admittedly incremental, the three China–LAC FTAs do bring China a bit closer to the WTO's ultimate goal of multilateral trade gains, not to mention China's own goal of achieving market economy status at the WTO in the near future.[28]

In short, as China is quickly on its way to becoming the largest economy in the world, the consequences of its increasing participation in bilateral FTAs and other subregional accords cannot be written off due to its developing country status. Although we are on decidedly new terrain with a rising major power that is some way from becoming a developed country proper, the policy trajectory reflected in table 4.1 suggests that China is gradually making its way toward twenty-first-century standards.

Motives

On the Asian side, the motives that have been attributed to the negotiation of cross-Pacific trade and investment accords suggest that we are also moving beyond neatly packaged explanations for why countries are choosing to depart from multilateralism. For instance, explanations in the literature for Japan's decision to negotiate an FTA with Mexico and Korea's decision to negotiate an accord with Chile assign significant weight to politics and diplomacy.[29] This concept is foreign to the US trade policy-making apparatus, at least as it applies to Latin America, where FTA negotiators arrive from Washington, DC, with a WTO-plus template and persist with few concessions.[30] Yet the overlapping outcomes between China's Latin American FTAs and those that the US, Japan, and Korea have negotiated with Latin American countries confirm that different motives and approaches can produce similar results. The overriding narrative in the literature on China's motives for pursuing FTAs in Latin America also rests largely on cross-Pacific diplomacy.[31] Nevertheless, as Yang Jiang writes, "there is no simple explanation for the Chinese interest in FTAs. . . . [E]conomic, political, and strategic competition can play a decisive role in China's FTA decisions."[32]

China's first formal policy statement on Latin America, issued in a 2008 white paper, more specifically reflects on the development challenges that are shaping its pursuit of FTAs with these particular countries.[33] Much more than diplomacy seems to be at stake here. First is China's concern over resource security and its need for Latin America's abundant raw materials to fuel its growth.[34] While an FTA in and of itself cannot entirely guarantee China's access to natural resources, when bundled within a strategic partnership, various other material incentives, and laced with soft-power rhetoric, China has secured access to raw materials from both countries.[35] Second is the PRC's 2008 policy paper on LAC, which prioritizes the pursuit of the One-China principle as fundamental to the establishment of closer relations with the Latin American region.

On the first count, China's FTAs with Chile and Peru speak directly to its own resource scarcity in copper, iron ore, and other minerals and hence the imperative to internationalize its development strategy. Raw materials comprise over 90 percent of Chile's and Peru's exports to China (see tables 2.6, 2.9). Still, why the effort to achieve WTO-plus standards within these accords? For Chile and Peru, the liberalization of services and investment undertaken within their respective FTAs with the US was of a one-shot nature, which most favors first-movers in the market but remains open to those that follow. At the outset Chile, in order to get its foot in the Chinese market, settled for a "WTO-minus" accord with China that covered just goods, and then it gradually moved forward with Beijing on successful negotiations over services and investment. For its part, China inched forward in its quest to achieve market economy status at the WTO.[36]

On the second count, the Costa Rica–China FTA embodies China's efforts to win recognition for its One-China policy in a subregion (Central

America) where the majority of states continues to recognize Taiwan. Although Costa Rica accounts for just 0.12 percent of China's total trade (exports plus imports), the minuscule trade and investment ties between the two countries were of no importance to China.[37] The highlights of this diplomatic coup include China's purchase of US$300 million in Costa Rican bonds in 2008; China's donation of US$83 million for the construction of a new soccer stadium in San José, completed in 2011; and the launching of a US$1.3 billion mixed capital venture between the China National Petroleum Corporation and Costa Rica's national oil refinery company for the expansion of Costa Rica's oil production capacity. Projections based on this project were rosy, estimating that on its completion Costa Rican oil production would go from eighteen thousand to sixty thousand barrels per day and up to five thousand new jobs would be created, 75 percent to be filled by Costa Rican workers.[38] However, the project foundered over a rigged feasibility study, budget irregularities, and opposition from environmental activists.

On the South American side, the motives for negotiating an FTA with China were quite different. Chile and Peru, as noted, were the first LAC countries after Cuba to formally recognize China in 1970 and 1971, respectively. Chile was also one of the most active LAC supporters of China's 1971 entry into the United Nations and its bid to accede to the WTO as well as the first country in the LAC region to offer the PRC market economy status. Peru, with the government's sale of its Hierro iron ore mine in 1992 to the Chinese state company Shouhang, for US$120 million, was the locus of the largest foreign investment the PRC had made at that time. Fast forward: in both cases the move to negotiate an FTA with China in the 2000s was fairly seamless. In fact, in both countries as well as in Costa Rica it was the negotiation of an FTA with the US that raised more domestic hackles within various economic sectors and among civil society organizations.

As a decade-long boom in commodity sales to China has been offset by the import of manufactured goods back from China, domestic producers in Chile and Peru lobbied their governments hard to export more nontraditional, higher value-added products to the Chinese market, to counter the traditional pattern of comparative advantage (see tables 2.6 and 2.9). The decision of each government to negotiate an FTA with China was further motivated by the goal of attracting Chinese FDI into efficiency and market-seeking investments as opposed to the current flood of incoming resource-seeking investment (mainly in Peru) limited to mineral extraction.[39] The negotiation of a bilateral FTA with China also raised the prospect that each could be transformed into a dynamic transport and service hub for trans-Pacific trade.[40] China sweetened these deals by accepting numerous exceptions in the domestic manufacturing sector in both countries. For China, these market access concessions to Chile and Peru represented such a minuscule percentage of its total trade in manufactured exports that the sacrifice was worth making in order to secure a steady supply of commodities from the two countries.

Since the launching of the Chile–China FTA in 2006 Chile's total trade with China has nearly quadrupled, from US$9.65 billion in 2006 to US$34.60 billion in 2017 (see table 2.6). China is now Chile's top trading partner, and Chile has run a trade surplus with China throughout this period.[41] At US$6.091 billion from 2000 to 2017, Chile's FDI inflows from China have been modest when compared with the other South America countries considered here;[42] this is partly because FDI in copper is China's main interest, and Chilean copper is largely state-held. Chilean policy makers, rather than opening up the copper sector to Chinese investors, are holding out in hopes of attracting nonresource-seeking FDI from China.[43] As of 2017 there were signs this was finally beginning to happen. Discussions are under way for Chinese outward FDI in Santiago's public transit network, and two Chinese companies have now acquired shares in Chilean wine businesses, including Viña San Pedro Tarapacá and the Bethwines Group.[44]

The time period since the implementation of the Peru–China FTA in 2010 has seen total trade between the two countries increase from US$13.34 billion in 2010 to US$20.49 billion in 2017 (see table 2.9), rendering China Peru's most important commercial partner. In terms of FDI, with five major mainland Chinese mining companies now operating in Peru, current estimates are that around US$12.37 billion in mining investments, amounting to about 25 percent of Peru's inward FDI, are under way.[45] Unlike Chile's, Peru's mining sector was privatized in the 1990s, and this has clearly facilitated Chinese entry into this sector. Peru has been less strict than Chile in limiting Chinese content in the latter's FDI inflows (labor, materials, engineering services, etc.). The Human Rights Council of the United Nations has received numerous complaints of human rights abuses by majority-held Chinese companies toward local indigenous populations living near oil, natural gas, and mining projects.[46] There need not be a trade-off between Chinese FDI inflows and the rights of Peru's indigenous groups, but this is a lesson to which political and economic elites in Peru have paid insufficient attention. In 2018 Chinese investors began expressing interest in more diverse projects in Peru, including the telecommunications, finance, and construction sectors. China's COSCO Shipping Holdings has committed to the building of a US$2 billion port on Peru's Pacific coast.[47]

Costa Rica's decision to negotiate an FTA with China was at first mainly responsive and made in the context of the numerous side payments China was offering in pursuit of its One-China policy. But Costa Rican policy makers, having invested heavily in innovation and technology clusters over the past two decades, thought this looked like a good deal. While Costa Rica's total trade with China was just US$1.7 billion at the outset of its FTA with China, by 2017 total trade between the two countries hit US$20.3 billion. Moreover, the bulk of that two-way trade is in higher value-added electrical and electronic equipment (see table 2.7) Approximately 34.8 percent of two-way trade is conducted in electrical machinery and electronic equipment, indicating that the possibilities for the expansion of intra-industry trade and cross-border production in high-tech operations between the two countries are strong. And given that Costa Rica now has FTAs in place with both the US and China, it could get a foothold in the formidable value chains that now define Pacific Basin trade in these higher value-added sectors. Even more so than Chile and Peru, Costa Rica now finds itself well situated to play both sides of the Pacific.

Although I have argued thus far that these developing–developing country accords between China and Latin America have approximated twenty-first-century standards, at the end of the day these are still developing countries. Thus a given country's endowment factors and its institutional landscape come more closely into play. In view of the enormous asymmetries between China and each of these three LAC countries, this point could not be more relevant. For example, of these three small, open economies Chile has the strongest trade ties, accounting for about 0.79 percent of China's total trade in 2016.[48] Conversely, China accounted for around 85 percent of Chile's combined copper and ore exports in 2016. Yet these asymmetries have not deterred any of these three countries from towing the line with their respective reform agendas since the early 1990s. Again, in contrast with Mexico's strategy of embracing the NAFTA agreement as a means to lock in recently implemented market reforms in the early 1990s, Chile, Costa Rica, and Peru forged bilateral FTAs with the US and with China once their respective reforms were firmly in place. In contrast with Mexico, all three countries negotiated an FTA with China from a position of strength.

Content

The Chile–China and the Peru–China FTAs accomplished two things. On the upside, because growth prospects for these small, open economies rest largely on efficiency and productivity gains, an FTA with China further bolstered their overall strategy to realize these goals.[49] On the downside, despite the lofty ambitions of each country to diversify its trade and incoming FDI from China, both signed on to a traditional comparative advantage development model with China based on the export of low value-added primary goods to China and the import of higher value-added Chinese goods back. In other words, the pattern of economic exchange within these two FTAs still rests largely on market access back and forth in traditional goods, although Chinese outgoing FDI in both countries did begin to diversify away from resource-seeking ventures in 2017. Moreover, the access achieved by both Chile and Peru to the Chinese market was considerable.

In terms of traded goods, the Chile–China FTA provided duty-free entry for 98 percent of Chile's exports to China, although some of the country's most successful agro-industrial exports (fruits and fish) were placed on a ten-year timeline for accessing the Chinese market.[50] On the import side, 50 percent of Chile's imports from China were granted duty-free access at the outset, and Chile was able to completely exclude 152 "sensitive products" (e.g., some textiles and garments and some major appliances).[51] Again, China agreed to forgo considerable industrial market access in exchange for Chile's steadily supplying raw materials to the PRC. In 2008 the governments of Chile and China signed a "Supplementary Agreement on Trade in Services of the Free Trade Agreement," which signaled China's increased willingness to tackle the new trade agenda (e.g., business services, telecommunications, and manufacturing services).[52] From there, the two governments completed an agreement on investment in 2012. Of note are the very few limitations set by Chile in terms of market access for services and national treatment for investors versus the numerous exceptions insisted upon by Chinese negotiators. As China continues to struggle in its efforts to gain market economy status at the WTO, asymmetries such as this one will have to be corrected.

The Peru–China FTA was formally implemented in March 2010, China hailing it as the most comprehensive FTA it had yet to sign, including coverage of labor and the environment.[53] Peruvian negotiators succeeded in extracting nearly four times the number of restrictions and exclusions in sensitive sectors than those secured by Chile.[54] In terms of market access, Peru was quite proactive in reducing tariffs on 99 percent of its exports to China, 83.5 percent of which entered the Chinese market duty free at the outset of the agreement. In return, 68 percent of China's exports to Peru were granted immediate market access. At the same time, Peru altogether excluded some 592 "sensitive products" in the textile, garment, shoes, and metal mechanics industries, which amounted to around 10 percent of the value of China's exports to Peru. For its part, China excluded just 1 percent of the value of Peru's exports. On the new trade issues, separate chapters on services and investment commit both sides to upholding national treatment, greater transparency, and the use of dispute settlement mechanisms in the event of a conflict.

The Costa Rica–China FTA, which could easily be mistaken as a populist bribe given its roots in the One-China policy, is anything but. Implemented in 2011, this FTA included an immediate tariff reduction on 60 percent of all goods traded between the two countries; an additional 30 percent of goods will have tariffs lowered gradually over the next five to fifteen years. By 2018, 90 percent of Costa Rican exports had duty-free access to the Chinese market. China's main exports that will benefit from the FTA include textiles, machines, electrical appliances, vegetables, fruits, automobiles, chemical products, raw fur, and leather. At the same time, Costa Rica will be able to freely export such products as electrical and electronics equipment, sugar, coffee, beef, pork, fruit juices, and jam. On the new trade agenda, Costa Rica will allow free services trade in forty-five sectors, including, for example, telecommunications, business services, construction, real estate, IT, and tourism, while China will open seven sectors in return, including IT services.[55] Costa Rica's comparatively lower market access at the outset of this FTA reflected its status as a higher value-added exporter to China versus the dominant raw material endowments of Chile and Peru.

Preliminary Outcomes

To summarize, although the motives for negotiating these developing–developing country accords varied on the part of China and the countries themselves, this did not disrupt the march toward greater coverage of investment and services on both sides of the Pacific. With the completion of separate accords on services and investment between China and Chile by 2012, and despite the market access exceptions agreed to by China in its accords with Chile and Peru, all three of these China–Latin American FTAs are in line with twenty-first-century standards. The question remains as to the ways in which these FTAs may contribute to theory building about bilateral versus multilateral approaches to trade liberalization as well as the significance of the empirical strides made by all of the participating parties. The asymmetries are such that one side's gains (those of the three small Latin American FTA partners) appear to be phenomenal while the other side's (China's) seem minuscule. Nevertheless, the sum of these accords amounts to much more than their individual parts.

In terms of theory building, only Chile offers a sufficient timeline to verify Baier's and Bergstrand's prediction that bilateral trade between two FTA partners can be expected to increase 100 percent within a decade.[56] Peru and Costa Rica, though, are on track to do so. As for the claim by Saggi and Yildiz that bilateral FTAs that involve large differences in size and GDP between the two partners can indeed constitute building blocks toward multilateral trade gains, all three of these FTAs are indisputably trade creating.[57] As small, open price-takers in the IPE, reform-minded countries like Chile, Costa Rica, and Peru have been left to their own devices to pursue the kinds of market access and efficiency gains once sought through the various GATT / WTO negotiating rounds. Peter Katzenstein theorized about the policy options of small open economies three decades ago, arguing that small states are best off by casting their fate with the global market.[58] In line with Katzenstein's argument, the three small states considered here have moved unilaterally on the liberalization front and bilaterally to harness these reforms to the markets of much bigger and more dynamic trade partners, and they have left the door wide open for the (increasingly unlikely) resumption of multilateral undertakings.

For Chile and Peru, however favorable the preliminary outcomes of their respective FTAs with China have been, these cross-Pacific accords taken together offer up two cautionary tales. First is the resort by each to a backdoor industrial policy by exempting a considerable chunk of the domestic manufacturing sector from Chinese competition within these FTAs. Economic history has shown that protectionism rarely leads to industrial restructuring of the kind called for here, and this is confirmed by estimates undertaken by Boston University's Working Group on Development and Environment in the Americas (GDEA). For example, GDEA data show that because of competition from China "Peru's apparel sector shrank from 47% of its exports (from 2003–2008) to 33% (from 2003–2013)," while the threat from Chinese competition continues to rise.[59] Chile is in the same boat. These exemptions won some political reprieve on the domestic front in the two countries, but policy makers in both are facing the reality that an FTA on its own cannot reverse the logic of old-fashioned comparative advantage which currently defines China's relationship with both Chile and Peru. As Ken Shadlen argued at the height of the GFC in 2008,[60] it will require an explicit, proactive industrial strategy backed by well-crafted policy tools to restore health to these fragile manufacturing sectors.

A second, related precaution concerns the persistent narrative in Chile and Peru about the need to diversify into higher value-added exports to China and to attract nonresource-related FDI inflows from China.[61] Despite China's diplomatic discourse of "expand and balance two-way trade," and "give a lot yet demand little" as well as some aforementioned signs of diversification with outgoing Chinese FDI, it is doubtful that Chile and Peru will fully achieve these respective goals.[62] Given the multiple FTAs that each country now holds with developed countries, a more fruitful course for both might be to focus on exporting all kinds of goods to the rest of the world. Although Costa Rica has overcome geographical and technological disadvantages, not to mention adverse economies of scale, its export of higher value-added goods to the Chinese market is the result of aggressive public policies and incentives that have been in place for more than two decades.[63] Thus Costa Rica now stands the better chance of integrating more tightly into dynamic Pacific Basin industrial production networks and value chains.

As noted, all three of these LAC countries have set their sights on deep integration into global markets, and the data on comparative economic performance from 2001 to 2018 presented throughout this book suggest this approach has served them quite well. Again, it is more likely that higher value-added export gains for both Chile and Peru remain to be made in regional and / or other global markets. With regard to the Chinese market, policy makers at both the Chilean and Peruvian embassies in Beijing have been successful in securing the necessary protocols for introducing new goods into China.[64] Chile, for example, is now the top exporter of tropical fruit to China and is second only to France in the export of wine to the Chinese market. Peru is exporting exotic fruits, canned seafood, and high-end alpaca clothing to China. None of this is high value-added, but it does constitute product diversification and may be as good as it is going to get for both countries in terms of conquering new niches in the Chinese market.

The Broader Implications for Latin America

To recapitulate, the beginning of the new millennium marked China's entry into the WTO, its need for massive commodity imports to fuel a new development phase, and a rapid takeoff in Chinese trade and investment in Latin America. Brisk Chinese demand pulled Latin America out of the lingering 2000–2003 recession, enabled the region to rebound quickly from the 2008–9 GFC, and helped to produce historically high average annual growth rates for a full decade.[65] In short, the China–Latin America relationship is now a permanent feature of the region's political economic landscape, and China remains a force to be reckoned with.

With the end of the China boom, the implications for the China–LAC relationship moving forward are twofold: first, in macroeconomic terms, historically high commodity prices and massive capital inflows offered these countries unprecedented room to maneuver, even if some were unable to effectively utilize it; second, China's deeper integration with the LAC region has upped the ante exponentially at the microeconomic level, showing that there are no shortcuts for the completion of those reforms that are instrumental in the attainment of higher productivity, efficiency, and sustainable growth.

Chile, Costa Rica, and Peru offer one scenario of institutional modernization and policy innovation. I have argued here that because of their significant reform advances and complementary endowment factors these countries were well positioned to pursue an FTA route in coping with the China challenge. But this option is obviously not for everyone. Brazil and Colombia have made periodic statements in this direction, but manufacturing interests and domestic lobbies in both countries have thrown up sizeable obstacles to the negotiation of an FTA with China, at least for the time being.[66] Apart from Costa Rica, Mexico and Central America have little to sell to China and face difficult export similarities with China in third markets, especially that of the US.[67] Argentina and Brazil, each in its own way, are reminiscent of earlier times, when the end of a commodity price bonanza triggered a full-blown macroeconomic crisis and the collapse of growth. The data I have presented throughout this book suggest that, in varying ways, the boom itself was a distraction to the larger LAC EEs in terms of reform backsliding and a lapse in efforts at economic restructuring. Nevertheless, the rise of China in the region continues unabated.

Since the 1990s the small open economies of Chile, Peru, and Costa Rica have sought to turn their weaknesses into strength. For Chile and Peru, this has meant the simultaneous pursuit of an outward trade model led by commodity exports and the constructing of institutions and economic reforms to support that model. For both, a reference point would be to follow in the path of successful developed-country commodity exporters like Canada and Australia. Notably, Chile rejected Washington Consensus pressures to privatize copper; the state kept a tight grip on foreign exchange and invested these funds productively. Of necessity, Peru privatized its blighted state mining companies in the 1990s, but subsequent macroeconomic and institutional reforms rendered this strategy sound.

In turn, Costa Rican policy makers have nurtured the development of an information and communication technology cluster since the mid-1990s. These three economies were thus able to secure an FTA with China because of complementary factor endowments and, in the case of Costa Rica, a chance for China to advance its One-China policy.[68] The fact that each country already had an FTA in place with the US enabled China to tread softly without appearing to upstage US power and interests in the Western Hemisphere.

As of 2016 China had completed thirteen bilateral FTAs and is in the process of negotiating several others.[69] Next to its other FTA partners, such as Singapore (2008), New Zealand (2008), and Australia (2014), it would be quite easy to write off the three bilateral FTAs discussed here as too small to succeed. Indeed, the huge asymmetries involved, the varying motives, and the developing–developing country nature of these China–LAC accords certainly gives cause for concern. My point, however, is that China's incorporation of the LAC region into its internationalized development strategy in the 2000s has opened up a new venue for economic integration, an opportunity that each of these small states has seized on. In doing so, Chile, Costa Rica, and Peru have chosen to meet the China challenge in the realm of international norms and binding treaties, which will afford them greater access to the Chinese market and a more predictable, stable relationship with their Chinese counterparts. They have also done so through a position of strength in terms of the institutional maturation and reform trajectory of each.

China's entry into the FTA fray in the 2000s requires that we rethink standing assumptions and upgrade our expectations concerning what can be accomplished between developing countries at the FTA negotiating table. In fact, these three developing–developing China–LAC FTAs have turned standing theories on their head, while also lending new weight to others. First, they support earlier findings that bilateral FTAs can be trade creating and that highly asymmetrical deals are likely to contribute to multilateral trade gains. Second, in contrast with earlier LAC experiences, they show that developing–developing bilateral accords can make progress in adopting items on the WTO's new trade agenda. Third, despite the widely varying motives for the pursuit of these bilateral deals, the outcomes for all three were still WTO-plus. Finally, it appears that these three small, open economies may be the only LAC countries to enjoy privileged access to both the Chinese and the US markets for some time to come. As serendipity would have it, these three price-takers in the global economy are now in a highly advantageous situation.

5

An Institutional Resource Curse
in Argentina and Brazil

I doubt that anyone in this country is more law-abiding than me.

Luiz Inácio Lula da Silva, former president of Brazil, 2003–10[1]

IN THE PERIOD JUST PRIOR TO THE 2003–13 boom growth and economic dynamism were essentially flat in Latin America, with the exception of Chile. Argentina's decade-long currency board and dollar–peso exchange rate peg had just come unhinged, and Brazil had yet to fully rebound from its own exchange rate meltdown in 1998–99. There were few signs that the dawn of the new millennium would constitute a takeoff for emerging economies (EEs) in Latin America and the Caribbean (LAC). And yet China's 2001 entry into the WTO, the recovery of the US economy, and rising growth rates in the OECD bloc all converged to prompt an unexpected turnaround: as mentioned throughout this book, China's 9–10 percent annual average growth rates and its intense demand for natural resources kicked off the region's biggest commodity lottery ever. Both Argentina and Brazil thrived on the explosion of soybean, oil, and mineral sales to China. Brazil captured the bulk of Chinese foreign direct investment (FDI) in LAC for further development of these sectors, investment bolstered by generous project loans from China's two big policy banks, the China Development Bank (CDB) and the China Export-Import Bank (CHEXIM).[2] This situation had everything to do with the incorporation of both countries into China's internationalized development strategy.

My grounds for considering these two cases together here have to do with their common resource endowments and the similar ties of trade, loans, and FDI that the two countries have forged with China. Moreover, just as the China boom was taking off, the countries launched economic strategies under the broad banner of developmentalism, as newly elected political leaders in both were anxious to disassociate themselves from the neoliberal, Washington Consensus (WC) policies that had preceded them in the 1990s. In Brazil this entailed the launching of three sequential plans, two under Workers' Party President Luiz Inácio Lula da Silva, or Lula (2003–10), and one under his Workers' Party successor, President Dilma Rousseff (2011–16). The goal of all three developmentalist plans was "to sustain a long productive development cycle based on investment, business competitiveness, and an increase in exports."[3] Especially under Lula, industrial policy, efficiency, and innovation were all back in vogue. Coined by some as the new developmentalism, the newness apparently had to do with the success of preceding policies of inflation stabilization and macroeconomic restructuring, which now lent credibility to such an effort.[4]

Argentina's renewed embrace of state intervention was more reactive and ad hoc, as the China boom took off in the immediate wake of the country's currency crash and its US$100 billion default on government-held debt. In the eyes of domestic public opinion, the implementation of WC reforms based on liberalization, privatization, and deregulation as well as the simultaneous adherence to IMF-directed neoliberal policies during the previous decade were all to blame. For Argentine policy makers, developmentalist policies seemed to constitute anything that was not neoliberal. Nevertheless, President Néstor Kirchner (2003–7), elected on a splinter coalition within the long-standing labor-backed Peronist Party, did cobble together an approach that has since been anointed developmentalist: "*Kirchnerismo* was a strategy for growth based on selective protectionism in the manufacturing sector and targeted state intervention through public works and credit expansion."[5] After a decade of steep currency appreciation under the dollar–peso peg, Kirchner's policy of exchange rate devaluation and unilaterally lowered debt payments meant that Argentina finally had some room to maneuver.

As sales to China exploded and foreign exchange reserves suddenly burgeoned, both Argentina and Brazil now had the ready cash to tackle long-standing challenges in the way of industrialization, income distribution, and economic growth. The data I have presented throughout this book tell the following story: For Argentina, average annual growth rates from 2003 to 2013 were spectacular, as were the gains in per capita GDP; Brazil's performance on both indicators was solid and certainly better when compared with the preceding period (see table 1.1). In addition, as I have argued (see chapter 3), both countries deftly weathered and quickly rebounded from the 2008–9 global financial crisis (GFC). These trends validate the argument of the Inter-American Development Bank (IDB) economist Ambrogio Cesa-Bianchi and his colleagues, who found that the positive effect of Chinese GDP growth on LAC countries had been increasing since 1990.[6] However, as Chinese growth slowed by 2–3 percentage points in 2013–14 and has remained steady at 6–7 percent of GDP since then, Argentina and Brazil have felt the full force of a negative GDP shock from China. For both countries, between 2014 and 2017 average growth rates were basically negative, per capita income dropped precipitously, and gross capital formation as a percent of GDP fell by 1–2 percentage points.

The data in table 1.1 present a puzzle with regard to the comparatively dismal economic performance of Argentina and Brazil in the post-2013 period. Although all six countries were exposed to the negative China shock that kicked in post-2013, the other four countries in the table have managed to remain on the positive side of the ledger in the postboom period. This includes Chile and Peru, which are even more dependent on commodity exports than Argentina and Brazil. What accounts for this differential performance? My answer throughout the book has been an institutional one, and in the particular cases of Argentina and Brazil this has meant the slowing of vital reforms and the neglect of domestic economic institutions during the China boom. I presented absolute numbers on institutional performance for all six countries considered here, based on data gathered by the World Bank, World Economic Forum, Transparency International, and the Heritage Foundation (see table I.5). On the basis of the World Bank's Worldwide Governance Indicators I presented relative measures of institutional performance over time with regard to both intracountry trends and the six LAC countries considered in this book in comparison (see fig. 1.1).

Whichever way you cut it, Argentina's institutional measures are dismal; Brazil does better than Argentina, but on two of the three measures in figure 1.1 it is outpaced by the three small open economies analyzed above (see chapter 4). Given their exceedingly rich factor endowments, we would have every reason to expect much better economic performance overall for Argentina and Brazil. Apart from common factor endowments, a shared development strategy, and similar ties with China, it is this institutional stagnation (Brazil) and backsliding (Argentina) that warrant the classification of these two countries under the rubric of an institutional resource curse. In the introduction I referred to the work of Halvor Mehlum and his coauthors, who argue that it is the quality of domestic institutions that most decisively explains differences in development outcomes between countries that are abundant in natural resources. This literature raises two interrelated questions that will inform my own analysis in this chapter: (1) In what ways might institutional weaknesses condition the effects of natural resource abundance on economic performance? (2) How might otherwise effective institutions deteriorate under the force of a commodity boom?[7]

The chapter proceeds along the following lines. The first section analyzes the rise of China in Brazil and Argentina with an emphasis on the post-2000 period. A second section reviews and analyzes the developmentalist model that both countries embraced at the turn of the millennium; a third section analyzes the institutional erosion that has occurred in both countries in the 2000s; a final section draws conclusions. With regard to each of these themes, first, I find that the explosion of investment and trade with China since the early 2000s was a necessary condition for explaining the dynamic take-off of both countries, but China's slowing growth after 2013 does not fully account for the economic depths to which Brazil and Argentina both fell in the wake of the boom. Second, the record shows that in both countries it was the implementation of reckless policies under the guise of "developmentalism" that exacerbated the post-2013 slowdown to the extent that Brazil went into a full-blown economic depression. Finally, I illustrate how "grabber-friendly" institutions, combined with corrupt and predatory politicians and policy makers, brought out the very worst elements of state and society in both countries.[8]

The Rise of China in Brazil and Argentina

There Is a History

I pointed out earlier that China's informal ties with Brazil and Argentina date back to the 1950s (see chapter 2), as the PRC's Radio Broadcasting Agency had secured permission to air pro-China Spanish-language programs in both countries.[9] By the mid-1960s, moreover, Argentina had sold over one million tons of wheat to China as Mao's misguided Great Leap Forward had morphed into the Great Famine. Brazil was already shipping iron ore to mainland China during this same period. Within the context of people-to-people contacts, Southern Cone citizens of all walks of life were hosted by China for educational, political, and cultural exchanges.[10] After military coups in Brazil in 1964 and Argentina in 1966 cross-Pacific relations cooled as the newly installed generals shared the rabid anticommunist sentiments of the US. However, China's rupture with the Soviets and the Cubans, combined with Mao's decision to side with the enemy of his enemies (i.e., the US) in the early 1970s, opened the floodgate for China's normalization of diplomatic relations with Argentina in 1972 and Brazil in 1974.[11]

By the mid-1970s trade had superseded political tensions, as Brazil became China's top LAC trade partner and Argentina was number two. Bound by their shared animosity toward the Soviets, China and the two countries saw their ties warm considerably as China launched its reforms in 1978. As in the case of General Augusto Pinochet in Chile, the Chinese leadership embraced other authoritarian hitmen from the Southern Cone, hosting General Jorge Rafael Videla of Argentina in 1980 and General João Figueiredo of Brazil in 1984. Both countries topped the itinerary for Premier Zhao Ziyang's pathbreaking visit to the region in 1985. Chinese leaders stressed their support for Argentina's claim over the Falkland / Malvinas Islands, and a number of joint development projects were launched in the spirit of solidarity.[12] In 1988, for example, a deal was struck for China and Brazil to jointly construct and launch two satellites, and a contract was signed for Argentina to build a model farm in China. Between 1980 and 1985 reciprocal credit lines were established to facilitate trade between China and Argentina.

The first major turning point came in 1993, when China designated Brazil its very first strategic partner (SP). Throughout the book I have referred to China's strategic partnerships as weakly defined instruments of Chinese foreign policy. Two Chinese scholars, Feng Zhongping and Huang Jing, note that the actual list of SPs is not reported by Beijing for fear of offending a nonpartner. They estimate that China has established SPs with some forty-seven countries, most of them since the early 2000s.[13] The first SP with Brazil, however, reflected the CCP's eagerness to mend China's diplomatic fences in the aftermath of the Tiananmen Square massacre. Like Mexico in the early 1990s, Brasilia welcomed China with open arms as most of the West stood by horrified. For that matter, in 1990 the Argentine president Carlos Menem had the distinction of being the first head of state in the world to visit China in the wake of Tiananmen. At any rate, nine of the ten China–LAC SPs subsequently forged are with countries that are abundant in those commodities that are essential for sustaining Chinese growth. The Costa Rica–China SP is the exception to this rule, as it is a product of the One-China policy.

Between 1993 and 2000 Brazil and Argentina continued to lead the LAC pack in the dollar value of trade with China: total Brazil–China trade over this period reached nearly US$16 billion, and total trade between Argentina and China hit around US$8.2 billion (see tables 2.4 and 2.5). Although outflows of Chinese FDI in South America would not take off until the 2010s, joint ventures began to proliferate between China and the two countries—for example, in lumber and iron ore production with Brazil and in fisheries with Argentina.[14] The trade balance was more or less in equilibrium between China and both countries during these two decades, but the complementarities of shipping raw materials to China and importing back manufactured goods began to wear thin. As China geared up for WTO entry in 2001 and accelerated its industrial export-led strategy, Brazil imposed import quotas on Chinese textiles in 1996.[15] Unlike Mexico, which had some minor success in exporting value-added goods to China during this period, the commercial relationship between China and Brazil and Argentina, respectively, veered little from this traditional comparative advantage pattern.

The China Boom

The domestic reaction to the rapid takeoff of commodity sales to China in both countries was one of disbelief, especially in Argentina, where the dire crisis of 2001–2 had invoked a justifiable sense of doom.[16] In 2003 alone Argentina's exports of soybeans to China had soared by 16 percent, and prices on the country's oil and energy resources were up 20 percent on the commodity price index. Thanks to Chinese demand, between 2001 and 2004 Brazil's trade surplus had gone from US\$2.6 billion to US\$25 billion. Granted, some of this surplus reflected compressed consumption due to Brazil's own economic slump at the time. Still, these figures in both countries broke all previous records.[17] By 2007 the total trade of each country with China over the 1993 to 2000 period was now on par with *annual* patterns of total trade between China and each country. From 2001 to 2017 total China–Argentina trade came to US\$95.8 billion, while total China–Brazil trade stood at US\$383.1 billion. Mexico's total trade with China was on par with Brazil's during this period. However, Mexico's total was weighted on the import side whereas Brazil has run a yearly trade surplus with China with the exception of 2007–8 (see table 2.5).

By 2016 China accounted for 13.1 percent of Argentina's trade, and Argentina 0.3 percent of China's trade; China accounted for 18.1 percent of Brazil's trade, and Brazil 1.8 percent of China's trade. Argentina's top exports to China were soybean, grains, seeds, and fruits (58 percent); animal, vegetable fats, and oils (17 percent); and mineral fuels, oils, and distillation products (9 percent) (see table 2.4). Its top imports from China were electrical and electronic equipment (30.5 percent); nuclear reactors, fuel elements, and isotope separators (21.8 percent); and organic chemicals (8.8 percent). Brazil's top exports to China were ores, slag, and ash (32 percent); soybean, grains, seeds, and fruits (33.2 percent); and mineral fuels, oils, and distillation products (10 percent). Its top imports from China were electrical and electronic equipment (31 percent); nuclear reactors, fuel elements, and isotope separators (19 percent); and organic chemicals (6 percent). Again, the export of manufactured goods to China has heretofore not been a part of these respective bilateral relationships. What is new is China's vigorous export of manufactured goods to both countries in the 2000s. Argentina has run a continual trade deficit with China since 2008.

Brazil

In earlier chapters I attributed China's deepening economic ties with its LAC SPs to its need for an internationalized development strategy to compensate for its serious natural resource deficit. If China did not import minerals, oil, and agricultural products, it would be unable to feed itself or to fuel the soon-to-be largest economy in the world. On this count, Brazil is China's jewel in the crown. The China–Brazil SP, which lay dormant for nearly a decade, came to life in the early 2000s and was upgraded to a Comprehensive Strategic Partnership (i.e., "non-fair-weather friends forever") in 2012.[18] From 2000 to 2017 China's outflow of FDI to Brazil was US$48.02 billion (see table I.3), and since 2005 Brazil has received a total of US$28.9 billion in loans from CDB and CHEXIM.[19]

If there is such a thing as a blue chip state-owned enterprise (SOE), China has cornered this market. The bulk of Chinese FDI inflows to Brazil is concentrated in oil, mining, and energy, in which a handful of Chinese SOE's dominate. This includes two of the top Chinese public oil companies, China Petroleum and Chemical (SINOPEC), and China National Petroleum Corporation (CNPC); China Three Gorges Corporation (CTG); State Grid Corporation of China; Wuhan Steel Processing Co Ltd (WISCO); and the Sinochem Group.[20] Most of the significant investments were made from 2009 on, for example, SINOPEC's "US$7.1 billion investment in the Brazilian operations of the Spanish firm Repsol YPF in exchange for a 40 percent share in the company's operations in the country."[21] In 2010 State Grid Corporation invested US$2.2 billion in seven Brazilian electricity transmission companies and thirteen transmission lines, rendering it the fourth largest energy transmission company in Brazil.[22] In 2015 CTG, the largest producer of hydroelectric power in the world, won the auction for a thirty-year concession to operate two hydroelectric power plants in Brazil, paying US$3.7 billion.[23]

The Belo Monte hydroelectric project, which will eventually transmit energy to four states in Brazil's southeast, began operating its first transmission line in 2016.[24] Brazil's National Development Bank (BNDES) funded 46 percent of this project, while CTG raised the remaining capital through a complex scheme of partnerships, mergers, and acquisitions. Once completed, Belo Monte hydroelectric dam will be the third largest dam in the world. On the upside, per BNDES' stipulation, this project drew largely on Brazilian suppliers and service providers and is expected to create as many as eight thousand jobs for Brazilian technical specialists and for national workers residing in nearby cities. On the downside, domestic opponents of this project question the ease with which its sponsors were able to obtain the necessary environmental license from the Brazilian Institute of Environment and Renewable Natural Resources. As the Brazilian economist Celio Hiratuka notes, "According to the impact study for the first transmission line, 1,725 hectares of native vegetation in Brazil's two largest biomes will be lost."[25]

Many of these mega-deals have been facilitated by loans from China's policy banks, which have financed such endeavors as pre-salt oil field development in Brazil's Santos basin (US$10 billion to Petrobras, Brazil's majority state-held oil company);[26] SINOPEC'S construction of the Gasene pipeline (US$750 million with counterpart funding from BNDES);[27] and US$1.2 billion for a soy processing plant. Although keen to invest in land to cultivate soybeans and corn for export back to the mainland, Chinese investors have been prohibited by the Brazilian government's 2010 law that clamped down on the sale of land to foreigners. Another mega-deal on China's wish list is the construction of a Twin Ocean Railroad that would connect an Atlantic port in Brazil with a Pacific port on the Peruvian coast. In July 2014 the governments of China, Brazil, and Peru signed a memorandum of understanding, and feasibility studies on this proposed interoceanic railway began in 2015. Since then, the project has stalled amid economic recession and political instability in Brazil and Peru. However, the biggest obstacle is environmental conservation, as the various routes considered would run through the Amazon rain forest in reserves that are "home to one of the most important areas of flora and fauna on the planet."[28]

The more recent shift in Chinese outflows of FDI into manufacturing, autos, and services in LAC has gone mainly toward Brazil. Some top market-seeking Chinese companies, for example, ZTE (telecom equipment), Huawei (telecom services, equipment, and networking), and Lenovo Think Pad, have already established a foothold in Brazil. Autos are a newer frontier, as Brazil, like China, has one of the largest domestic auto markets in the world. Some of these Chinese investments in autos are a response to incentives offered by the Brazilian government, for example, targeted programs to spur innovation and the tighter integration of this sector into global value chains. Many of these are greenfield investments by such Chinese companies as the Chery Automobile Company, the Jainghuai Auto Company, Great Wall Motors, and Geely. Unfortunately, Brazil's high tariffs on auto imports, meant to encourage foreign investors to set up and produce in local factories, have offset some of these efforts at industrial upgrading and increased dynamism. Some Chinese companies, for example, those operating in the services sector (e.g., information technology [IT], finance, and electronics), have gotten their foot in the Brazilian market through mergers and acquisitions and by assuming a minority position in larger projects. LAC's services sector has captured more than half of Chinese outflows of FDI to the region since 2013, and, again, Brazil has been the magnet for these investments.[29]

None of these deals came easily. However, the realization of proposed and planned projects has been a smoother process for Chinese investors in Brazil than in Argentina. This is so even though Brazil has much higher regulatory restrictions on incoming FDI than Argentina.[30] Moreover, Brazil upholds domestic laws that require public bidding on projects and has stood firm against China's efforts to insert high levels of its own content (labor, management, engineering services, and other material inputs).[31] On labor, for example, employment data gathered from 2000 to 2017 suggest that Chinese inflows of FDI to Argentina have created roughly 11,210 domestic jobs, whereas Chinese inflows of FDI into Brazil over this same period generated around 138,613 jobs.[32] Brazil's ready access to international capital markets and the institutional role of BNDES in cofinancing Chinese infrastructure have strengthened the country's position vis-à-vis Chinese investors.

Argentina, shut out of international capital markets from 2002 to 2015 and lacking the domestic equivalent of BNDES, is the opposite. China became a de facto lender of last resort for Argentina with the establishment of a currency swap fund for US$10.24 billion in 2009, raised to US$18.7 billion in 2018. Although the goal of a currency swap is to streamline bilateral trade by reducing transactions costs, since 2014 Beijing has allowed Argentina to tap into this fund to ease its liquidity crunch.[33] Otherwise, China has disbursed project financing for Argentina through engineering, procurement, and construction (EPC) contracts, mainly because Argentina has none of Brazil's financial flexibility and less of its indigenous expertise in the design of mega-development projects such as those discussed above. Under an EPC, Chinese firms guarantee the financing for a given project, but these funds can be transferred to local Chinese service providers and may never leave the mainland.[34] China has also made state-to-state loans to Argentina similar to those made to Ecuador and Venezuela, although some of these are now showing up in ledgers that indicate huge cash payments to Argentine politicians in exchange for the approval of a given Chinese-financed project.[35]

Argentina

Argentine policy makers in the post-GFC period embraced some measures, such as nationalization, capital controls, and multiple exchange rates, that were simply not appealing to any rational investor. One result is that Argentina has attracted around 25 percent of the outflows of Chinese FDI that Brazil has received and ranks third behind Peru as a destination for outflows of Chinese FDI into the LAC region (see table I.2). Argentina's total Chinese FDI from 2000 to 2017 was around US$11.87 billion, whereas this indicator for Peru in the same period was roughly US$19.34 billion.[36] Argentina, having received US$16.9 billion in loans from China's two policy banks, ranks fourth, behind Venezuela, Brazil, and Ecuador, as a recipient of Chinese lending.[37]

In 2011 the takeover of 80 percent of the Standard Bank of Argentina by the Industrial and Commercial Bank of China (ICBC), the largest of China's big four state-owned banks, rendered this the biggest Chinese financial sector investment in LAC to date. It also made ICBC the world's biggest bank by market value—not to mention a potential source of financing for cash-starved Argentina. In 2015 the People's Bank of China opened a renminbi, or yuan, clearinghouse through ICBC in Buenos Aires, as one of many efforts to internationalize the Chinese currency since the designation of the renminbi as a reserve currency at the IMF in 2016.

Chinese policy bank loans to Argentina began to flow in 2010 and were concentrated in several projects related to the national train system, hydroelectric dam construction, and renewable energy projects. By far the most successful venture in this portfolio was a US$10 billion CDB loan for the modernization of the national railway system. Here, new state-of-the-art Chinese-made trains and Chinese technical labor replaced dilapidated infrastructure that dated back to the 1970s.[38] In 2014 another US$2.1 billion loan was made by CDB and ICBC for the renovation of Argentina's Belgrano-Cargas freight line, which links Argentina with its neighbors to the north and west all the way to the Pacific coast.[39] This was just one of several major rail–freight corridors that had fallen into disrepair, and these upgrades promised to lower cargo transport costs and quicken delivery times in getting goods to China, in particular. According to government estimates, the modernization of these railways could increase the country's freight haul capacity by some 400 percent as soon as 2019.[40]

While all of these rail infrastructure projects have suffered from financial bottlenecks and bureaucratic delays on the Argentine side, they are gradually coming to fruition. Other sectors, such as mining, agriculture, and hydroelectric, have been less penetrable. To date, the outflow of Chinese FDI into Argentina has been concentrated in the oil sector. Chinese FDI in mining has been limited to share acquisition and purchases of smaller ventures. In agriculture, where Chinese investors are most interested in purchasing land for soybean production, the Argentine government joined step with Brazil and legislated a ban on land sales to foreigners in 2011.

Chinese FDI has thus shifted into agricultural trading companies, exemplified by the China Overseas Food Corporation's US$1.2 billion purchase of a sizeable Argentine soybean processing operation and a genetically engineered seed business in 2014.[41] As in Brazil, smaller Chinese investments have been made in Argentina by three of China's top tech companies, ZTE, Huawei, and Lenovo. In 2018, as an apparent tack-on to China's

Belt and Road Initiative, China's State Construction Engineering Corporation won a US$2.1 billion contract for highway construction in Argentina. As in the case of the Belgrano-Cargas freight line, the Argentine government signed on to a large percentage of Chinese input with this project, including engineering, construction, upgrades, and operational maintenance.

China's big three oil companies—SINOPEC, CNPC, and the China Offshore Oil Corporation (CNOOC)—have placed some of the biggest bets on Argentina.[42] The two largest acquisitions in the Argentine oil sector have been made by CNOOC and SINOPEC. In 2010 CNOOC purchased a 50 percent share in the Argentine firm Bridas for a breathtaking US$3.1 billion; the merging of the two combined the best skills of each in offshore exploration and production (CNOOC) and onshore operations (Bridas). As Kevin Gallagher writes, "Since Bridas has a 40 percent stake in PanAmerican Energy (PAE), this merger granted CNOOC access to Argentina's large Cerro Dragón petroleum reserve, operated by PAE."[43] At the same time, SINOPEC acquired Occidental Petroleum in Argentina in 2010 for US$2.6 billion and thereby gained the rights to explore some fifteen hundred wells across twenty-three separate sites in three of Argentina's oil-rich provinces (Chucut, Mendoza, and Santa Cruz).[44] As China–Argentina trade and investment ties continued to thicken, China upgraded its SP with Argentina to a Comprehensive Strategic Partnership in 2014.[45]

Despite the allocation of US$2.5 billion in 2014 by the CDB, ICBC, and the Bank of China, to begin the construction of hydroelectric dams in Argentina, these infrastructure projects were thrown into question by a change of administration in December 2015.[46] President Mauricio Macri, elected on a center-right ticket, had vowed to scrutinize the flurry of last-minute projects his predecessor had signed off on with the Chinese behind closed doors. As the newly elected executive saw it, Argentina's financial and diplomatic isolation from 2002 to 2015 had left it disproportionately dependent on China.[47] Macri thus went about repairing diplomatic relations with the US and the EU, including the resolution of outstanding debts still owed from the 2001 default, and he more carefully scrutinized hydroelectric projects in the construction pipeline. Most controversial were two major hydroelectric projects already under way on the Santa Cruz River, home of the Patagonia region and the Kirchners' power base. The ultimate cost of the two projects—one even named after Fernández de Kirchner's late husband, Néstor Kirchner—was estimated at US$21.6 billion, meaning a considerable debt burden for the country for years to come.[48]

As in the case of Brazil's Belo Monte hydroelectric dam, environmentalists had raised legitimate concerns that these two dams would inflict damages on the pristine ecosystem in Santa Cruz Province. Moreover, this scarcely populated province did not have the transmission capacity to handle the projected 1,740 megawatts of electricity to be generated by these hydroelectric projects.[49] China, however, was not to be deterred. Having dealt with the idiosyncrasies of the Fernández de Kirchner administration for eight years, the CDB had inserted a cross-default clause in its loan stating that the cancellation of these two mega-projects would mean the immediate halt of Chinese funding for completion of the crucial Belgrano-Cargas freight line. Because these dams are the largest ever to be built by a Chinese company (the Gezhouba Group) overseas, President Xi Jinping had a personal stake in their completion. In the end, "China agreed to lower the capacity of (the) dams by including fewer turbines and adding another transmission line. Conservation groups were also successful in forcing a new environmental assessment through the Argentine Supreme Court."[50] The projects went forward, representing just one underside to the China boom in Argentina. Assuming the eventual resolution of these conflicts, the estimated savings from replacing diesel and natural gas imports with hydroelectric energy are around US$1.1 billion annually.[51]

Debating the Effects of the Boom

There is a growing concern that in the course of the China boom from 2003 to 2013 both Argentina and Brazil have undergone a re-primarization of their export baskets and a deindustrialization of their respective economies. It is this very pattern that has fueled the neodependency critique on the evolving China–Latin America relationship. For these thinkers China has now become part of the core in the core–periphery relationship, the perpetuator of asymmetry and underdevelopment of the periphery, including the LAC region. In the introduction I rejected this notion as too simplistic and unable to account for the dynamic upward mobility of East Asian cases like Japan, Korea, and China itself. China's rise may have set the stage for patterns of reprimarization and deindustrialization in both countries, but domestic institutions and actors in Argentina and Brazil wrote the script. Moreover, if China is indeed the independent variable in this story, how then do we account for the absence of this same pattern of reprimarization in Mexico? Mexico's exports are under considerable threat from Chinese competition both at home and abroad, as witnessed in Mexico's huge trade deficit with China, but manufacturing exports and manufacturing value-added as a percent of GDP have basically held steady.

For others, the process of reprimarization dates back to the implementation of WC trade liberalization policies in the late 1980s and early 1990s in the LAC region, which was the first notch down in the deindustrialization process.[52] Defining deindustrialization as a "falling share of manufacturing employment and value-added in total employment and GDP . . . and a rising specialization in primary goods," Mario Castillo and Antonio Martins Neto argue that there is some evidence of this happening in Brazil, but less so in Argentina.[53] Commercial account liberalization in the 1990s was harsh on domestic industry in both cases and compounded by currency appreciation and the lack of public policies to facilitate structural adjustment. On the basis of their data and following Dani Rodrik's work on "premature de-industrialization,"[54] these same authors note that "manufacturing already achieved its peak in these countries, both in employment and value-added. Latin America is now similar to most developed countries, with a rising importance of services—a premature deindustrialization."[55] The catch here is that, in contrast to the developed countries, where manufacturing began to decline once per capita income had reached a range of US\$\$10–15,000, this process is occurring at much lower levels of per capita income in Argentina (US\$5,461) and Brazil (US\$5,202). Hence, the "premature" nature of this decline.

As in the developed countries, workers in Argentina and Brazil have moved from agriculture toward industry and are now shifting into services. While seen as a natural progression in the developed countries, where the move into services signified higher-paying and more knowledge-intensive work, the shift in Argentina and Brazil has been toward low-productivity and lower value-added services. Although Argentina has stood out thus far for its institutional neglect and rash policy approaches in the 2000s, it is actually Brazil that has experienced the deeper pattern of premature industrialization. In 1990 the share of primary goods in total Brazilian exports was 28 percent, while low- and medium-technology industries together accounted for 39 percent. By 2014 the share of primary goods in exports had jumped to 50 percent and that of low- and medium-technology industries was down to 23 percent.[56] The comparable figures for Argentina are 44 percent of primary goods in total exports in 1990 with an increase to 48 percent in 2014; interestingly, Argentina's share of medium-technology exports increased from 10 percent in 1990 to 22 percent in 2014.[57] However, despite this increase manufacturing employment in Argentina has fallen on par with that in Brazil.

What do these trends suggest about the China boom? First, the onset of deindustrialization in Brazil in particular was well under way before the explosion of commodity prices from 2003 to 2013. The boom further distracted policy makers from generating the kinds of reforms and cohesive industrial policies that would render the manufacturing sector more efficient and competitive. For example, Brazil's manufacturing value-added as a percent of GDP dropped from 15.3 percent in 2000 to 11.7 percent in 2016 (see table 1.2). This trend need not be a permanent one, but to reverse it would require the proper mix of policies and incentives. At the same time, Brazil exports just one-fifth of its manufacturing production, meaning there is plenty of room for the expansion of more competitive goods.[58] Second, the extent of re-primarization of the Argentine economy appears to have been exaggerated in the recent literature, as the increase in primary exports as a share of total exports was just 4 percent between 1990 and 2014. Argentina's manufacturing value-added as a percentage of GDP dropped from 17.8 percent in 2000 to 16.4 percent in 2016 (see table 1.2). The China boom drew out Argentina's agricultural exports but without the large loss in manufacturing value-added that Brazil registered. As for the rise of Argentina's share of low- and medium-technology exports, it is important to keep in mind the low starting point on this indicator in 1990.

Yet out of the intense global volatility and domestic economic turmoil of the 1990s there is a side story here. The findings of a comparative project on technological innovation in Brazilian and Argentine firms undertaken by a team of researchers at the Institute of Applied Economic Research in

Rio de Janeiro point to some advances in the specialization of medium and high-tech goods in both countries.[59] In Argentina the rise of these goods in the export sector is a spin-off of the massive infusion of FDI in agro-industry (soybeans) and energy (oil refineries, petrochemical complexes, steel and aluminum plants) since the 1990s. Consisting of fewer than four hundred companies, this higher tech segment accounted for 40 percent of Argentina's industrial output in 2007.[60]

In Brazil a similar process is occurring because of the application of technology to the natural resource and agribusiness sectors. While counting for just 1.7 percent of Brazilian manufacturing firms, this higher tech segment was responsible for 25.9 percent of total industrial revenue in 2007.[61] These higher tech segments in both countries are still reliant on the import of capital goods and IT to spur their own growth, a niche that Chinese exporters have readily captured. The cultivation of domestic suppliers should be a much stronger focus of industrial policy for both countries, as these firms still struggle to compete in global markets. Finally, the variation in deindustrialization versus re-primarization patterns between these two countries suggests the extent to which domestic variables—endowment factors, institutions, and political and economic actors—have shaped distinct outcomes within each.

Developmentalism, Southern Cone Style

Prelude

The onset of the China boom in 2003 saw both countries with newly elected leftist executives, Lula in Brazil and Néstor Kirchner in Argentina. Although the political economy literature is laced with references to this period as "post-neoliberal," there are important nuances between the market reforms embraced by the two countries in the 1990s.[62] These differences, in turn, shaped the varying content and emphases of the developmentalist programs that both administrations rolled out in the early 2000s.

Both countries faced the imperative to eradicate hyperinflation in the early 1990s, and both resorted to exchange rate–based stabilization plans, Argentina in 1991 and Brazil in 1994. Argentina took a more drastic approach, pegging the peso one-to-one to the US dollar under a new currency board and proceeding with both the tight monetary and fiscal policies advocated by the IMF as well as WC structural reforms based on liberalization, privatization, and deregulation. Having no successful history of state intervention in the post–World War II period and no Brazilian-style economic miracle (during the 1960s and 1970s) in its recent past, Argentina bought into the antistatist rhetoric that surged in the West as communist regimes collapsed in 1989–90.

Brazil, conversely, had more or less thrived on a state-led strategy all the way up to the 1982 debt shocks. Numerous industries (mining, steel, autos, petrochemicals, shoes, textiles, and aerospace, to name a few) had been nurtured by the state and become formidable domestic players in their own right. But the evaporation of easy external credit and the explosion of debt liabilities post-1982 also exposed the weaknesses of this strategy. This rendition of Brazil's state-led development model could no longer stay afloat; budget indexing and intragovernmental lending could no longer mask inflation or paper over the fiscal deficits. It was, moreover, quite late in the game for a country with Brazil's emerging power aspirations to be running an inflation rate in the neighborhood of 2,500 percent![63] In contrast with Argentina, Brazilian policy makers incorporated monetarist policies and market reforms into the ongoing statist model rather than jettisoning it altogether. Inflation stabilization was urgent, and it was accomplished by pegging the Brazilian real to the US dollar. Otherwise, Brazil's reforms proceeded in a manner akin to China's: gradual, sometimes pragmatic, and heterodox.

The IMF was involved in both of these market reform programs. In the case of Argentina, the IMF was closely engaged from the outset of the Convertibility Plan in 1991 all the way up to the 2002 crash, providing loans and technical assistance with fiscal, monetary, and banking sector reforms.[64] Despite the steep appreciation of the Argentine peso through the 1990s, the country's flagrant failure to meet designated fiscal targets, and the government's halfhearted implementation of structural reforms, the IMF stood by Argentina until the currency board met its dire end. Having dispersed two bailout loans totaling US\$23 billion in 2001 alone, the IMF was not able to save face.[65] The economy tanked, the country defaulted on its debts, and the fund's director of the Western Hemisphere Division was promptly fired. It was thus from a position of isolation and desperation that President Kirchner approached the Chinese about the possibility of securing a loan for Argentina to pay off its outstanding debt to the IMF.[66] President Hu Jintao demurred, without giving Argentina a straight answer or a loan, which set a prickly tone for Sino–Argentine relations from that point on.

In the case of Brazil, the IMF stepped in with a US$18 billion loan in 1999 to assist the country in defending against the financial contagion emanating from the crash of the Thai baht and the Russian ruble in 1997–98. Obviously, this attempt at proactive intervention failed to deter a massive devaluation of the Brazilian real later that same year. Nevertheless, in September 2002, with a possible Lula victory looming, the IMF arranged its largest loan yet: a US$30.4 billion standby agreement for Brazil to help quell jittery markets and capital outflows in anticipation of the Workers' Party victory.[67] Up through 2005 the fund provided technical assistance in designing Brazil's "macro prudential" economic policy framework based on tight monetary and fiscal policy. This combination of monetarist policy guidance from the IMF and Lula's more proactive developmentalist strategy resulted in "a hybrid paradigm in which some of the policy content of the Washington Consensus has been preserved intact, while some has been gutted and replaced with neo-developmentalist goals and policy instruments."[68]

What role did China play in these evolving developmentalist programs and approaches post-2003? In Argentina, apart from approaching China about financial assistance for debt repayment (including the possible purchase of Argentine bonds by the Chinese), the Kirchner team had also put out feelers for a US$20 billion mega-package from Beijing to launch a major capital investment campaign. After a flurry of memoranda back and forth and some interest shown by the Chinese in refurbishing the Argentine rail system, Beijing quietly withdrew, again offering neither a concrete answer nor a loan package.[69] Until 2010 China's involvement with Argentina was mainly on the demand side as the importer of large quantities of Argentine soybeans. In contrast, China was active on both the supply and demand side of Brazil's developmentalist project. The explosion of trade between the two countries garnered numerous agreements in space exploration, shipbuilding, aircraft production, gas pipeline construction, agribusiness, deep-sea oil exploration, and railway wagon cars for shipping iron ore.[70] By 2015 China was buying 67 percent of Brazil's soybean exports and importing a third of its iron ore from Brazil, and it had become the biggest consumer of Brazilian oil.

Brazil: Developmentalism as Continuity

As I noted above, in 1990 the share of primary goods in total Brazilian exports was 28 percent, while low- and medium-technology industries together accounted for 39 percent.[71] Brazil was running neck and neck with Mexico on this count, although Brazil's manufacturing growth was endogenous and built up steadily from the 1960s on. Mexico's industrial development has been exogenous in the sense that it relies on FDI in export-processing zones (maquilas), while domestic value-added as a share of exports has averaged 70 percent or less in the 2000s.[72] Brazil, a member of the BRIC (Brazil, Russia, India, and China) coalition of EEs and ranked as the eighth largest GDP in the global economy, has long enjoyed the image of an industrial powerhouse. Yet, as I mentioned previously, Brazil exports just one-fifth of its manufacturing production. Moreover, on indices of trade openness Brazil's economy ranked just 51.0 on a scale of 1–100 (with 100 being completely open) in 2000 versus scores of 85.8 and 70.4 for Chile and Peru, respectively.[73] Whereas Brazil's overall labor productivity had averaged annual growth rates of 4.25 percent from 1950 to 1975, this same indicator averaged just .66 percent from 1990 to 2011.[74]

Prior to Lula's inauguration in 2003, the government had made considerable inroads with macroeconomic stabilization, the currency had been reformed, and the IMF had provided a financial cushion to support the ongoing reform effort. For at least a decade prominent Brazilian economists had been decrying the undercapacity, inefficiency, and low global integration of Brazilian industry. The "renewed developmentalism" of the Lula team was based on a "mixture of market-oriented policies and a new emphasis on industrial competitiveness, the internationalisation of national champions, and a more robust dedication to innovation."[75] The locus of this developmentalist project was BNDES, the only Latin American counterpart to the formidable CDB. In their research on BNDES and the developmentalist thrust under Lula, Kathryn Hochstetler and Alfred Montero analyze the bank's loans in two divisions: industry and infrastructure from 2001 to 2011 and raw materials from 2009 to 2011:

> Energy-related spending was an especially large part of BNDES' loan portfolio from 2002 to 2011. . . . [S]ix of the eight largest loans in our data set were made to produce, generate, or distribute energy, and a seventh was to Transpetro for oil tanker ships. An especially large set of loans went to Petrobras and its subsidiary firms in 2009 to support the development of off-shore oil finds. Beyond the marquee loans to Petrobras and large electricity generation plants, there were hundreds of smaller loans for wind energy generation, ethanol plants and sugarcane plantations, and small hydroelectric plants.[76]

Whereas the main raw materials loans were in the range of US$2.5–5.2 billion each and spread across ten companies (including meatpacking, telecom technologies, and food processing), the industrial and infrastructure loans from 2002 to 2011 were smaller and disbursed across eight main companies that encompassed electrical machinery, civil engineering, electricity production, motor vehicles, sugarcane, food processing, and the manufacture of chemicals. At the height of the GFC in 2009 BNDES disbursed about US$70 billion, which represented half of the domestic banking system.[77] Although given the mandate to export, innovate, and internationalize and provided with plenty of other tax breaks and subsidized inputs to do so, Brazilian industry as a whole has continued to underperform. Rhys Jenkins notes that at its peak in 2005 Brazil carried a trade surplus of US$8 billion in manufactured goods, but by 2012 this had turned into a US$90 billion deficit.[78] About 29 percent of this manufacturing deficit could be attributed to displacement by Chinese manufactured imports. The sectors hit hardest have been leather, electronic products, office equipment, IT, and medical equipment.

Two countervailing forces have worked against Brazilian industry. First is the tight macro-prudent policy framework still in place, which relies on high interest rates to quell inflation.[79] High real rates of interest and capital account liberalization, in turn, have been a magnet for incoming capital flows. This, combined with the accumulation of unprecedented levels of foreign exchange reserves, has made it difficult for Brazil to maintain a competitive exchange rate. The most acute period of overvaluation of the currency, which favors imports over exports, was 2005 to 2012.[80] As I mentioned above, a competitive exchange rate was the lynchpin of the earlier rise of export-led industrialization in developmental states like Japan and Korea. During her first presidential term (2011–15) Dilma Rousseff launched a "New Macroeconomic Matrix," which sought a flexible downward adjustment of the Brazilian real to make it more conducive for exports. However, by this time the China boom was winding down, and Brazil was slipping into the equivalent of the Great Depression of the 1930s.

The second countervailing force is the role that intense demand from China has played in the rise of primary goods as a percent of exports in Brazil, from 28 percent in 1990 to 50 percent in 2014. The country's abundance of iron ore and oil is more strongly reflected in BNDES lending under Lula's new developmentalism than are outlays for industrial restructuring and innovation. The centrifugal pull of Chinese demand and the accompanying price hikes post-2003 superseded the industrial revamp Lula and Rousseff had sought to propel. China's "going out" and its keen interest in modernizing Brazil's infrastructure for its own extractive purposes—the electricity grid, iron ore rail transport, oil infrastructure—simply overwhelmed the Workers' Party vision of a twenty-first-century manufacturing renaissance. Hindsight suggests that the lines between Brazil's old and new developmentalism blurred under the China boom, including the government's protectionist concessions to industry.[81] Brazil has filed more antidumping complaints and restrictive measures against China than any other country, although this has done nothing to halt the manufacturing trade deficit or improve the competitiveness and outward orientation of domestic industry overall.[82]

Argentina: Developmentalism as Heist

The story of Argentina's economic survival and revival during the 2003–13 China boom may be one of the more interesting LAC political economy narratives yet.[83] Having struck out with Beijing in its search for external financing, the Kirchner team was able to secure a loan package of approximately US$10 billion from Venezuela between 2005 and 2008.[84] Additional funds were raised through a more concerted effort at tax collection and the imposition of a unilateral restructuring on about 75 percent of the country's outstanding external debt, which boosted GDP growth by lowering the country's debt service burden from 8 percent to 2 percent of GDP. Following the 2001–2 devaluation of the peso, policy makers were able to maintain a competitive exchange rate up until 2009.[85] This, combined with hefty Chinese demand for Argentine soybeans, prompted the aforementioned windfall in foreign exchange. The reinstatement of export taxes on a range of products in 2002 further fattened the revenue base and set the stage for Kirchner's neodevelopmentalist strategy.

In this respect, the timing on the modernization of Argentine soybean production could not have been more propitious. When the 2001–2 crisis exploded, Argentina had already become the world's third largest exporter of soybeans (after the US and Brazil), capturing 18 percent of the global market. It was, moreover, the top exporter of soy oil and soy meal. Historically, Argentine beef and wheat production had dominated markets for domestic consumption and agribusiness exports. However, heightened global demand for soybeans beginning in the 1980s had prompted a shift away from these traditional products, as powerful transnational commodity traders (Aceitera General Deheza, Bunge, Cargill, and Louis Dreyfus, or ABCD) capitalized on Argentina's natural habitat for soybean crops. Until the departure of Fernández de Kirchner in 2015 soybean exports were taxed at 35 percent and soy oil, soy meal, and biodiesel at 32 percent. Because soybeans are not consumed domestically in Argentina and their production is capital- and technology-intensive, opposition from labor and domestic producers in this sector is for the most part weak. Neal Richardson estimates that "export taxes comprised 8 to 11 percent of the Kirchner government's total tax receipts, and around two-thirds of this—nearly US$2 billion in 2006—came from soy exports."[86]

Argentina's poverty and unemployment rates were dire in 2002. The first prong of Néstor Kirchner's strategy was the expansion of income support programs and the pension system. On top of this was the subsidization of consumption and working-class wages. This included everything from food to energy (electricity, petroleum, and natural gas) to urban transport. The second prong was industrial policy, which included incentives for manufactured exports, selective protection, support for small and medium-sized firms, and efforts to channel cheaper credit to domestic industrial companies.[87] However, as Argentina's industrial policy turned to nonautomatic import licenses and chronic antidumping complaints against Chinese imports beginning in 2005, China exerted its market power.[88] Beijing declared Argentine soy oil to be contaminated with an impure solvent and temporarily halted these imports (estimated at US$2 billion annually) to the mainland in 2010.[89] Although resolved within six months, this disagreement triggered Argentina's first trade deficit with China, which persists to this day.

Soybean prices peaked in the wake of the global financial crisis in 2012 and then began their fall. Camelot under Néstor Kirchner quickly devolved into a new strain of export-backed populism under his spouse and successor, Cristina Fernández de Kirchner, who went to extraordinary lengths to maintain it through her two terms.[90] Under Argentine law the executive is not obligated to share export taxes with the provinces, which left both Kirchners free to channel "discretionary spending" to their core constituents— the urban unemployed and blue-collar workers.[91] Hit with falling commodity prices, the Fernández de Kirchner team also lost sight of the fiscal and monetary policies necessary to control inflation and maintain a competitive exchange rate. From 2009 on, currency appreciation, dwindling central bank reserves, and the increasing resort to financial repression (price controls, domestic currency rationing, and restrictions on capital outflows) became the flip side of the massive subsidization that had started in the throes of the 2001–2 crisis. Some 3 percent of GDP was spent on domestic energy subsidies alone during the two Fernández de Kirchner administrations, which reduced household electricity bills to as low as US$3 per month.

Although sitting on some of the world's largest shale oil and gas reserves, including the discovery of large deposits of shale oil and gas in the Vaca Muerta reserves in 2010, Argentina became an energy importer for the first time in thirty years in 2011. The country's energy import bill in 2012 alone was US$9.2 billion, and by 2014 the energy deficit was US$6.49 billion.[92] On top of the burgeoning of energy subsidies for consumers was the government's erratic policy making with regard to the tendering of energy infrastructure and exploration projects.[93] The Argentine government nationalized the former state oil company (YPF) in 2012, owned by the Spanish firm REPSOL, calling it a victory for "energy sovereignty."[94] Given the price distortions, opaque regulatory framework, and general unpredictability surrounding the Argentine energy sector, only the heavyweight Chinese oil companies have had the stomach to buy in to this environment in the 2010s. China is now the world's top importer of oil, and that demand is growing. As one Chinese colleague recently explained to me, the government message to the CEO's of these huge Chinese oil SOEs is "either go out or get fired." Hence, their willingness to venture into high-risk environments like those of Argentina and Venezuela, places where other foreign investors fear to tread.

There are distinct differences in the economic strategies employed by Brazil and Argentina during the China boom. In Brazil, Lula's new developmentalism had a strong institutional base in BNDES, and the effort to promote company innovation and an outward orientation was transparent and explicit, if not entirely cohesive.[95] The macro prudent economic policy framework worked at cross-purposes and ultimately hampered the quest to promote value-added exports with greater technological intensity. In Argentina, the strategy was based on the Kirchners' coalition of the urban unemployed and underemployed and blue-collar workers as well as the powerful ABCD trading companies, which have passed soybean export taxes on to weakly organized domestic producers.[96] Given the discretionary nature of this spending, developmentalism was whatever the Kirchners said it was. If there was an industrial policy, it was difficult to discern. As for China, Argentina had naively expected south–south solidarity and a lender-of-last-resort relationship that never gelled; with Brazil, China has been an active trade and investment partner since the onset of the China boom. Both countries have had trade conflicts with China, although the China–Argentina relationship has been more acrimonious.

A Twenty-First-Century Resource Curse: Grabber-Friendly Institutions and Politicians

I return here to the recent literature on the institutional resource curse, which has sought to explain varying outcomes between developing countries that are abundant in natural resources. This literature, as noted, has raised two interrelated questions: (1) in what ways might institutional weaknesses condition the effects of natural resource abundance on economic performance? and (2) how might otherwise effective institutions deteriorate under the force of a commodity boom?[97] Thus far I have relied on large time series databases from the World Bank, the World Economic Forum, Transparency International, the Heritage Foundation, and the World Bank's Worldwide Governance Indicators (which are an aggregate of thirty-two individual data sources provided by organizations such as survey institutes, think tanks, NGO's, international organizations, and private sector firms) (see table I.5 and fig. I.I). From these databases I have been able to substantiate broad insights about the nature and pace of institutional reform concerning the six countries in this study. Now I want to be more specific.

A decade ago Alejandro Portes and Lori Smith launched a research project on institutions and development in Latin America, the purpose of which was to move beyond narrow, economistic definitions of institutions as property rights.[98] Funded by the National Science Foundation, the project focused on three country case studies (Chile, Mexico, and Colombia) and devised hypotheses from the seminal literature on institutions and development.[99] Three bureaucratic agencies (the postal service, the stock exchange, and the civil aviation authority) were analyzed in-depth by teams of individual investigators who conducted intensive studies of each institution in each country. Two broad questions framed the process of hypothesis generation: (1) does the agency reflect the original institutional design and values for which it was created? (2) does it make a significant contribution to national development? From there, six specific hypotheses were set forth:

- Meritocratic recruitment and promotion
- Immunity from bribe taking and "capture" by special interests
- Absence of entrenched "islands of power" capable of subverting institutional rules to their own ends
- Proactivity, or the ability of the organization to involve itself with clients, users, and other relevant actors in its institutional environment

- Technological flexibility and openness to external innovation
- Countervailing power, either by the organization itself or its external allies, to prevent control by particularistic interests in the dominant classes[100]

Importantly, this project's findings on Chile and Mexico closely parallel the data trends presented here (see fig. 1.1). That is, Chile readily outscored the other two countries on all six hypotheses, whereas Mexico fell right in the middle or intermediate range of the scale.[101] What about Argentina and Brazil? The Argentine case is included in a follow-up publication by Portes and Smith, which employs the same methodology and hypotheses.[102] The one difference is that along with the three bureaucratic agencies studied intensively in the Chilean and Mexican cases, the Argentine case study incorporates a fourth agency: the National Tax Board. In this later study the Chilean and Mexican cases are replicated, with the addition of the health care system in both case studies. The same results hold for Chile and Mexico, while the Argentine case study similarly parallels the data reflected in both table I.5 and figure 1.1. The authors of the Argentina case study found that "the problems created by patronage practices in these institutions are common knowledge, as is the fact that eminently meritocratic and proactive organizations like the Argentine flagship airline Aerolíneas Argentinas were destroyed by military dictatorships and by neoliberalism. As a result, the new millennium has found the country with a dearth of solid, proactive institutions."[103]

Unfortunately, the Brazilian case is not included in the Portes and Smith project or database. Another, more recent project titled *States in the Developing World*, undertaken by Miguel Centeno and his colleagues, does tackle the Brazilian case study, with findings that are decidedly rosier than those reflected in table I.5 and figure 1.1 in this book.[104] Like Portes and Smith, the authors of the Brazilian case study—Katherine Bersch, Sérgio Praça, and Matthew M. Taylor—compare agencies within the state, specifically within the Brazilian federal bureaucracy.[105] They rightly critique an approach like my own for failing to detect important nuances; these authors articulate very specific measures with regard to two main variables, bureaucratic capacity and political autonomy. The departure point for Bersch et al.

is "the Weberian legal-rational state: a professional bureaucracy able to implement policy without undue external influence. . . . 'Professional' means the degree to which public servants specialize in a specific field. . . . The 'ability to implement policy' refers to the degree to which human resources are available and adequately remunerated. . . . 'Freedom from external influence' refers to freedom from particularistic pressures."[106]

Rather than focusing intensively on three or four select agencies within the bureaucracy, as the Portes and Smith project does, Bersch et al. gather public data on some 1.1 million federal employees and civil servants working within the Brazilian bureaucracy at the federal level. Bureaucratic capacity is measured by such variables as career strength, specialization, longevity, and remuneration, while political autonomy measures the politicization of appointments and partisan affiliation of nonappointed civil servants within each agency. With this sophisticated, mixed-methods approach, the authors find high capacity and autonomy within the usual suspects—the central bank, finance ministry, and foreign policy apparatus—but they also singled out an additional twenty-six federal-level agencies within this quadrant (including communications and the federal police) as ranking high on both capacity and autonomy. They also identified a number of well-functioning agencies that have high capacity but low autonomy and found that infrastructure agencies, on average, performed poorly on both measures. Celio Hiratuka confirms this last point on Brazilian infrastructure, which as a percent of GDP "falls well below other developing countries such as China and India . . . and even below the average of Latin America."[107]

Overall, the methodological design, research strategy, and databases compiled in these two institutional research projects—Portes and Smith as well as Centeno et al.—are dazzling. Together, they launch a completely new approach for future generations of scholars looking to make more accurate and fine-grained assessments of the role of institutions in the development process. From the Portes and Smith project, I stand vindicated on my institutional assessments of Argentina, Chile, and Mexico; but I also stand corrected by the more well-founded findings of Bersch et al. on the resilience and staying power of Brazilian state institutions. There is still more to say on how institutions fared in Argentina and Brazil during the China boom. The first question posed above—in what ways might institutional weaknesses condition the effects of natural resource abundance on economic performance?—applies directly to Argentina, whereas the second question— how might otherwise effective institutions deteriorate under the force of a commodity boom?—is apropos to Brazil.[108] In short, during the China boom both suffered an institutional resource curse of sorts.

In the case of Argentina it is indisputable that already weak institutions worsened further under the two administrations of Cristina Fernández de Kirchner. In this case, remarkably, it was the office of the executive that was the "grabber-friendly" institution during the China boom. Both the Central Bank of Argentina (BCRA) and the National Statistics and Census Institute (INDEC) were fair game for an executive that became increasingly desperate to fabricate favorable growth and low inflation rates and access funds for the massive subsidies needed to hold her support base together. In the case of Brazil, Petrobras, the national oil company (where the government owns 63.6 percent of voting shares and has an overall stake in the company of 47.6 percent), became the locus of a feeding frenzy on the part of Brazilian elites (politicians, policy makers, and private actors).[109] The graft, corruption, and outright theft from the coffers of Petrobras cost the company and the country the investment-grade rating that had been so hard-won since the launching of Brazil's economic reforms in the mid-1990s. The findings of Bersch et al. suggest that there is still ample institutional cohesion and integrity within the Brazilian state sector to overcome this debacle. The quote above on the gutting of Aerolíneas Argentinas and on the weaknesses of Argentina's institutional makeup is much less sanguine.

Argentina and the China Boom: Further Institutional Weakening

At the beginning of the twentieth century Argentina was the seventh largest economy in the world—a position Brazil, ironically, nearly occupies today. There is a broad consensus that widespread institutional decline and the erosion of economic / financial institutions in particular have been the dominant force in the country's downward mobility.[110] In *Why Nations Fail* Daron Acemoglu and James Robinson distinguish between countries that have cultivated institutions of investment and social inclusion versus those in which the institutional ethos that has evolved over time is one of extraction and social exclusion. These authors, interestingly, situate Brazil in the first category and Argentina in the second. They argue that prior to 1914 "Argentina experienced around fifty years of economic growth, but this was a classic case of growth under extractive institutions. . . . [I]t was not sustainable. . . . [T]he government is quite able to override property rights and expropriate its own citizens with impunity."[111] This quote sizes up the most recent spree of extraction under the two Kirchner presidencies, as soybean rents and proceeds from the nationalization of the country's pension system became the crucial glue for holding together a fragile, transient coalition. When this "model" collapsed, these same constituents bore the brunt of adjustment.

The massive subsidies and wage hikes from 2003 to 2013 placed a huge burden on the government's fiscal accounts, which, in turn, reignited inflation and macroeconomic instability. Rapidly escalating expenditures also fueled a constant demand for new revenues to cover them, and this was especially tricky given the country's international economic isolation. During the final year of his term Néstor Kirchner found a solution: direct executive intervention in INDEC. Remarkably, in 2007 the president fired a highly qualified statistician in charge of the consumer price division and replaced her with an economist who had little background in statistics. I quoted earlier the authors of the Argentine case study in the Portes and Smith project on institutions and development, who lamented the government's destructive interference in the country's once-sound flagship airline.[112] This suggests that some Argentine institutions are (or have been) less weak than others, and since the 1990s INDEC has stood out as one of the more integral and professional state entities. Its weakness, unfortunately, was revealed by the ease with which the executive was able to stampede through it.

From 2007 all the way up through Fernández de Kirchner's departure in December 2015 INDEC was coerced into reporting inflation data by the government's own method wherein goods with controlled prices were given a greater weight.[113] Protests from personnel within INDEC and within the Argentine congress led to the passage of a Senate bill that compelled Fernández de Kirchner's team to design a more accurate inflation index and restore INDEC's credibility. In 2011, however, the government levied stiff fines on three top Argentine economic consulting firms that estimated inflation at 25 percent annually, which contradicted the government's insistence that inflation was running at 10 percent per year.[114] The flaws of the new consumer price index prompted the IMF to begin formal censure proceedings for the first time ever, declaring that the manipulation of national statistics by the government was a breach of its articles of agreement with the fund.[115] It was left to President Mauricio Macri to clean up the mess within INDEC, which he set about doing.

One of the fiercest critics of Fernández de Kirchner's reckless economic policies was Martín Redrado, the president of the BCRA from 2004 to 2010. Like INDEC, BCRA was a bastion of competence and professionalism within a sea of otherwise weak government entities. In 2010, with inflation and consumer subsidies running amok, Fernández de Kirchner launched a new "Bicentennial Fund for Stability and Reduced Indebtedness" that she sought to finance with some US$6.57 billion in foreign reserves held by BCRA.[116] The idea, ostensibly, was to pay down the country's US$16 billion in debt obligations that were coming due for 2010 alone and to begin mending ties with the international financial community. However, Redrado denied the request because it would exacerbate inflation, and this violated the central bank's nominal independence. At the same time, the congress, with a newly installed opposition majority, objected to Fernández de Kirchner's request. It claimed that the legislature, not the executive, had the final say over the use of Argentina's approximately US$48 billion in foreign reserves (as of 2010). Not one to be easily deterred, the president issued an emergency decree that dismissed Redrado as the head of BCRA.

Although the courts immediately intervened with a ruling that reinstated Redrado as BCRA president and prohibited the executive from using reserves to pay down national debt, Redrado resigned shortly thereafter.[117] His replacement was a much less qualified ally of Fernández de Kirchner who further politicized the central bank, ran down reserves, and made no progress in getting Argentina back into the good graces of international capital markets. In fact, in 2014 the country suffered its second bond default within the new century. As in the case of INDEC, it was up to the incoming Macri team to restore integrity and economic rationale within the BCRA. Steven Levitsky and Maria Victoria Murillo write about this process as one in which institutions must continually be rebuilt on weak foundations.[118] While they refer largely to this challenge in the political realm, their argument holds for Argentina's economic institutions, where cyclical routings of the kind just described have become part of the narrative on the country's long-running decline.

Brazil and the China Boom: Erosion of Institutional Strength

The empirical research by Katherine Bersch and her colleagues makes a powerful argument for the resilience and integrity of nearly thirty Brazilian institutions operating at the federal level of government. This finding is echoed in the comprehensive case study of BNDES conducted by Kathryn Hochstetler and Alfred Montero. In addition, although based on skimpy evidence, Daron Acemoglu and James Robinson declare Brazil to be a country with inclusive economic and political institutions. They attribute this inclusiveness largely to the rise of the Workers' Party and the broad grassroots coalition it began building in the 1970s:

> Leaders such as Lula, along with the many intellectuals and opposition politicians who lent support to the party, sought to make it into a broad coalition. These impulses began to fuse with local social movements all over the country, as the party took over local governments . . . causing a sort of revolution of governance through the country. . . . More important, empowerment at the grass-roots level in Brazil ensured that the transition to democracy corresponded to a move toward inclusive political institutions . . . and the emergence of a government committed to the provision of public services, educational expansion, and a truly level playing field.[119]

Alas, Brazil's mass of *favela* (slum) dwellers, many of whom live on US$2.50 a day or less, may beg to differ with this rosy assessment. And Lula himself has been sent to prison for twelve years due to his role in Operation Car Wash, the massive corruption scheme that siphoned billions of dollars off of the books at Petrobras. Yet Acemoglu and Robinson are not entirely off base in their analysis of the Workers' Party. After all, this party pushed hard for an independent judiciary and attorney general, greater transparency and accountability, and the end of impunity for wealthy elites. Workers' Party leaders just never expected that their own infractions would be caught up in the snares of these new legal and political reforms. Facing mass anticorruption demonstrations in 2013, even prior to the eruption of

Car Wash, Rousseff instituted plea bargaining for the first time in Brazil. Prosecutors could now make deals with indicted and convicted crooks and reduce their jail time in exchange for information that resulted in the arrest of bigger criminals.[120] Thanks to all of these earlier legal reforms, Car Wash unraveled through a cascade of plea bargaining. It was, moreover, the country's "clean slate" law of 2010 that prompted the courts to ban an imprisoned Lula from running for a third presidential term in 2018.

Created in 1953 with a capital ownership structure of 51 percent public and 49 percent private, Petrobras was from the start envisioned as a state enterprise that would strive for private sector efficiency.[121] Due to the lack of significant reserve discoveries in Brazil, Petrobras gradually came to play two main roles: (1) the import and processing of crude oil from abroad, which added value to domestic consumption and exports; and (2) beginning in the 1970s the company carved out a niche for offshore exploration and drilling in Brazil and expanded its operations outside of the country. Together, these two strategies fostered the development of a capital goods industry in the Brazilian oil sector that generated skilled jobs and a push for technological innovation in offshore drilling. It took fifty-four years, but Petrobras finally struck black gold in 2007 with the discovery of some 20 to 110 billion barrels of oil in deepwater pre-salt reserves off the country's coast.[122] In 2010 Petrobras raised US$70 billion in the midst of booming oil prices, one of the biggest share sales in LAC history; by 2011 it was ranked as the eighth largest company in the global economy and the third largest energy company in the world.

In their enthusiasm, the two Workers' Party administrations under Lula and Rousseff together earmarked government funding for oil and energy infrastructure projects amounting to around US$826 billion between 2007 and 2014.[123] Petrobras was a main interlocutor in the disbursement of these funds. In order for the party to move its legislative package through an inchoate congress, it struck a deal with the long-standing and patently corrupt Brazilian Democratic Movement Party (PMDB), led by the interim president Michel Temer (2016–18). Notably, Temer's PMDB was given control of the international division of Petrobras, including the flow of funds channeled through that department. This was just one of many pockets of corruption within Petrobras. At the heart of the scandal was a pattern by which the company's executives were deliberately overpaying large, powerful contractors for the construction of refineries, exploration vessels, and drilling rigs. A main protagonist in this scheme was the powerful Odebrecht construction conglomerate, a multinational firm with its home base in Brazil. Odebrecht contractors forged clandestine agreements with Petrobras executives "to ensure they were guaranteed business on excessively lucrative terms if they agreed to channel a share of between 1% and 5% of every deal into secret slush funds."[124]

Plea bargain testimonies indicated that most of these corruption trails led back to Lula and the Workers' Party. At least US$5 billion was syphoned off Petrobras by its in-house executives, political parties, and individual politicians, by the contracting companies, and numerous other operatives involved in money laundering, transfers to Swiss bank accounts, and payment of nonmonetary bribes (luxury cars, yachts, high-priced works of art, pricy bottles of wine, etc.). With the inauguration of President Rousseff on the Workers' Party ticket in early 2011, Temer became the vice president of Brazil. Despite numerous allegations of his involvement in Car Wash, prosecutors were not able to build a solid case until after his term ended. Temer was convicted for the violation of electoral rules in 2016 and barred from running for office until 2024. However, by teaming up with his fellow criminal and the former speaker of Brazil's Chamber of Deputies, Eduardo Cunha, in maneuvering the impeachment of Rousseff for budgeting irregularities in 2016, Temer survived two congressional votes on whether he should face a criminal trial for other corruption charges while acting as interim president. Subsequent wiretapping of Temer and his cabinet revealed that Rousseff was actually impeached because she refused to call off the Car Wash investigation.[125]

Brazil is certainly no stranger to corruption. Yet the costs of the Car Wash scandal have been astronomical. Petrobras accounts for roughly 10 percent of Brazil's GDP and thus weighed heavily on the prolonged economic slowdown. The company had been weakened by Rousseff's policy of freezing domestic energy prices and subsidizing energy costs for consumers. The hit from plunging oil prices in 2014 was exacerbated by the need for Petrobras to write off US$17 billion in graft and overvalued assets a year later, rendering it the world's most indebted major oil company.[126] Again, both the company and the country have been stripped of their hard-earned investment grade ratings.[127] There is an institutional silver lining in that plea bargaining agreements have implicated more than eighteen hundred dirty politicians from over two dozen political parties in Brazil. Moreover, big mafiosos like Eduardo Cunha, Sergio Cabral (the former governor of the State of Rio de Janeiro), and Marcelo Odebrecht (the former head of the mammoth construction company that bears his name) are all in jail. Perhaps more than any other economic event within the EEs, the sudden shocking fall of Petrobras and with it the administration of Dilma Rousseff clearly signaled both the end of the China boom and the ills of the institutional resource curse.

What are we to make of these incredible stories of institutional theft (Petrobras), bashing (INDEC), and intrusion (BCRA)? In earlier times this material would have easily fit into the work of famous magical realist novelists from both countries, for example, Brazil's Jorge Amado and Argentina's Julio Cortázar. As a literary genre, magical realism is characterized by the inclusion of fantastic or mythical elements into seemingly realistic narratives. However, Argentina's grandiose hydroelectric projects built next to pristine Patagonian reserves, Brazil's grotesquely inflated energy construction contracts and the chain of bribery extending all the way to luxury cars, Rolex watches, and yachts—not to mention the massive fuel subsidies and wage hikes in both countries—are not phantoms. These and all of the other gimmicks I have written about in this chapter are real. They are especially real to the people of both countries who have lived with negative growth rates, high unemployment, and substantial losses at the level of per capita income since 2014 (see table 1.1).

I conclude with three insights concerning the China boom and the onset of the institutional resource curse in Argentina and Brazil. First, at the outset of this chapter I argued that the China boom was a necessary condition for the buoyant growth rates registered by each country from 2003 to 2013. My analysis also suggests that institutional incursions of the magnitude witnessed here were the flip side of the huge foreign exchange bonanza that suddenly accrued in state coffers. The uncanny timing of each country's high-tech soybean revolution with the spiking up of Chinese demand plus the major oil and gas discoveries (Brazil's offshore pre-salt reserves in 2007 and Argentina's Vaca Muerta shale oil and gas finds in 2010) that soon followed created a sense of financial invincibility that commodity lotteries tend to instill. During a fieldwork interview in Rio de Janeiro with a highly respected Brazilian economist in 2011, I asked about the possible longevity of the commodity boom. The answer I received: "Our horizon is now infinite."

Second, when comparing macroeconomic outcomes (see table 1.1) with institutional performance (see fig. 1.1) we have seen that the small open economies of Chile, Costa Rica, and, secondarily, Peru had advanced considerably on important institutional reforms prior to the boom, had stellar macroeconomic performance during the boom, and managed to avoid reform backsliding. In contrast, these same data show that in the period prior to 2003 neither Argentina nor Brazil had advanced sufficiently on the kinds of reforms that are essential to spur productivity and sustainable growth. Both, in fact, were just emerging from major financial crises when the boom struck. Argentina and Brazil were thus slower reformers, and there was indeed backsliding (Argentina) and stagnation (Brazil) on institutional reforms during the boom. The end of the boom, moreover, cannot entirely explain the very low funk that befell Argentina and Brazil. One reason is that commodity prices are still well above their preboom levels. In 2018, for example, soybeans were trading at about 30 percent above their 2000 base level; iron ore prices were nearly double their 2000 level in 2018; and, after plummeting from its \$95 / barrel peak in 2013, oil was holding in the range of about \$60 / barrel in 2018.

Finally, as I have argued throughout this chapter, answers to the dismal performance of Argentina and Brazil post-2013 can be found in the institutional milieu of both countries over the course of the China boom. The rise of China in both countries has had a paradoxical effect: it has quickly upped the ante and underlined the dire need for measures to promote efficiency and competitiveness, while also providing sufficient trade demand and capital inflows for both to gut key domestic economic institutions. The emergence of a new and compelling literature on institutions and development in Latin America tells us that Argentina's institutional neglect is the more egregious of the two cases, as do the aggregate data I have presented throughout this book.[128] In the case of Argentina, it is simply unimaginable that the executive office in other LAC EEs, for example, Brazil and Mexico, would dismiss a central bank president and proceed to run down the country's reserves.[129] Neither would the business sector in these other two LAC EEs stand for export taxes of the magnitude leveraged on Argentine commodity producers.[130]

At least on the institutional front, sanity partially prevailed in Argentina in December 2015 with the election of the center-right candidate and former mayor of Buenos Aires Mauricio Macri. Although Macri and his team failed to quell inflation, reactivate the economy, and restore jobs, they were able to reverse the worst of the damage done to INDEC and BCRA. Inflation stabilization was taken seriously, and international political and financial relations were repaired.[131] Unfortunately, the approximately US$16.5 billion in loans Macri managed to raise on international capital markets went toward debt repayment, not productive investment. Argentina's return to the IMF in mid-2018 and its signing on to another round of tired austerity measures suggests it is on the Greek route, where a decade-long effort at cutting one's way to growth has been an utter failure. The country's propensity thus far to accept Chinese project financing with high Chinese content (e.g., materials, engineering, and construction) and, to a lesser extent labor, is not going to do much to alleviate these economic woes. Then again, Argentina is not Greece, where EU rules and Eurozone membership have tied policy makers' hands and limited their macroeconomic options for exiting a long recession. Argentina's much richer factor endowments suggest it has the makings of a sound recovery, but domestic institutions and politics are still the worst enemies of reform.

As for Brazil, the aforementioned literature argues convincingly that the country's institutional vitality is intact, at least at the level of the federal government, including BNDES. Petrobras is slowly coming back from the depths to which it sank in 2014–15. The fact that the company is listed on the New York Stock Exchange means it is still subject to investigations from the US Department of Justice and the US Securities and Exchange Commission. Moreover, a number of individual investor lawsuits are still outstanding.[132] Investor pressures could well result in a reduction of the company's share of new discoveries from 30 percent to zero. Although the

Brazilian congress is making some weak-kneed efforts to reform itself, this does not include the lifting of immunity for the sizeable number of sitting politicians that should be in jail for crimes related to the Car Wash scandal.[133] The irony that an independent, committed judiciary emerged from the Workers' Party's earlier reforms is not lost on prosecutors, who are fighting a continual battle to bring the culprits to justice.[134] It will be difficult to take a Brazilian economic comeback seriously until sitting politicians have been served their due justice.

6

Ratcheting Down the Industrial Ladder in Mexico

Some foreigners with full bellies and nothing better to do engage in finger-pointing at us. . . . First, China does not export revolution; second, it does not export famine and poverty; and third, it does not mess around with you. So what else is there to say?

Xi Jinping, *Wall Street Journal*, October 19, 2010[1]

SINCE GAINING ITS INDEPENDENCE from Spain in 1821, Mexico was most at odds with the US due to the latter's imperialistic stance and chronic interference. As the Mexican historian Enrique Krauze has written, "The first and most serious offense was of course the American invasion of Mexico in 1846 and the subsequent Mexican–American War, which resulted in Mexico losing more than half of its territory."[2] However, nearly 150 years down the line, the US–Mexico relationship had matured, as reflected in the implementation of the North American Free Trade Agreement (NAFTA) between Canada, Mexico and the US in 1994. At the turn of the new millennium it was China that had become more problematic for Mexico, as reflected in the acerbic comments made by Xi Jinping (quoted in the epigraph above) while visiting the country prior to assuming the Chinese presidency in March 2013. Until the mid-1990s the two countries had enjoyed a cordial bilateral relationship on issues ranging from academic exchanges to science and technology collaboration. Unfortunately, for reasons I elaborate on here, this earlier goodwill has all but eroded.[3]

More immediately, with the Republican clean sweep in the November 2016 US elections, the US–Mexico relationship also took a new and unexpected nosedive. The presidential candidate Donald Trump won over the hard-hit US rust belt by laying blame for factory closings and lost jobs almost entirely at the feet of NAFTA. Remarkably, with little hard data and even less serious analysis or debate, Trump's rallying cry was to renegotiate NAFTA and strike a "better deal" for the US.[4] In the same essay quoted above, Krause continues: "The victory of Mr. Trump has changed all the rules. With Mexico, a new period of confrontation has arisen, not military but surely commercial, diplomatic, strategic, social and ethnic. Trump is essentially calling for a confrontation between the countries."[5] Thus in the run-up to its own presidential election in 2018 Mexico found itself wedged quite uncomfortably between the two largest and most powerful players in the global economy.

Mexico's dilemma stands in stark contrast to the other country case studies analyzed above. We've seen that Chile, Costa Rica, and Peru have institutionalized their respective relationships with China through the negotiation of separate bilateral free trade agreements (FTAs) with the US, on the one hand, and with China on the other hand. The stringency of the US FTA for each country falls mainly in the realm of the World Trade Organization's (WTO) new trade agenda (services, investment, and intellectual property rights, or IPRs); each country's FTA with China includes coverage of some of these issues while also loosening constraints in the agricultural and manufacturing sectors. For Peru and Chile, in particular, exceptions allowed by China in terms of access to each country's domestic manufacturing sector have been offset by massive mineral and agricultural sales to the Chinese market. Strikingly, all three of these small players have locked in access to the two largest markets in the global economy and are set to ride out the benefits.

Argentina and Brazil likewise have been more successful than Mexico when it comes to managing their bilateral relationship with China. Periodic trade spats and antidumping complaints aside, both countries have gained immensely from their complementary endowment factors vis-à-vis China. For both, China is now the top export destination. Like many marriages, it is far from perfect, but trade and investment integration will continue to bind both countries to China—for better or for worse. The remnants of the institutional resource curse Argentina and Brazil suffered in different ways during the height of the China boom from 2003 to 2013 are now the headache of new administrations in each country. In both cases policy makers must reverse the institutional decay that set in during the China boom and credibly strengthen basic norms around rule of law, regulatory quality, and control of corruption (see table I.5). This institutional backsliding is not inherent to either country's relationship with China. Rather, these weaknesses are an offshoot of long-standing institutional neglect and policy missteps that are endogenous to both countries.

Where does this leave Mexico, which has neither the complementary factor endowments enjoyed by Argentina and Brazil nor the institutionalized relationship with China that Chile, Costa Rica, and Peru have built up over time? In this chapter I begin by analyzing Mexico's own reform trajectory and the process by which NAFTA was embraced by domestic elites in the early 1990s as a way to lock in neoliberal policies at the outset of the reform process. While subtle at first, the other side of Mexico's trade liberalization and deeper integration with the US was its heightened vulnerability to China's massive export drive. Second, I trace the effect of China's WTO entry on the Mexican economy, as well as the latter's success in extracting hefty protectionist side payments from China as a condition for Mexico's vote for the former's WTO accession. Third, I explore other aspects of the China-Mexico relationship in the 2000s, including the ways in which China's rapid economic rise in the Western Hemisphere dampened the expected gains from NAFTA and exacerbated tensions between Mexico and the US. Certainly nothing could have prepared Mexico, a middling economic actor at best, for the woes it has faced from the administrations of Trump in the US and Xi in China.

Two conceptual themes underpin this analysis. First, in my effort to explain the contradictions and subpar outcomes of Mexico's neoliberal-industrial development strategy I return to Ha-Joon Chang's work *Kicking Away the Ladder: Development Strategy in Historical Perspective*.[6] The critical window for Mexico is the period between 1986 and 1994, which included the country's accession to the General Agreement on Tariffs and Trade (GATT) in 1986, its jettisoning of industrial promotion polices in the early 1990s, and the implementation of NAFTA in 1994. As Chang would put it, Mexico literally kicked away the ladder of state guidance for industrial promotion, reducing such tools as public credit, tax breaks, trade tariffs, and so on. However, just as Mexican policy makers were preaching the merits of economic liberalism, China was ramping up on these very policies of state-led industrial promotion. At the same time, China undertook a cluster of reforms that both modernized its macro- and microeconomic policy approaches and prepared the country for accession to the WTO in 2001.[7] China's unbridled success as a manufacturing exporter spawned the need for an internationalized development strategy, the second theme that runs through this chapter.

Throughout I have argued that China has of necessity internationalized its development strategy in order to compensate for its serious natural resource deficit and to feed the world's largest domestic population. For the handful of Latin American countries (LAC) with rich natural resource endowments (Argentina, Brazil, Chile, and Peru), Chinese demand has generated massive revenues and sizeable Chinese loans and direct investment in resource-related infrastructure and transportation networks. LAC, as a middle-income developing region, has provided buoyant demand for China's finished consumer goods and its intermediate inputs for manufacturing. Again, Mexico is the odd one out, as its incorporation into China's internationalized development strategy has mainly been on the import side. This is evident in the massive trade deficit Mexico has accrued with China over the past twenty-five years. The adversarial nature of the China–Mexico relationship drives home the risks of a hands-off industrial development strategy for the latter. It also raises concerns about Mexico's future growth prospects, despite the belated launching of major economic reforms in 2012–14.

NAFTA as a Development Strategy for Mexico: Reform Lock-In or Straightjacket?

Prelude to NAFTA

The Mexican case raises any number of tempting counterfactuals. What if, for example, political leaders and policy makers had been able to resist excessive external borrowing in the 1970s and maintain the country's impressive industrialization program and growth momentum? What if the authorities had opted for GATT entry in 1979–80, when more favorable returns were offered from Geneva, including the option for a more gradual trade opening? What if former president Carlos Salinas de Gortari (1988–94) had stuck with his original declaration that a NAFTA-style arrangement was not feasible and in fact contrary to Mexico's short- and medium-term interests?[8] What if policy makers had streamlined and sharpened industrial policy tools in the earlier 1990s and not deep-sixed them altogether? Alas, as warning signs went unheeded and more promising routes were not taken, Mexico lost the economic dynamism that had carried it through the postwar era up to through the 1970s. However, the low growth and paltry per capita gains that have persisted since the early 1980s were far from predetermined. These policy failures have been self-inflicted.

In just one decade, from 1982 to 1992, Mexico went from being virtually bankrupt to completing the negotiations for NAFTA entry. The country's "golden age of industrialization" had long faded, as the 1982 debt shocks pulled the rug out from under the last vestiges of the import-substitution-industrialization strategy.[9] In addition, as inflation surged, the country's long-touted stabilizing development model had been exhausted. Like most debt-saddled countries in the region Mexico was compelled to turn to the International Monetary Fund (IMF) for policy advice and financial assistance. While the traditional apparatchiks in the long-standing Revolutionary Institutional Party (PRI) had always bristled at the fund's neoliberal policy prescriptions, a rift emerged within the ruling party between the old guard and a new generation of more highly educated technocrats who were rising in the party ranks. In the 1970s the administration of Luis Echeverría had created the National Council of Science and Technology (CONACYT), which began funding scholarships for study abroad. The first generation to benefit from mainly US university training began entering the halls of government in the 1980s, a time when the ruling party and the state were still one and the same.

At the outset of the 1982 crisis Mexico's average weighted tariff was 100 percent, public spending had spun out of control, and the government had nationalized the banks in an effort to halt the massive flight of capital from the country. While it hardly required an Ivy League graduate degree to grasp the depths to which the Mexican economy had sunk, this new generation had its own ideas about the need to carry out deep economic and institutional reforms. Most came with neoclassical economic training and a strong conviction about the merit of markets over state intervention. As Nora Hamilton observes:

> In the Salinas administration [1988–94], Salinas himself had received an M.A. in Public Administration, and an M.A. and a Ph.D. in Economics at Harvard; Pedro Aspe, Secretary of Finance, had a Ph.D. from MIT; Emilio Lozoya, Secretary of Energy and Mines, received a degree in Public Administration at Harvard; Ernesto Zedillo, Secretary of Education (and later president), had a Ph.D. from Yale, as did Jaime Serra Puche, Secretary of Commerce and chief NAFTA negotiator. Educated in the same universities as their U.S. counterparts, they shared a free market, internationalist approach to economics.[10]

The three pillars of the Washington Consensus (WC), liberalization, privatization, and deregulation, were quickly adopted post-1988. By 1992 the trade and capital accounts, including the Mexican stock market, had been liberalized, state-owned enterprises had been sold off, and the banking system was largely reprivatized. Key government ministries had been overhauled, fiscal and monetary accounts had been tightened, the country's US$48 billion external debt had been restructured and service payments reduced under the 1989 Brady Plan. With the modernization of the Mexican stock exchange and the issuing of new bonds backed by the US Treasury (Brady Bonds) as part of the external debt restructuring, portfolio investment poured into Mexico. Yet most of this capital was highly mobile (stocks and bonds); inflows of FDI increased by around 57 percent from 1989 to 1993, while hot portfolio capital inflows to Mexico jumped 8,000 percent during this same time.[11] The peso, which was anchored tightly to the US dollar in 1987, rapidly appreciated under the thrust of these massive capital inflows.

The sophisticated academic credentials that had accumulated within the Salinas team meant that no one within that inner circle could have possibly deemed this toxic economic scenario to be sustainable. Growth averaged

2.8 percent annually under the Salinas *sexenio,* but this was hardly transformative. Why not devalue the currency and push off with an assertive Asian-style export-led growth strategy? Instead, with the end of the Cold War in 1989, the pending economic liberalization of the former Soviet bloc, and the failure of significant amounts of direct private investment—both international and domestic—to materialize, policy makers moved in the opposite direction. Despite decades of mutual suspicion and diplomatic acrimony between Mexico and the US, Salinas buried the hatchet and aggressively pursued the negotiation of NAFTA as a way to signal the durability of the country's newly minted market reforms.

NAFTA was a game changer in numerous respects. For the very first time the US had agreed to negotiate an FTA that included a developing country. Moreover, with just three countries at the negotiating table, NAFTA broke through the impasse on liberalizing trade-related services and investment that had slowed multilateral negotiations at the Uruguay Round (1986–94). It covered agriculture and IPRs, created its own dispute settlement mechanisms for trade and investment, and, in two separate side agreements, paid lip service to labor rights and environmental protection. The sheer size and promise of NAFTA prompted reticent GATT members to return to Geneva and finalize the Uruguay Round agreement in 1994, including the creation of the WTO the following year. This was arguably the defining foreign economic policy triumph of Bill Clinton's presidency (1992–2000). The same could have been said about Salinas, at least until the bottom dropped out of the Mexican economy less than a year into NAFTA. The bubble burst with the December 1994 peso crash, the collapse of the domestic banking system, and revelations of graft, money laundering, and the billions stowed by some of NAFTA's "winners" in offshore bank accounts. Salinas himself sought exile in Ireland.

NAFTA in Principle

NAFTA's proponents grounded the agreement in the tenets of economic integration theory,[12] arguing that the rapid liberalization of trade and investment would unleash market forces and propel Mexico into the ranks of the developed world.[13] First, it was held that the elimination of barriers at the border would promote scale economies related to greater specialization, increased technological capabilities, and a more efficient deployment of those factors for which Mexico has a comparative advantage. Second, it was argued that the merging of Mexico's abundant factors (relatively cheap labor and natural resource inputs) with the capital, technology, and expertise the US brought to the table would trigger a dynamic pattern of economic convergence among the three members.

In a nutshell, the NAFTA accord, along with the side agreements on labor standards and environmental protection, promoted the free flow of goods, investment, and services within the North American bloc over a fifteen-year time period that ended in 2009. In line with WTO rules, most barriers came down in the first ten years of the agreement. Tariffs and nontariff barriers were eliminated on 65 percent of North American goods by the five-year point; tariff reductions on automobiles occurred over a ten-year period, with the rules-of-origin stipulation that such vehicles must meet a 62.5 percent local content requirement in order to qualify.[14] In the agricultural sector, sensitive products were put on a fifteen-year liberalization schedule that ended in 2009.

As for the liberalization of investment and trade in services, NAFTA adopted the principle of national treatment for member countries, removed performance requirements, and created dispute settlement mechanisms to arbitrate investment conflicts. The latter reflects the extent to which NAFTA was as much about the promotion of investment flows in North America as it was about spurring free trade. However, NAFTA still fell short of its mandate to liberalize substantially all trade between the three partners. First, administered protection persists in the setting of hefty percentages for local content under NAFTA's rules of origin in such sectors as autos, high-tech products, and textiles and apparel. Second, as in the case of the 1988 Canada–US agreement that preceded NAFTA, little progress was made toward the elimination of antidumping policies and countervailing duties— which have been all too prevalent. Although the very point of entering into an agreement like NAFTA is to institutionalize the rules and norms that govern economic exchange among the partner countries and deter the frivolous resort to such trade remedies, US domestic lobbies in particular insisted on maintaining antidumping remedies in the agreement.

NAFTA in Practice

NAFTA's critics have arguably done a better job of advertising its failures than its proponents have done in touting the gains that have underpinned North American integration since the early 1990s. At the aggregate level it would be difficult to paint NAFTA as anything but a mild success, at least when judged according to its own goals: the creation of a free trade area in which all three partners have pursued an economic growth strategy via the liberalization of goods, capital, and services among themselves. Since NAFTA's implementation, regional trade increased from roughly US$290 billion to more than US$1.1 trillion in 2016, and US inflows of FDI to Mexico similarly surged from US$15 billion to well over US$100 billion today.[15] Some of the negative hype surrounding NAFTA has to do with the lofty promises made by political leaders versus the impacts of these trade and investment figures at the aggregate level.

The wage, distributional, and labor market effects of NAFTA are tricky to measure, given all the other variables at play. With regard to the US–Mexico relationship in particular, I side with Gary Hufbauer and his colleagues at the Peterson Institute for International Economics in Washington, DC, who argue, "Since the Mexican economy is less than one-tenth of the US economy, it is not plausible that trade integration could dramatically shape the giant US economy, even though trade integration could exert a substantial impact on the relatively small Mexican economy."[16] It was the opposite message that helped Trump win the presidency, even if the hard evidence points to technological adaptation and the China trade shock as the more likely culprits for job losses in the US.[17] Rising US trade with Mexico can explain only "about 5 percent of the job churn" in the US market.[18] Nevertheless, this did not stop team Trump from demanding the negotiation of a new US–Mexico–Canada Agreement (USMCA), "the first free trade agreement negotiated by the United States that raises rather than lowers barriers to trade and investment."[19] Finalized by all three countries in late 2018, USMCA must first gain the approval of the US Congress.

To be clear, NAFTA has been completely implemented for nearly a decade. It could certainly use some updating and revision to address continuing bottlenecks, including the lack of an explicit and shared competition policy in North America as well as the long wait at the border for truck shipments heading north to the US. Perhaps the more glaring failure of North American integration has been Mexico's lackluster growth, averaging just 2.5 percent annually in the NAFTA era. As the least developed of the three NAFTA members, Mexico was expected to suffer the largest adjustment costs but also realize the biggest gains. This enthusiast projection spilled over to the OECD, which granted Mexico entry in May 1994. Again, according to NAFTA's largely neoclassical trade narrative, Mexico would readily advance up the industrial and technological learning curve, substantially increase its annual growth of per capita and aggregate income, and more authentically approximate the macro- and microeconomic indicators of the OECD bloc.

In chapters 1 and 3 we saw just how far from the truth these suppositions turned out to be. Mexico rashly kicked away its own ladder of state guidance for industry and technology development, ostensibly locked in its market reforms, and in exchange secured privileged access to the US market. Exports to the US market have been the main motor of Mexican growth, but the obvious geographical advantages have proved ephemeral in the absence of badly needed structural reforms and a cohesive progrowth strategy: "Investments in research and development, for instance, have failed to materialize in both the public and private sectors. Government spending on infrastructure has dropped to its lowest level in seven decades . . . leaving an unreliable network of ports, highways and even internet connections across the country. Burdensome regulation and corruption stifle investment, while the nation's banks lent far less than their Latin American peers, leaving small companies to scramble for credit."[20]

The NAFTA accord, in and of itself, has not turned out to be a straight-jacket for Mexico. Rather, Mexican policy elites painted themselves into a corner by embracing NAFTA prematurely, well before their ambitious market reforms had been consolidated. These same elites also mistook NAFTA for a development strategy proper. Ironically, the triumph of securing this groundbreaking deal distracted subsequent Mexican administrations from carrying out the considerable backlog of reforms that would be required for the country to thrive in the global economy—NAFTA or no NAFTA. The trade deal alone and the neoliberal macro- and microeconomic policy approaches that framed it have failed to trigger the kind of transformation that PRI policy makers had promised. Nor could NAFTA help deter Chinese exports from barreling into US market niches in both Mexico and the US that were once solidly North American.

Although some bilateral tensions with the US have been a steady-state reality under NAFTA, no one could have predicted the full-metal jacket approach toward Mexico that the Trump administration has adopted. The South American countries considered in this book have been able to pivot more toward China, which, in light of Washington's hostile rhetoric, is now looking like a more viable economic and diplomatic alternative. Mexican officials have likewise recognized the necessity of improving the country's bilateral ties with China. However, in the 2018 USMCA draft agreement the US foreclosed the option of formalizing stronger ties with China by insisting that both Mexico and Canada give six-months' notice to Washington in the event that either intends to launch trade negotiations with a "non-market economy" (USMCA, Article 32.10), that is, China. In the event that the USMCA never makes it off the floor of the House of Representatives, with its newly elected 2018 midterm Democratic majority, the White House has dangled the threat of a US withdrawal from NAFTA altogether. What options might Mexico have moving forward?

The Political Economy of China-Mexico Relations, 1990–2018

As I noted earlier, Mexico was one of the first countries to sell wheat to China in the early 1960s, as Mao's Great Leap Forward deteriorated into grain shortages and a severe famine. Moreover, former Mexican president Echeverría's fiery speech before the UN General Assembly in 1971 had smoothed the way for China's entry into that entity the same year. The normalization of Mexico's diplomatic relationship with China was forged in 1972, and from there followed a personal invitation from Premier Zhou Enlai for Echeverría to visit China, making him the very first Latin American head of state to do so. Soon thereafter an exhibition of Aztec artifacts sponsored by Mexico's first ambassador to China traveled to Shanghai and Beijing, drawing wide praise from the Chinese public.[21] Up through the

1970s Mexico was in step with the PRC on calls for a New International Economic Order and greater respect for third world sovereignty. Mexico was the first country to welcome high-level Chinese delegations in the immediate wake of the 1989 Tiananmen Square tragedy, while most of the West condemned China for its brutal student massacre.

The first real sign of trouble on the bilateral front appeared in the early 1990s, as Mexico began registering a trade deficit with China (it has never once abated since). Although China was a mere speck on Mexico's economic horizon at this time, it would proceed to bump Mexico down to third place in the ranking of US trade partners in 2003, and—completely unfathomable at the time—the China–Mexico trade deficit would hit US\$67.4 billion by 2017.[22] Understandably, back in the early 1990s PRI technocrats were still operating in a short-term mode, trying to coordinate their market shock strategy with negotiations for NAFTA accession. However, no longer the least of Mexico's worries, China has single-handedly invoked a contradictory set of trade policies on the part of the Mexican government: "free trade" with its numerous FTA partners versus massive protectionism leveraged against Chinese goods since 1993.

Despite the acute pain of adjustment and restructuring in the wake of the 1994 peso crisis, Mexico stuck to its neoliberal guns in the implementation of NAFTA. The devaluation triggered a surge of exports and restoration of growth, spawning data that point to the period from 1995 to 2003 as Mexico's heyday under NAFTA. On this count, the country's economic performance appeared to at least partially vindicate neoclassical theories of economic integration.[23] Still, outside of NAFTA, policy makers embraced protectionism to an unusual extent. The country's most-favored-nation tariffs with its non-FTA partners were among the highest in the region, and its protectionist measures directed toward China were off the chart.[24] None of this, however, helped to slow either China's entry into the North American market or its accession to the WTO.

As the China boom in Latin America took off from 2003 to 2013, the similarity of Chinese and Mexican manufactured exports would unleash fierce competition between the two countries, exacerbated by Mexico's weak reform record. In this section, I begin with an analysis of NAFTA's heyday in the 1990s from the Mexican standpoint, including the wielding of a double-edged sword based on trade liberalization and protectionism. I then turn to the effect of China's WTO entry on Mexico and the latter's inability to generate effective policy responses, including the delay of structural reforms that were essential for better withstanding the China boom. I finish with a critique of China–Mexico relations in the new millennium. One of the added pressures of the US-led USMCA, should it come to fruition, would be the greater stress this will place on the China-Mexico relationship.[25] In particular, Mexico's current account would be hit simultaneously by ever-rising manufactured imports from China and slowing exports to the US due to the mercantilist nature the USMCA draft accord.

NAFTA'S Heyday for Mexico, 1995–2003

I reviewed the comparative economic performance of China's six Latin American strategic partners covered in this book from 2001 to 2017 (see table 1.1) and came to the conclusion that Mexico has been a laggard in terms of institutional reform and aggregate and per capita growth. Interestingly, the country's growth under NAFTA from 1995 to 2003, an annual average rate of around 2.1 percent, was lower than the average for the 2003–17 period. At the time, this was seen as acceptable given the post–peso crisis loss of about 6.2 percent of GDP in 1995; and Mexico had made it through the worst of the US recession from 2001 to 2003. Per capita GDP had nearly doubled between 1995 and 2003, and Mexico's macroeconomic indicators appeared to be converging toward those of the US.[26] Inflation and interest rates, after soaring in the wake of the 1994 crisis, were in the single-digit range by 2003, and the currency had stabilized under a new floating exchange rate regime.

Although this performance was respectable in light of the trials the country had faced and overcome since the 1982 debt shocks, it turned out that this was as good as it was going to get for Mexico. From 2003 on, per capita GDP growth virtually stalled, meaning that things actually worsened on this front, especially when compared with the other five countries analyzed in this book (see table 1.1). Mexico's NAFTA heyday was thus very short-lived. Some of Mexico's early trade deficit with China can be chalked up to clashing currency policies, with China running a cheap exchange rate that favored exports versus a steeply appreciating Mexican peso that served as a magnet for imports. But even after the peso's devaluation in 1994–95 Mexico's trade deficit with China persisted. As I mentioned earlier, China had also begun ramping up its structural reforms during this period, with an eye toward WTO entry by 2001.

At the NAFTA negotiating table Mexico had agreed to forgo any of the developing country exceptions that typically applied under the GATT. With policy makers' avowed blind faith in free trade, this meant that Mexico would white-knuckle it through the NAFTA-related pain of further liberalization and leave the adjustments to market forces. Implicitly, all three NAFTA partners assumed that Mexico would continue to forge ahead with crucial structural and institutional reforms (e.g., strengthening property rights, upholding rule of law, implementing antitrust measures). We have seen that Mexico had made some measured progress with institutional reforms by 2002 (see fig. 1.1). But this modernization was arguably offset by the explosion of the China boom and Mexico's misfortune to be on the losing side of it. Policy makers first lashed out in 1993–94 by imposing antidumping duties on a wide range of Chinese products, including footwear, textiles, garments, toys, bicycles, hand tools, electronics, and chemicals. This affected nearly three thousand items, with duties running as high as 1,105 percent in some cases:

> The measures were aimed at excluding China from the Mexican market. Mexico was able to set such sweeping and unprecedentedly severe antidumping duties because China was not a party to the General Agreement on Tariffs and Trade. Superficial injury examinations were conducted and non-market economy treatment was applied, which allowed for the imposition of extremely high anti-dumping duties. . . . Mexico's policy toward China—no other country was subject to such high amounts of duty or to anti-dumping duties on so many goods—caused distortions in trade, as many importers opted to apply circumvention or transshipment practices or obtain judicial relief in order to avoid paying anti-dumping duties.[27]

With the creation of the WTO in 1995 and China's plan to accede to it as soon as possible, the clock was ticking on this protectionist game. Thus began a two-pronged strategy on Mexico's part, as policy makers simultaneously sought to block China's entry into the WTO *and* to pursue a number of FTAs with the likes of Japan, the European Union (EU), Chile, and Peru. The Clinton administration's 1994 proposal to negotiate a Free Trade Area of the Americas (FTAA) by 2005 was another thorn in Mexico's side, as this would cut further into its privileged access to the US market. Without openly seeking to thwart the FTAA, Mexican officials did little to move this project forward.[28] The country's assertive outreach for new bilateral FTA partners was meant to diversify its trade and investment ties away from heavy dependence on the US market. At the same time, however, Mexico continued to covet these US ties.

In the run-up to China's WTO accession, thirty-seven WTO members had requested bilateral negotiations with China prior to signing on to a multilateral agreement. This obviously included WTO heavyweights like the US and the EU, both of which differed with China over such matters as agricultural subsidies, retail and distribution, trading rights, and insurance permits. By 1999 most differences had been ironed out, leaving the completion of a bilateral understanding with Mexico as China's last barrier to WTO entry.[29] In 2000 the ruling PRI party lost the presidential elections for the first time since 1929. This long-overdue transition to democracy ushered in President Vicente Fox on the center-right National Action Party (PAN) ticket, and this changing of the guard slowed the completion of the bilateral understanding between China and Mexico. Chinese officials no doubt saw this changing of the guard as an opportunity to secure a better deal in its negotiations with Mexico, although this was not to be. If anything, Sino–Mexican trade relations worsened, as Mexico insisted on a thirteen-year period of protection for its domestic market. In August 2001 China countered with a five-year extension maximum, and both sides walked away from the table.

Domestic reports in the Chinese and Mexican media at that time reflect the differing approach of the two countries to their standoff over China's WTO entry. The state-controlled Chinese media spoke in platitudes, whereas in the Mexican press the gloves came off.[30] The final deal struck between the two countries reflected these differing stances, with China taking a midterm approach to accessing the Mexican market and Mexican policy makers looking for quick fixes to stanch the inflow of Chinese imports. In September 2001 a bilateral agreement was signed which gave Mexico a six-year respite, allowing it to maintain duties (which openly violated WTO rules) still in place on hundreds of Chinese exports in the aforementioned sectors and China agreeing not to contest these at the WTO during this period.[31] In 2002 Mexico and China established a "high-level group" to work toward a better trade balance.[32] But in 2003 Chinese exports to the US market surpassed those of Mexico, bumping the latter to third place in the ranking of US trading partners. All of these factors combined to set the China–Mexico bilateral relationship on an ambiguous, contentious path for the twenty-first century, a path marked by Eastern euphemisms and Western acrimony.

The Effect of China's WTO Entry on Mexico

In their pathbreaking article "The China Shock," David Autor, David Dorn, and Gordon Hanson write that "China's emergence as a great economic power has induced an epochal shift in patterns of world trade."[33] Although their analysis pertains to the effect of the rise of China on the developed countries, the authors further state that "China made comparable gains in penetration by detailed sectors across numerous countries."[34] We have seen that this was certainly true for both Argentina and Brazil, meaning that Mexico has no pride of place in the country-by-country struggle to survive and succeed in the face of the China shock. In the LAC region Mexico has arguably been hit the hardest, and there is plenty to support this claim. Yet what stands out in this case is Mexico's continually weak policy responses to the worsening indicators—including its overreliance on self-defeating protectionism against Chinese goods—and the perpetual failure of politicians and policy makers to undertake key structural reforms as well as promotional policies that could better enable Mexico to withstand the China shock. Here I want to review the trade data and the extent of China's encroachment on both Mexico's home market and its long-standing export niches in the US market; and elaborate on the inability of Mexican political leaders and policy makers to generate a proactive response to the China shock.

Displacement and Disillusion

To summarize, both China and Mexico have made tremendous strides as exporters of manufactured goods since the early 1990s. Mexico transformed its export profile from one that was highly dependent on oil and related natural resources in 1980 to a formidable exporter of manufactured goods by the turn of the new century. In bringing about this shift, policy makers relied largely on the country's 1994 accession to NAFTA, which resulted in deep trade and financial liberalization. FDI inflows, mainly from US companies, became the driving force for technology transfer and the country's move up the value-added industrial learning curve. The state wrote itself out of this strategy, relegating the country's productive transformation to market forces. China's path to becoming an industrial exporter was quite different, with the state promoting and financing this strategy, including technology acquisition and adaptation. In preparation for WTO entry China began with unilateral trade liberalization, and, upon its accession to the WTO, its trade with the entire world market exploded. Unlike Mexico's, China's fate as an industrial exporter in the post-1978 reform period has never depended on a single country or market.

The limitations of Mexico's neoliberal industrial-exporter strategy were evident even prior to NAFTA's implementation. Unilateral trade liberalization moved forward apace in the period between the country's 1986 GATT entry and the 1994 NAFTA accession but with little of the preparation and structural adjustment that had occurred during China's trade opening prior to its WTO entry. Mexico's macroeconomic policy, with an overvalued exchange rate and rapid expansion in commercial and consumer credit, was a boon for imports—from both the US and China. The painful 1994 devaluation of the peso reversed the US–Mexico trade balance into a surplus for Mexico, and this has remained the case since the takeoff in cross-border production. Major US companies like Northrup Grumman, Honeywell, Alcoa, Goodrich, and the big three US auto companies (General Motors, Chrysler, and Ford), to name only a few, are essentially coproducing manufactured goods with assembly contractors in Mexico. Value is thereby added to these products, and they are then shipped back to the home market for finalization. This is the basic logic of intraregional production under NAFTA.

The US trade deficit with Mexico has been spurred partly by the dollar's appreciation in the 2000s, but between 12 and 20 percent of these "exports" from Mexico are then reexported from the US to the rest of the world.[35] Despite the insistence of the Trump administration that these reexports should count as part of the US trade deficit with Mexico and therefore constitute a "bad deal" for the US, a sizeable portion of value-added still accrues in the US. Given the posturing by the US Bureau of Economic Analysis about the need to recalculate the trade figures, mainly in ways that would validate the increased protectionism within the USMCA draft agreement, estimates on the percentage of US value-added contained in Mexico's exports to the US range anywhere from 14 to 40 percent.[36] This rancorous discourse on the US trade deficit with Mexico has served to bolster Washington's a priori assumptions rather than illuminate the intricacies of measuring trade statistics under complex conditions of coproduction, assembly contracting, and regional integration.

Again, the China–Mexico saga has been in play since the early 1990s, when China's growing trade surplus with Mexico triggered hefty antidumping duties on Chinese goods. The reasons for China's trade surplus have changed over time. At first, exchange rate misalignment was the culprit, with China running a very undervalued currency up until the early 2000s, and Mexico maintaining an overvalued exchange rate. As I noted earlier, however, the massive peso devaluation of 1994 did not make a dent in Mexico's trade deficit with China. China's entry into the WTO struck another blow to this deficit, as it gained most-favored-nation access to world markets.[37] Between 2001 and 2004 Mexico's trade deficit with China jumped by some US$10 billion.[38] At the outset of the China boom in 2003 Mexico's export similarity index with China stood at 25.1 versus 17.4 for Brazil and 7.0 for Argentina.[39] Because more than 80 percent of Mexico's exports are destined for the US market, this became a second battlefront for Mexican producers now faced with unprecedented competition from China in the US market.

With WTO membership finally in hand and its unabashed state-led promotion of exports, R&D, and technological adaptation in high gear, China has plowed through the very sectors (electronics and parts, telephone equipment, and apparel) that Mexico once claimed as its own in the US market. Between 2002 and 2008, for example, Mexico's share of the US import market slipped by 11 percent, while China's share rose by 50 percent.[40] With China advancing exponentially, Enrique Dussel Peters and Kevin Gallagher have calculated the rapid pace at which China is displacing not only Mexico in the US market but also US exports to the Mexican market.[41] Following the methodology devised by Sanjaya Lall, John Weiss, and Hiroshi Oikawa, Dussel and Gallagher define a "partial threat" to a product / subsector when exports to the US market from both LAC and China are growing, but China's are growing at a faster clip.[42] A "direct threat" occurs when China's exports to the US market are growing but LAC's are declining:

> 96% of United States manufacturing exports to Mexico, which represent 62% of total exports to Mexico, are under [direct] threat from China. . . . In the case of Mexican manufactures, 52% of Mexican exports to the United States are under direct threat, and 29% are under partial threat. The only sector in which Mexico is not under threat from China or is gaining market share with respect to China is in relation to cars, trucks and related parts and accessories. This is because such items are physically heavy to transport from China and because the North American auto sector enjoys protection under NAFTA.[43]

There is no simple explanation for Mexico's pattern of falling so far behind China on export competitiveness, the bilateral trade balance, and a range of other economic indicators. For the casual observer this might come as a surprise, as the financial press periodically touts Mexico's strengths as an exporter of high value-added goods.[44] After all, Mexico ranks closer to China than any of the other LAC emerging economies (EEs) in terms of the "revealed comparative advantage" of its manufacturing sector. We have also seen that since 2000 Mexico has outperformed the other LAC EEs on such measures as manufactured exports as a percent of GDP and the percent of value-added that Mexican manufacturing contributes to GDP (see table 1.2). Mexico is, in fact, the only Latin American country to rank among the top twenty developing countries in terms of the technological content of its manufactured exports. Yet since 1980 Mexico's average rates of aggregate and per capita GDP growth have been downright anemic, in both absolute and relative terms. Obviously, Mexico's neoliberal industrial-export model has been no match for China's state-led economic strategy. What went wrong?

Today's cross-border assembly-contractor strategy sprang from the earlier *maquiladora* program launched by Mexico in the 1960s. The program offered tax breaks to US companies looking to reduce costs by outsourcing part of the production line to Mexico. NAFTA eliminated the various tariff and duty drawback schemes of the earlier maquila program and established the aforementioned rules of origin to prevent foreign investors from using Mexico as an easy jump-off platform for entering the US market.[45] Over time these joint investment strategies among North American firms became more sophisticated, as scale economies and intra-industry specialization fostered an increasingly dynamic pattern of export-led growth. The guarantee of permanently low trade barriers held special appeal for producers on both sides of the border, and business lobbies in the leading sectors (autos, electronics, and machinery) on both sides pushed hardest for NAFTA.

Going in to NAFTA the structural legacy of the maquilas was concentration on mainly "low value-added activities which provide minimal opportunities for upgrading, few linkages to domestic manufacturing or suppliers, and strong incentives to keep labor costs low."[46] In the early 1990s social scientists in the Western Hemisphere had begun to theorize about the benefits of tackling these bottlenecks such that developing countries could transform cross-border interfirm networks, or "global commodity chains," into fully integrated export manufacturing modules.[47] This view, however, was informed by the East Asian experience in such sectors as textiles, autos, and electronics, an approach that depended on strong state guidance and targeted incentives along every link in the production chain.[48] For Mexico to get into this game the government would have to design a cohesive and proactive public policy framework to transform this sector from an export-processing logic to a dynamic platform for industrial production.

At the outset of the Enrique Peña Nieto administration in 2012, the incoming policy team acknowledged the need for a complete overhaul of Mexico's industrial sector and committed to a new industrial policy of sorts.[49] However, the corresponding national development plan for 2013–18 was ambiguous in that it committed to the promotion and strengthening of manufacturing subsectors where a considerable competitive advantage had already accrued (aerospace, medical equipment, autos, and auto parts). Proposals for stronger state sponsorship in areas where the market has failed (small and medium enterprises, human capital investment and skill acquisition, access to affordable credit, and so on) were rejected. While readily recognizing these weaknesses as obstacles to higher growth, the 2013–

18 development plan continued to weigh on the side of market mechanisms for their resolution. As the Peña Nieto *sexenio* and the designated timeline for the development plan ended, the results for the manufacturing sector were the same: select industries with high levels of FDI inflows and competitive advantage are thriving, while the other, mostly domestic companies are simply surviving.

At the top of Mexico's manufacturing sector are industries that have done smashingly well, among them aerospace, medical devices, and autos / auto parts (boxes 6.1, 6.2, 6.3).[50] As the narratives in the boxes indicate, Mexico's Ministry of Economy has targeted six regions for government support, which includes funds for research and innovation from CONACYT.[51] The channeling of these funds to the state level in these select regions has spurred dynamic public–private partnerships that unite local universities, companies, development planning entities, and technical training institutes. I have visited the Baja California cluster a number of times, and what stands out is the sophistication of company managers, the vision and commitment of state- and city-level policy makers (in Tijuana and Ensenada), and the professionalism of those working within the local universities and technical training institutes.[52] This impressive network has been replicated across the six designated regions, and these clusters exemplify Mexico's manufacturing elite.

However, the narratives in the boxes also reflect that the companies involved in this exciting manufacturing transformation are mostly foreign. Moreover, only the largest, most privileged Mexican companies have been able to integrate into these networks, and these firms have been privy to all kinds of government promotion and benefits.[53] As for the local companies in these cluster regions, contractors with a steadily increasing share of knowledge and skill intensity embedded these top-of-the-line assemblers into their operations. Yet outside of this vibrant esprit de corps the pickings are quite thin. Herein lie the hundreds of small and medium-sized companies that during the "golden age of industrialization" formed the backbone of Mexico's manufacturing sector. Since the late 1980s the repeal of industrial policy, Mexico's NAFTA accession, and China's WTO entry have cumulatively worked to decimate these traditional domestic companies. Just as the large, cash-rich companies have had ready access to both public and

Box 6.1. Aerospace

Starting from virtually nil at the turn of the century, aerospace is now a $5 billion export industry in Mexico which employs some thirty-one thousand people. The Ministry of Economy is coordinating a national plan based on the strengths of six regions. Chihuahua is to build on its vocation for precision-machined products, while Baja California looks to attract knowledge-process outsourcing. Attracting foreign aerospace companies has been key to this process. Cessna, for example, produces electrical components for its Citation business jets in Chihuahua, and Honeywell makes jet engine components in Mexicali. Mexican companies such as Volare Engineering and Soisa, which make airplane interiors and seats, are growing alongside these international firms.

Various regional centers vie to attract foreign aviation firms and to develop domestic suppliers. Local authorities proudly promote the triple helix concept, whereby governments and universities promote industrial development. Plantronics, a Santa Cruz, California, firm, is just one example of this concept in action. The company moved product design operations to Tijuana and now coordinates its R&D with engineering students from nearby universities. The company hires some of these students, and Mexico's National Science and Technology Council (CONACYT) provides research funding. This strategy has brought several Plantronics products to market.

State technical universities are ramping up their aerospace design and engineering resources. Universidad Tecnológica de Tijuana's recent half-million-dollar investment in the French company Dassault trains students to produce and use Dassault's 3D aircraft design software.

With Mexico graduating one hundred thousand engineers annually, three times as many per capita as the US, the capacity for design in Mexico is promising. Honeywell has a design center in Mexicali, and General Electric employs thirteen hundred engineers in Querétaro to design commercial airliner turbines. With the US capturing 59 percent of the world's aerospace and defense market, Mexico's access to the US market is essential to future success. In addition to its NAFTA/USMCA advantages, Mexico holds a privileged position in the highly regulated US market through its Bilateral Air Safety Arrangement and membership in the forty-one-nation Wassenaar Arrangement for regulation of defense industry products. With 20 percent annual growth in this sector since 2004, hopes are high that Mexico will reach its goal of exporting $12 billion in aerospace products by the end of the decade.

Source: Carol Wise and Joshua Tuynman, "NAFTA @ 20: A Bittersweet Celebration," *Americas Quarterly* (Winter 2014): 26–31.

Box 6.2. High Mix / Low Volume Medical Devices

The relatively short distance to the US market gives Mexico a huge advantage in High Mix/Low Volume manufacturing in medical devices. American managers and customers of factories in Mexico are in the same time zone, a short flight away for executives, and a door-to-door truck drive away for products.

The shorter time from order to final delivery means Mexican manufacturers can integrate themselves more easily into the supply chains of cross-border manufacturing operations, without the lengthy turnaround time involved in working with parts shipped overseas.

High Mix/Low Volume contract manufacturers like Oncore, Creation Technologies, and SMTC are often global businesses with operations in China and elsewhere but use their Mexican factories to supply their NAFTA/USMCA customers. Assembly operations run on a build-to-order basis. A particular assembly line is configured and reconfigured throughout the week to make different products for different customers.

This allows flexibility throughout the supply chain for large manufacturers and enables companies to get products to customers on an as-needed basis. DJ Orthopedics (DJO), with headquarters in San Diego and two thousand employees at its manufacturing facilities in Tijuana, uses its cross-border operations to offer customers second-day delivery of custom-built medical devices. DJO can take a customer order in the morning, build the product that day, and drive it across the border to send for next-day delivery via FedEx.

However, no amount of efficiency can reverse the adverse conditions that plague Mexican producers at the border. There, northward trade flows continue to battle deficient highway infrastructure and a thick web of bureaucracy. Lacking enough lanes, northbound cross-border traffic jams stretch well into the middle of the business district in Tijuana. Mexican shipping companies can operate north of the border, but regulatory hurdles keep many from doing so. Mexican and American companies have profited by the speed of business between the two countries, but there is plenty of room for improvement.

Source: Carol Wise and Joshua Tuynman, "NAFTA @ 20: A Bittersweet Celebration," *Americas Quarterly* (Winter 2014): 26–31.

Box 6.3. Auto Parts / Automotive Sector

Mexico's geographic proximity to the US gives it a clear advantage over China in the automotive market. Since Chevy Silverado pickup trucks weigh in at over two tons apiece, it is a lot cheaper to ship them to the US. The advantage of shipping costs, along with the regulatory and intellectual property protections under NAFTA, means Mexico exports $53 billion worth of automobiles and parts to the US annually, compared with China's $12 billion.

Mexican automobile production has flourished under NAFTA, tripling since 1994 to three million cars and trucks annually. Mexico has outpaced Britain, France, Spain, and Canada to become the world's eighth largest automobile producer. The industry as a whole produces 23 percent of Mexico's exports, providing around 579,000 jobs—40 percent of all automotive manufacturing jobs in North America. If passed by the US Congress, the drafted United-States-Mexico-Canada-Agreement (USMCA) of 2018 would replace NAFTA and significantly raise minimum wages and content requirements (from 62.5 percent to 75 percent) in the auto industry. This, plus the stipulation that higher content must come from the US market, will put a damper on these dynamic Mexican figures.

All auto production in Mexico is by foreign companies, as Mexico sold off its floundering state-owned VAM car company in 1989. Nissan is the top producer, followed by Volkswagen, General Motors, Ford, and Chrysler. The location of their operations in Mexico has enabled European and Japanese carmakers to abide by NAFTA's 62.5 percent local content rule. More important, these foreign producers can access high-quality, low-cost production without having to pay transoceanic shipping costs. At $2 to $6 per hour, Mexican assembly line workers make about one-seventh as much as autoworkers in the US. Again, higher wages and content requirements will cut into the gains registered thus far.

The lower wages in Mexico rankle unionized workers in the United States, and hence the efforts of the Trump administration to dictate wage policies in the Mexican auto industry via the USMCA. When two of the big three US automakers required a government rescue during the 2008–9 global financial crisis, it became apparent that lower costs would be the only way to save the overall industry. But higher wages in Mexico will not compensate for the country's small consumer market for new cars, especially when sellers there have to compete with used cars from the United

States. The market for imported used American cars—some registered, some not—is estimated at six hundred thousand per year and slightly higher than the number of Mexican-made automobiles sold domestically.

Source: Carol Wise and Joshua Tuynman, "NAFTA @ 20: A Bittersweet Celebration," *Americas Quarterly* (Winter 2014): 26–31.

private funding, so the smaller, cash-strapped firms are in need of a helping hand from both the government and local private lenders.

In the absence of a cohesive public policy framework that explicitly integrates the bulk of Mexico's small and medium-sized companies into the vibrant production-export networks described (see boxes 6.1, 6.2, 6.3), these high-flying global value chains have taken off without sufficient participation from domestic companies and suppliers. Over time the weakness of forward and backward linkages, that is, the low value-added contained in goods produced for export by smaller domestic firms, has trapped Mexico in a low-wage, low-growth rut for two decades.[54] The NAFTA production value chain is disproportionately reliant on foreign inputs on the Mexican side, and, as Dussel and Gallagher have aptly argued, a rapidly growing share of intermediate goods for production is coming from China. Some of this market stress does indeed have to do with the effect of China's WTO entry on the Mexican economy. However, related problems in the way of sluggish growth, compressed manufacturing wages, and a burgeoning informal economy for workers and small producers also pertain to the insistence of political and economic elites that industrial policy should favor sectors and firms with an established competitive edge.

Chronic Reform Delays

Earlier we saw that the timing on Mexico's buildup to the 1994 peso crisis coincided with China's launching of sweeping structural reforms that aptly prepared it for WTO entry. This was especially unfortunate for Mexico, where the fallout from the 1994 currency crash had thrown policy makers back into a short-term crisis mode. This was the opposite mindset of Chinese reformers during this period. The peso debacle also marked the end for the PRI's seventy-one consecutive years of single-party rule. As mentioned, voters finally opted for an alternative in 2000, electing Vicente Fox from the center-right National Action Party (PAN). The PAN made huge promises on the reform front, vowing to tackle the pending structural reforms and thereby push annual economic growth into the 7 percent range. Yet, the reform tasks inherited by Fox (2000–2006) were waylaid by the unexpected difficulties that arose between the country's first democratically elected executive, a minority government, and the divided congress he was handed.[55] The PRI, moreover, had won enough seats in the lower house of congress to thwart the slated reform agenda.

By the 2003 midterm elections, Fox was effectively a lame duck. This meant the delay of crucial competitiveness measures in the realm of energy sector modernization, fiscal restructuring, labor market mobility, and stronger technical support and credit access for those small and medium-sized firms that provide the bulk of Mexican employment. It is no coincidence that China began to quickly advance within the North American market and displace Mexico at this point in time. China's WTO entry may have triggered the process of Mexico's displacement in the US market, but this shift was also due to the former's lower corporate tax rates, cheaper utility inputs, and increasing value-added with higher technological input. China, in other words, had an explicit and formidable trade and competition strategy while Mexico did not.

The 2006 presidential elections saw the success of another center-right PAN candidate, Felipe Calderón (2006–12). While Calderón proved to be more politically adroit in navigating a divided congress, the pace of reform remained tediously slow and far too incremental. The big-ticket reforms— energy, infrastructure, labor, education, and a serious fiscal overhaul— barely saw the light of day. Like his predecessor, Calderón was a lame duck by the 2009 midterm elections. A clear bust on the reform front, the two consecutive PAN administrations were also host to some alarming reversals. Public safety deteriorated, as parts of the country had fallen prey to organized criminal gangs engaged in drug and arms trafficking. By 2009 Mexico had fallen seventeen points in Transparency International's global ranking of corruption perceptions, putting it at 89 out of 180 countries.[56]

After sitting out two administrations the PRI recaptured the executive office in 2012. True to its historic practices, the party had recast itself, this time in a pro-reform, twenty-first-century image. The youthful president Peña Nieto came out swinging with an ambitious structural reform package launched under the auspices of a new cross-party political pact (Pacto por México). By early 2015 the bulk of these reforms had been passed by the congress, and the government was poised to move into the implementation stage: "Mr. Peña Nieto's first year and a half in office were marked by one success after another, passing a series of landmark initiatives like opening the country's oil industry to private investment and boosting competition in industries like telephones and TV. The International Monetary Fund and others have praised Mexico, and its president, as a model for other emerging markets."[57] Policy makers still faced the enormous hurdle of overhauling the ministries and establishing the proper regulatory oversight to govern these reforms, but the domestic political economic trajectory was more favorable than it had been in years.[58]

Nevertheless, Peña Nieto, too, was a lame duck by the end of his third year in office.[59] The specter of the old PRI—ruthless, corrupt, and autocratic—could simply not be repressed. The disappearance of forty-three student protestors from Ayotzinapa Rural Teachers' College in the state of Guerrero in September 2014 remains a mystery, although figuratively speaking the fingerprints of state authorities are all over this tragedy.[60] While a landmark anticorruption bill was approved in congress, the president vetoed a transparency provision for recipients of government contracts. Shady fund transfers, hidden real estate holdings, and the cannibalization of big infrastructure tenders by party officials were all still very much a part of the PRI's repertoire. Almost as an afterthought for Mexican officials, China–Mexico relations sunk to a new low.

China–Mexico Relations in the New Millennium: Hollowing Out?

Strategic Partners since 2003

In early 2013 President Peña Nieto became the country's third chief executive in the new millennium to announce an effort to forge stronger and

better ties with the PRC.[61] As I noted, Mexico had extracted high protectionist side payments from China in return for supporting its 2001 bid to enter
the WTO. Having set high tariffs on Chinese products until 2008 and ex-
tended the transition time to 2011, this was hardly a propitious start for the
collegial relationship that both sides had touted since the launching of a
strategic partnership (SP) in 2003. China's SPs are difficult to nail down.
The euphemisms and clichés are present, but we are left to induce China's
motives for bringing Mexico into its SP fold. Three equally important reasons come to mind: (1) China will need Mexico's vote to achieve full market
economy status (MES) at the WTO; (2) Mexico's recent opening up of its oil
and natural gas reserves for exploration and development by foreign investors is of special interest to China; and (3) like most countries and firms
operating in the Mexican market, the appeal of using Mexico as a production platform for accessing the US market.

As for my first proposed reason, China's MES quest, a key article in China's 2001 WTO Protocol of Accession stated that it would be granted MES
by December 2016. Yet that date has come and gone, and neither the US
nor the EU has been willing to graduate China from its current nonmarket
economy status ranking. The difference between these two labels is significant for China, as an upgrade to MES concerns the latitude that other
states would have in calculating whether China should be subject to antidumping complaints. If China had a full-fledged MES label, its trade partners would find it much harder to justify antidumping measures. Mexico
may be a small fish in this pond, but it is a tenacious one.[62] All five of the
other LAC SPs considered in this book have appeased China by conceding
it MES status in the context of finalizing trade and investment deals. But
interestingly, market economy treatment has not been formally legislated
into any of these Latin American jurisdictions.[63] This means that these LAC
SPs continue to file antidumping complaints against China. Mexico has
been quite vocal about opposing MES for China, which is perhaps the one
area where it is in agreement with the Trump administration.[64]

As for Chinese access to Mexico's oil and natural gas holdings, this process
is now under way. After more than seven decades of state control over the
oil sector, Mexico held its first big auction for foreign bidders in December
2016. In Round One, China National Offshore Oil Corporation (CNOOC),

the third largest of China's top three oil companies, won two contracts to drill in the Perdido Fold Belt situated close to the US border in the Gulf of Mexico: "CNOOC's bold move into Mexico came with the offer of an additional royalty of 17.01 percent—way above the 3.1 percent threshold stipulated by the government."[65] Round Two tenders were offered in July 2017. Here, China's Shandong Kerui Oilfield Service Group secured three new drilling areas in partnership with two other companies.[66] On China's side, the record has shown that its LAC SPs run more smoothly when access to key natural resources comes into play. For Mexico, these contracts, along with numerous others won by companies outside of North America, signal an important opportunity to diversify away from its overall dependence on the US market.[67]

On the use of NAFTA as a platform for accessing the US market, my third theoretical reason, a formidable lineup of foreign producers has perfected this strategy to an art. China, despite its expressed interest in investing in Mexico and its willingness to adhere to NAFTA's hefty rules of origin, has not. As I discussed earlier, China's de facto entry into the North American market has consisted largely of competitive displacement of Mexican exports to the US market and of US exports to the Mexican market. China, in other words, has very effectively inserted itself into cross-border value chains on the trade side while committing little FDI in Mexico within these high value-added sectors.[68] This is not for lack of trying. The very essence of NAFTA has been for foreign companies to invest in Mexico with the explicit purpose of exporting back to the US, regional, and global markets. In this case, the explosion of Mexico's trade deficit with China and the perpetually low percentage of goods that Mexico exports back to China continue to cast a cloud over the bilateral relationship.

Despite the forging of an SP between the two countries in 2003, a running anti-China narrative has continued in the Mexican media. Although the ink had barely dried on the September 2001 agreement that significantly protected Mexican producers from Chinese competition, local fear over the pending 2008 termination of the agreement was already circulating in the media.[69] One of the few favorable stories concerning the PRC had to do with the rise in China's manufacturing wages and the near wage parity between the two countries by 2009—no matter that Mexican wages had basically flatlined.[70] Since the launching of the China–Mexico SP in 2003, a flurry of supplementary bilateral accords have been signed, and China's Ministry of Commerce and Mexico's Secretariat of the Economy convened a permanent Bilateral Commission and three High-Level Groups to focus generally on the strengthening of trade and investment ties between the two countries.[71] Together, China and Mexico have contributed to a US$2.4 billion Mexico–China Fund, and in 2013 the two countries established an action program between the United States of Mexico and the People's Republic of China to Enhance a Comprehensive Strategic Association.[72] These various ventures have thus far come to naught.

Why So Little Chinese FDI in Mexico?

Argentina and Brazil, as I've noted, have had their own fair share of trade spats with China, to the extent that 90 percent of Argentina's protectionist measures in 2008 were directed at the PRC![73] Yet this did not deter China from investing vigorously in both countries. In the period between 2000 and 2018 total Chinese FDI in Brazil was approximately US$48.5 billion, and in Argentina over the same period it was about US$12.5 billion (see table I.3). Until the aforementioned oil exploration tenders won by China in 2017, total inflows of Chinese FDI to Mexico stood at approximately US$3 billion. What accounts for this slowness in the momentum of Chinese inflows of FDI to Mexico? Certainly the eleven years of protection against Chinese imports did not help. Mexico now ranks third, behind Brazil (first) and Argentina (second), in the filing of trade remedies against China at the WTO. However, inflows of Chinese FDI in these other two countries seem to have taken on a life of their own despite these trade conflicts.

The literature on Chinese FDI in Latin America sheds light on a number of other possible obstacles at work here. As R. Evan Ellis writes, "Chinese companies have confronted a range of problems, from submitting inadequate bids in competitive technical procurements, to difficulties with the local partners that they have associated themselves with, and the elimination or de-funding of projects by Latin American governments before they could be taken forward."[74] Language barriers, legal glitches, difficult labor relations, environmental concerns, and dealing effectively with the local communities that will be most impacted are some of the additional pitfalls that both a LAC host government and a given Chinese company face when looking to invest. In the case of Mexico, two other key factors seem to have been at play: the country's consolidation of an export-led industrial model prior to the rise of China in the 2000s, and its decision to kick away the ladder of state support and offer limited policy guidance for this model.

To their credit, Mexican policy makers and economic elites came out of the 1980s with a determination to rely less on oil and raw material exports and to pursue growth led by high value-added industrial goods. By the time Beijing had formulated its go out strategy and Chinese firms were being pushed to invest abroad, Mexico was understandably looking to attract FDI into its industrial sector. We have seen from chapter 5 that the mainstay of FDI in Brazil and Argentina has been in primary resources, although Brazil in particular is starting to attract manufacturing FDI from China. In these two countries, we also saw that the bulk of Chinese firms entering these markets are state-owned enterprises (SOEs) and that they come with strong backing from China's policy banks—China Development Bank (CDB) and China Export-Import Bank (CHEXIM). In Brazil private counterpart financing has been easier to secure than in Mexico, and Brazil's National Development Bank (BNDES) is frequently involved in supporting these funding packages. Although the Mexican government has nurtured the high-tech blue chip sectors that now top the country's industrial export profile, its largesse has stopped there. Big-ticket FDI projects like the ones China has sought to pursue in Mexico simply have no CDB or CHEXIM counterpart to spur them to completion.

The English-language financial news is full of "red elephant" stories across the region, and Mexico is no exception. The two most publicized failures have been the Dragon Mart Cancún project and the abrupt cancellation of the China Railway Construction Corporation's contract to build a 130-mile bullet train from Mexico City to the high-tech industrial hub of Querétaro to the north. The Dragon Mart Cancún project was a mega-mall that would have covered fourteen hundred acres just two miles from the Caribbean Sea. Modeled after Dragon Mart Dubai, launched in 2004, this multimillion dollar project was envisioned to be the second largest venue for Chinese retail products outside of China: "Plans called for Dragon Mart to house 3,040 exhibition spaces for Chinese-produced electronics, software, toys, clothing, home-building supplies and other goods."[75] Backed by a Mexican–Chinese partnership and promising to create five thousand plus Mexican jobs, builders broke ground on the project in 2014. Soon thereafter Mexican environmental groups and domestic producers of these same goods succeeded in halting the project. To date, a partially constructed Dragon Mart Cancún now sits defunct on pristine land that borders the Caribbean.[76]

The Mexico City–Querétaro bullet train was agreed to and then canceled by the Mexican government within less than a week's time. For varying reasons China's planned high-speed train projects have fallen on rough times across the world.[77] However, the 2014 US$4.4 billion contract to construct a bullet train in Mexico became embroiled in a domestic Mexican corruption inquiry. China's government-controlled media broke with its usual custom of putting a positive spin on the country's troubled relationship with Mexico and openly expressed its shock and anger at the abrupt cancellation of the project.[78]

A third infrastructure project is the Chicoasén II hydroelectric power plant in the southern state of Chiapas, launched by a China-led consortium involving Mexican partners. Although the contract was awarded in 2015, this project has since faced twenty-three local work stoppages due to social, political, environmental, financial, and technical conflicts that have yet to be resolved.[79] In light of these recent failures, the aforementioned success of Chinese companies in bidding on Rounds One and Two of Mexico's oil field auctions could be a game changer for China–Mexico relations on the FDI front. At least for now China's winning of large oil drilling tenders seems to have ruffled none of the local opposition that has frozen Chicoasén II in place and killed Dragon Mart Cancún and the Mexico City–Querétaro bullet train.

To be sure, Mexico has had a number of successful smaller-scale Chinese investments in mining, telecommunication, banking, and manufacturing.[80] By 2015 nonmetallic mineral mining accounted for 35.4 percent of Chinese FDI inflows to Mexico, the banking sector another 29.5 percent, and machinery / equipment services for commercial activities represented 26.2 percent. Although Mexico is no longer considered a mining powerhouse, the riches are still there: Chinese investors are now digging for copper (Huaxi Group, Jinchuan Group,), gold (Shangnan Qingshan Mining

Company Ltd.), and other ores in Mexico. In the telecommunication sector, the Chinese telecom giant Huawei has its Latin American headquarters in Mexico City, where it supports and builds networks for Mexico's top companies in this sector. In banking, the Industrial and Commercial Bank of China (ICBC) received the necessary permit in 2014 to operate in Mexico and now does so under the name ICBC Mexico. In manufacturing, China's Lenovo Group opened a computer assembly plant in Monterrey in 2009 and in 2014 opened an office in Guadalajara for customer support services. Finally, in 2015 China Shipping Container Lines opened its corporate offices in Mexico City and operates the Pacific coast ports of Manzanillo and Lázaro Cárdenas.

What's NAFTA Got to Do with It?

On July 17, 2017, the Office of the US Trade Representative (USTR) issued a "Summary of Objectives for the NAFTA Renegotiation."[81] The report blamed NAFTA for the explosion of the US trade deficit with Mexico, thousands of factory closings, and the stranding of millions of jobless US workers. The USTR committed to promote truly fair trade, including "the elimination of unfair subsidies, market-distorting practices by state owned enterprises, and burdensome restrictions of intellectual property."[82] As I mentioned earlier in this chapter, these claims formed the economic pillar of the Trump presidential campaign in 2016 without offering a shred of empirical evidence. Again, analyses by well-respected economists remind us that NAFTA accounts for a very small percent of US GDP. Moreover, it is widely agreed that China's 2001 entry into the WTO and the rise of workplace automation delivered the biggest shocks to the US industrial belt.[83] Nevertheless, the USTR report espoused mercantilist ambitions that have now been enshrined in the 2018 USMCA draft agreement.

These goals run up against some long-standing textbook fundamentals about what can and cannot be accomplished through trade policy and regional integration. The US trade deficit with Mexico, for example, cannot be rectified through any of the measures written into the USMCA draft agreement. In fact, lower barriers to entry into the US market (i.e., lower rules of origin) and major investments in rail, highways, and port infrastructure to facilitate the flow of goods back and forth across the US–Mexico border would go much further toward reducing the bilateral deficit. However, rational, empirically based policy solutions are not what Trump's NAFTA renegotiation proceedings were all about. Rather, the NAFTA renegotiation and Trump's insistence on building a new US$25 billion wall along the border (on top of the US$7 billion, 652-mile fence constructed under George W. Bush)[84] were bullet points on a to-do list of campaign promises to be checked off prior to the 2018 midterm elections in the US. As the NAFTA renegotiation morphed into a trade war against China, Japan, the EU, and seemingly the world, even staunch constituents in the Trump heartland were scratching their heads.[85]

When NAFTA and the Mexican people themselves were first vilified by Trump on the presidential campaign trail, it was commonly assumed that Mexico would be the main loser in the event of a US withdrawal from NAFTA. However, after nearly a quarter century of cross-border investment, coproduction and intra-industry trade under NAFTA, none of the three countries would walk away unscathed. For instance, some 20 percent of US agricultural exports go to Mexico from states like Kansas and Wisconsin, amounting to US$18 billion in 2016.[86] The US auto sector may be the hub for Canadian and Mexican auto production, but Mexico offers cost and location advantages that enable US companies to produce models that would be cost-prohibitive in the US: "Since 1994, low labour costs, unfettered access to the U.S. market and free-trade deals covering another 44 countries have propelled Mexico to become the world's seventh largest car manufacturer," a supply chain that supports more than 750,000 jobs.[87] Similarly, US companies in aerospace, medical instruments, computers, and electronics have all woven themselves into sophisticated value and supply chains with a seamless flow of parts and goods moving across North American borders (see boxes 6.1, 6.2, 6.3).

In short, the USMCA draft agreement reflects little knowledge or concern about these realities of trade and investment integration under NAFTA. The imposed NAFTA renegotiation did get Mexican policy makers to consider a Plan B, which at face value means diversifying away from the country's heavy dependence on the US market. While this theme has intermittently arisen for more than a century as a matter of public discourse in Mexico, it is now time to get serious about it. The most obvious step toward diversification would be for Mexico to export more of its rich natural resources, now that the country has proven itself a formidable export-led industrializer. Two major oil deposits have been discovered just since the opening of the oil sector to private developers. One of these, Zama, is considered to be among the twenty top oil discoveries in the past two decades: "After the consortium recoups development costs, Mexico will receive royalties and taxes totaling about 80 percent of oil and gas produced—to be worth more than $1 billion a year."[88]

Vastly increased oil sales to China and the rest of the world would be a start toward a viable Plan B. Increased agricultural sales to China and the rest of the LAC region are also a concrete possibility. If Chile can become the top exporter of tropical fruits to China, displacing Thailand, there is no reason Mexico cannot up its game on this front. Mexico has secured the complicated hygiene protocols required by Beijing for exporting, among other things, grapes, avocados, blackberries, raspberries, corn, cranberries, pork, beef, and tequila, and a number of other products are in the queue to be approved. In 2015 Mexico's agricultural exports to China grew 24 percent over the previous year, and this is one sector where the balance leans in Mexico's favor.[89] Mining is another example of untapped export potential. Although Mexico ranks in twelfth place globally for its mineral wealth, in their rush to shift to an export-led industrial model policy makers have lost sight of this fact. As mentioned, Chinese companies are already active in mining for copper and gold in Mexico, and the country is abundant in manganese, zinc, bismuth, silver, and molybdenum.

There is no reason Mexico, like Brazil, could not pursue a two-pronged strategy of promoting raw material exports to China while also seeking Chinese investment in infrastructure, manufacturing, and services. This is not to say that the goal of exporting higher value-added goods to China should be forsaken by Mexico or, for that matter, Brazil. However, herein lies a legitimate reason for delaying MES for China at the WTO: its high nontariff barriers to market entry for the kinds of value-added products that EEs like Mexico and Brazil could export to the Chinese market.[90] Since its entry into the WTO a long list of countries, including the US and EU bloc, has been in line to gain deeper access to the Chinese market in terms of direct investment and higher value-added exports. There are no two ways about it: China's adherence to the GATT / WTO's most-favored-nation and reciprocity norms has sorely lagged. This drawback, along with Washington's mercantilist approach to the renegotiation of NAFTA, has left Mexican policy makers and producers scrambling to diversify the country's trade and investment relations.

As far as Mexico is concerned, the past quarter century has been one game changer after another. Just as the country's entry into NAFTA had been completely implausible in the debt-ridden 1980s, its displacement by China in the US market was equally unforeseen in the early 2000s. From the shift to an impressive manufacturing export-led development model, to the transition to democracy in 2000, to the return of the disgraced Revolutionary Institutional Party in 2012—these trends have all been dramatic. They have not, however, been especially transformational, and this raises the nagging question as to why not? The one constant over this entire period has been mediocre growth at both the aggregate and per capita levels. For all its apparent economic bravado in terms of buoyant FDI inflows and the high percentage of industrial exports over GDP, the Mexican political economy has underperformed since the 1982 debt shocks. I have attributed this to the decision of political and economic elites to kick away the ladder of state guidance and support in the early 1990s. In no way was the country properly prepared to withstand and benefit from the formidable competition augured by its entry into NAFTA.

Nevertheless, policy makers have muddled their way through with the delegation of industrial restructuring and technology adaptation to FDI inflows. This approach has been exacerbated by the running of a tight macroeconomic policy that has excluded all but the biggest players in the market from accessing affordable credit. Political and economic elites have been able to shelter themselves from the China shock, slow-walking crucial reforms across a range of sectors and issue areas (energy, telecom, fiscal policy, and antitrust) and embracing absurd levels of protection in sectors vulnerable to Chinese competition. The government's failure to incentivize restructuring in these sensitive sectors, which is also the domain of smaller and medium-sized firms, has left them all the more vulnerable now that Mexico's import barriers against China have been brought into line with the WTO. The Mexican government, as we saw earlier, also mishandled the 2008–9 global financial crisis, raising interest rates for fear of inflation rather than engaging in the kinds of hands-on counter-cyclical fiscal policies at the outset that spared huge GDP losses in the rest of the countries discussed in this book. After a 9 percent drop in GDP during that first year of the crisis the Central Bank shifted course, but the damage to per capita GDP was already done.

In his upbeat book *The Fix* Jonathan Tepperman generously declares the reforms of the Peña Nieto administration as "changes [that] have set Mexico up for explosive growth in the near future—a future that could materialize as soon as oil prices recover and the government brings corruption and crime under some sort of control."[91] True enough, this is the first administration to frontload and push through reforms of this breadth and substance in so many issue areas (education, elections, labor, banking, taxes, telecom, and economic competition). Ending the state monopoly over petroleum exploration and extraction was the coup de grace. However, for these reforms to become more than packages of new policies they must be rooted in sound domestic institutions. Peña Nieto and his change team chose not to seriously tackle crucial issues like rule of law and anticorruption, areas in which Mexico is competing with Argentina and Brazil for the worst rankings among the countries considered here.

The July 2018 presidential election shuffled the chairs on the deck by electing for the first time ever an independent coalition, led by President Andrés Manuel López Obrador (AMLO). Like Lula in Brazil, AMLO won on the third try with a victory driven largely from the bottom up. Unlike Lula and his Workers' Party, AMLO's National Regeneration Movement (MORENA) was a coalition that gelled around the bitterness, frustration, and anger invoked by the political impunities and dreary economic indicators I've detailed here. A former mayor of Mexico City, AMLO, his party, and its allies won an absolute majority in the congress. After twenty-four years of divided government and reform blockage, this means that AMLO and his team have considerable leeway to bring the previous administration's reforms to full fruition and to tackle the basic institutional frailties discussed here. Although foreign economic policy was the black box in the MORENA platform, this is also an opportunity for Mexico to get down to business with an authentic China strategy, one that could seriously tap into the latent economic potential and offer geopolitical respite from an increasingly hostile US.

7

Latin America's Pivot toward Asia

A bosom buddy afar brings distant lands near.

Chinese proverb[1]

The Argument

In this book I have offered a conceptual framework for explaining the motivation for China's assertive economic integration with select LAC countries since the turn of the new millennium; and I have analyzed the preliminary effects of this integration with theoretical constructs that borrow from the field of development economics. From the standpoint of the Western Hemisphere, I dispute hawkish, so-called realist interpretations of China's rise in Latin America as a security threat or affront to US hegemony. Realists fret that China's rapid economic catch-up with the US and its aggressive military buildup could destabilize the world order. It is true that China could wreak havoc on the international system but perhaps for reasons that have more to do with some of the inherent weaknesses in the Chinese economy. For example, the rapid and deleterious effects of the US trade war on China in 2018 suggest that a significant slowdown in China's growth is a real possibility, and this could be similarly disruptive to the international political economy. Michael Beckley elaborates on this economic risk: "Chinese businesses . . . use roughly two times more capital and five times more labor than U.S. companies to generate the same level of output. More than one-third of China's industrial capacity is wasted. More than half of its R&D spending is stolen. Nearly two-thirds of its infrastructure projects cost more to build than they will ever generate in economic returns."[2]

On China's part, I argue that it has of necessity internationalized its development strategy in order to compensate for the country's serious natural resource deficit. Chinese policy makers face the daunting tasks of having to feed the world's largest domestic population, and to fuel the soon-to-be largest economy in the world. Latin America is, in fact, a latecomer to China's internationalized development strategy, as the PRC has already established similar ties with countries in Africa and Southeast Asia for these very reasons. Given its continued status as an emerging economy (EE), the gist of the China–LAC relationship has been developmental in nature. China's ten designated strategic partners in LAC represent the bulk of trade, loans, and foreign direct investment (FDI) outflows from China to the region. For the region as a whole, China is now the most important trade partner after the US. Through numerous joint ventures China is contributing to the development of select LAC countries to render them stronger partners in the provision of primary exports and the kinds of market opportunities China needs in order to propel its own growth and development.

On the political economic impact of the rise of China in LAC, I situate my analysis of the effects of tighter integration with China on the LAC region within the context of the 2003–13 commodity boom, the bust from 2014 to 2017, and at present the aftermath. I identify three separate political economy scenarios that have been accentuated within those countries that have the strongest trade links and FDI inflows from China: the first scenario is the decision by Chile, Costa Rica, and Peru to institutionalize their respective relationships with China through the negotiation of separate bilateral free trade agreements (FTAs) with the PRC; the second scenario is the institutional resource curse that struck Argentina and Brazil in the throes of the China boom; and the third scenario is Mexico's competitive disadvantage vis-à-vis China as it persists with an FDI-driven, hands-off, export-led industrial strategy. With regard to all three of these scenarios, I dispute the critique of neodependency scholars, who overlook the fact that the LAC region is considerably more industrialized and macro-economically stable than in days of old. More to the point, given their emphasis on the structure of international capitalism as the driving factor, dependency scholars, neo- or otherwise, are still at a loss to explain the profound economic transformation of countries like Japan, Korea, and China that once occupied the purported periphery.

I offer three takeaway points based on the political economy scenarios just mentioned. First, contrary to the view expressed by some, the only new China–LAC relationship among the country cases considered here is that between the PRC and Costa Rica, and this is explicitly based on the One-China policy. Otherwise, the record shows that China and the other five countries analyzed have had a rich set of exchanges that date back to the 1950s. With the exception of Mexico in the earlier era, these LAC countries ran a surplus exporting raw materials to China. This pattern has held up to today, which suggests path dependence in the relationship the four South American countries have maintained with China. In the case of Mexico, value-added electrical equipment and electronic goods averaged 10.3 percent of its total exports to China between 2001 and 2017, whereas Chinese exports to Mexico in these same categories averaged 43 percent during this same period.[3] There is simply no good explanation—beyond its neoliberal industrial strategy—for Mexico's inability to attract market-seeking FDI inflows from China and to increase its share of value-added exports to China.

This segues into my second point, which is the passivity of all six countries in the face of rising competition from China. Mexico's first trade deficit with China appeared in 1993 and has continued to deepen ever since. The country's main policy response has been protectionism, rendering its export-led industrial strategy as pseudo-neoliberal: free trade with its various FTA partners and a myriad of protectionist measures directed toward China. Argentina and Brazil have also played the protectionist game, filing numerous antidumping complaints against China at the WTO and imposing licenses on Chinese imports. Of note here are the tremendous room to maneuver afforded by the China boom and the opportunity for human agency in undertaking the kinds of promotional policies that would strengthen a given country's ability to benefit most from its increased interaction with China. Take, for example, the case of environmental protection and oversight. A running theme in this book is the ease with which Chinese-backed infrastructure projects received the go-ahead by host governments.

Elizabeth Economy notes the corruption that plagues China's own environmental assessment agency, which means that the burden for environmental protection falls squarely on the shoulders of LAC policy makers.[4]

My third point concerns the success of the three, small open economies—two of which, Chile and Peru, are still largely dependent on primary exports. In the period between 2001 and 2018 average growth rates for these countries were 3.8 percent to 5 percent, versus average growth rates of 2.0 percent to 2.4 percent for Argentina, Brazil, and Mexico during this same time period (see table 3.1). In hindsight, the decision of Chile, Costa Rica, and Peru to enter into separate bilateral FTAs with China was a prudent one. These are the only LAC countries to enjoy privileged access to both the US and Chinese markets. However, neither are these FTAs with China the kinds of neoliberal blueprints touted by the economics establishment in the early 1990s. At the negotiating table Chile and Peru won rapid access to the Chinese market and numerous industrial sector exceptions for their domestic manufacturers. Through the institutionalization of their respective relationships with China each has succeeded in securing market access for additional value-added products.

As for Costa Rica, despite its low level of trade with China to date, some 77 percent of its exports to that market consist of electrical and electronic parts. Its shift to diplomatic recognition of China in 2007 has brought with it a grand design for the merging of Costa Rican and Chinese high-tech production in a planned special economic zone (SEZ) that would include the creation of distribution centers to service global suppliers. This may be grandiose, given how little progress has been made to date on establishing the proposed SEZ.[5] But the lack of progress does not detract from the fact that Costa Rican policy makers have set their sights on a worthwhile prize.

The Big Picture

Throughout this book I have emphasized that the China–LAC relationship is a work in progress. The data on comparative economic performance confirm how quickly gains can turn into losses in the aftermath of a commodity boom. For the more industrialized LAC EEs, the costs of misguided policies and institutional deterioration (Argentina and Brazil) or stagnation (Mexico) have proven quite steep, especially in per capita terms. For Argentina and Brazil the backsliding on reform indices and the exceedingly poor postboom economic performance highlight the extent to which opportunities for policy experimentation and innovation were squandered. Mexico's mediocre performance all the way through the boom and into the aftermath is also self-inflicted. Policy makers there settled into a low-productivity rut and have held on to an FDI-driven, export-led industrial strategy long past the evidence of its failure to raise national living standards and sustain healthy growth. The three small, open economies have deliberately promoted growth, per capita GDP gains, and capital formation. In doing so, they have pushed past the minimalist dictates of neoliberalism, harnessed domestic institutions to the task of export-led development, and molded the terms of their respective FTAs with China in ways that recognize the need for a proactive policy stance.

Nevertheless, the postboom period has highlighted the considerable reforms on which all six countries need to buckle down. An international comparison with the performance of other developing regions during the China boom provides an important reality check. The peak period of growth for the LAC region was 2003–7, and it averaged 5.4 percent a year. During this same time span the average annual growth rate for the developing countries and EEs was 7.4 percent; this includes sub-Saharan Africa, Central Asia, all of the other Asian subregions, and the transition economies of Eastern Europe.[6] Peru is the only breakout case in the LAC region, as it grew at an annual average rate of 6.2 percent from 2003 to 2013, and it increased gross fixed-capital formation as a percent of GDP from an annual average of 21.6 percent between 2003 and 2013 to 23.4 percent in the 2014–16 period (see table 1.1). All of the other countries analyzed saw a decrease in average annual rates of gross fixed-capital formation between these two periods. From 2014 to 2016 Argentina's average annual rate of gross fixed-capital formation was just 16.8 percent, and Brazil's was 17.9 percent.

Of all the lost opportunities suffered by LAC during the China boom, these low investment rates are one of the most glaring. An annual average rate of 25 percent of GDP is considered the minimum necessary in order for gross fixed-capital formation to propel catch-up growth, and only Peru approximated this level. Moreover, the averages that appear for the countries in this book (see table 1.1) pale next to China's average annual gross fixed-capital formation rate of 45 percent of GDP during the boom.[7] Throughout, we have seen that China stands ready to invest in all six LAC countries. This, however, has been no panacea. For example, in the midst of a capital drought and international isolation, Argentina agreed to the construction of two Chinese-financed hydroelectric projects, riding roughshod over environmental warnings and placing few limits on the use of Chinese engineering services and capital goods.[8] One of the PRC's planned investments in Costa Rica, an oil refinery, has fallen apart over environmental disputes and mutual allegations of corruption.[9] As we have seen, Chinese efforts to invest in Mexico's auto and retail sectors, not to mention a roughly US$4 billion bullet train, all came to naught. It took the opening of Mexico's oil sector for China to land the big investment tenders in that country, but this is repetitious of Brazil and Peru, where Chinese inflows of FDI are heavily concentrated in natural resources and endeavors related to oil and mineral extraction.

Investment drives growth, and growth, when harnessed to progressive distributional policies, is necessary for both absolute and relative income gains. Until recently, country-specific advances made in both poverty reduction and per capita income had been widely touted as a positive offshoot of the China boom. But because this growth "was not coupled with significant improvements in classic regional bottlenecks such as savings, investment, and productivity," these social inroads and the emergence of a new LAC middle class due to the China boom are still on fragile ground.[10] Per capita income gains have already taken a hit in the postboom period (see table 1.1); for now, the reduction in poverty rates, which went from a peak of 48.4 percent in 1990 to 28 percent in 2014, is still holding steady.[11] The reversal of fortune is especially acute in Argentina, where massive subsidies were highly regressive, benefiting all consumers of fuel and electricity rather than targeting those most in need. In Brazil, Workers' Party leaders may have been sincere, but the generous wage increases went well above the gains in productivity during the boom (as did those in Argentina). The expansion of government-backed consumer credit and an explosion in social expenditures pushed state budgets well beyond their limits. After five years of retrenchment, civil society in both countries has been especially vocal about this phenomenon of diminishing gains and a lot more pain.

The slowdown since 2014 has confirmed, once again, that dynamic, sustainable growth will elude LAC until the export basket incorporates more technology-intensive goods.[12] In the case of Chile and Peru, this would mean the greater application of technology to natural resource production and modern services.[13] In the other four manufacturing exporters the task is to return to more active productive-sector strategies geared toward educational improvement, increased funds for R&D, infrastructure upgrading, and incentives for much higher levels of investment overall. Three of the LAC EEs, Argentina, Brazil, and Mexico, as I've discussed above, articulated an industrial policy during the China boom. Argentina's "new developmentalist" policy was difficult to discern, given all of the subsidies and opaque budgeting practices; Brazil's developmentalist industrial policy was run through the country's National Development Bank and was more transparent but unable to break old patterns of exaggerated funding for natural resources over industry; Mexico has an explicit promotional policy for information technology, but this favors foreign-owned companies and domestic assembly contractors that have already been highly successful within this subsector. None of this adequately addresses the plight of small and medium-sized firms, the need to incorporate these firms more assertively into supply and value chains, or the skill deficit in the industrial sector of these respective economies.

What might this mean for the China–LAC relationship moving forward? On the demand side, this book has shown that Chinese demand for LAC's rich commodities has held steady. In 2018 total China–LAC trade hit an all-time high of US$306 billion, while FDI inflows and lending from China's policy banks began to level off. This slowing of capital flows is plausibly due to China's Belt and Road (BRI) commitments the world over and to the uncertainties wrought by the US trade war on China that began in 2018. On the supply side and despite the regional rhetoric of striving to export more diversified value-added goods to the Chinese market, it is incumbent on LAC policy makers and political leaders to push through the necessary reforms and design the proper incentives to achieve this goal. The three small, open economies, as we've seen, have pursued their own promotional strategy through the negotiation of bilateral FTAs with China. Mired in deep recession since 2014, Argentina and Brazil continue on a passive-aggressive status quo relationship with China, one based on complementary comparative advantage (passive) and a steady onslaught of trade remedies filed against China at the WTO (aggressive). Mexico, with China as its second largest trading partner, has fixated on the risks of this phenomenon and done little, in fact, to capitalize on the inherent opportunities. At the same time, as much as China talks the talk on globalization and free trade, it has its own surreptitious ways of keeping higher value-added imports at bay.[14] This is why its quest to win market economy status at the WTO has failed to gain wide support.

The bottom line is that the three more industrialized LAC EEs are going to have to fight for access to the Chinese market just like everybody else. For reasons analyzed throughout this book, Argentina, Brazil, and Mexico were not able to seize the opportunities for reform and restructuring opened up by the China boom. The LAC region as a whole is projected to continue to grow more slowly than the other developing and emerging countries. However, as I have argued throughout, such underachievement is not structurally predetermined. Rather, it depends on the tenacity and leadership of politicians and policy makers within each of these countries to advance policies that promote "technology upgrading, high-quality education, significant diversification of trade with China, betting on strong regional integration processes, and heavy investing in physical infrastructure."[15] These, argues José Antonio Ocampo of Columbia University, "are, together, the structural keys to dynamic long-term growth in Latin America."

LAC's Pivot toward Asia

In late January 2018, just as Secretary of State Rex Tillerson was trumpeting a revival of the imperialistic Monroe Doctrine as the guidepost for US–Latin American relations, China and the Community of 33 Latin American and Caribbean States (CELAC) held their second ministerial meeting of the China–CELAC Forum in Santiago, Chile. As Tillerson ranted about arms trafficking, drug running, and illegal aliens penetrating the US–Mexico border, the China–CELAC ministerial meeting—a follow-up to the first such forum hosted by Beijing in 2015—approved a joint action plan for cooperation from 2019 to 2021 and a special declaration on China's BRI. The BRI, launched by President Xi in 2013, promotes stronger infrastructure links between Asia and Europe along the old Silk Road, with billions of dollars of infrastructure investment in roads, ports, and railways. Africa has since been included, and now the CELAC nations have been invited to join. The joint action plan identifies areas of common interest in the realm of renewable energy, science and technology, infrastructure, the environment, and greater connectivity between land and sea.[16]

One proposal is to construct a fiber-optic cable across the Pacific Ocean to improve connectivity. Reality check: One of the first BRI contracts negotiated within LAC—a US$2.1 billion bid won by China's State Construction Engineering Corporation for highway construction in Argentina—fell far afield from this lofty goal. The gesture to include LAC, however, contrasts sharply with the constant stream of US insults toward the region in the Trump era. No sooner had the US electoral college votes been tallied up in favor of candidate Trump on November 8, 2016, than China made its move to fill what was sure to be a US leadership void in both Asia and Latin America.

True to form, Trump, upon taking office, pulled the US out of the Trans-Pacific Partnership (TPP)—once a pillar of President Barack Obama's "pivot toward Asia"—and followed through on his campaign vow to renegotiate the North American Free Trade Agreement (NAFTA) in ways more favorable to the US. The eleven remaining TPP members (Australia, Brunei, Canada, Chile, Japan, Malaysia, Mexico, New Zealand, Peru, Singapore, and Vietnam), regrouped and have agreed on a Comprehensive and Progressive Agreement for Trans-Pacific Partnership (CPTPP) which covers about 15 percent of the global economy. Now approved by all eleven member nations, CPTPP will cut tariffs on goods and services flowing between member markets, and it covers labor and environmental standards. China, which is not a member, has an open door to join.

At the same time, China is moving forward with the negotiation of its Regional Comprehensive Economic Partnership (RCEP). Launched in November 2013, RCEP includes the ASEAN countries (Brunei, Cambodia, Indonesia, Lao PDR, Malaysia, Myanmar, Philippines, Singapore, Thailand, and Vietnam), which together have a free trade agreement (FTA) with

China and the five other states that have existing FTAs with ASEAN (Australia, India, Japan, South Korea, and New Zealand). In the best of all possible worlds, these two mega-deals—RCEP and CPTPP—would be formally merged. In this world, where major economic powers are vying to control the content and membership of large regional accords, the two deals are moving forward in tandem.

Whereas TPP was all about advancing quickly on the new trade agenda (services, investment, and intellectual property rights), including the removal of opaque barriers to government-procurement contracts and foreign direct investment, RCEP is expected to move more gradually on the old trade agenda, including tariff reductions and greater market access.[17] The RCEP is considered more gradual and mercantilist, whereas CPTPP is designed along the more liberal economic lines of the WTO. In a comparative analysis of these two mega-regional agreements, Yifei Xiao argues that the two are actually linked by a "competitive and mutually stimulating relationship."[18] Especially in light of the overlapping membership of Australia, Brunei, Japan, Malaysia, New Zealand, Singapore, and Vietnam in both of these regional schemes, these countries can simultaneously gain deeper entry into the Chinese market and plausibly reap the best of what both deals have to offer.

Policy makers in Chile and Peru grasped the benefits of this competitive regionalism immediately upon the quashing of the TPP by Trump, and both promptly reached out to China about becoming a part of the RCEP scheme. Both countries also pushed hard for the revival of TPP. Costa Rica is now in the queue to join both schemes. The three LAC EEs have yet to chart a visible course that would afford them greater access to the Chinese market, in particular. Argentina and Brazil are hamstrung by their membership in the moribund Southern Cone Common Market (Mercosur), which limits external negotiations to the bloc as a whole. Mexico, again, is the odd one out. Mexico's trade deficit with China is roughly the size of its trade surplus with the US. Even if the NAFTA renegotiation has been less damaging than Mexican policy makers and producers feared, there is nothing to prevent President Trump from pulling the US out of NAFTA, especially if the US Congress jettisons the renegotiated US–Mexico–Canada

(USMCA).[19] Mexico's former economy minister Ildefonso Guajardo ac-knowledged that "Mexico has to have a means of integrating itself with the Asia-Pacific (region)" and that policy makers will "weigh the merits of the China-backed Regional Comprehensive Economic Partnership (RCEP)."[20]

However, if the USMCA does survive, the US has foreclosed the option of Mexico joining RCEP, insisting that both Mexico and Canada must give six-months' notice to Washington in the event that either intends to launch trade negotiations with a "non-market economy," read, China. At this point Mexico's best option for maximizing on China's internationalized develop-ment strategy is to go back to the numerous bilateral entities that have been created and deals that have been struck and add some meat to these bones. In the event the USMCA comes to fruition, its restrictions can be circum-vented by working through the High-Level Groups and the Bilateral Com-mission and by tapping into the US$2.4 billion Mexico–China Fund man-aged by the World Bank's International Finance Corporation. While some have declared these various venues a failure, this naysaying is premature. Pre-USMCA, Mexican policy makers were halfhearted in their efforts to max-imize on China–Mexico trade and investment relations. Now, as USMCA threatens higher North American barriers for both insiders and outsiders and as Washington ratchets up the economic hostility toward Beijing, Mex-ico has little choice but to pursue deeper economic and diplomatic ties with China.

As Tillerson made his way south on the February 2018 LAC tour, bash-ing China and touting the Trump administration's "America First" stance, the unimaginable happened: more than one LAC policy official publicly de-fended and lauded their country's respective partnership with China.[21] Apart from the headline-grabbing news of trade, loans, and FDI flowing from China to LAC, there are numerous signs of China's integrating construc-tively within the region. I have already discussed the two China–CELAC fora, one in 2015 and the other in 2018. Even if just a tenth of the numerous project proposals announced comes to fruition, the context is one of com-mon goals and mutual respect.[22] In the meantime millions of Brazilian shoppers are buying on Alibaba's AliExpress website (roughly the Chinese equivalent of Amazon); Beijing-based Ofo, a bicycle sharing company, is looking to invest in Mexico; Argentines and Chileans are driving Chinese-made cars; and the Chinese are buying up Peru's "maca root," akin to ginseng, in gold-rush fashion.

The big China boom is over. And yet two decades into the new millennium the horizon for any number of other enriching ties in China–LAC relations does indeed seem to be wide open. While the opportunities for closer economic integration may be infinite, so too are the risks. This book has shown that "success" has varied according to issue areas, sectors, and projects across these countries. Moreover, the best outcomes have stemmed from China-related endeavors where rule of law, regulatory oversight, and a clear strategy exist on the Latin American side. As security hawks in the Trump administration have redefined China as a global competitor that engages in predatory economic policies and accused it of trying to "decouple" Latin America from the US, Latin American leaders of all political stripes have been wise to keep their heads down. As a region, LAC has much to gain from its pivot toward Asia. The task ahead is to work smarter and more efficiently on the China relationship, while simultaneously tackling the backlog of pending reforms on the domestic front.

NOTES

Introduction

1. Quoted in Raul Zibechi, "China Stakes Its Claim in Latin America," *Counter-Punch*, March 16, 2015, http://www.counterpunch.org/2015/03/16/china-stakes-its-claim-in-latin-america/.

2. Based on the average of twelve Latin American annual GDP growth rates. World Bank Development Indicators, available at http://data.worldbank.org/.

3. John Williamson, "From Reform Agenda to Damaged Brand Name," *Finance and Development* (September 2003), 10–13.

4. See Leslie Armijo, Carol Wise, and Saori Katada, "Lessons from the Country Case Studies," in *Unexpected Outcomes: How Emerging Economies Survived the Global Financial Crisis*, ed. Carol Wise, Leslie Armijo, and Saori Katada (Washington, DC: Brookings Institution Press, 2015); and Eduardo Lora, "Structural Reforms in Latin America: What Has Been Reformed and How to Measure It," Inter-American Development Bank, Research Department, Working Paper 466, 2001.

5. Armijo, Wise, and Katada, "Lessons from the Country Case Studies," 212.

6. Manuel Pastor and Carol Wise, "Good-bye Financial Crash, Hello Financial Eclecticism: Latin American Responses to the 2008–09 Global Financial Crisis," *Journal of International Money and Finance* 52 (April 2015): 200–217.

7. Ambrogio Cesa Bianchi, M. Hashem Pesaran, Alessandro Rebucci, and Tengteng Xu, "China's Emergence in the World Economy and Business Cycles in Latin America," *Economía* 12, no. 2 (2012): 32.

8. "Brazil Takes Off," *The Economist*, November 9, 2009, http://www.economist.com/node/14845197.

9. "IMF: Better than Expected Rebound for Argentina," *Buenos Aires Herald*, April 12, 2011, http://www.buenosairesherald.com/article/64170/imf-better-than-expected-rebound-for-argentina.

10. Clifford Kraus, "Oil Glut Grows and Takes a Toll on the Economy," *New York Times,* January 16, 2016, A1.

11. Gustavo Ribeiro, "Brazil Emerges from Recession Weaker than It Was Before," *The Brazilian Report,* March 2, 2018, https://brazilian.report/money/2018/03/02 /brazil-recession-economy-weaker/; Jayson McNamara, "IMF: Argentina's Recession to Continue in 2019 with 1.7% Slump," *Buenos Aires Times,* January 1, 2019, https://www.batimes.com.ar/news/economy/imf-argentina-recession-to-continue -in-2019-with-17-slump.phtml.

12. "Argentina Gets Biggest Loan in IMF's History at $57 Billion," *The Guardian,* September 26, 2018, https://www.theguardian.com/world/2018/sep/26/argentina -imf-biggest-loan.

13. "Economic Snapshot for Latin America," *Focus Economics,* May 15, 2019, http:// www.focus-economics.com/regions/latin-america.

14. Guillermo Perry and Alejandro Forero, "Latin America: The Day After. Is This Time Different?" Documentos CEDE 46, Centro de Estudios sobre Desarrollo Económico, University of the Andes, Bogotá, Colombia, December, 2014.

15. Rocio Cara Labrador, "Venezuela: The Rise and Fall of a Petrostate," Council on Foreign Relations, Backgrounder, January 24, 2019, https://www.cfr.org/back grounder/venezuela-crisis.

16. Economic Commission for Latin America and the Caribbean (ECLAC), *First Forum of China and the Community of Latin American and Caribbean States* (Santiago: ECLAC, 2015).

17. A good starting point on this literature is R. Evan Ellis, *China in Latin America: The Whats and Wherefores* (Boulder: Lynne Rienner Press, 2009); Kevin P. Gallagher and Roberto Porzecanski, *The Dragon in the Room: China and the Future of Latin American Industrialization* (Stanford: Stanford University Press, 2011); Kevin Gallagher, *The China Triangle: Latin America's China Boom and the Fate of the Washington Consensus* (New York: Oxford University Press, 2016); Adrian H. Hearn and José Luis Léon-Manríquez, eds., *China Engages Latin America: Tracing the Trajectory* (Boulder: Lynne Rienner Press, 2011); Rhys Jenkins, *How China Is Reshaping the Global Economy* (New York: Oxford University Press, 2019); Margaret Myers and Carol Wise, eds., *The Political Economy of China–Latin America Relations in the New Millennium* (New York: Routledge Press, 2016).

18. John J. Mearsheimer and Stephen M. Walt, "The Case for Offshore Balancing: A Superior U.S. Grand Strategy," *Foreign Affairs* 95, no. 4 (July/August 2016): 71.

19. See, for example, Alexandre de Freitas Barbosa, "China and Latin America: Strategic Partnership or Latter-Day Imperialism?" in *China's New Role in Africa and the South,* ed. Dorothy-Grace Guerrero and Firoze Manji (Oxford: Fahamu Books, 2008); Jaime Ortiz, "Déjà vu: Latin America and Its New Trade Dependency . . . This Time with China," *Latin American Research Review* 47, no. 3 (2012): 175–90; Ruben Laufer, "Argentina–China: New Courses for an Old Dependency," *Latin American Policy* 4, no. 1 (2013): 123–43; Alicia Puyana and Agostina Costantino,

"Chinese Land Grabbing in Argentina and Colombia," *Latin American Perspectives* 42, no. 6 (2015): 105–19.

20. Gustavo A. Flores-Macías and Sarah E. Kreps, "The Foreign Policy Consequences of Trade: China's Commercial Relations with Africa and Latin America, 1992–2006, *Journal of Politics* 75, no. 2 (2013): 357–71.

21. Georg Stuver, "'Bereft of Friends'? China's Rise and Search for Political Partners in South America," *Chinese Journal of International Politics* 7, no. 1 (2014): 148.

22. One of the biggest doubters I met while researching this book was the very prominent political science professor Pan Wei, the director of the Center for Chinese and Global Affairs, Peking University.

23. Jeffry Frieden, *Debt, Development and Democracy: Modern Political Economy and Latin America, 1965–1985* (Princeton: Princeton University Press, 1991), 235.

24. Feng Zhongping and Huang Jing, "China's Strategic Partnership Diplomacy: Engaging with a Changing World," European Strategic Partnerships Observatory, Working Paper 8, June 2014. Using a broader definition, Georg Struver estimates that China has thus far established partnership relations with sixty-seven individual countries. See Georg Struver, "China's Partnership Diplomacy: International Alignment Based on Interests or Ideology," *Chinese Journal of International Politics* 10, no. 1 (2017): 31–65.

25. Yanran Xu, *China's Strategic Partnerships in Latin America: Case Studies of China's Oil Diplomacy in Argentina, Brazil, Mexico and Venezuela, 1990 to 2015* (Lanham, MD: Lexington Books, 2017).

26. UNDP, "Sustainable Development Goals (SDGs)," available at http://www.undp .org/content/undp/en/home/sdgoverview/post-2015-development-agenda.html; Kevin Gallagher, *The China Triangle*, 72.

27. Bushra Bataineh, Michael Bennon, and Francis Fukuyama, "Beijing's Building Boom," *Foreign Affairs*, May 21, 2018, https://www.foreignaffairs.com/articles /china/2018-05-21/beijings-building-boom.

28. Author's calculation of six selected LAC countries, based on trade data from https://comtrade.un.org/data/.

29. Enrique Dussel Peters, "Monitor of China's OFDI in Latin America and the Caribbean 2018," March 21, 2018, available at http://www.redalc-china.org/monitor /images/pdfs/menuprincipal/DusselPeters_MonitorOFDI_2018_Eng.pdf.

30. Barbara Stallings, "Chinese Foreign Aid to Latin America: Trying to Win Friends and Influence People," in *The Political Economy of China–Latin American Relations in the New Millennium*, ed. Margaret Myers and Carol Wise (New York: Routledge Press, 2016), 78.

31. Kevin Gallagher and Margaret Myers, "China–Latin America Finance Database," Inter-American Dialogue, Washington, DC, 2019, available at http://www.the dialogue.org/map_list/.

32. Rebecca Ray, Kevin Gallagher, and Rudy Sarmiento, "China–Latin America Economic Bulletin 2016 Edition," 4.

33. Gregor Aisch, Josh Keller, and K. K. Rebecca Lai, "The World According to China," *New York Times,* July 24, 2015, http://www.nytimes.com/interactive/2015/07/24 /business/international/the-world-according-to-china-investment-maps.html.

34. Stephen B. Kaplan and Michael Penfold, "China-Venezuelan Economic Relations: Hedging Venezuelan Bets with Chinese Characteristics," Washington, DC: Wilson Center, Latin America Program, February, 2019), 27.

35. James Kynge, Michael Peel, and Ben Bland, "High-speed Dream Hits the Buffers," *Financial Times,* July 18, 2017, 9.

36. For a detailed analysis of China's much earlier foray into Africa, for example, see Deborah Brautigam, *The Dragon's Gift: The Real story of China in Africa* (Oxford: Oxford University Press, 2009).

37. Yang Ge, " 'Belt and Road Drives Into Argentina With $2 billion Contract,' " *Caixin,* August 10, 2018, https://www.caixinglobal.com/2018-08-10/belt-and-road-drives -into-argentina-with-2-billion-contract-101313794.html.

38. Leonardo Stanley, "Argentina's Infrastructure Gap and Financial Needs: The Role of China," in *Building Development for a New Era: China's Infrastructure Projects in Latin America and the Caribbean,* ed. Enrique Dussel Peters, Ariel C. Armony, and Shoujun Cui (Mexico, D.F.: Red Académica de América Latina y el Caribe sobre China and the University of Pittsburgh, 2018), 77–101.

39. "Chinese Consortium to Build Fourth Panama Canal Bridge," *Reuters,* July 29, 2018, https://www.reuters.com/article/panama-china/chinese-consortium-to-build -fourth-panama-canal-bridge-idUSL1N1UP05W; and Guyana, Department of Public Information, August 16, 2018, http://dpi.gov.gy/guyana-signs-onto-chinas-road -and-belt-initiative/.

40. "China's Belt and Road Initiative Is Falling Short," *Opinion: The FT View,* July 29, 2018, https://www.ft.com/content/47d63fec-9185–11e8-b639–7680cedcc421.

41. Tom Hancock, "China Renegotiated $50 billion in Loans to Developing Countries," *Financial Times,* April 29, 2019, https://www.ft.com/content/0b207552 -6977-11e9-80c7-60ee53e6681d.

42. Margaret Myers, "The Reasons for China's Cooling Interest in Latin America," *Americas Quarterly,* April 23, 2019, https://www.americasquarterly.org/content /how-beijing-sees-it.

43. Gallagher and Porzecanski, *The Dragon in the Room,* 8.

44. Yuan Yang and Lucy Hornby, "China Admits Almost All Its Computer Chips Are Imported," *Financial Times,* July 20, 2018, 3.

45. Sven-Uwe Mueller and Fan Li, "Chinese Infrastructure Projects in Latin America and the Caribbean: The Experience of the Inter-American Development Bank," in *Building Development for a New Era: China's Infrastructure Projects in Latin America and the Caribbean,* ed. Enrique Dussel Peters, Ariel C. Armony, and Shoujun Cui (Mexico, D.F.: Red Académica de América Latina y el Caribe sobre China and the University of Pittsburgh, 2018), 164–79.

46. Ray, Gallagher, and Sarmiento, "China–Latin America Economic Bulletin 2016 Edition," 5.

47. See, for example, Martin Jacques, *When China Rules the World* (New York: Penguin Press, 2009), and Michael Fenby, *Will China Dominate the 21st Century?* (Cambridge: Polity Press, 2014).

48. Mark Blyth, "Global Trumpism," *Foreign Affairs*, November 15, 2016, https://www.foreignaffairs.com/print/1118798.

49. Jude Webber and John Paul Rathbone, "Tillerson Extols 19th-Century Foreign Policy in Latin America," *Financial Times*, February 2, 2018, https://www.ft.com/content/bdaee8d2-07c3-11e8-9650-9c0ad2d7c5b5.

50. Chairman Dan Burton, "Opening Statement," Hearing on China's Influence in the Western Hemisphere, Subcommittee on the Western Hemisphere, Committee on International Relations, US House of Representatives, April 6, 2005.

51. Zachary Keck, "The U.S. Renounces the Monroe Doctrine," *The Diplomat*, November 21, 2013, http://thediplomat.com/2013/11/the-us-renounces-the-monroe-doctrine/.

52. Andres Oppenheimer, "China Is Becoming More Popular than the U.S. in Many Latin American Countries," *Miami Herald*, April 24, 2019, https://www.miamiherald.com/news/local/news-columns-blogs/andres-oppenheimer/article22962 1934.html.

53. The data cited in this paragraph can be found in Catherine A. Theohary, "Conventional Arms Transfers to Developing Nations, 2008–2015," Congressional Research Service, December 19, 2016, available at https://fas.org/sgp/crs/weapons/R44716.pdf.

54. Ted Piccone, "The Geopolitics of China's Rise in Latin America," Paper 2, Geoeconomics and Global Issues, Brookings Institution, November 2016, 24.

55. Ibid., 8–9.

56. Ernesto Londoño, "From a Space Station in Argentina, China Expands Its Reach in Latin America," *New York Times*, July 28, 2018, https://www.nytimes.com/2018/07/28/world/americas/china-latin-america.html.

57. Allan Nixon, "China's Growing Arms Sales to Latin America," *The Diplomat*, August 24, 2016, https://thediplomat.com/2016/08/chinas-growing-arms-sales-to-latin-america/?allpages=yes&print=yes.

58. Michael Beckley, "Stop Obsessing About China," *Foreign Affairs*, September 21, 2018, https://www.foreignaffairs.com/articles/china/2018-09-21/stop-obsessing-about-china.

59. ECLAC, *First Forum of China and the Community of Latin American and Caribbean States*, 28.

60. Joseph Y. S. Cheng, "Latin America in China's Contemporary Foreign Policy," *Third World Quarterly* 36, no. 4 (2007): 500–528.

61. Francisco Urdinez, Fernando Mouron, Luis L. Schenoni, and Amancio J. de Oliveira, "Chinese Economic Statecraft and US Hegemony in Latin America," *Latin American Politics and Society* 58, no. 4 (2016): 3.

62. Lei Yu, "China's Strategic Partnership with Latin America: A Fulcrum in China's Rise," *International Affairs* 91, no. 5 (2015): 1048.

63. Tracy Wilkinson, "Russia and China, Heavily Invested in Venezuela, Warily Watch the Political Turmoil," *Los Angeles Times,* January 25, 2019, https://www.latimes .com/world/europe/la-fg-venezuela-russia-china-20190125-story.html.

64. June Teufel Dreyer, "From China with Love: P.R.C. Overtures in Latin America," *Brown Journal of World Affairs* 12, no. 2 (Winter/Spring 2006): 90.

65. Mearsheimer and Walt, "The Case for Offshore Balancing: A Superior U.S. Grand Strategy."

66. This term first appeared in a 1977 article in *The Economist* and referred to the decline of the Dutch manufacturing sector due to the discovery and development of natural gas in the late 1950s. As high natural gas prices triggered a foreign exchange boom and, in turn, currency appreciation, industrial exports, and jobs languished. See "The Dutch Disease," *The Economist,* November 26, 1977, 82–83.

67. Omar Sánchez, "The Rise and Fall of the Dependency Movement: Does It Inform Underdevelopment Today?" *Estudios Interdisciplinarios de América Latina y el Caribe* 14, no. 2 (2003), http://eial.tau.ac.il/index.php/eial/article/view/893/946.

68. These numbers come from Arthur Kroeber, *China's Economy: What Everyone Needs to Know* (Oxford: Oxford University Press, 2016), 9–10.

69. See https://tradingeconomics.com/china/gdp-per-capita-ppp. Unlike conventional measures of per capita GDP, purchasing power parity (PPP) accounts for national differences in the cost of living. Based on this measure and given China's radically lower domestic prices, in 2014 the International Monetary Fund announced that China's per capita GDP based on PPP had surpassed that of the US. No one was more vehemently in disagreement with this notion than China itself. See Matt Schiavenza, "China Surpasses US in Purchasing Power, But Americans Don't Need to Worry," *International Business Times,* October 8, 2014, https://www .ibtimes.com/china-economy-surpasses-us-purchasing-power-americans-dont -need-worry-1701804.

70. "Meet the Latin Americans Making It Big In China," *Americas Quarterly,* April 23, 2019, https://www.americasquarterly.org/content/meet-latin-americans-making -it-big-china-2.

71. Dussel Peters, "Monitor of Chinese OFDI in Latin America and the Caribbean 2018," available at http://www.redalc-china.org/monitor/images/pdfs/menu principal/DusselPeters_MonitorOFDI_2018_Eng.pdf.

72. The seminal work on this is Raúl Prebisch, *The Economic Development of Latin America and Its Principal Problems* (New York: United Nations, Department of Social Affairs, 1950).

73. Author's interview with Andrés Campos, Senior Business Developer, Ensenada Economic Development Commission, Ensenada, Baja California, Mexico, July 28, 2016.

74. See Sunil Mani, "Have China and India Become More Innovative since the Onset of Reforms in the Two Countries?" in *Transformation and Development: The Political Economy of Transition in India and China,* ed. Amiya Kumar Bagchi and An-

thony P. D'Costa (New Delhi: Oxford University Press, 2012); and Gallagher and Porzecanski, *The Dragon in the Room*, chapter 3.

75. Ortiz, "Déjà vu: Latin America and Its New Trade Dependency," 188.

76. Prebisch, *The Economic Development of Latin America.*

77. Robert Devlin, "China's Economic Rise," in *China's Expansion into the Western Hemisphere: Implications for Latin America and the United States*, ed. Riordan Roett and Guadalupe Paz (Washington, DC: Brookings Institution Press, 2008), 137–39. Also see Ricardo Hausmann, "How to Make the Next Big Thing," *Scientific American*, 308, no. 5 (May 2013), 36–37.

78. See "The Dutch Disease," *The Economist*, November 26, 1977, 82–83.

79. Andres Schipani, "Venezuela Army Tightens Grip as Food Riots Grow," *Financial Times*, July 29, 2016, 30.

80. Mauricio Cárdenas, "Curbing Success in Latin America." April 14, 2011, available at https://www.brookings.edu/opinions/curbing-success-in-latin-america/.

81. Perry and Forero, "Latin America: The Day After," 22.

82. CEPALSTAT, "Exports of Manufactured Products According to Their Share in the Total: Latin America and Caribbean," 2014, available at http://interwp.cepal.org/sisgen/ConsultaIntegrada.asp?IdAplicacion=6&idTema=119&idIndicador=1911&idioma=i.

83. Daniela Prates, Barbara Fritz, and Luiz Fernando de Paula, "Brazil at a Crossroads: A Critical Assessment of Developmentalist Policies," in *The Brazilian Economy since the Great Financial Crisis of 2007/2008*, ed. Philip Arestis, Carolina Baltar, and Daniela Prates (London: Palgrave Macmillan, 2017), 9–39.

84. Halvor Mehlum, Karl Moene, and Ragnar Torvik, "Institutions and the Resource Curse," *Economic Journal* 116, no. 1 (2006): 1–20.

85. Terry Lynn Karl, *The Paradox of Plenty: Oil Boom and Petro-States* (Berkeley and Los Angeles: University of California Press, 1997), 11–13; Michael Ross, "What Have We Learned about the Resource Curse?" *Annual Review of Political Science* 18 (2015): 248–50.

86. Daron Acemoglu and James Robinson, *Why Nations Fail: The Origins of Power, Prosperity, and Poverty* (New York: Crown Business, 2012).

87. Mehlum, Moene, and Torvik, "Institutions and the Resource Curse," 2–3.

88. Shawn Donnan, " 'Doing Business' Survey at World Bank Has a New Look, but China Will Still Not Be Happy," *Financial Times*, October 28, 2014, https://www.ft.com/content/f7b1fb0b-d183-38d7-a46f-432cd0a175ae.

89. Yuen Yuen Ang, "The Real China Model: It's Not What You Think It Is," *Foreign Affairs*, June 29, 2018, https://www.foreignaffairs.com/print/1122584.

90. Karl, *The Paradox of Plenty*, 11–13.

91. Douglass North, *Institutions, Institutional Change, and Economic Performance* (New York: Cambridge University Press, 1990), 98–99.

92. Ariel Armony and Julia C. Strauss, "From Going Out (zou chuqu) to Arriving In (desembarco): Constructing a New Field of Inquiry in China–Latin America Relations," *China Quarterly* 209 (2012): 1.

Chapter 1. Dragonomics

1. Deng Xiaoping, *Selected Works of Deng Xiaoping* (Beijing: People's Publishing House, 1993), 374. Cited in Hu Angang, *China in 2020: A New Type of Superpower* (Washington, DC: Brookings Institution Press, 2011), 10.

2. Rebecca Ray and Kevin Gallagher, "China–Latin America Economic Bulletin 2015 Edition," Working Group on Development and Environment in the Americas, Global Economic Governance Initiative, Discussion Paper 2015–9, Boston University, September 2015.

3. Barry Naughton, "A Political Economy of China's Economic Transition," in *China's Great Economic Transformation*, ed. Loren Brandt and Thomas G. Rawski (Cambridge: Cambridge University Press, 2008); Nicholas R. Lardy, *Markets over Mao: The Rise of Private Business in China* (Washington, DC: Peterson Institute for International Economics, 2014); and Arthur Kroeber, *China's Economy: What Everyone Needs to Know* (Oxford: Oxford University Press, 2016).

4. Francis Fukuyama, "Exporting the Chinese Model." *Project Syndicate* 12 (2016), available at https://www.project-syndicate.org/onpoint/china-one-belt-one-road -strategy-by-francis-fukuyama-2016–01?barrier=accesspaylog.

5. Charles Clover, "IMF's Lagarde Warns China on Belt and Road Debt," *Financial Times*, April 18, 2018, https://www.ft.com/content/8e6d98e2–3ded-11e8-b7e0 -52972418fec4.

6. Owen Churchill, "Mike Pompeo Warns Panama and Other Nations about Accepting China's 'Belt and Road' Loans," *South China Morning Post*, October 18, 2018, https://www.scmp.com/news/china/diplomacy/article/2169449/mike-pompeo -warns-panama-and-other-nations-about-accepting.

7. Naughton, "A Political Economy of China's Economic Transition," 116.

8. This refers to exchanges occurring between private, nongovernmental parties and was a cornerstone of the PRC's outreach to LAC up through the normalization of relations with these countries.

9. Cecil Johnson, *Communist China and Latin America, 1959–1967* (New York: Columbia University Press, 1970); Frank Dikotter, *Mao's Great Famine: The History of China's Most Devastating Catastrophe, 1958–1962* (New York: Walker, 2010).

10. Marisela Connelly and Romer Cornejo Bustamante, *China–América Latina: Génesis y desarrollo de sus relaciones* (Mexico, D.F.: El Colegio de Mexico, 1992), 133–35; Johnson, *Communist China and Latin America, 1959–1967*, 15–21.

11. William A. Joseph, "China's Relations with Chile under Allende: A Case Study of Chinese Foreign Policy in Transition," *Studies in Comparative Communism* 18, no. 2 (1985): 140.

12. Hongying Wang, "The Missing Link in Sino–Latin American Relations," *Journal of Contemporary China* 24, no. 95 (2015): 922–42.

13. Luciano Ciravegna, *Promoting Silicon Valleys in Latin America: Lessons from Costa Rica* (New York: Routledge, 2012).

14. Economic Commission for Latin America and the Caribbean (ECLAC), *First*

Forum of China and the Community of Latin American and Caribbean States (Santiago: ECLAC, 2015).

15. Simon Romero, "China's Ambitious Rail Projects Crash into Harsh Realities in Latin America," *New York Times,* October 3, 2015, http://www.nytimes.com/2015 /10/04/world/americas/chinas-ambitious-rail-projects-crash-into-harsh-realities -in-latin-america.html?_r=0. Also see Adam Chimienti and Benjamin Creutzfeldt, "Who Wants What for Latin America: Voices for and against the China-backed Extractivist Development Model," in *The Political Economy of China–Latin America Relations in the New Millennium,* ed. Margaret Myers and Carol Wise (New York: Routledge, 2016).

16. Minxin Pei, *China's Trapped Transition: The Limits of Developmental Autocracy* (Cambridge: Harvard University Press, 2006); Elizabeth C. Economy, *The Third Revolution: Xi Jinping and the New Chinese State* (New York: Oxford University Press, 2018).

17. Robert O. Keohane and Joseph S. Nye, "Power and Interdependence Revisited," *International Organization* 41, no. 4 (1987): 725–53.

18. Jonathan Kirshner, "The Tragedy of Offensive Realism: Classical Realism and the Rise of China," *European Journal of International Relations* 18, no. 1 (2010): 53–75; Robert Kagan, *The Jungle Grows Back: America and Our Imperiled World* (New York: Knopf, 2018).

19. John Mearsheimer, "Can China Rise Peacefully?" *National Interest,* October 24, 2014.

20. John Ikenberry, "The Rise of China and the Future of the West," *Foreign Affairs* 87, no. 1 (January/February, 2008): 23–37.

21. Kurt M. Campbell and Ely Ratner, "The China Reckoning: How Beijing Defied American Expectations," *Foreign Affairs* 97, no. 2 (March/April 2018): 60–70.

22. Ibid., 62.

23. Mark Weisbrot and Jake Johnston. "Voting Share Reform at the IMF," Center for Economic and Policy Research, April 2016, available at http://cepr.net/images /stories/reports/IMF-voting-shares-2016–04.pdf.

24. For more detail on this matter, see Cynthia Roberts, Leslie Elliott Armijo, and Saori N. Katada, *The BRICS and Collective Financial Statecraft* (New York: Oxford University Press, 2018).

25. Oliver Stuenkel, *Post-Western World* (Cambridge: Polity Press, 2016), 122–23.

26. R. Evan Ellis, "China: Latin America and the Emerging Ideological Struggle of the 21st Century," *Global Americans,* June 17, 2018, available at https://theglobal americans.org/2018/06/latin-america-and-the-emerging-ideological-struggle -of-the-21st-century/.

27. Mearsheimer, "Can China Rise Peacefully?" 20.

28. The highlights of this literature include Chalmers Johnson, *MITI and the Japanese Miracle: The Growth of Industrial Policy, 1925–1975* (Palo Alto: Stanford University Press, 1982); Alice Amsden, *Asia's Next Giant: South Korea and Late Industrialization* (New York: Oxford University Press, 1989); Robert Wade, *Governing the Mar-*

ket: Theory and the Role of Government in East Asian Industrialization (Princeton: Princeton University Press, 1990); Stephan Haggard, *Pathways from the Periphery* (Ithaca: Cornell University Press, 1990); Meredith Woo-Cumings, ed., *The Developmental State* (Ithaca: Cornell University Press, 1999); and Ha-Joon Chang, *The East Asian Development Experience* (London: Zed Books, 2006).

29. Vogel, *Deng Xiaoping and the Transformation of China*, 294 (Kindle Edition).
30. Ministry of Foreign Affairs of Japan, "Treaty of Peace and Friendship between Japan and the People's Republic of China," available at http://www.mofa.go.jp /region/asia-paci/china/treaty78.html.
31. Ezra F. Vogel, "Can China and Japan Ever Get Along?" in *The China Questions: Critical Insights into a Rising Power*, ed. Jennifer Rudolph and Michael Szonyi (Cambridge: Harvard University Press, 2018), 111 (Kindle Edition).
32. See, for example, Peter Evans, "Predatory, Developmental, and Other Apparatuses: A Comparative Political Economy Perspective on the Third World State," *Sociological Forum* 4, no. 4 (1989): 561–87; and Atul Kohli, *State-Directed Development: Political Power and Industrialization in the Global Periphery* (New York: Cambridge University Press, 2004).
33. Arthur Kroeber, *China's Economy: What Everyone Needs to Know* (New York: Oxford University Press, 2016), 9–16.
34. Hu Angang, *China in 2020: A New Type of Superpower* (Washington, DC: Brookings Institution Press, 2011), 9.
35. Inter-American Development Bank (IDB), *Japan and Latin America and the Caribbean* (Washington, DC: IDB, 2013), 22–23.
36. Coordinated Direct Investment Survey (CDIS) extracted from IMF Data Warehouse on March 23, 2014.
37. Enrique Dussel Peters, "Characteristics of Chinese Overseas Foreign Direct Investment in Latin America (2000–2012)," *Contemporary International Relations* 23, no. 5 (2013): 105–29.
38. Isaac Stone Fish, "Why Does the U.S. Still Give Millions of Dollars in Aid to China?" *Huffington Post*, July 15, 2013, http://www.huffingtonpost.com/2013/07 /15/aiding-and-abetting_n_3598712.html; Steven Lee Myers and Motoko Rich, "Shinzo Abe Says Japan Is China's 'Partner,' and No Longer Its Aid Donor," *New York Times*, November 5, 2018, https://www.nytimes.com/2018/10/26/world/asia /shinzo-abe-china-japan.html.
39. Deborah Brautigam and Kevin Gallagher, "Bartering Globalization: China's Commodity-Backed Finance in Africa and Latin America," *Global Policy* 5, no. 3 (2014): 346–52.
40. William J. Norris, *Chinese Economic Statecraft: Commercial Actors, Grand Strategy, and State Control* (Ithaca: Cornell University Press, 2016). Also see Wei Liang, "Pulling the Region into its Orbit? China's Economic Statecraft in Latin America," *Journal of Chinese Political Science*, January 2019, https://doi.org/10.1007 /s11366-018-09603-w.
41. Jennifer Hughes, "China's March of the Milestones Is Having a Cumulative Im-

pact," *Financial Times*, October 7, 2016, 24; Dan McCrum, "Opportunities and Risks as China Becomes Too Big to Ignore," *Financial Times*, June 23, 2017, 22.

42. Emma Dunkley, "China Inc's Habit of Shelving Stocks Is a 'Visceral' Issue, Says Head of MSCI," *Financial Times*, June 5, 2018, 19.

43. Joseph Nye, "America Still Holds the Aces in Its Poker Games with China," *Financial Times*, November 3, 2017, 9.

44. Steven Liao and Daniel McDowell, "Redback Rising: China's Bilateral Swap Agreements and Renminbi Internationalization," *International Studies Quarterly* 59, no. 3 (2015): 401–22.

45. Yanran Xu, *China's Strategic Partnerships in Latin America: Case Studies of China's Oil Diplomacy in Argentina, Brazil, Mexico and Venezuela, 1990 to 2015* (Lanham, MD: Lexington Books, 2017).

46. Evan Medeiros, *China's International Behavior: Activism, Opportunism, and Diversification* (Santa Monica, CA: Rand Corporation, 2009).

47. Gastón Fornés and Álvaro Méndez, *The China–Latin America Axis*, 2d ed. (London: Palgrave Macmillan, 2017), 57–58.

48. I thank my USC colleague Stan Rosen for this insight.

49. Ministry of Foreign Affairs, Republic of China (Taiwan), available at http://www .mofa.gov.tw/en/AlliesIndex.aspx?n=DF6F8F246049F8D6&sms=A76B7230 ADF29736.

50. Barbara Stallings, "Chinese Foreign Aid to Latin America: Trying to Win Friends and Influence People," in *The Political Economy of China–Latin American Relations in the New Millennium*, ed. Margaret Myers and Carol Wise (New York: Routledge Press, 2016), 84.

51. Ibid., 86.

52. Merriden Varrall, "Chinese Views on China's Role in International Development Assistance," *Pacific Affairs* 86, no, 2 (2013): 233–34.

53. Charles Wolf, Xiao Wang, and Eric Warner, *China's Foreign Aid and Government-Sponsored Investment Activities* (Santa Monica, CA: Rand Corporation, 2013).

54. Enrique Dussel Peters, *Monitor of China's OFDI in Latin America and the Caribbean 2018* (Mexico, D.F.: Academic Network of Latin America and the Caribbean and China, March 21, 2018). Following this author, I use the term OFDI (outflows of foreign direct investment) rather than FDI, as the latter includes both inflows and outflows, available at http://www.redalc-china.org/monitor/images /pdfs/menuprincipal/DusselPeters_MonitorOFDI_2018_Eng.pdf.

55. Stallings, "Chinese Foreign Aid to Latin America."

56. Gallagher and Myers, "China–Latin America Finance Database."

57. Rebecca Ray, Kevin Gallagher, and Rudy Sarmiento, "China–Latin America Economic Bulletin 2016 Edition," 4.

58. Dussel Peters, *Monitor of Chinese OFDI in Latin America and the Caribbean 2018.*

59. Wolf, Wang, and Warner, *China's Foreign Aid and Government-Sponsored Investment Activities*, 26. These authors also state that Chinese foreign aid to Latin America totaled $186 billion from 2001 to 2011, 29!

60. Stallings, "Chinese Foreign Aid to Latin America," 71–72.

61. Ibid., 78.

62. Ibid., 81–86.

63. Ricky Singh, "Dominica Breaks Ties with Taiwan; Establishes Ties with China," *Jamaica Observer,* March 31, 2004, http://www.jamaicaobserver.com/news/57940 _Dominica-breaks-with-Taiwan—establishes-ties-with-China.

64. Max Corden and Peter Neary, "Booming Sector and De-industrialization in a Small Open Economy," *Economic Journal* 92 (December 1982): 825–48.

65. Elaine Moore and Andres Schipani, "Venezuela Keeps Paying Foreign Lenders Despite Blackouts and Food Queue Riots," *Financial Times,* June 10, 2016, 1; Jonathan Kaiman, "Controversial Ecuador Oil Deal Lets China Stake an $80-million Claim to Pristine Amazon Rainforest," *Los Angeles Times,* January 29, 2016, http://www.latimes.com/world/mexico-americas/la-fg-ecuador-china-oil-20160129 -story.html.

66. Gallagher and Myers, "China–Latin America Finance Database."

67. Brautigam and Gallagher, "Bartering Globalization," 350–51; Kejal Vyas, "China's President Pledges Continued Aid to Venezuela; China Has Given More Than $40 Billion in Loans since 2008, in Exchange for Oil," *Wall Street Journal,* July 21, 2014, https://www.wsj.com/articles/chinas-president-pledges-continued-aid -to-venezuela-maduro-1405974441.

68. Stephen Kaplan, "Banking Unconditionally: The Political Economy of Chinese Finance in Latin America," *Review of International Political Economy* 23, no. 4 (2016): 643–76.

69. Norris, *Chinese Economic Statecraft.*

70. Feng Zhongping and Huang Jing, "China's Strategic Partnership Diplomacy: Engaging with a Changing World," European Strategic Partnerships Observatory, Working Paper 8, June 2014, 7.

71. Ibid., 16.

72. Ibid., 13.

73. Jonathan Wheatley, "Lawsuit Shows China Losing Patience with Venezuela," *Financial Times,* December 6, 2017, https://www.ft.com/content/d627460a-da8e -11e7-a039-c64b1c09b482.

74. Stephen B. Kaplan and Michael Penfold, "China–Venezuelan Economic Relations: Hedging Venezuelan Bets with Chinese Characteristics," Washington, DC: Wilson Center, Latin America Program, February, 2019), 5; Margaret Myers, "China Bets on Venezuelan Mining," Inter-American Dialogue Blog, August 7, 2017, available at http://www.thedialogue.org/blogs/2017/08/china-bets-on-venezuelan -mining/.

75. "China, Mexico Eye Comprehensive Cooperation," *Xinhua News,* September 30, 2014, http://news.xinhuanet.com/english/china/2014–09/30/c_133684699.htm.

76. J. David Richardson, "Empirical Research on Trade Liberalization with Imperfect Competition: A Survey," NBER Working Paper No. 2883, March 1989; and Gary

Clyde Hufbauer and Jeffrey Schott, *NAFTA: An Assessment* (Washington, DC: Institute for International Economics, 1993), 23–25.

77. Don Bogler, "Andean Economies Prove Resilient in Face of Regional Woes," *Financial Times*, September 15, 2015. See: http://www.ft.com/cms/s/3/8ec1c738 -5b86-11e5-9846-de406ccb37f2.html#axzz3nId4AJkt.

78. Peter J. Katzenstein, *Small States in World Markets* (Ithaca: Cornell University Press, 1985), 24.

79. Kenneth Sokoloff and Stanley Engerman, "History Lessons: Institutions, Factor Endowments, and Paths of Development in the New World," *Journal of Economic Perspectives* 14, no. 3 (2000): 217–32.

80. Juan Carlos Moreno-Brid and Stefanie Garry, "Economic Performance in Latin America in the 2000s," in *Why Latin American Nations Fail: Development Strategies in the 21st Century*, ed. Esteban Pérez Caldentey and Matías Vernengo (Oakland: University of California Press, 2017), 149.

81. Author's interviews with former Chilean trade negotiator Osvaldo Rosales (June 14, 2011, in Santiago, Chile); former Peruvian trade minister Mercedes Araoz (interviewed on June 21, 2011, in Lima, Peru); and Laura Dachner, Economic Affairs, Costa Rican embassy, Washington, DC (April 11, 2013).

82. China Ministry of Commerce (MOFCOM), "China FTA Network," available at http://fta.mofcom.gov.cn/english/index.shtml.

83. Chinese government, *China's Policy Paper on Latin America and the Caribbean* (Beijing: Chinese Government, 2008), available at http:// english.gov.cn/official /2008-11/05/content_1140347.htm.

84. Jeffrey D. Wilson, "Resource Security: A New Motivation for Free Trade Agreements in the Pacific–Asia Region," *Pacific Review* 25, no. 4 (2012): 429–53.

85. Ganeshan Wignaraja, Dorothea Ramizo, and Luca Burmeister, "Assessing Liberalization and Deep Integration in FTAs: A Study of Asian–Latin American FTAs," *Journal of East Asian Economic Integration* 17, no. 4 (2013), 408–11.

86. Carol Wise, "Playing Both Sides of the Pacific," *Pacific Affairs* 89, no. 1 (2016): 84–85.

87. Monica DeHart, "China–Costa Rica Infrastructure Projects: Laying the Groundwork for Development?" in *Building Development for a New Era: Chinese Infrastructure Projects in Latin America and the Caribbean,* ed. Enrique Dussel Peters, Ariel Armony, and Shoujun Cui (Mexico, D.F.: Red Académica de América Latina y el Caribe sobre China and the University of Pittsburgh, 2018), 3–23.

88. Ken Shadlen, "Globalisation, Power, and Integration: The Political Economy of Regional and Bilateral Trade Agreements in the Americas," *Journal of Development Studies* 44, no. 1 (2008): 16–17.

89. Joe Leahy, "Temer's Travails Set the Stage for Brazil's Political Freak Show," *Financial Times*, August 4, 2017, https://www.ft.com/content/f184d694-7925-11e7 -a3e8-60495fe6ca71?mhq5j=e4.

90. Joe Leahy and Andres Schipani, "Brazil Puts Its Faith in Bolsonaro's Free Market

Conversion," *Financial Times*, October 29, 2018, https://www.ft.com/content /e769d796-daf8-11e8-9f04-38d397e6661c?emailId=5bdc61a1860fc 30004557c55&segmentId=45cc9415-bda1-0201-0786-d4cf471c8ced.

91. Halvor Mehlum, Karl Moene, and Ragnar Torvik, "Institutions and the Resource Curse," *Economic Journal* 116, no. 1 (2006): 1–20.

92. Manuel Pastor and Carol Wise, "Stabilization and Its Discontents: Argentina's Economic Restructuring in the 1990s," *World Development* 27, no. 3 (1999): 477–503.

93. Michael Ross, "What Have We Learned about the Resource Curse?" *Annual Review of Political Science* 18 (2015): 248–50.

94. Kathryn Hochstetler and Alfred Montero, "The Renewed Developmental State: The National Development Bank and the Brazil Model," *Journal of Development Studies* 49, no. 11 (2013): 1484–99.

95. Ha-Joon Chang, *Kicking Away the Ladder: Development Strategy in Historical Perspective* (London: Anthem Press, 2003).

96. Ibid., 4–5.

97. Kevin P. Gallagher and Lyuba Zarsky, *The Enclave Economy: Foreign Investment and Sustainable Development in Mexico's Silicon Valley* (Boston: MIT Press, 2007), 48.

98. Carol Wise, "Unfulfilled Promise: Economic Convergence under NAFTA," in *Requiem or Revival? The Promise of North American Integration*, ed. Isabel Studer and Carol Wise (Washington, DC: Brookings Institution Press, 2007), 27–52.

99. Brian Winter, "This Man Is Brilliant: So Why Doesn't Mexico's Economy Grow Faster?" *Americas Quarterly*, July 20, 2016, http://www.americasquarterly.org /content/man-brilliant-so-why-doesnt-mexicos-economy-grow-faster.

100. Xinhua News, "Days to WTO Entry Numbered," *Xinhuanet*, August 23, 2001, http://news.xinhuanet.com/english/20010823/443326.htm.

101. Kevin Gallagher and Enrique Dussel Peters, "China's Economic Effects on the US–Mexico Trade Relationship," in *China and the New Triangular Relationship in the Americas*, ed. Enrique Dussel Peters, Adrian Hearn, and Harley Shaiken (Miami: Center for Latin American Studies, University of Miami, 2013), 38–39.

102. Gallagher and Porzecanski, *The Dragon in the Room*.

Chapter 2. A Slow Thaw across the Pacific

1. Quoted in William Ratliff, "Chinese Communist Cultural Diplomacy toward Latin America," *Hispanic American Historical Review* 49, no. 1 (1969): 55.

2. Marisela Connelly and Romer Cornejo Bustamante, *China–América Latina: Génesis y desarrollo de sus relaciones* (Mexico, D.F.: El Colegio de Mexico, 1992), 59–61.

3. Cecil Johnson, *Communist China and Latin America, 1959–1967* (New York: Columbia University Press, 1970), 37–39.

4. Connelly and Cornejo Bustamante, *China–América Latina: Génesis y desarrollo de sus relaciones*, 68–69; Johnson, *Communist China and Latin America*, 164–65.

5. Robert North Belmont, *The Foreign Relations of China*, 3rd ed. (North Scituate, MA: Duxbury Press, 1978), 194.

6. Connelly and Cornejo Bustamante, *China–América Latina: Génesis y desarrollo de sus relaciones*, 115–16.

7. Gustavo Gorriti, *Sendero: Historia de la guerra milenaria en el Perú* (Lima: Editorial Apoyo, 1991); June Teufel Dreyer, "From China with Love: P.R.C. Overtures in Latin America," *Brown Journal of World Affairs* 12, no. 2 (Winter/Spring 2006): 86.

8. This would include, for example, Douglas M. Johnston and Hungdah Chiu, *Agreements of the People's Republic of China, 1949–1967: A Calendar* (Cambridge: Harvard University Press, 1968); Hungdah Chiu, *Agreements of the People's Republic of China: A Calendar of Events, 1966–1980* (New York: Praeger, 1981); Peter P. Cheng, ed., *A Chronology of the People's Republic of China from October 1, 1949* (Totowa, NJ: Littlefield, Adams, 1972); and Peter P. Cheng, ed., *A Chronology of the People's Republic of China, 1970–1979* (Metuchen, NJ: Scarecrow Press, 1986).

9. Jorn Dosch and David S. G. Goodman, "China and Latin America: Complementarity, Competition, and Globalisation," *Journal of Current Chinese Affairs* 41, no. 1 (2012): 6–7.

10. Margaret MacMillan, "Nixon, Kissinger, and the Opening to China," in *Nixon in the World: American Foreign Relations 1969–1977*, ed. Fredrik Logevall and Andrew Preston (Oxford: Oxford University Press, 2008).

11. He Li, "China's Growing Interest in Latin America and Its Implications," *Journal of Strategic Studies* 30, no. 4–5 (2007): 833–62.

12. Kevin Gallagher, *The China Triangle: Latin America's China Boom and the Fate of the Washington Consensus* (New York: Oxford University Press, 2016), chap. 6.

13. Author's interviews with Ambassador Sergio Ley, former Mexican ambassador to China, Mexico City, March 9, 2011; Ambassador Pablo Cabrera, former Chilean ambassador to China, Santiago, Chile, June 14, 2011; Ambassador Luiz Agosto de Castro Neves, former Brazilian ambassador to China, Rio de Janeiro, Brazil, July 5, 2011; Ernesto Taboada, president of the China–Argentine Business Council, Buenos Aires, Argentina, June 30, 2011.

14. I thank my USC colleague Stan Rosen for his very insightful comments on this chapter.

15. Carol Wise, *Reinventing the State: Economic Strategy and Institutional Change in Peru* (Ann Arbor: University of Michigan Press, 2003), 85–87.

16. Frank Mora, "The People's Republic of China and Latin America: From Indifference to Engagement," *Asian Affairs* 24, no. 1 (1997): 35–58.

17. Johnson, *Communist China and Latin America*, 50–51.

18. Ratliff, "Chinese Communist Cultural Diplomacy toward Latin America," 55.

19. Victor Alba, "The Chinese in Latin America," *China Quarterly* 5 (March 1961): 57.

20. Mora, "The People's Republic of China and Latin America," 38–39.

21. Ratliff, "Chinese Communist Cultural Diplomacy toward Latin America," 66.

22. Johnson, *Communist China and Latin America, 1959–1967*, 9.

23. Ratliff, "Chinese Communist Cultural Diplomacy toward Latin America," 68.

24. Ernst Halperin, "Peking and the Latin American Communists," *China Quarterly* 29 (January 1967): 118–20.

25. William E. Ratliff, "Communist China and Latin America, 1949–1972," *Asian Survey* 12, no. 10 (1972): 850.

26. Mora, "The People's Republic of China and Latin America," 40.

27. Nicholas R. Lardy, *Markets over Mao: The Rise of Private Business in China* (Washington, DC: Peterson Institute for International Economics, 2014), 39.

28. Frank Dikotter, *Mao's Great Famine: The History of China's Most Devastating Catastrophe, 1958–1962* (New York: Walker, 2010), 328–29.

29. Johnson, *Communist China and Latin America, 1959–1967*, 14–21.

30. Rosemary Thorp, *Progress, Poverty and Exclusion: An Economic History of Latin America in the 20th Century* (Washington, DC: Inter-American Development Bank, 1998), 318.

31. Mora, "The People's Republic of China and Latin America," 40.

32. Timothy Cheek, *Mao Zedong and China's Revolutions: A Brief History with Documents* (New York: Bedford/St. Martin's, 2002), 104.

33. Wolfgang Bartke, *China's Economic Aid* (London: Hurst, 1975), 23.

34. Belmont, *The Foreign Relations of China*, 181.

35. Connelly and Cornejo Bustamante, *China–América Latina: Génesis y desarrollo de sus relaciones*, 130–31.

36. He Li, *Sino–Latin American Economic Relations* (New York: Praeger, 1991), 25.

37. Ibid., 23–24.

38. Connelly and Cornejo Bustamante, *China–América Latina: Génesis y desarrollo de sus relaciones*, 133–35; Johnson, *Communist China and Latin America, 1959–1967*, 15–21.

39. Peter Van Ness, *Revolution and Chinese Foreign Policy* (Berkeley and Los Angeles: University of California Press, 1970), 147.

40. Ratliff, "Communist China and Latin America, 1949–1972," 860.

41. Hu Angang, *China in 2020: A New Type of Superpower* (Washington, DC: Brookings Institution Press, 2011), 18.

42. Mora, "The People's Republic of China and Latin America," 41–42.

43. Henry Kissinger, *On China* (New York: Penguin, 2012), 202.

44. Li, *Sino–Latin American Economic Relations*, 54.

45. Michael Reid, *Forgotten Continent: The Battle for Latin America's Soul* (New Haven: Yale University Press, 2007), 107–15.

46. Bartke, *China's Economic Aid*, 10–11.

47. William A. Joseph, "China's Relations with Chile under Allende: A Case Study of Chinese Foreign Policy in Transition," *Studies in Comparative Communism* 18, no. 2 (1985), 137.

48. Mora, "The People's Republic of China and Latin America," 41.

49. Joseph, "China's Relations with Chile under Allende," 140.

50. Li, *Sino–Latin American Economic Relations*, 41.
51. Connelly and Cornejo Bustamante, *China–América Latina: Génesis y desarrollo de sus relaciones*, 139–40.
52. Ibid., 110–12.
53. Mora, "The People's Republic of China and Latin America," 42.
54. Sebastian Edwards, *Crisis and Reform in Latin America: From Despair to Hope* (Washington, DC: World Bank, 1995), 17.
55. Mora, "The People's Republic of China and Latin America," 43.
56. See, for example, Johnston and Chiu, *Agreements of the People's Republic of China, 1949–1967;* Chiu, *Agreements of the People's Republic of China;* Cheng, ed., *A Chronology of the People's Republic of China from October 1, 1949;* Cheng, ed., *A Chronology of the People's Republic of China, 1970–1979;* FBIS, *Daily Report: People's Republic of China;* and *Daily Report: Latin America, 1980–1990;* and various issues of *Xinhua News*, available at http//news.xinhuanet.com/English.
57. Gorriti, *Sendero: Historia de la guerra milenaria en el Perú;* Dreyer, "From China with Love: P.R.C. Overtures in Latin America."
58. Frank Mora, "Sino–Latin American Relations: Sources and Consequences, 1977–1997," *Journal of Interamerican Studies and World Affairs* 41, no. 2 (1999): 97–98.
59. Wolfgang Deckers, "Latin America: How the Chinese See the Region," *Pacific Review* 2, no. 3 (1989): 246–51.
60. Mora, "Sino–Latin American Relations: Sources and Consequences, 1977–1997," 101.
61. "The Legacy of 1968 Continues to Burn in Mexico," *Stratfor Global Intelligence*, May 21, 2018, available at https://worldview.stratfor.com/article/legacy-1968-continues-burn-mexico.
62. Mapped out by the Chinese leadership before 1949, the five principles are (1) mutual respect for each other's territorial integrity and sovereignty; (2) mutual non-aggression; (3) mutual noninterference in each other's internal affairs; (4) equality and mutual benefit; (5) peaceful coexistence. See Sophie Richardson, *China, Cambodia, and the Five Principles of Peaceful Coexistence* (New York: Columbia University Press, 2010).
63. Mora, "Sino–Latin American Relations: Sources and Consequences, 1977–1997," 111.
64. Feng Zhongping and Huang Jing, "China's Strategic Partnership Diplomacy: Engaging with a Changing World," European Strategic Partnerships Observatory, Working Paper 8, June 2014, 10.
65. Joan M. Nelson, ed., *Intricate Links: Democratization and Market Reforms in Latin America and Eastern Europe* (Washington, DC: Overseas Development Council, 1994).
66. Barry Naughton, "A Political Economy of China's Economic Transition," in *China's Great Economic Transformation*, ed. Loren Brandt and Thomas G. Rawski (Cambridge: Cambridge University Press, 2008), 116.

67. Lardy, *Markets over Mao*, 72–76.
68. Manuel Pastor and Carol Wise, "The Origins and Sustainability of Mexico's Free Trade Policy," *International Organization* 48, no. 3 (1994): 459–89.
69. Roberto Hernández Hernández, "Economic Liberalization and Trade Relations between Mexico and China," *Journal of Current Chinese Affairs* 41, no. 1 (2012): 51–52.
70. International Bar Association (IBA) Divisions Project Team, "Anti-Dumping Investigations against China in Latin America," IBA, 2010, 34, available at http://www.ibanet.org/ENews_Archive/IBA_Jan_2010_ENews_AntiDumping_investigations_against_China.aspx.
71. Alexandre De Freitas Barbosa, "Rising China and Its Impacts on Latin America: Strategic Partnership or a New International Trap?" Paper presented at the VIII Reunión de la Red de Estudios de América Latina y el Caribe sobre Asia–Pacífico, Bogotá, August 22–28, 2008, 18–19.
72. Kevin Gallagher and Roberto Porzecanski, *The Dragon in the Room: China and the Future of Latin American Industrialization* (Stanford: Stanford University Press, 2010).
73. Leslie Armijo, Carol Wise, and Saori Katada, "Lessons from the Country Case Studies," in *Unexpected Outcomes: How Emerging Economies Survived the 2008–09 Global Financial Crisis*, ed. Carol Wise, Leslie Armijo, and Saori Katada (Washington, DC: Brookings Institution Press, 2015), 221.
74. The Chilean data are cited from the Central Bank of Chile, available at http://www.bcentral.cl/estadisticas-economicas/series-indicadores/index_se.htm; the Peruvian data are cited from US Department of Commerce (available at http://tse.export.gov/) and Peru's Ministry of Foreign Commerce and Tourism, available at http://www.mincetur.gob.pe/newweb/Default.aspx?tabid=2315.
75. Peter Nolan, *China and the Global Economy: National Champions, Industrial Revolution, and the Big Business Revolution* (New York: Palgrave, 2001), 73.
76. Carol Wise, "De la apatía a la vigilancia: La política del desarrollo energético en el Perú," *Apuntes*, no. 56/57 (Lima 2005): 17–18.
77. China National Petroleum Corporation, *CNCP in Latin America* (Beijing: CNPC, 2013), http://www.cnpc.com.cn/en/America/CNPC_Latin_America.shtml.
78. Li, *Sino–Latin American Economic Relations*, 159–60.
79. The quote is from R. W. Apple, "Analysis: Plenty of Process, But Little Progress," *New York Times*, October 30, 1997, http://partners.nytimes.com/library/world/103097us-china-assess.html; also see Helene Cooper, "China Holds Firm on Major Issues in Obama's Visit," *New York Times*, November 17, 2009, http://www.nytimes.com/2009/11/18/world/asia/18prexy.html.
80. Thorp, *Progress, Poverty and Exclusion*, 87–93.
81. World Development Indicators, available at http://databank.worldbank.org/data/home.aspx.
82. Dosch and Goodman, "China and Latin America: Complementarity, Competition, and Globalisation."

83. These insights are based on confidential interviews I conducted in Lima, Peru, and Santiago, Chile, in June 2011 and on my interview with Andreas Pierotic, Prochile, Chilean embassy in Beijing, April 1, 2015. The former Chilean trade negotiator Osvaldo Rosales (interviewed on June 14, 2011, in Santiago, Chile) and the former Peruvian trade minister Mercedes Araoz (interviewed on June 21, 2011, in Lima, Peru) offered particularly helpful insights.

84. See Romer Cornejo, Francisco Javier Haro Navejas, and José Luis Léon-Manríquez, "Trade Issues and Beyond: Mexican Perceptions on Contemporary China," *Latin American Policy* 4, no. 1 (2013): 57–75.

Chapter 3. From State to Market

1. Raúl Prebisch, *Towards a Dynamic Development Policy for Latin America* (New York: United Nations, 1963), 3.

2. Kevin Gallagher, *The China Triangle: Latin America's China Boom and the Fate of the Washington Consensus* (New York: Oxford University Press, 2016), chap. 2.

3. Ezra Vogel, *Deng Xiaoping and the Transformation of China* (Cambridge: Harvard University Press, 2011), 372 (Kindle Edition).

4. David Landes, "Why Europe and the West? Why Not China?" *Journal of Economic Perspectives* 20, no. 2 (2006): 3–22.

5. Sebastian Edwards, *Crisis and Reform in Latin America: From Despair to Hope* (Washington, DC: World Bank, 1995), 17.

6. On Chile, see Alejandro Foxley, *Latin American Experiments in Neoconservative Economics* (Berkeley and Los Angeles: University of California Press, 1983); on Mexico, see Roberto Newell and Luis Rubio, *Mexico's Dilemma: The Political Origins of Economic Crisis* (Boulder: Westview Press, 1984).

7. Victor Bulmer-Thomas, *The Economic History of Latin America since Independence*, 2d ed. (Cambridge: Cambridge University Press, 2003), 250–51.

8. Michael Kryzanek, *U.S.–Latin American Relations*, 4th ed. (Westport, CT: Praeger, 2008), 55–56.

9. Michael Reid, *Forgotten Continent: The Battle for Latin America's Soul* (New Haven: Yale University Press, 2007), 84–86.

10. Kryzanek, *U.S.–Latin American Relations*, 68–69.

11. Jeffrey Taffet, *Foreign Aid as Foreign Policy: The Alliance for Progress in Latin America* (New York: Routledge, 2007).

12. See Patrice Franko, *The Puzzle of Latin American Development*, 3d ed. (New York: Rowman and Littlefield, 2007), 14–15.

13. Kryzanek, *U.S.–Latin American Relations*, 69–70.

14. Jerome Levinson and Juan de Onís, *The Alliance that Lost Its Way* (Chicago: Quadrangle Books, 1970), 307.

15. This entity was renamed the Economic Commission for Latin America and the Caribbean (ECLAC) in 1984 to recognize its expanded focus on the Caribbean region, http://www.cepal.org/sites/default/files/pages/files/eclac_booklet.pdf.

16. See Raúl Prebisch, *The Economic Development of Latin America and Its Principal Problems* (New York: United Nations, Department of Social Affairs, 1950).

17. Bulmer-Thomas, *The Economic History of Latin America since Independence*, 234–35.

18. Hans Singer, "The Distribution of Gains between Investing and Borrowing Countries," *American Economic Review* 40, no. 2 (1950): 473–85.

19. See Edwards, *Crisis and Reform in Latin America*, 44–45.

20. Rosemary Thorp, *Progress, Poverty and Exclusion: An Economic History of Latin America in the 20th Century* (Washington, DC: Inter-American Development Bank, 1998), 318.

21. Nicolás Ardito Barletta, "Managing Development and Transition," in *Managing the World Economy: Fifty Years after Bretton Woods*, ed. Peter B. Kenen (Washington, DC: Institute for International Economics, 1994), 183–84.

22. Barbara Stallings, *Banker to the Third World: U.S. Portfolio Investment in Latin America, 1900–1986* (Berkeley and Los Angeles: University of California Press, 1987).

23. Jeffry Frieden, *Debt, Development and Democracy* (Princeton: Princeton University Press, 1991), 254.

24. Ibid., 245.

25. Inter-American Development Bank (IDB), *Economic and Social Progress in Latin America* (Washington, DC: IDB, 1988), 541.

26. Karen Remmer, "Elections and Economics in Contemporary Latin America," in *Post-Stabilization Politics in Latin America,* ed. Carol Wise and Riordan Roett (Washington, DC: Brookings Institution Press, 2003).

27. Miles Kahler, "Orthodoxy and Its Alternatives," in *Economic Crisis and Policy Choice,* ed. Joan Nelson (Princeton: Princeton University Press, 1990).

28. Mark Blyth, *Austerity: The History of a Dangerous Idea* (New York: Cambridge University Press, 2013), 212–13.

29. Andrés Velasco, "The State and Economic Policy in Chile: 1952–92," in *Chilean Economic Policy: Lessons and Challenges,* ed. Barry Bosworth, Rudiger Dornbusch, and Raúl Labán (Washington, DC: Brookings Institution Press, 1994).

30. Mario Marcel, "Effectiveness of the State and Development Lessons from the Chilean Experience," in *Chile: Recent Policy Lessons and Emerging Challenges,* ed. Guillermo Perry and Danny Leipziger (Washington, DC: World Bank, 1999).

31. Edwards, *Crisis and Reform in Latin America*, 33–39.

32. Henry Kissinger, *On China* (New York: Penguin, 2012), 321.

33. Vogel, *Deng Xiaoping and the Transformation of China*, 420 (Kindle Edition).

34. This section draws on Hu Angang, *China in 2020* (Washington, DC: Brookings Institution Press, 2011); Justin Yifu Lin, *Demystifying the Chinese Economy* (New York: Cambridge University Press, 2011); Barry Naughton, *Growing Out of the Plan: Chinese Economic Reform, 1978–1993* (New York: Cambridge University Press, 1995); and Vogel, *Deng Xiaoping and the Transformation of China.*

35. Naughton, *Growing Out of the Plan*, 70–74.

36. Ezra F. Vogel, "Can China and Japan Ever Get Along?" in *The China Questions:*

Critical Insights into a Rising Power, ed. Jennifer Rudolph and Michael Szonyi (Cambridge: Harvard University Press, 2018).

37. See, for example, Yasheng Huang, *Capitalism with Chinese Characteristics* (New York: Cambridge University Press, 2008); and, Yuen Yuen Ang, *How China Escaped the Poverty Trap* (Ithaca: Cornell University Press, 2016).

38. Sebastian Heilmann, "Policy Experimentation in China's Economic Rise," *Studies in Comparative and International Development,* no. 1 (2008): 1–26.

39. John Williamson, "What Washington Means by Policy Reform," in *Latin American Adjustment: How Much Has Happened?* ed. John Williamson (Washington, DC: Institute for International Economics, 1990).

40. Joshua Cooper Ramo, *The Beijing Consensus: Notes on the New Physics of Chinese Power* (London: Foreign Policy Centre, 2004).

41. Jeffrey D. Sachs and John Williamson, "External Debt and Macroeconomic Performance in Latin America and East Asia," *Brookings Papers on Economic Activity* 82, no. 2 (1985): 523–73; Alice Amsden, *Asia's Next Giant: South Korea and Late Industrialization* (New York: Oxford University Press, 1989); Stephan Haggard, *Pathways from the Periphery: The Politics of Growth in the Newly Industrializing Countries* (Ithaca: Cornell University Press, 1990); and Gary Gereffi and Donald Wyman, eds., *Manufacturing Miracles: Paths of Industrialization in Latin America and East Asia* (Princeton: Princeton University Press, 1990).

42. Lin, *Demystifying the Chinese Economy,* 264–66. Also see, for example, Gerald Segal, "Does China Matter?" *Foreign Affairs* 78, no. 5 (1999): 24–36.

43. Ramo, *The Beijing Consensus,* 11–12.

44. Scott Kennedy, "The Myth of the Beijing Consensus," *Journal of Contemporary China* 19, no. 65 (2010), 462.

45. William Easterly, *The Elusive Quest for Growth: Economists' Adventures and Misadventures in the Tropics* (Cambridge: MIT Press, 2002), 23.

46. John Williamson, "From Reform Agenda to Damaged Brand Name," *Finance and Development* 40. no. 3 (September 2003): 10–13; and John Williamson, "A Short History of the Washington Consensus," in *The Washington Consensus Reconsidered,* ed. Narcís Serra and Joseph E. Stiglitz (New York: Oxford University Press, 2008).

47. See Yasheng Huang, "Rethinking the Beijing Consensus," *Asia Policy* no. 11 (January 2011): 1–26; Suisheng Zhao, "The China Model: Can It Replace the Western Model of Modernization?" *Journal of Contemporary China* 19, no. 65 (2010): 419–36; and Barry Naughton, "China's Distinctive System: Can It Be a Model for Others?" *Journal of Contemporary China* 19, no. 65 (2010): 437–60.

48. Kennedy, "The Myth of the Beijing Consensus," 469.

49. Ibid., 469–70.

50. Ibid., 472.

51. Email communication with Arthur Kroeber, February 15, 2016.

52. Nicholas Lardy, *Markets over Mao: The Rise of Private Business in China* (Washington, DC: Peterson Institute for International Economics, 2014), chap. 3; Elizabeth

C. Economy, *The Third Revolution: Xi Jinping and the New Chinese State* (New York: Oxford University Press, 2018), 106–10.

53. Minxin Pei, *China's Trapped Transition: The Limits of Developmental Autocracy* (Cambridge: Harvard University Press, 2006); Yasheng Huang, *Capitalism with Chinese Characteristics;* Yuen Yuen Ang, *How China Escaped the Poverty Trap.*

54. Yuen Yuen Ang, "The Real China Model: It's Not What You Think," *Foreign Affairs* June 29, 2018, https://www.foreignaffairs.com/print/1122584.

55. See, for example, T. J. Pempel, "The Developmental Regime in a Changing World Economy," in *The Developmental State,* ed. Meredith Woo-Cumings (Ithaca: Cornell University Press, 1999), 138–47; Ha-Joon Chang, *The East Asian Development Experience* (London: Zed Books 2006), chap. 2.

56. "China's Data: Superstition Ain't the Way, *The Economist,* September 1, 2016, http://www.economist.com/news/finance-and-economics/21706272-why-do-people-still-pay-rapt-attention-chinas-unsatisfactory-growth-statistics?frsc=dg|c.

57. "Stand Up for 'Doing Business,'" *The Economist,* May 25, 2013, http://www.economist.com/news/leaders/21578397-president-world-bank-should-support-one-its-most-useful-products-stand-up-doing.

58. Reid, *Forgotten Continent,* chap. 6, offers a very thoughtful critique along these lines.

59. Jonathan Tepperman, *The Fix: How Countries Use Crises to Solve the World's Worst Problems* (New York: Tim Duggan Books, 2016), 180.

60. Eduardo Lora and Ugo Panizza, "Structural Reform in Latin America under Scrutiny," Inter-American Development Bank Research Department, Working Paper no. 466, 2001.

61. The countries included in fig. 3.1 are Argentina, Bolivia, Brazil, Chile, Colombia, Costa Rica, Ecuador, El Salvador, Guatemala, Honduras, Jamaica, Mexico, Paraguay, Peru, Trinidad & Tobago, Uruguay, and Venezuela.

62. Carol Wise, "Introduction: Latin American Politics in the Era of Market Reform," in *Post-Stabilization Politics in Latin America,* ed. Carol Wise and Riordan Roett (Washington, DC: Brookings Institution Press, 2003), 11–15.

63. Moisés Naím, "Fads and Fashions in Economic Reforms," *Foreign Policy Magazine,* October 26, 1999.

64. Gallagher, *The China Triangle,* chap. 2.

65. Eduardo Lora, "What Makes Reforms Likely? Timing and Sequencing of Structural Reforms in Latin America," Inter-American Development Bank Research Department, Working Paper no. 424, 2000.

66. See, for example, Zhao, "The China Model," and Naughton, "China's Distinctive System."

67. Angang, *China in 2020,* 1.

68. Ibid., 10–11.

69. William Overholt, *The Rise of China: How Economic Reform Is Creating a New Superpower* (New York: W. W. Norton, 1993), 46.

70. See Steven L. Chan, "The Rise of China: How Economic Reform Is Creating a New Superpower by William H. Overholt," *Boston College Third World Law Journal* 15, no. 1 (1995): 211–23.

71. Susan Shirk, *The Political Logic of Economic Reform in China* (Berkeley and Los Angeles: University of California Press, 1993), 336–39.

72. Yingyi Qian, "How Reform Worked in China," in *In Search of Prosperity*, ed. Dani Rodrik (Princeton: Princeton University Press, 2003), 297–333.

73. Lardy, *Markets over Mao*, chap. 3.

74. The Global Competitiveness Report 2013–14 assesses the competitiveness of 148 economies, providing insight into the drivers of their productivity and prosperity. The report, considered the most comprehensive assessment of national competitiveness worldwide, examines twelve variables: institutions, infrastructure, macroeconomic environment, health and primary education, higher education and training, goods market efficiency, labor market efficiency, financial market development, technological readiness, market size, business sophistication, and innovation, available at http://reports.weforum.org/the-global-competitiveness-report-2013-2014/.

75. This index averages the country's percentile rankings on ten topics: starting a business, dealing with construction permits, getting electricity, registering property, getting credit, protecting investors, paying taxes, trading across borders, enforcing contracts, and resolving insolvency—giving equal weight to each topic, available at http://doingbusiness.org/rankings.

76. WGI is produced by the Revenue Watch, Brookings Institution, World Bank Development Research Group, and the World Bank Institute. It reports aggregate and individual governance indicators for 215 countries. The indicators are based on information from thirty-two individual data sources provided by organizations such as survey institutes, think tanks, NGOs, international organizations, and private sector firms. They track six main dimensions of governance: Voice and Accountability, Political Stability and Absence of Violence, Government Effectiveness, Regulatory Quality, Rule of Law, and Control of Corruption, available at http://info.worldbank.org/governance/wgi/index.aspx#home.

77. Ang, *How China Escaped the Poverty Trap*, 16.

78. Gallagher, *The China Triangle*, chap. 2.

79. This section draws on Wise, Armijo, and Katada, eds., *Unexpected Outcomes*, chaps. 1, 9.

80. Shaun Breslin, "Chinese Financial Statecraft and the Response to the Global Financial Crisis," in *Unexpected Outcomes*, Wise, Armijo, and Katada, eds., 36.

81. Carol Wise, "Argentina's Currency Board: The Ties that Bind?" in *Exchange Rate Politics in Latin America*, ed. Carol Wise and Riordan Roett (Washington, DC: Brookings Institution Press, 2000), 103.

82. Cheng Hoon Lim et al., "Macroprudential Policy: What Instruments and How to Use Them?" IMF Working Paper 11/238, Washington, DC, 2011.

83. Kevin Gallagher and José Antonio Ocampo, "IMF's New Views on Capital Controls," *Economic and Political Weekly* 48, no. 12 (2013): 10.

84. Joshua Aizenman, "Foreword," in *Unexpected Outcomes,* Wise, Armijo, and Katada, eds., viii–ix.

85. Natalie Kitroeff, "A Manufacturing Boom Lifts More than Mexico," *Los Angeles Times,* August 21, 2016, A1.

86. See, for example, Robert Devlin and Graciela Moguillansky, "What's New in Industrial Policy in Latin America," Policy Research Working Paper 6191, The World Bank Development Economics Office of the Chief Economist, September 2012; and Inter-American Development Bank and Eduardo Stein, *Rethinking Productive Development: Sound Policies and Institutions for Economic Transformation* (New York: Palgrave Macmillan, 2014).

87. Jorge Guajardo, Manuel Molano, and Dante Sica, *Industrial Development in Latin America: What Is China's Role?* (Washington, DC: Atlantic Council, 2016).

88. Xiaolan Fu, *China's Path to Innovation* (Cambridge: Cambridge University Press, 2015).

89. Economy, *The Third Revolution,* chap. 5.

90. "Beijing Sets Its Sights on New Industries," *Financial Times,* Special Section on "Investing in Chendu," August 19, 2016, 2; Eva Dou, "After 1,000 Year Slumber, China Vows to Invent Again," *Wall Street Journal,* December 6, 2016, http://www .wsj.com/articles/after-1-000-year-slumber-china-vows-to-invent-again-1481042748.

91. Barry Eichengreen, Donghyun Park, and Kwanho Shin, "Growth Slowdowns Redux: New Evidence on the Middle-Income Trap," National Bureau of Economic Research, Working Paper 18673, January 2013, p. 10, available at http://www.nber .org/papers/w18673.

92. Gallagher and Porzecanski, *The Dragon in the Room,* 2.

93. Jonathan D. Ostry, Prakash Loungani, and Davide Furceri, "Neoliberalism: Oversold?" *Finance and Development* 53, no. 2 (June 2016): 40.

94. Landes, "Why Europe and the West? Why Not China?" For opposing points of view, see Janet Abu-Lughod, *Before European Hegemony* (New York: Oxford University Press, 1989), and Kenneth Pomeranz, *The Great Divergence: Europe, China and the Making of the Modern World Economy* (Princeton: Princeton University Press, 2000).

95. Dou, "After 1,000 Year Slumber, China Vows to Invent Again."

Chapter 4. Making Openness Work

1. Marco Vinicio Ruiz, Andrés Rebolledo, and Eduardo Ferreyros, "How to Negotiate with China," *Integration and Trade,* no. 40 (June 2016): 117.

2. ASEAN, or the Association of Southeast Asian Nations, is comprised of Brunei, Burma/Myanmar, Cambodia, Indonesia, Laos, Malaysia, the Philippines, Singapore, Thailand, and Vietnam.

3. Ministry of Foreign Affairs, "China FTA-Network," November 25, 2016, available at http://fta.mofcom.gov.cn/english/fta_qianshu.shtml.

4. Ed Crooks, "Manufacturing Output Has Hit Record Highs, But Employment in

the Sector Is in Long-term Decline as Businesses Rely on Automation," *Financial Times*, November 25, 2016, 9.

5. Kevin Granville, "The Trans-Pacific Partnership Trade Accord Explained," *New York Times*, October 5, 2015, http://www.nytimes.com/2015/10/06/business /international/the-trans-pacific-partnership-trade-deal-explained.html?_r=0.

6. "The Collapse of TPP: Trading Down," *The Economist*, November 19, 2016, http:// www.economist.com/news/asia/21710287-big-free-trade-deals-demise-leaves -worrying-void-asia-trading-down.

7. Gardiner Harris and Keith Bradsher, "China's Influence Grows in Ashes of the Trans-Pacific Trade Pact," *New York Times*, November 20, 2016, 11.

8. Rana Foroohar, "America First, International Trade Last," *Financial Times*, November 20, 2017, 9.

9. Yifei Xiao, "Competitive Mega-regional Trade Agreements: Regional Comprehensive Economic Partnership (RCEP) vs. Trans-Pacific Partnership (TPP)," April 20, 2015, *College Undergraduate Research Electronic Journal*, University of Pennsylvania, available at http://repository.upenn.edu/curej/194. Also see Pradumna B. Rana and Xianbai Ji, "The Asia-Pacific's Response to Rising U.S. Protectionism," *Global Memo*, Council of Councils, Council on Foreign Relations, March 27, 2018, https://www.cfr.org/councilofcouncils/global_memos/p39181.

10. An earlier version of this chapter appeared as Carol Wise, "Playing Both Sides of the Pacific: Latin America's Free Trade Agreements with China," *Pacific Affairs* 89, no. 1 (2016): 75–101.

11. J. David Richardson, "Empirical Research on Trade Liberalization with Imperfect Competition: A Survey," NBER Working Paper No. 2883, March 1989; Gary Clyde Hufbauer and Jeffrey Schott, *NAFTA: An Assessment* (Washington, DC: Institute for International Economics, 1993), 23–25.

12. Mercosur's members are Argentina, Brazil, Paraguay, Uruguay, and Venezuela (which has been suspended since the dissolution of the democratic regime there in 2017); Andean Community members are Bolivia, Colombia, Ecuador, and Peru. See Laura Gómez Mera, *Power and Regionalism in Latin America: The Politics of Mercosur* (Notre Dame: University of Notre Dame Press, 2013), and "Mercosur RIP," *The Economist*, June 14, 2012, http://www.economist.com/node/21558609.

13. Composed of 161 members, 117 of which are developing countries, the WTO was created from the General Agreement on Tariffs and Trade in 1995 and tasked with, among other things, expanding the coverage of international trade agreements to include the protection of intellectual property rights and trade-related services and investment flows. Not all member countries have signed on to these newer trade agenda items, hence in this chapter the term "WTO+" refers to those trade agreements which do cover these new agenda items or go even deeper, for example, with new rules to govern e-commerce and digital trade, https://www .wto.org/english/thewto_e/whatis_e/ wto_dg_stat_e.htm.

14. Heritage Foundation Economic Freedom Index, available at http://www.heritage .org/index/ranking.

15. These insights are based on my interviews with the former Chilean trade negotiator Osvaldo Rosales (interviewed on June 14, 2011, in Santiago, Chile) and the former Peruvian trade minister Mercedes Araoz (interviewed on June 21, 2011, in Lima, Peru).

16. Rolando Avendano, Angel Melguizo, and Sean Miner, *Chinese FDI in Latin America: New Trends with Global Implications* (Washington, DC: Atlantic Council and OECD Development Centre, 2017), 6.

17. See Michael G. Plummer, "'Best Practices' in Regional Trading Agreements: An Application to Asia," *World Economy* 30, no. 12 (2007): 1771–96; and Maria Garcia, "Resources and Trade: Linking the Pacific through Bilateral Free Trade Agreements," *Journal of World Trade* 47, no. 2 (2013): 329–58.

18. For classic statements on FTAs in the post–Cold War era, see Robert Z. Lawrence, *Regionalism, Multilateralism, and Deeper Integration* (Washington, DC: Brookings Institution Press, 1996); and John Whalley, "Why Do Countries Seek Regional Trading Agreements?" in *Regionalization of the World Economy*, ed. Jeffrey A. Frankel (Chicago: University of Chicago Press, 1997).

19. Whalley, "Why Do Countries Seek Regional Trading Agreements?"

20. Manuel Pastor and Carol Wise, "The Origins and Sustainability of Mexico's Free Trade Policy," *International Organization* 48, no. 3 (1994): 459–89; Helen Milner, "Industries, Governments, and Regional Trade Blocs," in *The Political Economy of Regionalism*, ed. Edward D. Mansfield and Helen Milner (New York: Columbia University Press, 1997).

21. Barbara Kotschwar, "Mapping Investment Provisions in Regional Trade Agreements," in *Regional Rules in the Global Trading System*, ed. Kati Suominen and Robert Teh (New York: Cambridge University Press, 2009).

22. Ibid.

23. Mark Manger, *Investing in Protection: The Politics of Preferential Trade Agreements between North and South* (Cambridge: Cambridge University Press, 2009), 19.

24. Ibid.

25. Juan Carlos Gachúz, "Chile's Economic and Political Relationship with China," *Journal of Current Chinese Affairs* 41, no. 1 (2012): 133–54; Rubén González-Vicente, "The Political Economy of Sino–Peruvian Relations: A New Dependency?" *Journal of Current Chinese Affairs* 41, no. 1 (2012): 97–131.

26. Scott Baier and Jeffrey Bergstrand, "Do Free Trade Agreements Actually Increase Members' International Trade?" *Journal of International Economics* 71 (2007): 92.

27. Kamal Saggi and Halis Murat Yildiz, "Bilateralism, Multilateralism, and the Quest for Global Free Trade," *Journal of International Economics* 81 (2010): 27. Also see Peter A. Petri, Michael G. Plummer, and Fan Zhai, *The Trans-Pacific Partnership and Asia-Pacific Integration: Quantitative Assessment* (Washington, DC: Peterson Institute for International Economics, Policy Analyses in International Economics no. 98, 2012).

28. Nargiza Salidjanova, "China's Trade Ambitions: Strategy and Objectives behind

China's Pursuit of Free Trade Agreements," US–China Economic and Security Review Commission, Staff Research Report, May 28, 2015, 24.

29. On Japan, see Mireya Solís and Saori N. Katada, "The Japan–Mexico FTA: A Cross-Regional Step in the Path towards Asian Regionalism," *Pacific Affairs* 80, no. 2 (2007): 279–301; on Korea, see Sung-Hoon Park and Min Gyo Koo, "Cross-Regional Partnership: The South Korea–Chile FTA and Its Implications," *Pacific Affairs* 80, no. 2 (2007): 259–78.

30. The author's interviews with Felipe Ortiz de Zevallos, the former Peruvian ambassador to the US and with members of the Peru–US FTA negotiating team, Lima, May 29, 2009; and with Ricardo Duarte, president of the Colombia–China Chamber of Commerce, Bogotá, June 27, 2012.

31. Elaine S. Kwei, "Chinese Trade Bilateralism: Politics Still in Command," in *Bilateral Trade Agreements in the Asia-Pacific,* ed. Vinod K. Aggarwal and Shujiro Urata (New York: Routledge, 2006); Guoyou Song and Wen Jin Yuan, "China's Free Trade Agreement Strategies," *Washington Quarterly* 35, no. 4 (2012): 112; and Garcia, "Resources and Trade: Linking the Pacific through Bilateral Free Trade Agreements."

32. Jiang Yang, "China's Competitive FTA Strategy: Realism on a Liberal Slide," in *Competitive Regionalism: FTA Diffusion in the Pacific Rim,* ed. Mireya Solís, Barbara Stallings, and Saori Katada (Basingstoke, UK: Palgrave Macmillan, 2009), 216.

33. Chinese Government, *China's Policy Paper on Latin America and the Caribbean,* 2008, available at http://english.gov.cn/official/2008–11/05/content_1140347.htm.

34. Jeffrey D. Wilson, "Resource Security: A New Motivation for Free Trade Agreements in the Pacific–Asia Region," *Pacific Review* 25, no. 4 (2012): 429–53.

35. Joshua Kurlantzick, *China's Charm Offensive: How China's Soft Power Is Transforming the World* (New Haven: Yale University Press, 2007).

36. Salidjanova, "China's Trade Ambitions," 24.

37. The author's interview with Laura Dachner, Costa Rican embassy on April 11, 2013, Washington, DC.

38. Monica DeHart, "China–Costa Rica Infrastructure Projects: Laying the Groundwork for Development?" in *Building Development for a New Era: Chinese Infrastructure Projects in Latin America and the Caribbean,* ed. Enrique Dussel Peters, Ariel Armony, and Shoujun Cui (Mexico, D.F.: Red Académica de América Latina y el Caribe sobre China and the University of Pittsburgh, 2018), 11–14.

39. These insights are based on my confidential interviews conducted in Lima, Peru, and Santiago, Chile, in June 2011. The former Chilean trade negotiator Osvaldo Rosales and the former Peruvian trade minister Mercedes Araoz offered particularly helpful insights.

40. Stephen Hoadley and Jiang Yang, "China's Cross-Regional FTA Initiatives," *Pacific Affairs* 80, no. 1 (Summer 2007): 327–48.

41. IMF, *Directions of Trade Statistics Yearbook.*

42. Enrique Dussel Peters, *Monitor of Chinese OFDI in Latin America and the Caribbean 2018*, 6, available at http://www.redalc-china.org/monitor/images/pdfs/menu principal/DusselPeters_MonitorOFDI_2018_Eng.pdf.

43. My interview with Andreas Pierotic, Prochile (Export Promotion Bureau), Chilean embassy in Beijing, April 1, 2015.

44. "Large Chinese Companies Continue to Show Interest in Chilean Agribusiness," *InvestChile*, January 9, 2018, https://investchile.gob.cl/large-chinese-companies -continue-to-show-interest-in-chilean-agribusiness/.

45. Dussel Peters, *Monitor of China's OFDI in Latin America and the Caribbean 2018*, 6.

46. "CooperAcción participa del Foro Empresas y Derechos Humanos en Ginebra," Cooperacción, November 26, 2018, http://cooperaccion.org.pe/cooperaccion -participa-del-foro-empresas-y-derechos-humanos-en-ginebra/.

47. "China's COSCO to Build $2 Billion Shipping Port in Peru," *Reuters*, June 1, 2018, https://www.reuters.com/article/us-peru-china/chinas-cosco-to-build-2-billion -shipping-port-in-peru-ambassador-idUSKCN1IX5WW.

48. Salidjanova, "China's Trade Ambitions," 15.

49. Sebastian Edwards, "The Andean Pact Reforms: How Much Progress? How Far to Go?" in *The Andean Community and the United States,* ed. Miguel Rodriguez, Patricia Correa, and Barbara Kotschwar (Washington, DC: Organization of American States, 1998), 9–43.

50. Gachúz, "Chile's Economic and Political Relationship with China," 149–50.

51. Jonathan R. Barton, "The Chilean Case," in *China and Latin America: Economic Relations in the Twenty-First Century,* ed. Rhys Jenkins and Enrique Dussel Peters (Bonn: German Development Institute, 2009), 244.

52. For a summary of this supplementary agreement on services, see http://fta.mof com.gov.cn/topic/enchile.shtml.

53. Full details available at http://www.mincetur.gob.pe/newweb/Portals/0/comercio /tlc_china/docs/Informes _Finales_TLC_Peru-China.pdf.

54. My confidential interviews with members of the Peruvian negotiating team for the Peru–China FTA, Lima, May 29, 2009.

55. For further detail, see "China–Costa Rica FTA Comes Into Effect," *China Briefing,* August 2, 2011, http://www.china-briefing.com/news/2011/08/02/china-costa-rica -fta-comes-into-effect.html#sthash.aNHZirtF.dpuf.

56. Baier and Bergstrand, "Do Free Trade Agreements Actually Increase Members' International Trade?" 92.

57. Saggi and Yildiz, "Bilateralism, Multilateralism, and the Quest for Global Free Trade," 27.

58. Peter J. Katzenstein, *Small States in World Markets* (Ithaca: Cornell University Press, 1985).

59. Rebecca Ray and Kevin Gallagher, "China–Latin America Economic Bulletin 2015 Edition," Working Group on Development and Environment in the Americas, Global Economic Governance Initiative, Discussion Paper 2015–9, Boston University, September 2015, 9.

60. Ken Shadlen, "Globalisation, Power, and Integration: The Political Economy of Regional and Bilateral Trade Agreements in the Americas," *Journal of Development Studies* 44, no. 1 (2008): 1–20.

61. My interviews with Ambassador Pablo Cabrera, the former Chilean ambassador to China, Santiago, Chile, June 14, 2011; the former Chilean trade negotiator Osvaldo Rosales, Santiago, Chile, June 14, 2011; the former Peruvian trade minister Mercedes Araoz, Lima, Peru, June 21, 2011; and comments made by the current Peruvian ambassador to China, Juan Carlos Capuñay, China and Latin America Working Group, "China–Latin American Relations in 2015: Beyond Complementarity?" Sponsored jointly by the Inter-American Dialogue and Peking University, March 30, 2015, Beijing.

62. Garcia, "Resources and Trade: Linking the Pacific through Bilateral Free Trade Agreements (FTAs)," 336–37.

63. Luciano Ciravegna, *Promoting Silicon Valleys in Latin America: Lessons from Costa Rica* (New York: Routledge, 2012).

64. My interviews with Andreas Pierotic, Prochile, Chilean embassy in Beijing, April 1, 2015; and Diana Pita, PromPeru, Peruvian embassy in Beijing, April 1, 2015.

65. Carol Wise, Leslie Armijo, and Saori Katada, eds., *Unexpected Outcomes: How Emerging Economies Survived the 2008–09 Global Financial Crisis* (Washington, DC: Brookings Institution Press, 2015).

66. Salidjanova, "China's Trade Ambitions," 22; and author's interview with Ricardo Duarte, the president of the Colombia–China Chamber of Commerce, Bogotá, June 27, 2012.

67. Rolando Avendano and Jeff Dayton-Johnson, "Central America, China, and the US: What Prospects for Development?" *Pacific Affairs* 88, no. 4 (2015): 813–47. My interview with Felipe Jesús de García Aguayo, Promexico (Mexican Export Agency), Mexican embassy, Beijing, April 2, 2015.

68. My interview with Laura Dachner of the economic affairs division at the Costa Rican embassy in Washington, DC, April 11, 2013.

69. "China FTA Network," Ministry of Commerce, Beijing, http://fta.mofcom.gov.cn/english/.

Chapter 5. An Institutional Resource Curse in Argentina and Brazil

1. "The Petrobras Scandal: Defendant-in-chief," *The Economist*, August 6, 2016, http://www.economist.com/news/americas/21703295-remarkable-downfall-most-important-brazilian-defendant-chief?frsc=dg%7Cc.

2. Kevin Gallagher and Margaret Myers, "China–Latin America Finance Database," Inter-American Dialogue, Washington, DC, 2018, available at http:// http://www.thedialogue.org/map_list/.

3. Maria Cristina Pereira de Melo and Jair do Amaral Filho, "The Political Economy of Brazil–China Trade Relations, 2000–2010," *Latin American Perspectives* 42, no. 1 (2015): 68.

4. Ben Ross Schneider, *Designing Industrial Policy in Latin America: Business–State Relations and the New Developmentalism* (New York: Palgrave Macmillan, 2015).

5. Christopher Wylde, "State, Society and Markets in Argentina: The Political Economy of *Neodesarrollismo* under Néstor Kirchner, 2003–2007," *Bulletin of Latin American Research* 30, no. 4 (2011): 6.

6. Ambrogio Cesa-Bianchi, M. Hashem Pesaran, Alessandro Rebucci, and Tengteng Xu, "China's Emergence in the World Economy and Business Cycles in Latin America," *Economía* 12, no. 2 (2012): 1–75.

7. Halvor Mehlum, Karl Moene, and Ragnar Torvik, "Institutions and the Resource Curse," *Economic Journal* 116, no. 1 (2006): 1–20; also see Michael Ross, "What Have We Learned about the Resource Curse?" *Annual Review of Political Science* 18 (2015): 248–50.

8. Mehlum, Moene, and Torvik, "Institutions and the Resource Curse," 2–3.

9. Cecil Johnson, *Communist China and Latin America, 1959–1967* (New York: Columbia University Press, 1970), 14–21.

10. People-to-people contact refers to exchanges occurring between private, nongovernmental parties and was the cornerstone of the PRC's outreach to LAC up through the normalization of relations with these countries.

11. Hungdah Chiu, *Agreements of the People's Republic of China: A Calendar of Events, 1966–1980* (New York: Praeger, 1981).

12. Wolfgang Deckers, "Latin America: How the Chinese See the Region," *Pacific Review* 2, no. 3 (1989): 246–51.

13. Feng Zhongping and Huang Jing, "China's Strategic Partnership Diplomacy: Engaging with a Changing World," European Strategic Partnerships Observatory, Working Paper 8, June 2014, 7.

14. He Li, *Sino–Latin American Economic Relations* (New York: Praeger, 1991), 159–60.

15. Alexandre De Freitas Barbosa, "Rising China and Its Impacts on Latin America: Strategic Partnership or a New International Trap?" Paper presented at the VIII Reunión de la Red de Estudios de América Latina y el Caribe sobre Asia–Pacífico, Bogotá, August 22–28, 2008, 18–19.

16. Pablo Adreani, "China, en el centro de la escena agrícola," *La Nación*, January 11, 2003. See: http://www.lanacion.com.ar/465114-china-en-el-centro-de-la-escena -agricola.

17. These figures are cited from various issues of the *Economist Intelligence Unit*, Country Reports on Argentina and Brazil from 2001 to 2005.

18. "China, Brazil Issue Joint Statement on Strengthening Partnership," *Global Times*, June 22, 2012, http://www.globaltimes.cn/content/716492.shtml.

19. Gallagher and Myers, "China–Latin America Finance Database."

20. Enrique Dussel Peters, *Monitor of Chinese OFDI in Latin America and the Caribbean 2018*, 6, available at http://www.redalcchina.org/monitor/images/pdfs/menu principal/DusselPeters_MonitorOFDI_2018_Eng.pdf.

21. R. Evan Ellis, *China on the Ground in Latin America* (New York: Palgrave Macmillan, 2014), 33.

22. Kevin Gallagher, *The China Triangle: Latin America's China Boom and the Fate of the Washington Consensus* (New York: Oxford University Press, 2016), 54.

23. "China Three Gorges' Acquisition of Hydro-Projects in Brazil Will Increase Leverage; Ratings Unaffected," *Moody's Investors Services,* December 4, 2015, https://www.moodys.com/research/Moodys-China-Three-Gorges-acquisition-of-hydro-projects-in-Brazil—PR_340294.

24. This paragraph draws on Celio Hiratuka, "Chinese Infrastructure Projects in Brazil: Two Case Studies," in *Building Development for a New Era; Chinese Infrastructure Projects in Latin America and the Caribbean,* ed. Enrique Dussel Peters, Ariel Armony, and Shoujun Cui (Mexico, D.F.: Red Académica de América Latina y el Caribe sobre China and the University of Pittsburgh, 2018), 130–34.

25. Ibid., 132.

26. "Closer Financial Ties Lift China–Brazil Oil Ties to New Level," *Xinhua News,* June 20, 2015, http://news.xinhuanet.com/english/2015–06/20/c_134343534.htm.

27. Ellis, *China on the Ground in Latin America,* 69.

28. Hiratuka, "Chinese Infrastructure Projects in Brazil: Two Case Studies," 136.

29. Rolando Avendano, Angel Melguizo, and Sean Miner, *Chinese FDI in Latin America: New Trends with Global Implications* (Washington, DC: Atlantic Council and OECD Development Centre, 2017), 14.

30. Ibid., 3.

31. Stephen B. Kaplan, "Banking Unconditionally: The Political Economy of Chinese Finance in Latin America," *Review of International Political Economy"* 23, no. 4 (2016): 643–76.

32. Dussel Peters, *Monitor of China's OFDI in Latin America and the Caribbean 2018,* 6.

33. Ken Parks, "Argentina Central Bank Borrows $814 Million under China Currency Swap; Argentina Taps Lines as Reserves Quickly Approach Multi-Year Low," *Wall Street Journal,* October 30, 2014, https://www.wsjcom/ articles/argentina-central-bank-borrows-814-million-under-china-currency-swap-1414704667; "Argentina Receives Second Currency Swap from China," *Reuters,* November 17, 2014, https://www.reuters.com/article/argentina-reserves-china/update-1-argentina-receives-second-currency-swap-from-china-idUSL2N0T72RD20141117.

34. Leonardo Stanley, "Argentina's Infrastructure Gap and Financial Needs: The Role of China," in *Building Development for a New Era: China's Infrastructure Projects in Latin America and the Caribbean,* ed. Enrique Dussel Peters, Ariel C. Armony, and Shoujun Cui, 79–80.

35. Daniel Politi, "Bags of Cash in Argentina," *New York Times,* August 3, 2018, https://www.nytimes.com/2018/08/03/world/americas/argentina-corruption-investigation.html.

36. Dussel Peters, *Monitor of Chinese OFDI in Latin America and the Caribbean 2018.*

37. Gallagher and Myers, "China–Latin America Finance Database."

38. "China-Made Trains Cover All Argentina's Long-Distance Lines," *Xinhua News,* December1,2015,http://news.xinhuanet.com/english/2015–12/01/c_134872792. htm; "Argentina Revamps Rail Transport with China's Help," *Xinhua News,* April 13, 2017, http://news.xinhuanet.com/english/2017–04/13/c_136205317.htm.

39. Keith Barrow, "Argentina's Roadmap to a Rail Revival," *International Railway Journal,* November 29, 2016, http://www.railjournal.com/index.php/central-south -america/argentinas-roadmap-to-a-rail-revival.html.

40. Stanley, "Argentina's Infrastructure Gap and Financial Needs,"90.

41. Ellis, *China on the Ground in Latin America,* 40.

42. Dussel Peters, *Monitor of Chinese OFDI in Latin America and the Caribbean 2018.*

43. Gallagher, *The China Triangle,* 53–54.

44. Ellis, *China on the Ground in Latin America,* 32.

45. "China, Argentina Upgrade Ties to Comprehensive Strategic Partnership," *Global Times,* July 19, 2014, http://www.globaltimes.cn/content/871428.shtml.

46. Gallagher and Myers, "China–Latin America Finance Database."

47. Luke Patey, "China Made Mauricio Macri a Deal He Couldn't Refuse," *Foreign Policy,* January 24, 2017, http://foreignpolicy.com/2017/01/24/china-made-mauricio -macri-a-deal-he-couldnt-refuse/.

48. Ellis, *China on the Ground in Latin America,* 69.

49. Patey, "China Made Mauricio Macri a Deal He Couldn't Refuse."

50. Ibid.

51. Stanley, "Argentina's Infrastructure Gap and Financial Needs," 85.

52. José Raimundo Trindade, Paul Cooney, and Wesley Pereira de Oliveira, "Industrial Trajectory and Economic Development: Dilemma of the Re-primarization of the Brazilian Economy," *Review of Radical Political Economy* 48, no. 2 (2016): 1–18.

53. Mario Castillo and Antonio Martins Neto, "Premature Deindustrialization in Latin America," ECLAC, Productive Development Series no. 205, Santiago, Chile, June 2016, 12.

54. Dani Rodrik, "Premature Deindustrialization," NBER Working Paper no. 20935, Cambridge, Massachusetts, February 2015.

55. Castillo and Martins Neto, "Premature Deindustrialization in Latin America," 11–12.

56. Ibid., 17.

57. Ibid., 16.

58. Gallagher, *The China Triangle,* 101.

59. João Alberto De Negri and Lenita Maria Turchi, eds., *Technological Innovation in Brazilian and Argentine Firms* (Rio de Janeiro: Institute of Applied Economic Research, 2007).

60. Bernardo Kosacoff, "Microeconomic Behavior in High Uncertainty Environments: The Case of Argentina," in *Technological Innovation in Brazilian and Argentine Firms,* ed. João Alberto De Negri and Lenita Maria Turchi, 75–76.

61. Wilson Suzigan, João Alberto De Negri, and Alexandre Messa Silva, "Structural Change and Microeconomic Behavior in Brazilian Industry," in *Technological In-*

novation in Brazilian and Argentine Firms, ed. João Alberto De Negri and Lenita Maria Turchi, 43.

62. Jewellord Tolentino Nem Singh, "Towards Post-Neoliberal Resource Politics? The International Political Economy of Oil and Copper in Brazil and Chile," *New Political Economy* 19, no. 3 (2014): 329–58; Christopher Wylde, "Post-Neoliberal Developmental Regimes in Latin America: Argentina under Cristina Fernández de Kirchner," *New Political Economy* 21, no. 3 (2016): 322–41.

63. See Carol Wise and Maria Antonieta del Tedesco Lins, "Macroprudence versus Macroprofligacy: Brazil, Argentina, and the Global Financial Crisis," in *Unexpected Outcomes: How Emerging Economies Survived the Global Financial Crisis*, ed. Carol Wise, Leslie Armijo, and Saori Katada (Washington, DC: Brookings Institution Press, 2015), 154.

64. "The Role of the IMF in Argentina: 1991–2002," International Monetary Fund, July 2003, available at https://www.imf.org/External/NP/ieo/2003/arg/index.htm#1.

65. "Argentina's Debt Restructuring: A Victory by Default?" *The Economist*, March 3, 2005, http://www.economist.com/node/3715779.

66. Gonzalo S. Paz, "Argentina and Asia: China's Reemergence, Argentina's Recovery," in *Reaching Across the Pacific: Latin America and Asia in the New Century*, ed. Cynthia J. Arnson and Jorge Heine (Washington, DC: Woodrow Wilson Center for International Scholars, 2014), 160–61.

67. "Brazil: Helping Calm Financial Markets," International Monetary Fund, November 21, 2007, available at https://www.imf.org/external/np/exr/articles/2007/112107.htm.

68. Cornel Ban, "Brazil's Liberal Neo-developmentalism: New Paradigm or Edited Orthodoxy?" *Review of International Political Economy* 20, no. 2 (2013): 320.

69. Andrés López and Daniela Ramos, "The Argentine Case," in *China and Latin America: Economic Relations in the Twenty-First Century*, ed. Rhys Jenkins and Enrique Dussel Peters (Bonn, Germany: German Development Institute, 2009), 153; Mariano Obarrio, "De aquel 'megaanuncio' quedó muy poco," *La Nación*, June 1, 2005, http://libproxy.usc.edu/login?url=https://search-proquest-com.libproxy2.usc.edu/docview/335119360 ?accountid=14749.

70. This summary draws on various issues of *Xinhua News*, available at http://news.xinhuanet.com/english/.

71. This section draws on Ban, "Brazil's Liberal Neo-developmentalism"; Kathryn Hochstetler and Alfred Montero, "The Renewed Developmental State: The National Development Bank and the Brazil Model," *Journal of Development Studies* 49, no. 11 (2013): 1484–99; Tolentino Nem Singh, "Towards Post-Neoliberal Resource Politics?; Jenkins, "Is Chinese Competition Causing Deindustrialization in Brazil?" *Latin American Perspectives* 42, no. 6 (2015): 42–63; and Daniela Prates, Barbara Fritz, and Luiz Fernando de Paula, "Brazil at a Crossroads: A Critical Assessment of Developmentalist Policies," in *The Brazilian Economy since the Great Financial Crisis of 2007/2008*, ed. Philip Arestis, Carolina Baltar, and Daniela Prates (London: Palgrave Macmillan, 2017), 9–39.

72. Castillo and Martins Neto, "Premature Deindustrialization in Latin America," 18.

73. Armijo, Wise, and Katada, "Lessons from the Country Case Studies," in *Unexpected Outcomes,* 220.

74. Castillo and Martins Neto, "Premature Deindustrialization in Latin America," 20.

75. Hochstetler and Montero, "The Renewed Developmental State," 1484.

76. Ibid., 1490–91.

77. Joe Leahy and Andrea Schipani, "Brazil's Development Bank BNDES Faces Reform, *Financial Times,* August 30, 2017, https://www.ft.com/content/493f4a68-8c72-11e7-a352-e46f43c5825d.

78. Jenkins, "Is Chinese Competition Causing Deindustrialization in Brazil?" 50–52.

79. For this insight I thank Marcelo José Nonnenberg, Senior Research Economist, Instituto de Pequisa Econômica Aplicada, Rio de Janeiro, Brazil.

80. Prates, Fritz, and Fernando de Paula, "Brazil at a Crossroads."

81. "China Urges Brazil against Trade Remedy Measures," *Xinhua News,* July 15, 2016, http://news.xinhuanet.com/english/2016–07/15/c_135516254.htm.

82. Jenkins, "Is Chinese Competition Causing Deindustrialization in Brazil?" 59.

83. This section draws on Neal P. Richardson, "Export-Oriented Populism: Commodities and Coalitions in Argentina," *Studies in Comparative International Development* 44, no. 3 (2009): 228–55; Tomás Bril-Mascarenhas and Alison E. Post, "Policy Traps: Consumer Subsidies in Post-Crisis Argentina," *Studies in Comparative International Development* 50, no. 1 (2015): 98–120; Eduardo Daniel Oviedo, "Argentina and China: An Analysis of the Actors in the Soybean Trade and Migratory Flows," *Journal of Chinese Political Science* 20, no. 3 (2015): 243–66; Wylde, "State, Society and Markets in Argentina; Wylde, "Post-Neoliberal Developmental Regimes in Latin America"; and José Luis Machinea and Lucio Castro, "Argentina, the US, and China," in *China, the United States, and the Future of Latin America,* ed. David B. H. Denoon (New York: New York University Press, 2017).

84. Wise and Tedesco Lins, "Macroprudence versus Macroprofligacy," 160.

85. Roberto Frenkel and Martín Rapetti, "Five Years of Competitive and Stable Real Exchange Rate in Argentina 2002–2007," *International Review of Applied Economics* 22, no. 2 (2008): 215–26.

86. Richardson, "Export-Oriented Populism," 242. Also see Steven Levitsky and Maria Victoria Murillo, "Argentina: From Kirchner to Kirchner," *Journal of Democracy* 19, no. 2 (2008): 19.

87. Wylde, "State, Society and Markets in Argentina," 439.

88. "China Urges Argentina to Lift Import Restrictions on Chinese Goods," *Xinhua News,* March 9, 2009.

89. Jude Webber, "Argentina Soy Rift with China Grows," *Financial Times,* April 5, 2010, https://www.ft.com/content/da759292-40d7-11df-94c2-00144feabdco.

90. See Richardson, "Export-Oriented Populism," 238–39.

91. My interview with Ricardo Carciofi, Director, Institute for Latin American and Caribbean Integration, Inter-American Development Bank, Buenos Aires, Argen-

tina, June 27, 2011. Also see Bril-Mascarenhas and Post, "Policy Traps: Consumer Subsidies in Post-Crisis Argentina," 111–12.

92. Christian Folgar, *The New Argentina: Time to Double Down on the Energy Sector?* (Washington, DC: Atlantic Council, 2016), 3.

93. "Argentina's Economy: Its Cold Outside," *The Economist*, August 13–19, 2016, http://www.economist.com/news/americas/21704824-battle-over-utility-bills -mauricio-macris-first-big-crisis-its-cold-outside?frsc=dg%7Cc.

94. "Flogging a Dead Cow," *The Economist*, July 27, 2013, http://www.economist .com/news/americas/21582304-recently-nationalised-oil-company-agrees-big -foreign-investment-flogging-dead-cow.

95. Albert Fislow, *Starting Over: Brazil since 1985* (Washington, DC: Brookings Institution Press, 2011), 79–80.

96. Oviedo, "Argentina and China: An Analysis of the Actors in the Soybean Trade and Migratory Flows," 248.

97. Mehlum, Moene, and Torvik, "Institutions and the Resource Curse," 1–20; also see Ross, "What Have We Learned about the Resource Curse?" 248–50.

98. Alejandro Portes and Lori D. Smith, "Institutions and Development in Latin America: A Comparative Analysis," *Studies in Comparative International Development* 43, no. 2 (2008): 101–28.

99. See, for example, Peter Evans, *Embedded Autonomy: States and Industrial Transformation* (Princeton: Princeton University Press, 1995); Stephan Haggard, "Institutions and Growth in East Asia," *Studies in Comparative International Development* 38, no. 4 (2004): 53–81; and Albert O. Hirschman, *The Strategy of Economic Development* (New Haven: Yale University Press, 1958).

100. Portes and Smith, "Institutions and Development in Latin America," 108–9.

101. Ibid., 125.

102. Alejandro Portes and Lori D. Smith, eds., *Institutions Count: Their Role and Significance in Latin American Development* (Berkeley and Los Angeles: University of California Press, 2012).

103. Alejandro Grimson, Ana Castellani, and Alexander Roig, "Institutional Change and Development in Argentina," in *Institutions Count*, 56.

104. Miguel Centeno, Atul Kohli, and Deborah J. Yashar, eds., *States in the Developing World* (Cambridge: Cambridge University Press, 2017).

105. Katherine Bersch, Sérgio Praça, and Matthew M. Taylor, "Bureaucratic Capacity and Political Autonomy within National States: Mapping the Archipelago of Excellence in Brazil," in *States in the Developing World*.

106. Ibid., 161.

107. Hiratuka, "Chinese Infrastructure Projects in Brazil," 128.

108. Mehlum, Moene, and Torvik, "Institutions and the Resource Curse"; also see Ross, "What Have We Learned about the Resource Curse?"

109. Kenneth Rapoza, "Brazil Oil Firm Petrobras Slowly Rising from Pits of Hell," *Forbes*, January 8, 2018, See https://www.forbes.com/sites/kenrapoza/2018/01 /08/brazil-oil-firm-petrobras-slowly-rising-from-pits-of-hell/#435204d7588e.

110. Nauro Campos, Menelaos G. Karanasos, and Bin Tan, "From Riches to Rags and Back: Institutional Change, Financial Development and Economic Growth in Argentina since 1890," *Journal of Development Studies* 52, no. 2 (2016): 206–23.

111. Daron Acemoglu and James A. Robinson, *Why Nations Fail* (New York: Crown Business, 2012), 385–86.

112. Grimson, Castellani, and Roig, "Institutional Change and Development in Argentina," in *Institutions Count*, 56.

113. "Accusations of Manipulation Greet Argentine Inflation Data," *Euroweek*, August 10, 2007, 1.

114. "Don't Lie to Me, Argentina," *The Economist*, February 25, 2012, http://www.economist.com/node /21548242.

115. "Sancionó el FMI a la Argentina," *La Nación*, February 1, 2013, http://www.lanacion.com.ar/1551002-sanciono-el-fmi-a-la-argentina.

116. "Central Bank Robbery," *The Economist*, February 4, 2010, http://www.economist.com/node/15469820.

117. Moffett and Cowley, "Court Reinstates Fired Central-Bank Chief—Argentina's Constitutional Crisis Escalates as Judge Blocks Kirchner from Using Reserves to Pay National Debt," *Wall Street Journal*, January 9, 2010, A7.

118. Steven Levitsky and Maria Victoria Murillo, "Lessons from Latin America: Building Institutions on Weak Foundations," *Journal of Democracy*, no. 2 (2013): 93–107.

119. Acemoglu and Robinson, *Why Nations Fail*, 459–60.

120. Jonathan Watts, "Operation Car Wash: The Biggest Corruption Scandal Ever?" *The Guardian*, June 1, 2017, https://www.theguardian.com/world/2017/jun/01 /brazil-operation-car-wash-is-this-the-biggest-corruption-scandal-in-history.

121. This paragraph draws on Tolentino Nem Singh, "Towards Post-Neoliberal Resource Politics?"

122. Susana Moreira, "The Impact of Brazil's Expanding Hydrocarbon Reserves and Its Relations with the US and the PRC," in *Sino–U.S. Energy Triangles: Resource Diplomacy under Hegemony*, ed. David Zweig and Yufan Hao (New York: Routledge, 2015), 185–87.

123. Tolentino Nem Singh, "Towards Post-Neoliberal Resource Politics?" 345.

124. Watts, "Operation Car Wash: The Biggest Corruption Scandal Ever?"

125. Ibid.

126. Paul Kiernan, "Brazil's Petrobras Writes Off $17 Billion," *Wall Street Journal*, April 23, 2015, A1.

127. "Brazil Stripped of Investment Grade Rating as Crisis Deepens," Reuters, December 16, 2015, http://www.reuters.com/article/us-brazil-ratings-fitch-idUS KBN0U00AR20151217.

128. This point is further substantiated in Katherine Bersch, *When Democracies Deliver: Governance Reform in Latin America* (Cambridge: Cambridge University Press, 2019).

129. Machinea and Castro, "Argentina, the US, and China," 188.

130. Jenkins, "Is Chinese Competition Causing Deindustrialization in Brazil?" 59.

131. John Paul Rathbone, "Argentina's Brief Window for Reform Opens Up," *Financial Times*, September 16, 2016, https://www.ft.com/content/4c6b123c-5805 -11e6-9f70-badea1b336d4.

132. Rapoza, "Brazil Oil Firm Petrobras Slowly Rising from Pits of Hell."

133. "Brazil's Congress Starts to Reform Itself," *The Economist*, October 14, 2017, https://www.economist.com/newsamericas/21730206-clean-up-sleazy-political -system-will-require-lot-more-work-brazils-congress-starts.

134. Andres Schipani, "Brazil Graft Probe at Risk of Sabotage," *Financial Times*, November 26, 2017, https://www.ft.com/content/da7fcc7a-cef6-11e7-b781-794ce 08b24dc.

Chapter 6. Ratcheting Down the Industrial Ladder in Mexico

1. Cited by Jeremy Page, "China Anoints Its Next Leader," *Wall Street Journal*, October 19, 2010, A1.

2. Enrique Krauze, "Trump Threatens a Good Neighbor," *New York Times*, January 17, 2017, https://www.nytimes.com/2017/01/17/opinion/trump-threatens-a-good -neighbor.html. Also see Michael Reid, *Forgotten Continent: The Battle for Latin America's Soul* (New Haven: Yale University Press, 2007), 74–75.

3. See Roberto Hernández Hernández, "Economic Liberalization and Trade Relations between Mexico and China," *Journal of Current Chinese Affairs*, no. 1 (2012): 49–96, and Romero Cornejo, Francisco Javier Haro Navejas, José Luis León-Manríquez, "Trade Issues and Beyond: Mexican Perceptions on Contemporary China," *Latin American Policy* 4, no. 1 (2013): 57–75.

4. Shawn Donnan, "Nafta Revisited: Renegotiation of Trade Deal Tops Agenda," *Financial Times*, January 24, 2017, 2.

5. Krauze, "Trump Threatens a Good Neighbor."

6. Ha-Joon Chang, *Kicking Away the Ladder: Development Strategy in Historical Perspective* (London: Anthem Press, 2003). Also see Erik. S. Reinert, "The Role of the State in Economic Growth," *Journal of Economic Studies* 26, no. 4/5 (1999): 268–326.

7. Barry Naughton, "A Political Economy of China's Economic Transition," in *China's Great Economic Transformation*, ed. Loren Brandt and Thomas Rawski (New York: Cambridge University Press), 91–135.

8. See Manuel Pastor and Carol Wise, "The Origins and Sustainability of Mexico's Free Trade Policy," *International Organization* 48, no. 3 (1994): 459.

9. I borrow this term from Juan Carlos Moreno-Brid and Jaime Ros, *Development and Growth in the Mexican Economy* (New York: Oxford University Press, 2009), chap. 5.

10. Nora Hamilton, *Mexico: Political, Economic, and Social Evolution* (New York: Oxford University Press, 2011), 110–11.

11. Manuel Pastor, "Pesos, Policies, and Predictions," in *The Post-NAFTA Political*

Economy: Mexico and the Western Hemisphere, ed. Carol Wise (College Park: Pennsylvania State University Press, 1998), 125.

12. See Roberto Bouzas and Jaime Ros, "The North–South Variety of Economic Integration," in *Economic Integration in the Western Hemisphere,* ed. Roberto Bouzas and Jaime Ros (Notre Dame: University of Notre Dame Press, 1994), 1–45.

13. This section draws on Carol Wise and Joshua Tuynman, "NAFTA @ 20: A Bittersweet Celebration," *Americas Quarterly* (Winter 2014): 26–31.

14. To be eligible for NAFTA's preferences, goods must (1) be produced entirely within the NAFTA bloc; (2) incorporate only those non-NAFTA materials that are sufficiently processed in North America to qualify for a tariff reclassification; and (3) satisfy a minimum-content rule. See Gary Hufbauer and Jeffrey Schott, *NAFTA Revisited: Achievements and Challenges* (Washington, DC: Peterson Institute for International Economics, 2005).

15. James McBride, "NAFTA's Economic Impact," *CFR Backgrounders,* Council on Foreign Relations, January 24, 2017, http://www.cfr.org/trade/naftas-economic-impact/p15790.

16. Gary Hufbauer, Cathleen Cimino, and Tyler Moran, *NAFTA at 20: Misleading Charges and Positive Achievements* (Washington, DC: Peterson Institute for International Economics, Policy Brief 14–13, 2014), 1.

17. David H. Autor, David Dorn, and Gordon H. Hanson, "The China Shock: Learning from Labor-Market Adjustment to Large Changes in Trade," *Annual Review of Economics,* 8 (2016): 205–40.

18. Hufbauer, Cimino, and Moran, *NAFTA at 20,* 5.

19. Jeffrey Schott, "For Mexico, Canada, and the United States, a Step Backwards on Trade and Investment," October 2, 2018, *Reuters,* https://piie.com/blogs/trade-investment-policy-watch/mexico-canada-and-united-states-step-backwards-trade-and.

20. Azam Ahmed and Elisabeth Malkin, "Mexicans Are Nafta Winners? It's News to Them," *New York Times,* January 4, 2017, https://www.nytimes.com/2017/01/04/world/americas/mexico-donald-trump-nafta.html?smprod=nytcore-iphone&smid=nytcore-iphone-share.

21. Adrian H. Hearn, *Diaspora and Trust: Cuba, Mexico, and the Rise of China* (Durham: Duke University Press, 2016), 2.

22. These figures are cited from chapter 2, table 2.8, available at https://globaledge.msu.edu/countries/mexico/tradestats.

23. Bela Balassa, *The Theory of Economic Integration* (New York: Routledge Revivals, 2012).

24. Jaime Zabludovsky and Sergio Gómez Lora, "Beyond the FTAA," in *Requiem or Revival? The Promise of North American Integration,* ed. Isabel Studer and Carol Wise (Washington, DC: Brookings Institution Press, 2007), 95.

25. Ana Swanson and Joshua Partlow, "US, Mexico Appear to Take First Steps toward Renegotiating NAFTA, Document Suggests," *Washington Post,* February 2, 2017,

https://www.stripes.com/news/us/us-mexico-appear-to-take-first-steps-toward
-renegotiating-nafta-document-suggests-1.452112.

26. Carol Wise, "Unfulfilled Promise: Economic Convergence under NAFTA," in *Requiem or Revival? The Promise of North American Integration,* 34–35.

27. "Anti-dumping Duty Agreement Marks New Dawn for Trade with China," International Law Office, October 24, 2008, available at http://www.internationallaw office.com/Account/Login.aspx?ReturnUrl=http%3a%2f%2fwww. international lawoffice.com%2fNewsletters%2fInternational-Trade%2fMexico%2fVzquez
-Tercero-y-Asociados%2fAnti-dumping-duty-agreement-marks-new-dawn-for
-trade-with-China.

28. Zabludovsky and Gómez Lora, "Beyond the FTAA."

29. "Days to WTO Entry Numbered," *Xinhuanet,* August 23, 2001, http://news.xin huanet.com/english/ 20010825/444228A.htm; "China Still Has Two Barriers Ahead Before Its WTO Entry," *Xinhuanet,* August 7, 2001, http://news.xinhuanet .com/english/20010816/440584.htm.

30. "Sino–Mexican Relations More Close than Before: Mexican President," *Xinhuanet,* June 7, 2001, http://news.xinhuanet.com/english/20010607/416348.htm; Rebeca Céspedes, "Desconfía de China la industria nacional—Temen los productores de acero mexicanos la competencia del país asiático," *Reforma,* November 9, 2001, 13; and Jason Booth and Matt Pottinger, "China exporta deflación," *El Norte,* November 23, 2001, 8.

31. Economist Intelligence Unit (EIU), "EIU Country Report: Mexico," October 2001, 29.

32. "Mexico, China Create High-Level Group for Exports," *Xinhuanet,* September 13, 2003, http://news.xinhuanet.com/english/2003–09/13/content_1079534.htm.

33. Autor, Dorn, and Hanson, "The China Shock," 205.

34. Ibid., 219.

35. "Lies, Damned Lies, and . . . The Sanctity of Trade Statistics," *The Economist,* February 23, 2017, http://www.economist.com/news/finance-and-economics/2171 7431-bilateral-trade-flow-data-are-misleading-reported-tweak-will-not-help?frsc =dg|c.

36. Robert Koopman et al., "Giving Credit Where Credit Is Due: Tracing Value Added in Global Production Chains," National Bureau of Economic Research, Working Paper 16426, Cambridge, MA. September, 2010, 8.

37. The prime source on the effect of China's WTO accession on the Mexican economy is Enrique Dussel Peters, "The Implications of China's Entry into the WTO for Mexico," Global Issue Papers No. 24, Heinrich Boll Stiftung Foundation, November 2005. Also see Enrique Dussel Peters and Kevin P. Gallagher, "NAFTA's Uninvited Guest: China and the Disintegration of North American Trade," *CEPAL Review* 110 (2013): 83–108.

38. Further detail on this can be found in table 2.8.

39. Robert Devlin, "China's Economic Rise," in *China's Expansion into the Western*

Hemisphere: Implications for Latin America and the United States, ed. Riordan Roett and Guadalupe Paz (Washington, DC: Brookings Institution Press, 2008), 117–21.

40. Ralph Watkins, "The China Challenge to Manufacturing in Mexico." Paper presented at "Global Perspectives Conference: Focus on China," Ellard School of Management, University of Arizona, April 2009.

41. Dussel Peters and Gallagher, "NAFTA's Uninvited Guest," 89–92.

42. Sanjaya Lall, John Weiss, and Hiroshi Oikawa, "China's Competitive Threat to Latin America: An Analysis for 1990–2002," *Oxford Development Studies* 33, no. 2 (2007): 163–94.

43. Dussel Peters and Gallagher, "NAFTA's Uninvited Guest," 90.

44. See, for example, Damien Cave, "As Ties with China Unravel, U.S. Companies Head to Mexico," *New York Times,* May 31, 2014, https://www.nytimes.com /2014/06/01/world/americas/as-ties-with-china-unravel-us-companies-head-to -mexico.html.

45. Sylvia Maxfield and Adam Shapiro, "Assessing the NAFTA Negotiations: U.S.– Mexican Debate and Compromise on Tariff and Nontariff Issues," in *The Post-NAFTA Political Economy,"* ed. Carol Wise, 87–88.

46. Jennifer Bair and Enrique Dussel Peters, "Global Commodity Chains and Endogenous Growth: Export Dynamism and Development in Mexico and Honduras," *World Development* 34, no. 2 (2005): 206–7.

47. Gary Gereffi and Miguel Korzeniewicz, eds., *Commodity Chains and Global Capitalism* (Westport, CT: Praeger, 1994).

48. Mushtaq H. Khan and Stephanis Blankenburg, "The Political Economy of Industrial Policy in Asia and Latin America," in *Industrial Policy and Development,* ed. Mario Cimoli et al. (New York: Oxford University Press, 2009).

49. See Juan Carlos Moreno-Brid, "Industrial Policy: A Missing Link in Mexico's Quest for Export-led Growth," *Latin American Policy* 4, no. 2 (2013): 216–37; and Fundación Colosio, *El futuro que vemos: Memoria de los encuentros por el futuro de México* (Mexico, D.F.: Fundación Colosio, 2013).

50. See Wise and Tuynman, "NAFTA @ 20: A Bittersweet Celebration," 27–29.

51. Mariana Rangel Padilla, "Developing Countries in the Digital Era: State and Business Interactions for Industrial Upgrading," PhD diss., School of International Relations, University of Southern California, Los Angeles, September 17, 2017.

52. The cluster in the state of Baja California, for example, includes Andrés Campos, Director, Ensenada Economic Development Commission; Al Chu, President for International Affairs, Aerospace Cluster of Baja California; Flavio Olivieri, Executive Director at Cali Baja Bi-national Mega-Region; Rafael Solorzano, Former Director of Economic Development for the City of Tijuana; and Armando Vega, Production Manager, DJ Ortho, Tijuana.

53. See Adrian Hearn, "Mexico, China, and the Politics of Trust," *Latin American Perspectives* 42, no. 2 (2015): 122.

54. OECD, "Participation of Developing Countries in Global Value Chains," OECD

Trade Policy Paper No. 179, 2015, 17. Also see Jude Webber, "Adjusting to the 'New Normal,'" *Financial Times*, March 25, 2017, 9.

55. Manuel Pastor and Carol Wise, "The Lost Sexenio: Vicente Fox and the New Politics of Economic Reform in Mexico," *Latin American Politics and Society* 47, no. 4 (2005): 135–60.

56. Economist Intelligence Unit, *Country Report: Mexico*, December 2009, 3.

57. David Luhnow, "Mexico's Leader's Woes Follow Him to China," *Wall Street Journal*, November 10, 2014, http://libproxy.usc.edu/login?url=http://search.proquest .com.libproxy1.usc.edu/docview/1622159346?accountid=14749.

58. Jonathan Tepperman, "How Mexico's President May Have Rescued His Country," *Washington Post*, October 17, 2016, https://www.washingtonpost.com/opinions /how-mexicos-president-may-have-rescued-his-country/2016/10/14/5154235a -8ff1-11e6-9c52-0b10449e33c4_story.html?utm_term=.599d5d5b2287.

59. Shannon Young, "Another Dent in Enrique Peña Nieto's Reform Agenda," *Americas Quarterly*, June 2019, http://www.americasquarterly.org/content/another-dent -enrique-pena-nietos-reform-agenda.

60. Denise Dresser, "Can Mexico Be Saved? The Peril and Promise of López Obrador," *Foreign Affairs* 97, no. 5 (2018): 164; Jorge Ramos, "Another Mexican Revolution," *New York Times International Edition*, September 17, 2018, S3.

61. Silvia Garduño, "Buscan rehacer nexo con China—Renueva Peña Nieto diálogo político," *Reforma*, April 2, 2013, 7.

62. Alfredo González, "Amenaza Dragón con nuevo ataque—Siderurgia," *El Norte*, October 30, 2016, 18.

63. International Bar Association (IBA) Divisions Project Team, "Anti-Dumping Investigations against China in Latin America," IBA, 2010, 5–6, available at http:// www.ibanet.org/ENews_Archive/IBA_Jan_2010_ENews_ AntiDumping_inves tigations_against_China.aspx.

64. William Mauldin, "U.S. to Review China Trade Status," *Wall Street Journal*, March 31, 2017, A1.

65. Jude Webber, "China Bets Big on Mexican Oil with Deepwater Wins," *Financial Times*, December 5, 2016, https://www.ft.com/content/7fa65584-dcf9-3e61-9740 -982ee9b71208.

66. David Alire Garcia, "Demand at Mexico Onshore Oil and Gas Auction Spurs Output Hopes," *Reuters*, July 13, 2017, https://www.reuters.com/article/us-mexico-oil -sun-god-idUSKBN19X28Z.

67. Gregory Meyer, Jude Webber, and Anjli Raval, "Hurricane Exposes Energy World's Achilles Heel," *Financial Times*, September 1, 2017, 20.

68. Enrique Dussel Peters and Samuel Ortiz Velásquez, "El Tratado de Libre Comercio de América del Norte, contribuye China a su integración o desintegración?" in *La Nueva relación comercial de América Latina y el Caribe con China*, ed. Enrique Dussel Peters (Mexico, D.F.: RED ALC-China, UDUAL y UNAM/Cechimex, 2016), 245–308.

69. Rebeca Céspedes, "Derribarán protección contra China en 2008," *Palabra*, May 9, 2003, 13.

70. Ulises Díaz, "Acortan salarios brecha con China—Estiman especialistas ventaja para México," *Reforma*, December 28, 2009, 12.

71. "China, Mexico Sign 7 Cooperation Accords," *Xinhua News*, January 25, 2005, http://news.xinhuanet.com /english/2005–01/25/content_2506034.htm; "Xi Raises Proposals for Maintaining Sino–Mexico Economic, Trade Development," *Xinhua News*, November 2, 2009, http://news.xinhuanet.com/english/2009-02 /11/content_ 10800144.htm.

72. "China, Mexico Vow to Enhance Political Dialogue," *Xinhua News*, May 6, 2013, http://news.xinhuanet.com/english/china/2013–06/05/c_132432564.htm.

73. R. Evan Ellis, *China on the Ground in Latin America* (New York: Palgrave Macmillan, 2014), 131.

74. Ibid., 152.

75. Cecilia Sanchez, "Mexico Halts Chinese Mega-Mall Project After Damage to Environment," *Los Angeles Times*, January 28, 2015, http://www.latimes.com/world /mexico-americas/la-fg-mexico-closing-chinese-megamall-20150128-story.html.

76. Edmund Downie, "The Dragon Mart Fiasco Still Haunts China–Mexico Relations," *The Diplomat*, January 24, 2017, http://thediplomat.com/2017/01/the-dragon-mart -fiasco-still-haunts-china-mexico-relations/.

77. James Kynge, Michael Peel, and Ben Bland, "High-Speed Dream Hits the Buffers," *Financial Times*, July 18, 2017, 9.

78. "China Railway Construction 'Extremely Shocked' by Mexico's Scrapping of Rail Deal," *Xinhua News*, November 9, 2014, http://news.xinhuanet.com/english/china /2014–11/09/c_133776727.htm; "Chinese Firm Files for Compensation over Suspended Railway Project," *Xinhua News*, February 9, 2015, http://news.xinhuanet .com/english/2015–03/28/c_134105227.htm.

79. Enrique Dussel Peters, "Chinese Infrastructure Projects in Mexico," in *Building Development for a New Era: China's Infrastructure Projects in Latin America and the Caribbean,* ed. Enrique Dussel Peters, Ariel C. Armony, and Shoujun Cui (Mexico, D.F.: Red Académica de América Latina y el Caribe sobre China and the University of Pittsburgh, 2018), 67–68.

80. This paragraph draws on Ellis, *China on the Ground in Latin America,* and Enrique Dussel Peters and Samuel Ortiz Velásquez, *Monitor of China's OFDI in Mexico* (Mexico, D.F.: Academic Network of Latin America and the Caribbean and China, 2016), 24–25.

81. USTR, "Summary of Objectives for the NAFTA Renegotiation," Washington, DC, July 17, 2017.

82. Ibid., 3.

83. Autor, Dorn, and Hanson, "The China Shock"; Hufbauer, Cimino, and Moran, *NAFTA at 20.*

84. "The 652.6 Miles of Fences on the Southwest Border," *Washington Post*, July 7, 2017, https://www. washingtonpost.com/politics/the-6526-miles-of-fences-in-the

-southwest-border/2015/07/17/e4e4e674-2c40-11e5-a5ea-cf74396e59ec_graphic
.html?utm_term=.e920ca2cd681.

85. Jude Webber, Shawn Donnan, and Demitri Sevastopulo, "Business Readies for Worst in NAFTA Talks," *Financial Times*, September 1, 2017, 2.

86. Shawn Donnan, "FT Big Read. Agriculture," *Financial Times*, August 18, 2017, 7.

87. Peter Campbell and Jude Webber, "Trump to Give Mexican Car Trade a Bumpy Ride," *Financial Times*, January 5, 2017, 13.

88. Christopher Helman, "CEO Says Oil Find Is 'Multiples of What We thought,'" *Forbes*, July 13, 2017, https://www.forbes.com/sites/christopherhelman/2017/07/13/ceo-says-mexico-oil-find-is-multiples-of-what-we-thought/#618f63dc3a77.

89. Ye Shuhong and Mao Pengfei, "LatAm–China Agricultural Cooperation Thrives," *Xinhuanet*, December 15, 2015, http://news.xinhuanet.com/english/2015-12/15/c_134918341.htm.

90. Silvia Pavoni, "China Not Such a Champion of Global Trade," *Financial Times*, May 8, 2017, https://www.ft.com/content/cbe2a1a8–30ed-11e7-9555-23ef563ecf9a; and Thomas L. Friedman, "Trump Lies, China Thrives," *New York Times*, June 7, 2017, https://www.nytimes.com/2017/06/07/opinion/trump-china-trade.html?mcubz=0&_r=0.

91. Jonathan Tepperman, *The Fix: How Countries Use Crises to Solve the World's Worst Problems* (New York: Tim Duggan Books, 2016), 180.

Chapter 7. Latin America's Pivot toward Asia

1. Quoted in Ernesto Londoño, "From a Space Station in Argentina, China Expands Its Reach in Latin America," *New York Times*, July 28, 2018, https://www.nytimes.com/2018/07/28/world/americas/china-latin-america.html.

2. Michael Beckley, "Stop Obsessing about China," *Foreign Affairs*, September 21, 2018, https://www.foreignaffairs.com/articles/stop-obsessing-about-china.

3. "Top Products Data" sourced from ComTrade Database. Export/Import totals and categories sorted from top one hundred commodity categories worldwide.

4. Elizabeth C. Economy, *The Third Revolution: Xi Jinping and the New Chinese State* (New York: Oxford University Press, 2018), 173–74.

5. Monica DeHart, "China–Costa Rica Infrastructure Projects: Laying the Groundwork for Development?" in *Building Development for a New Era; Chinese Infrastructure Projects in Latin America and the Caribbean*, ed. Enrique Dussel Peters, Ariel Armony, and Shoujun Cui (Mexico, D.F.: Red Académica de América Latina y el Caribe sobre China and the University of Pittsburgh, 2018), 17–18.

6. José Antonio Ocampo, "Latin America's Mounting Development Challenges," in *Why Latin American Nations Fail*, ed. Esteban Peréz Caldentey and Matías Vernango (Berkeley: University of California Press, 2017), 125.

7. Kevin Gallagher, *The China Triangle: Latin America's China Boom and the Fate of the Washington Consensus* (New York: Oxford University Press, 2016), 113–14.

8. José Luis Machinea and Lucio Castro, "Argentina, the US, and China," in *China,*

the United States, and the Future of Latin America, ed. David B. H. Denoon (New York: New York University Press, 2017), 194.

9. "Study Sank $1.3 bn Refinery Project with China: Costa Rica," *Daily Mail Online,* April 20, 2016, http://www.dailymail.co.uk/wires/afp/article-3551024/Study-sank -1-3-bn-refinery-project-China-Costa-Rica.html.

10. Osvaldo Rosales, "Is There a LatAm–US–China Economic Triangle?" in *China, the United States, and the Future of Latin America,* ed. David B. H. Denoon, 36.

11. Ocampo, "Latin America's Mounting Development Challenges," 123.

12. Jaime Ortiz, "Déjà vu: Latin America and Its New Trade Dependency . . . This Time with China," *Latin American Research Review* 47, no. 3 (2012): 175–90.

13. Ocampo, "Latin America's Mounting Development Challenges," 134.

14. Silvia Pavoni, "China Not Such a Champion of Global Trade," *Financial Times,* May 8, 2017, https://www.ft.com/content/cbe2a1a8-30ed-11e7-9555-23ef563ecf9a.

15. Ocampo, "Latin America's Mounting Development Challenges," 136.

16. "Spotlight: China, CELAC Seeks Common Ground for Future Development at Ministers' Meeting," *Xinhuanet,* January 23, 2018, http://www.xinhuanet.com /english/2018–01/23/c_136918365.htm.

17. "The Collapse of TPP: Trading Down," *The Economist,* November 19, 2016, http:// www.economist.com/news/asia/21710287-big-free-trade-deals-demise-leaves -worrying-void-asia-trading-down.

18. Yifei Xiao, "Competitive Mega-Regional Trade Agreements: Regional Comprehensive Economic Partnership (RCEP) vs. Trans-Pacific Partnership (TPP)," April 20, 2015. *College Undergraduate Research Electronic Journal,* University of Pennsylvania, available at http://repository.upenn.edu/curej/194.

19. Shawn Donnan, "New NAFTA May Not Fulfill Trump Promises," *Los Angeles Times,* August 29, 2018, C1.

20. "Mexico Sees Trade Deals in TPP Leftovers, Flags China Opportunity," *Reuters,* November 22, 2016, https://www.reuters.com/article/us-usa-trump-mexico/mexico -sees-trade-deals-in-tpp-leftovers-flags-china-opportunity-idUSKBN13H1ZV.

21. "Perú defiende a China tras críticas de EE.UU. sobre su influencia en la región," *Gestión,* February 7, 2018, https://gestion.pe/economia/peru-defiende-china -criticas-ee-uu-influencia-region-226664.

22. Jingzhou Tao, "Headline Numbers Rarely Add Up in China Trade Deals," *Financial Times,* February 6, 2018, 9.

INDEX

Page numbers followed by *t, f, b,* or *n* refer, respectively to tables, figures, boxes, and notes.